Kyoto

"All you've got to do is decide to go and the hardest part is over.

So go!"

TONY WHEELER, COFOUNDER – LONELY PLANET

D0841065

Kate Morgan,
Rebecca Milner

Contents

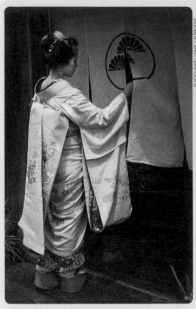

(left) **Geisha p167** Spot geisha in the old town.

(above) **Higashiyama p86** Wander this area's lovely lanes.

(right) **Tea ceremony p179** Take part in the age-old ritual.

Imperial Palace & Around p78

Northwest Kyoto p112

Arashiyama & Sagano p118

Northern Higashiyama p100

Downtown Kyoto p62

Gion & Southern Higashiyama p86

Kyoto Station & South Kyoto p54

Welcome to Kyoto

Kyoto is old Japan writ large: atmospheric temples, sublime gardens, traditional teahouses and geisha scurrying to secret liaisons.

Japan's Spiritual Heart

This is a city of some 2000 temples and shrines: a city of true masterpieces of religious architecture, such as the splendour of Kinkaku-ji (the famed Golden Pavilion) and the cavernous expanse of Higashi Hongan-ji. It's where robed monks shuffle between temple buildings, prayer chants resonate through stunning Zen gardens, and the faithful meditate on tatami-mat floors. Even as the modern city buzzes and shifts all around, a waft of burning incense, or the sight of a bright vermillion *torii* gate marking a shrine entrance, are regular reminders that Kyoto remains the spiritual heart of Japan.

A Trip for the Tastebuds

Few cities of this size pack such a punch when it comes to their culinary cred, and at its heart is Nishiki Market ('Kyoto's kitchen'). Kyoto is crammed with everything from Michelin-starred restaurants, chic cocktail bars, cool cafes and sushi spots to food halls, *izakaya* (Japanese pub-eateries), craft-beer bars and old-school noodle joints. Splurge on the impossibly refined cuisine known as *kaiseki* while gazing over your private garden, taste the most delicate tempura in a traditional building, slurp down steaming bowls of ramen elbow-to-elbow with locals, then slip into a sugar coma from a towering *matcha* sundae.

A City of Artisans

While the rest of Japan has adopted modernity with abandon, the old ways are still clinging on in Kyoto. With its roots as the cultural capital of the country, it's no surprise that many traditional arts and crafts are kept alive by artisans from generation to generation. Wander the streets downtown, through historic Gion and past *machiya* (traditional Japanese townhouses) in the Nishijin textile district to find ancient speciality shops from tofu sellers, *washi* (Japanese handmade paper) and tea merchants, to exquisite lacquerware, handcrafted copper *chazutsu* (tea canisters) and indigo-dyed *noren* (hanging curtains).

Cultural Encounters

If you don't know your *matcha* (powdered green tea) from your *manga* (Japanese comic), have never slept on a futon or had a bath with naked strangers, then it doesn't matter as this is *the* place to immerse yourself in the intricacies of Japanese culture. Whether you watch *matcha* being whisked in a traditional tea ceremony, spend the night in a ryokan, get your gear off and soak in an onsen, join a raucous *hanami* (cherry-blossom viewing) party or discover the art of Japanese cooking – you'll come away one step closer to understanding the unique Japanese way of life.

Why I Love Kyoto

By Kate Morgan, Writer

Having visited Kyoto many times, it still surprises and delights me. No matter how often I hear the 'nightingale floors' squeak beneath my feet at Nijō-jō, pad barefoot across tatami mats in ryokan, sip *matcha* in centuries-old tearooms, cycle through Arashiyama's bamboo forest or drink convenience-store beer on the banks of the Kamo-gama, it's a city I could never tire of. Yes, it's an ancient Japanese woodblock print come to life with its geisha and impossibly pretty cherry-blossom trees, but it's also a university town with a youthful feel and modernity breathing down its traditional neck.

For more about our writers, see p224

Top: Woman in traditional dress, Arashiyama Bamboo Grove (p121)

Kyoto's
Top 10

1

Kinkaku-ji (p114)

1 Talk about eye candy: the gold-plated main hall of this immensely popular temple in northwest Kyoto is probably the most impressive sight in the entire city. The hall rises above its reflecting pond like an apparition and if you're lucky enough to be here on a bright sunny day, you almost need sunglasses to look at it. The surrounding gardens and cosy teahouse Sekka-tei are also worth a visit here. Go early on a weekday morning to avoid the crush of people that descend on the temple each day.

⊙ *Northwest Kyoto*

Fushimi Inari-Taisha (p56)

2 This sprawling Shintō shrine is arguably one of Japan's most arresting visual spectacles. Thousands of vermilion *torii* (entrance gate to a Shintō shrine) line paths that criss-cross this mountain in southeast Kyoto. Visit the main hall and then head up the hill towards the summit. Be prepared to be utterly mesmerised. If you have time, do the circular pilgrimage route around the top of the mountain. And don't be afraid to get lost – that's part of the fun at Fushimi.

⊙ *Kyoto Station & South Kyoto*

GOWITHSTOCK / SHUTTERSTOCK ©

PATRYK KOSMIDER / SHUTTERSTOCK ©

Gion District (p89)

3 Gion, Kyoto's traditional entertainment district, is the best place in the city to catch a glimpse of 'old Japan'. With no fewer than three geisha districts scattered about, you stand a good chance of spotting a geisha (known as *geiko* in Kyoto) scurrying to an appointment. But geisha are only part of the story here: Gion also contains some of the most picturesque lanes in Kyoto, including Shimbashi. And don't forget Minami-za Theatre, the city's traditional kabuki theatre.

◉ *Gion & Southern Higashiyama*

Ginkaku-ji (p102)

4 A paradise tucked at the base of the Higashiyama mountains, Kyoto's famed Silver Pavilion is everything a Buddhist temple ought to be. The eponymous pavilion looks over a tranquil pond, and the stroll garden is sublime. Make your way past the unique sand mounds (used to reflect moonlight into the main hall for moon-viewing ceremonies), then climb the pathway to a lookout that offers panoramic views over the entire city. The autumn foliage here is among the best in the city.

◉ *Northern Higashiyama*

Chion-in (p88)

5 Called by some 'the Vatican of Pure Land Buddhism', this temple complex is a thriving hub of religious activity. The 24m-high San-mon gate is one of the largest wooden tower gates in Japan. The main hall is an imposing and impressive building, though is closed to the public until 2019. Wander the gardens visiting the collection of temple buildings here and allow yourself to be transported to blissful realms by the chanting of the monks. Then head up the hill to admire the enormous 70-tonne temple bell.
ABOVE: MONKS AT CHION-IN

◉ *Gion & Southern Higashiyama*

Kaiseki Cuisine
(p36)

6 In a city blessed with excellent dining options, one not to be missed is the refined and elegant experience of *kaiseki* cuisine. *Kaiseki* consists of a number of small courses, largely vegetarian, served on exquisite dinnerware where the preparation and service is as outstanding as the food itself. Diners are usually served in private rooms at speciality restaurants, such as the highly regarded Kikunoi (p95), and many ryokan serve *kaiseki* for guests. Prices can be steep when it comes to this Japanese haute cuisine but it's guaranteed to be a meal of a lifetime.

✗ *Eating*

Ōkōchi Sansō *(p120)*

7 While tourists descend on the nearby Bamboo Grove like paparazzi snapping photos of a big-wig celebrity, Arashiyama's Ōkōchi Sansō sits out of the limelight like a star waiting to be discovered. This charming estate is the former home of the famous samurai film actor from the 1920s, Ōkōchi Denjirō. The sprawling gardens here invite lazy wandering and there are fine views from the top of the hill. Take a break in the traditional teahouse with *matcha* (green powdered tea; pictured right) and a sweet, and relish your escape from the crowds.

⊙ *Arashiyama & Sagano*

Daitoku-ji *(p80)*

8 Carefully raked gravel representing rippling water, stylised arrangements of rocks, pruned trees, lush moss and dripping water — just one of these Zen garden features would be enough to have you feeling calm and contemplative, but here you have a mini world of them. Daitoku-ji is a complex of wandering lanes and subtemples with some of the most beautiful *kare-sansui* (dry landscape) gardens hidden inside their gates. It serves as the Rinzai Daitoku-ji school of Zen Buddhism headquarters and you'll be hard-pressed to find anywhere quite so meditative and atmospheric.

⊙ *Imperial Palace & Around*

Downtown Shopping (p73)

9 You could lose yourself for days among Downtown Kyoto's boutique-filled backstreets – a beacon for shopaholics – before asking, 'Temples? What temples?'. Hours can be whiled away just in the *bentō* box or stationery section of department stores before seeking out the kimono display or trying on the latest fashion. Once you discover the many traditional artisanal stores dotted around selling everything from centuries-old lacquerware to bright *wagasa* (waxed-paper umbrellas), you'll be hunting down the luggage shops for something to take it all home in.

🔒 *Downtown Kyoto*

Nishiki Market (p65)

10 Nishiki Market positively oozes old Japan atmosphere and you can imagine what it was like here before someone decided to attach the word 'super' to the word 'market'. Get off the temple trail and head here to discover some of the best and bizarre ingredients that go into Kyoto cuisine. Wander past stalls hawking slimy, shiny, slithering and spicy goods and try your best to work out what it is you're looking at. You can also grab a street-food snack or shop for high-end kitchenware and knives at Aritsugu.

◉ *Downtown Kyoto*

What's New

Kyoto Ukiyo-e Museum

In the heart of Downtown Kyoto, this small museum showcases a rotating collection of *ukiyo-e* (woodblock prints), as well as Hokusai's *Great Wave Off Kanagawa* permanently on display. (p66)

Foreigner-friendly Taxis

Kyoto's new foreigner-friendly taxis offer English-speaking drivers and credit-card payments. You'll find the taxi stands in front of Kyoto Station. (p187)

Cool Design Hostels

Hip new hostels have been sprouting up all over the city, from design-savvy 'pods' to beds in between bookshelves. (p145) (p147)

Four Seasons Hotel

The much anticipated Four Seasons hotel has established itself as a popular luxury option right in the Higashiyama sightseeing district. It doesn't disappoint: it's centred around an 800-year-old pond and gardens and the rooms are simply beautiful. (p148)

Craft Beer

Craft beer has certainly taken off in Kyoto and the number of bars dedicated to showcasing Japanese beer is growing every day. The Kyoto Brewing Company taproom is a great place to start taste testing. (p60)

Suiran Hotel

Arashiyama's newest luxury hotel sits in a private riverside spot and has comfortable contemporary rooms with open-air baths. (p150)

Kyoto Railway Museum

Trainspotters won't want to miss a trip to this excellent interactive museum, popular with kids and adults. (p58)

ROHM Theatre Kyoto

The renovated Kaikan Theatre has transformed into the ROHM Theatre Kyoto, a striking piece of architecture in the Okazaki-kōen area hosting everything from opera to comedy shows. (p110)

Specialty Coffee

A clutch of modern cool cafes roasting their own single-origin beans are popping up in Kyoto, such as Weekenders downtown. (p71)

Kyoto Tower Sando

The Kyoto Tower building was transformed in 2017 and now houses a basement food hall, souvenir shops and sushi-making workshops. (p59)

Maiko Performances

A number of new *maiko* (apprentice geisha) and geisha performances are now available, offering a more affordable option for visitors than some of the more traditional offerings. (p98)

For more recommendations and reviews, see **lonelyplanet.com/kyoto**

Need to Know

For more information, see Survival Guide (p181)

Currency
Yen (¥)

Language
Japanese

Visas
Visas are issued on arrival for most nationalities for stays of up to 90 days.

Money
ATMs available in major banks, post offices and 7-Eleven stores. Credit cards accepted in most hotels and department stores, but only some restaurants and ryokan.

Mobile Phones
Mobile phones can be rented online or at the airport for making voice calls. Prepaid data-only SIM cards can be purchased and used with unlocked smartphones.

Time
Japan Standard Time (GMT/UTC plus nine hours)

Tourist Information
Kyoto Tourist Information Center (p192) has bus and city maps, transport information and English-speaking staff.

Daily Costs

Budget: Less than ¥10,000
➡ Dorm bed: ¥3000

➡ Two simple restaurant meals: ¥2200

➡ Train/bus transport: ¥1200

➡ One temple/museum admission: ¥500

➡ Snacks, drinks, sundries: ¥1000

Midrange: ¥10,000– 25,000
➡ Double room in a midrange hotel: ¥12,000

➡ Two midrange restaurant meals: ¥5000

➡ Train/bus transport: ¥1200

➡ Two temple/museum admissions: ¥1000

➡ Snacks, drinks, sundries: ¥2000

Top End: More than ¥25,000
➡ Five-star hotel/ryokan accommodation: ¥30,000

➡ *Kaiseki* restaurant meal: ¥10,000

➡ Train/bus transport: ¥1200

➡ Two taxi rides: ¥3500

➡ Two temple/museum admissions: ¥1000

Advance Planning

Several months before Make accommodation reservations if you are travelling in cherry-blossom season (March and April) or the autumn-foliage season (October and November).

One month before Book at popular restaurants to avoid missing out, particularly for high-end *kaiseki* restaurants and Michelin-starred places.

At least a week before Send your postcard off to book a visit to one of the city's best gardens, Saihō-ji.

Useful Websites

Lonely Planet (www.lonely planet.com/kyoto) Destination information, hotel bookings, traveller forum and more.

Kyoto Visitor's Guide (www. kyotoguide.com) Great all-around Kyoto info.

HyperDia (www.hyperdia.com) Train schedules in English.

Kyoto Travel Guide (www.kyoto. travel) Excellent resource on all things Kyoto.

WHEN TO GO

Kyoto is crowded in the cherry-blossom (late March to early April) and autumn-foliage (November) seasons; be sure to advance book your accommodation.

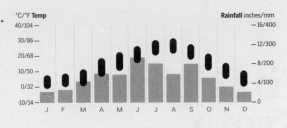

Arriving in Kyoto

Kansai International Airport
JR Haruka Airport trains to Kyoto Station (¥2850, 1¼ hours); Kansai International Airport Limousine buses to Kyoto Station (¥2550, about 1½ hours); shared MK taxi vans to hotels, inns and houses in Kyoto (¥4200, around 1½ hours).

Osaka International Airport
Osaka Airport Transport buses to Kyoto Station (¥1310, 55 minutes); shared MK taxi vans to hotels, inns and houses in Kyoto (¥2900, around one hour).

Kyoto Station *Shinkansen* (bullet trains) from Tokyo to Kyoto Station take about 2½ hours and cost around ¥13,080 for an unreserved seat. There are also *shinkansen* from cities such as Hiroshima, Osaka, Nagoya and Yokohama.

For much more on **arrival** see p182

Getting Around

Kyoto is a compact city with an excellent public transport system.

Subway Gets you quickly between north and south (the Karasuma subway line stops at Kyoto Station) or east and west (the Tōzai subway line runs between Higashiyama and the west side of the city).

Bus For destinations not well served by the subway lines (including sights in the northwest of the city, like Kinkaku-ji).

Bicycle A brilliant way to explore Kyoto (the city is mostly flat).

Walking Kyoto is a walker's paradise.

Taxi For short trips, late at night, or if you've got heavy luggage, a taxi is your best bet.

Car There's no need to hire a car; in fact, it's far more trouble than it's worth. Perhaps only handy for excursions out of the city.

For much more on **getting around** see p184

Sleeping

Kyoto has a wide range of accommodation, with some of the best ryokan (traditional Japanese inns) in Japan. Five-star and boutique hotels are well represented, along with cheaper business hotels and hip hostels. You'll also find plenty of guesthouses, some capsule hotels and the odd youth hostel scattered about.

Useful Websites

Lonely Planet (lonelyplanet.com/japan/hotels) Recommendations and bookings.

Japanese Guesthouses (www.japaneseguesthouses.com) A site that specialises in ryokan bookings

Jalan (www.jalan.net) Popular Japanese discount accommodation site, searchable in English.

For much more on **sleeping** see p141

First Time Kyoto

For more information, see Survival Guide (p181)

Checklist

➡ Organise an International Driving Permit if you plan to rent a car to drive to some of the surrounding areas.

➡ Inform your debit-/credit-card company you're heading away.

➡ Check airline baggage restrictions.

➡ Make restaurant reservations for high-end places.

What to Pack

➡ Slip-on shoes, as you'll be taking off your shoes a lot.

➡ Some medications can be difficult to find or challenging to work out what's what if you don't speak Japanese, so bring any medications you might need.

➡ Downloading a useful language app, such as VoiceTra (http://voicetra. nict.go.jp), will come in handy when dealing with language barriers.

Top Tips for Your Trip

➡ Splurge on *kaiseki* (Japanese haute cuisine) at lunch. Many elite *kaiseki* restaurants offer lunch menus that are almost half the price or less than what you'll find at dinner. And you'll still get to taste the same quality of food.

➡ Spend at least one night in a ryokan (traditional Japanese inn). Kyoto is the best place to try this quintessential Japanese experience.

➡ Avoid getting 'templed out'. Pick the temples you'd like to visit most on your trip and savour the experience rather than trying to tick as many off your list as you can.

➡ Learn some basic Japanese phrases. Kansai dialect is spoken in Kyoto so try impressing the locals by saying *ōkini* instead of the usual *arigatō*, meaning thank you.

What to Wear

Casual clothes are fine but you'll want to pack something a bit smarter for nights out to high-end restaurants.

There is no specific dress code for entering temples or shrines but you'll be taking your shoes off most of the time, so you probably won't want to be wearing a holey pair of socks. If you don't like the idea of slipping your feet into sweaty shared slippers, be sure to carry a pair of socks with you if you're wearing sandals during the summer months.

Kyoto can get stifling hot during summer so wear light, loose-fitting clothes, along with a sunhat as there is usually not a lot of shade in temple gardens and grounds.

Be Forewarned

➡ Kyoto is generally a very safe city and crime is rare. Use common sense and follow the same precautions you normally would.

➡ Take care when crossing the street or exiting restaurants, hotels and shops onto the pavement; there's almost always someone on a bicycle coming your way.

Guided Tours

Kyoto Cycling Tour Project
(p185) Offers a range of guided cycling tours across the city, including to Fushimi Inari-Taisha and a Kinkaku-ji to Arashiyama tour.

Ninja Food Tours (www. ninjafoodtours.com) Taste your way around the city with tours of Nishiki Market and a night tour of bars and restaurants.

Kyoto Free Walking Tour
(www.kyotofreewalkingtour. com) English-speaking guides run daily free two-hour walking tours. Schedules are posted online a few days before.

Taxes & Refunds

There is an 8% consumption tax on retail purchases in Japan (scheduled to increase to 10% in October 2019). Many shops in Kyoto offer tax-free shopping for purchases over ¥5000 (look for a sticker in the window). You must show your passport to prove that you have a short-stay visa.

Tipping

➡ Tipping is not done in Japan and is never expected.

➡ At high-end restaurants and hotels a 10% service charge is usually added to the bill.

Sushi set

Etiquette

Japan is well known for its etiquette, though as a visitor to Kyoto you are not expected to know everything. However, it does pay to familiarise yourself with a few of the main dos and don'ts.

Shoes Off You're required to remove your shoes at many of the city's temples, some museums and most ryokan, hotels and restaurants that have tatami-mat areas. Sometimes slippers are provided. Never wear shoes or slippers on tatami mats.

Temples & Shrines There is no dress code for religious sites in Kyoto but do remain respectful and speak quietly.

Queueing You'll see neat orderly queues formed when waiting for the bus, on the subway platform, at busy restaurants etc. Queue-jumping is a big no-no, so get in line.

Chopsticks Never leave them sticking upright in your bowl and never pass food from yours to another person's chopsticks; this is only done during funeral rituals.

Top Itineraries

Day One

Southern Higashiyama (p86)

 Start your Kyoto experience by heading to the city's most important sightseeing district – Southern Higashiyama contains the thickest concentration of worthwhile sights in Kyoto. Kick off with **Chion-in** and **Shoren-in** before a wander through **Maruyama-koen**.

> ✘ **Lunch** At Hisago (p95) go for the house speciality, *oyako-donburi*.

Southern Higashiyama (p86)

 Walk off your lunch with a stroll through the lanes of **Ninen-zaka and Sannen-zaka**, stopping in at teahouses and boutiques. Then head to one of the city's premier sights, **Kiyomizu-dera**. Spend the afternoon fully exploring this delightful temple.

> ✘ **Dinner** Get your first taste of an *izakaya* at Gion Yuki (p94).

Southern Higashiyama (p86)

 After dinner you'll want to spend your first evening taking in the atmospheric **Gion** district and keeping an eye out for geisha shuffling around the traditional lantern-lit streets. Round off the evening with a drink at the **Gion Finlandia Bar**.

Day Two

Northern Higashiyama (p100)

☀ There's a lot of ground to cover and a number of excellent temples to explore in Northern Higashiyama. Beat the crowds with an early visit to **Ginkaku-ji** before making your way along the **Path of Philosophy** to the splendid **Eikan-do** temple and exploring the vast **Nanzen-ji** temple complex and gardens.

> ✘ **Lunch** Fuel up on a tasty bowl of noodles at Hinode Udon (p109).

Downtown Kyoto (p62)

☼ Take a break from temples and head to the downtown area to check out the famous **Nishiki Market**; don't miss the world-renowned chef's knives for sale at **Aritsugu** here. Carry on shopping in this area along the Teramachi covered arcade and the department stores on Kawaramachi-dōri and Shijo-dōri.

> ✘ **Dinner** Try the delicious delicacy *unagi* (eel) at Kyōgoku Kane-yo (p67).

Downtown Kyoto (p62)

 For an after-dinner stroll, make your way along atmospheric **Ponto-chō**, stop in for a drink at **Atlantis** or grab a takeaway refreshment at the nearest convenience store and head for the Kamo-gama to hang out riverside.

Ryōan-ji (p115)

Day Three

Northwest Kyoto (p112)

 Jump on a bus bound for the northwest temples of Kyoto. Kick off with a wander through the peaceful grounds of the temple complex **Ninna-ji** before exploring the famous rock garden of **Ryōan-ji** nearby. Take the bus or walk 20 minutes to one of the city's most well-known sights, **Kinkaku-ji**. Admire the stunning golden temple and the Zen garden.

 Lunch Tasty noodle dishes at Gontaro (p117).

Arashiyama & Sagano (p118)

Grab a taxi and head west to the Arashiyama and Sagano district, which has a dense concentration of first-rate sights. Start at **Tenryū-ji** and stroll through the famed **Arashiyama Bamboo Grove** and on to lovely **Ōkōchi Sansō**. Continue temple-hopping in the hills, stopping to check out **Jōjakkō-ji**, **Nison-in** and as far as **Giō-ji**, or **Adashino Nenbutsu-ji** if you have the stamina. Work your way back to the main strip or take a bus if your legs need a rest.

Dinner Book ahead at one of the city's finest, Kitcho Arashiyama (p127).

Downtown Kyoto (p62)

Head back to spend what's left of your evening wandering down bar-and-nightlife-filled pretty Kiyamachi-dōri and end the night with a gin cocktail at **Nokishita 711** or further down at sophisticated **Bar K6**.

Day Four

Kyoto Station & South Kyoto (p54)

 While the immediate Kyoto Station area doesn't offer much in the way of sightseeing, head a little further south on day four to see two absolutely stunning attractions: **Tōfuku-ji** (don't forget to enter the Hōjō Garden) and **Fushimi Inari-Taisha**. Head back to the station to marvel at the architecture if you haven't taken time to do this already.

Lunch Take your pick of nine ramen joints at Kyoto Rāmen Kōji (p59).

Imperial Palace & Around (p78) & Downtown Kyoto (p62)

From Kyoto Station, take the subway or board a bus for **Daitoku-ji**, a maze of lanes with tucked-away temples featuring incredible Zen gardens. Spend your time wandering around before jumping back on the subway to the Imperial Palace Park (p81) for a stroll around the lovely expansive grounds, then head back downtown for a spot of dinner.

Dinner Book in advance for delicate tempura at Yoshikawa (p71).

Downtown Kyoto (p62)

 After dinner, head over to **Sake Bar Yoramu** to get an education in sake while taste testing, or drop into the intimate hidden-away **Bar Rocking Chair** for expertly made cocktails.

If You Like...

Temples & Shrines

Nanzen-ji A world of Zen temples and subtemples scattered amid the trees. (p103)

Ginkaku-ji The famed 'Silver Pavilion' boasts one of Kyoto's finest gardens. (p102)

Hōnen-in A secluded retreat a short walk from the perpetually crowded Ginkaku-ji. (p105)

Kinkaku-ji A golden apparition rises above a tranquil reflecting pond – arguably Kyoto's most impressive single sight. (p114)

Tenryū-ji This temple takes *shakkei* (borrowed scenery) to a new level – it borrows the entire sweep of Arashiyama's beautiful mountains. (p121)

Daitoku-ji Each subtemple at this Zen complex has a sublime garden: a must for garden lovers with an aversion to crowds. (p80)

Myōshin-ji This is a walled complex containing many fine subtemples and one of Kyoto's most famous gardens, Taizō-in. (p115)

Kurama-dera Climb a path lined with towering cedar trees to this mountain temple in the hills north of the city. (p129)

Chion-in A vast Pure Land Buddhist temple – the Vatican of Japanese Buddhism. (p88)

Shōren-in The crowds usually give this Southern Higashiyama temple a miss – don't make that mistake. (p92)

Museums

Kyoto National Museum The special exhibits here are often spectacular and the permanent

Cherry blossoms along the Path of Philosophy (p105)

TOOYKRUB / SHUTTERSTOCK ©

collection is a good introduction to Japanese art. (p91)

National Museum of Modern Art The permanent collection is small but interesting and the special exhibits are usually excellent. (p105)

Kyoto International Manga Museum If you are a fan of Japanese manga (comics), you simply must make a pilgrimage to this fine downtown museum. (p66)

Kyoto Railway Museum Train-spotters, and their kids, will love this fantastic museum showcasing everything from steam trains to *shinkansen*. (p58)

Fureai-Kan Kyoto Museum of Traditional Crafts Get an education on Kyoto's arts and crafts. (p107)

Kyoto Ukiyo-e Museum Check out some of Japan's big-name *ukiyo-e* (woodblock print) artists' work at this one-room museum downtown. (p66)

Raku Museum For anyone with an interest in ceramics, this small museum is dedicated to the art of Raku pottery with stunning pieces on display. (p81)

Geisha & Maiko Performances

Miyako Odori Held in April, this is the grandest of all Kyoto geisha dances. If you are in town, ensure you *do not miss it*. (p96)

Kamogawa Odori Held in May by the Ponto-chō geisha district, this is a small-scale but charming geisha dance. (p73)

Maiko Theatre Small modern venue near Gion hosting intimate *maiko* (apprentice geisha) performances at more affordable prices. (p98)

Kyō Odori The Miyagawa-chō geisha district holds its dance in April and it's a must-see affair. (p96)

Maiko Dinner Show Yasakadori Enraku Dinner and all-you-can-drink *maiko* shows held in a traditional restaurant. (p96)

Kitano Odori Held up north in the Kamishichiken geisha district every April, this is a quaint and touching dance. (p117)

Gion Odori The only major geisha dance held in autumn (November), this is put on by the Gion Higashi geisha district. (p96)

Traditional Culture

Club Ōkitsu Kyoto Get acquainted with an incense and tea ceremony in a beautiful old villa. (p85)

Camellia Tea Experience Learn to whisk up a cup of *matcha* (powdered green tea) as you watch an elegant tea ceremony be performed. (p99)

Gion Corner A great sampler of a bunch of traditional Japanese arts, if you can see past the tourists snapping photos on iPads. (p98)

Minami-za Kyoto's main kabuki theatre is the place to see the visual spectacle of kabuki - or see the main Kaomise kabuki event at ROHM Theatre Kyoto if Minami-za is still undergoing renovations. (p96)

Shunkō-in Achieve a sense of peace and calm as you are introduced to Zen Buddhism meditation by a monk in a lovely old temple. (p117)

Shopping & Markets

Tenjin-san Market Held on the 25th of each month at Kitano Tenman-gū, there are always

For more top Kyoto spots, see the following:
➡ Eating (p35)
➡ Drinking & Nightlife (p41)
➡ Entertainment (p44)
➡ Shopping (p46)
➡ Temples & Shrines (p48)

treasures hidden among the bric-a-brac here. (p117)

Kōbō-san Market Held on the 21st of each month at Tō-ji, this is a good market for used kimonos and antiques. (p61)

Nishiki Market Kyoto's main downtown food market is a must-see attraction, with plenty of souvenir shops scattered among the food shops. (p65)

Asahi-dō A complex of stores near Kiyomizu-dera with packed shelves of pottery by some of Japan's up-and-coming artists. (p98)

Zōhiko A treasure trove of sumptuous Japanese lacquerware. (p73)

Wagami no Mise This Japanese paper *(washi)* specialist is a dreamland for creative types. (p74)

Ippōdō Tea Kyoto's finest tea shop is worth a visit for the ambience and aroma alone. (p74)

Tsujikura Delicate *wagasa* (waxed-paper umbrellas) in production since the 17th century. (p77)

Green Spaces

Ryōan-ji Ponder the meaning of the 15 magical rocks at Japan's most famous Zen garden. (p115)

Tōfuku-ji This abstract expressionist garden is like none other in Kyoto – and it also happens to be one of the city's most beautiful. (p57)

Kyoto Botanical Gardens The cherries in these expansive gardens are superb and the greenhouse contains some exquisite orchid species. (p82)

Ginkaku-ji The gardens at the 'Silver Pavilion' have it all: luxuriant moss, a bamboo forest, a waterfall, a pond and maples that turn crimson in November. (p102)

Katsura Rikyū The garden at this detached imperial villa is sublime; for fans of Japanese gardens, a pilgrimage here is a must. (p125)

Ōkōchi Sansō Wander the paths and admire the views over the city, the maple leaves and the wonderful hidden contemplative corners of this Arashiyama villa. (p120)

Saihō-ji One of the city's best gardens, the nickname for this temple is Koke-dera (Moss Temple) and this place more than lives up to its name. (p125)

Maruyama-kōen Take some time from the bustle of Gion by wandering the paths here past lovely gardens and a central carp-filled pond. (p92)

Takara-ga-ike-kōen This expansive locals' park in the north of the city is a great spot for a picnic or you can take to the water on a paddle boat. (p83)

Kameyama-kōen The perfect place to escape the Arashiyama crowds – you can meander along walking trails or just sit and take in the scenery. (p121)

Architecture

Katsura Rikyū Connoisseurs often rank this imperial villa as the finest example of Japanese traditional architecture. (p125)

Ōkōchi Sansō Perched on a hillside overlooking Arashiyama and Kyoto, this traditional villa with spectacular gardens is the stuff of dreams. (p120)

Byōdō-in One of the few extant examples of Heian-period architecture, Byōdō-in will make you wish that a lot more survived. (p136)

Gion Head to the preserved streets of this entertainment district: Hanami-kōji and Shimbashi, both lined with lovely traditional wooden buildings. (p89)

Nishijin Kyoto's weaving district, Nishijin is home to the thickest concentration of *machiya* (traditional Japanese townhouses) in the city. (p83)

Kyoto Station A stark contrast to the traditional side of the city with its steel-and-glass cathedral-like building. (p57)

Kyoto State Guest House One for those with a keen interest in architecture is this modern take on a traditional Japanese building. (p82)

Scenic Strolls

Kurama The climb to the mountain temple of Kurama-dera is a classic (continue to Kibune if possible). (p129)

Fushimi Inari-Taisha Paths lined with *torii* (entrance gate to a Shintō shrine) criss-cross this

mountain shrine in Southeast Kyoto. (p56)

Kyoto Imperial Palace Park If you prefer your strolling on the flat, the broad arcades of Kyoto's Central Park are just the ticket. (p81)

Kamo-gawa riverbank Make like a local and take your morning or evening constitutional on the banks of Kyoto's main river. (p63)

Path of Philosophy (Tetsugaku-no-Michi) The stroll along this canal in Northern Higashiyama is beautiful in any season. (p105)

Views

Kyoto Tower Get your bearings with panoramic city views from atop this iconic tower. (p57)

Ōkōchi Sansō Take in mountain views from the hill behind this villa in Arashiyama. (p120)

Daimonji-yama Sweat it up on the climb to the top of Daimonji-yama and be rewarded with views over the city. (p108)

Kiyomizu-dera Fantastic views from the broad verandah of the main hall of this popular temple. (p90)

Arashiyama Monkey Park Panoramic views of Kyoto once you're done monkeying around. (p124)

Fushimi Inari-Taisha Climb through row upon row of *torii* to the top of the hill for sweeping city views. (p56)

Shūgaku-in Rikyū Imperial Villa Great views of the surrounding mountains from the upper level of these villa gardens. (p107)

Month By Month

January

Kyoto comes to life after the lull of the New Year holiday (things open on 2 or 3 January). It's cold, but not too cold for travelling and the city is uncrowded.

✲✲ Hatsumōde

The first three days of the New Year (1 to 3 January) are when Kyotoites make the all-important first Shintō shrine visit of the year. Kyoto's three most popular shrines for this are Yasaka-jinja, Heian-jingū and Fushimi Inari-Taisha. Transport will be crowded.

🏃 Tōshiya (Archery Contest)

Held at Sanjūsangen-dō on the Sunday closest to 15 January. Hundreds of kimono-clad archers gather for a competition of accuracy and strength.

February

It's still cold in February and snow is possible in the city (but usually melts by noon). The mountains north of the city may be covered in snow all month.

✲✲ Setsubun Matsuri at Yoshida-jinja

Held on *setsubun* (2, 3 or 4 February; check with the TIC, p189), this festival marks the last day of winter. People climb to Yoshida-jinja in Northern Higashiyama to watch a huge bonfire in which old good-luck charms are burned. The action starts at dusk.

March

By March it's starting to warm up. Plums usually bloom in mid-March and the cherry blossoms usually start to emerge by month's end.

April

Spring is in full swing by April, although mornings and evenings can still be chilly. The cherry blossoms usually peak in early April, which means thick crowds in the sightseeing districts.

🏃 Cherry Blossom Viewing

Hanami (cherry-blossom viewing parties) take place all over town when the cherries blossom in early April. Top spots include Maruyama-kōen, Kyoto Imperial Palace Park and the Kamo-gawa riverbanks. In the evening, join the crowds on Gion's Shimbashi.

May

May is one of the best months to visit Kyoto. It's warm and sunny, and the blossoms are blooming. Note the Golden Week holidays (29 April to 5 May) and book well in advance.

★彡 Yabusame at Shimogamo-jinja

The annual *yabusame* (horseback archery) event on 3 May is one of the most exciting spectacles in Kyoto. Held on Tadasu-no-mori, the tree-lined approach to Shimogamo-jinja.

★彡 Aoi Matsuri (Hollyhock Festival)

This major festival on 15 May involves a procession of imperial messengers in ox carts and 600 people dressed in traditional costume. The procession starts at Kyoto Imperial Palace and heads for Shimogamo-jinja where ceremonies take place. It sets out again to finish at Kamigamo-jinja.

June

June is a lovely time to visit Kyoto – it's warm but not sweltering and the new green on the trees is beautiful. However, it's also the wettest month, so expect humidity and occasional downpours.

★彡 Takigi Nō

Held at Heian-jingū on 1 to 2 June, this is a festival of *nō* drama held by flaming torchlight in the outdoor courtyard.

July

When the rainy season ends in late June or early July, the heat cranks up and it can be very hot and humid. Still, if you don't mind sweating a bit, travel is perfectly possible.

★彡 Gion Matsuri

One of Japan's biggest festivals, Gion Matsuri's main event is held on 17 July, when festival floats are hauled through Downtown Kyoto during the morning. On the three preceding evenings, huge crowds flock to the Shijō-Karasuma area to inspect the floats parked on the streets.

August

August is hot and humid in Kyoto, but the skies are usually sunny and most tourist sites are uncrowded, except during the O-Bon holiday in mid-August – book ahead.

★彡 Daimon-ji Gozan Okuribi

Held on 16 August to bid farewell to the souls of ancestors. Fires are lit at night in the form of Chinese characters on five mountains. The main fire is the character for *dai* (great), on Daimonji-yama. Watch from the Kamo-gawa or Yoshida-yama riverbanks.

★彡 Tōki Matsuri

Kyoto's largest ceramics fair, held 7 to 10 August from 9am to 10pm, is ideal for snapping up bargains, especially late on the last day. The market runs along Gojō-dōri, between Kawabata and Higashiōji. It's a 10-minute walk from Gojō Station on the Keihan line.

September

Sometime in mid-September, the heat breaks, cool breezes arrive and temperatures become very pleasant in Kyoto. Skies are generally clear, making it a great time to travel.

★彡 Karasu Zumō

Held at Kamigamo-jinja on 9 September, this festival, which is also called 'crow wrestling', sees young boys compete in bouts of sumo.

☆ Kyoto International Manga Anime Fair

Kyomaf is the largest event of its kind in Western Japan with displays of the latest manga and performances by anime voice actors. Held in mid-September at Miyako Messe and Kyoto International Manga Museum (http://kyomaf.kyoto).

October

October is one of the best months to visit: the weather can be warm or cool and it's usually sunny. The leaves start changing colour at the end of the month, particularly in the hills.

★彡 Jidai Matsuri (Festival of the Ages)

One of Kyoto's big three festivals features more than 2000 people dressed in costumes ranging from the 8th to the 19th centuries parading from the Kyoto Imperial Palace to Heian-jingū on 22 October.

★彡 Kurama Hi Matsuri (Kurama Fire Festival)

Mikoshi (portable shrines) are carried through the streets of Kurama, accompanied by young men in loincloths bearing giant flaming torches. The festival climaxes in the evening on 22 October at Yuki-jinja. Trains to and from Kurama

(Top) A costumed participant in the Jidai Matsuri
(Bottom) Cherry-blossom-viewing party, Maruyama-kōen (p92)

COWARD_LION / GETTY IMAGES ©

SEAN PAVONE / SHUTTERSTOCK ©

will be packed; go early and return late.

☆ Kyoto Experiment

This contemporary performing arts festival is held every autumn, usually in October and November, and runs for around three weeks featuring experimental art, dance and theatre performances in venues across the city. The main venue is the ROHM Theatre Kyoto (https://kyoto-ex.jp).

November

November rivals October and April/May as the best time to visit. Skies are clear and temperatures are pleasantly cool. Foliage usually peaks late in the month and the city gets crowded.

December

December is cool to cold in Kyoto. The autumn foliage may still be good early in the month. Most shops, museums and restaurants shut down from 29 or 30 December, but transport runs and accommodation is open. Almost all temples and shrines stay open throughout.

🎎 Ōmisoka (New Year's Eve)

People gather in their homes on 31 December to feast, then visit local temples to ring temple bells before heading to their local shrine to pray for a lucky year. Bell ringing happens around midnight. Yasaka-jinja and Heian-jingū are great places to enjoy the action.

Kyoto by the Seasons

Kyoto is highly attuned to the seasons – a maiko (apprentice geisha) has a different hair pin for every month of the year – and your travel plans should be too. Make the most of your time here by seeking out the experiences and tastes that define each season.

Spring-themed lunch box for cherry-blossom viewing

NANA777777 / SHUTTERSTOCK ©

Spring (March to May)

Whether you go for the pale-pink confetti bursts of the Yoshino cherries along the Path of Philosophy (p105) or the sight of a single, rouge-coloured *shidare-zakura* (weeping cherry) draped over the wall at Ryōan-ji (p115), cherry-blossom season is an enchanting time to be in Kyoto. While the cherries seem to get all the attention, Kyoto's gardens are full of flowers and fresh green all season long. Spring is the most popular time to visit, so you'll either need to be strategic about when to go where – or willing to go with the crowds.

What to See & Do

Late April and early May is the time for azaleas and wisteria; late May and early June for irises. The gardens at Heian-jingū (p107) and Nijō-jō (p64) are both excellent spots for all these late-spring blooms, while Byōdō-in (p136) is known particularly for its wisteria and Kinkaku-ji (p114) for its irises. From mid- to late June, during the rainy season, the hydrangeas come out; see them at Sanzen-in (p131). April is also when most of the city's geisha dances (p44) take place.

The *sakura* (cherry blossoms) are notoriously fickle, but your best bet is the first week of April. They can start blooming as early as late March and usually last 10 days to two weeks – peaking dramatically towards the end, before dropping their petals in a pink carpet.

Maruyama-kōen (p92) is hands-down Kyoto's most iconic *hanami* (cherry-blossom viewing parties) spot and the best place to experience the mass bacchanal that is cherry-blossom season. Particularly famous here is the *yozakura* (night cherry blossoms), when the trees are illuminated after dark and the sake-soaked picnics go on long into the night.

Heian-jingū has a big variety of cherry trees, including many *beni-shidare-zakura* (red weeping cherry blossoms), which bloom slightly later than most other kinds. The banks of the Kamo-gawa (p63) are lined with cherry trees that form a pink tunnel in early April; this is a popular place for a stroll.

Serious *hanami* picnickers get an early start to secure a prime spot. (But unless you've got a big group, you can usually find a good sliver of ground whenever you turn up.) Popular spots usually draw food and drink vendors. You can also get everything you need for a picnic – a plastic ground sheet, food and drinks – from the convenience store. Or go upscale and stock up on picnic supplies at the *depachika* (department store food floors) at Takashimaya and Daimaru. Just remember to pack a warm layer; it can still be surprisingly cold this time of year after the sun drops.

What to Eat & Drink

Look for pretty, cherry-themed treats like *sakura-mochi* (sticky rice cake flavoured with cherry blossom and wrapped in a cherry-tree leaf) and *sakura-yu* (an infusion of pickled cherry blossoms). Spring is the season for fresh shoots, stalks and buds, like *takenoko* (bamboo shoots) and *fuki* (butterbur), which are harvested from the mountains. Try dishes like *sansai soba* (soba topped with mountain vegetables) or *sansai tempura* (batter-fried mountain vegetables). In mid-May, head to Ippōdō Tea (p74) for *shin-cha,* fresh tea from the first harvest of the season.

Summer (June to August)

Summer is the season for festivals. There are the big ones, like the Gion Matsuri (p24) and the Daimon-ji Gozan Okuribi (p24), but also a whole calendar full of smaller ones, like the Takeiri-eshiki (Bamboo-cutting Ritual) at Kurama-dera (p129) and the Taue-sai (Rice-planting Festival) at Fushimi Inari-Taisha (p56). Summer really brings out Kyoto's traditional side: lots of people, young and old, wear colourful *yukata* (light cotton kimono) to hit the festivals. Summer is hot and sticky in Kyoto, which can be trying, but the locals have come up with some ingenious ways to make the most of it.

What to See & Do

Kyoto marks the start of summer with a festival (of course), the Nagoshi no Harae (Purification Ritual of Summer's Passing) on 30 June. Shrines erect *chinowa,* large grass wreaths, which visitors walk through to be cleansed of their misdeeds from the first half of the year. Kitano Tenman-gū (p115) is popular for this.

Mossy Giō-ji (p123) looks lovely and lush after the rains of early summer. In July, head to Heian-jingū (p107) to see the water lilies. Or escape the heat with a walk in the hills, around the villages of Kurama and Kibune (p129).

Summer firework shows are a tradition around Japan; the best displays near Kyoto are in Kameoka City and Nantan City. From July through mid-September, *ukai* (traditional cormorant fishing) takes place in Arashiyama (p53).

What to Eat & Drink

In summer, restaurants along the Kamogawa, such as Tōsuirō (p70) and Fujino-ya (p70), set up *kawayuka,* terraces suspended on stilts over the riverbank, for al fresco dining. Up in the foothills north of the city, in Kibune, restaurants like Hirobun (p131) offer dining on *kawadoko* – temporary platforms set up just inches above the Kibune-gawa. (It's best to book ahead for these experiences.)

If there is one food associated with Kyoto in summer it is *hamo* (pike conger), which is traditionally eaten around the Gion festival. Festivals also mean *yatai* (food stalls), where you can get all kinds of inexpensive sweet and savoury goodies.

Another surefire sign of summer is cooling *kakigōri* (shaved ice with toppings of condensed milk, sweet red beans or fruit-flavoured syrups); many cafes and teahouses serve it. Other seasonal teahouse treats include *warabi mochi* (bracken jelly) and *kudzu-kiri* (arrowroot noodles). This is also the time of year to go crazy with those *matcha* (powdered green tea) parfaits at Karafuneya Coffee Sanjō Honten (p68) and Saryo Suisen (p67).

Autumn (September to November)

Autumn is a popular time for Japanese travellers to visit Kyoto. There's *kōyō* (autumn foliage season), most notably the deep red maples, that colour Kyoto's gardens from mid-November to early December. There's also the Kyoto Heritage

PATRICK FOTO / SHUTTERSTOCK ©

Autumn foliage

Preservation Association's Autumn Special Exhibit, when 20 or so historic structures generally closed to the public – like Tōji's five-storey pagoda – open their doors. This, along with events like the Jidai Matsuri (p24) and Kyoto Experiment (p25), makes autumn the ideal time to be in Kyoto for history buffs and culture vultures.

What to See & Do

Kyoto's top spot for *momiji-gari* (seeing the maples in autumn) is Eikan-dō (p104). For most of November, when the leaves are at their peak, the temple stays open until 8.30pm with illuminated grounds. Other places with good displays include: Kiyomizu-dera (p90), Arashiyama (p53), Giō-ji (p123), Tōfuku-ji (p57) and Ōhara's Jakkō-in (p133). Fair warning: all of these will draw crowds. There are also the bright-yellow gingko trees at Nishi Hongan-ji (p57).

Another long-cherished Kyoto tradition is *tsukimi* – moon viewing. Events are held on and around *jugoya,* the 15th day of the 8th month on the old lunar calendar (which falls in September or October of the modern calendar), at shrines and temples, including Daikaku-ji (p124), Shimogamo-jinja (p81), Kamigamo-jinja (p82) and Kitano Tenman-gū (p115).

The Autumn Special Exhibit takes place over roughly 10 days in late October and early November (for details see www.kobunka.com). This is a rare opportunity to see important works of art on temple walls and sliding doors that, for preservation reasons, can't be shown year-round. The places that open are different each year.

What to Eat & Drink

Autumn food is wonderfully earthy, with all kinds of mushrooms (including, if you

---

NEED TO KNOW

Special Openings At various times during the year sights, eg subtemples, that are normally closed to the public open their doors. Ask for details at a tourist information centre.

Seasonal Delicacies Sample the flavours of the season by booking a *kaiseki* dinner. Visit Toraya Karyō Kyoto Ichijō (p84) for seasonal *wagashi* (Japanese sweets).

Cherry Blossoms Monitor the *hanami* forecast here: www.kyuhoshi.com/japan-cherry-blossom-forecast.

want to splurge, highly prized *matsutake*), plus chestnuts, pumpkin and persimmons. In honour of the autumn full moon, it's customary to eat *tsukimi-dango* (round white rice cakes).

Winter (December to February)

Winter isn't the obvious time to visit Kyoto, but it is certainly not without its charms. Snow falls a few times a year, most often in January and February, and a coat of snow can have just as magical an effect on the city as the cherry blossoms – all the better because you won't have to share it with as many people. While winter is the least popular time to visit and the city can take on a forlorn appearance stripped of its vegetation, this time of year is conducive to the kind of private moments that can be hard to come by in Kyoto today.

What to See & Do

Should it snow, make a beeline for Kinkaku-ji (p114) – the golden temple really pops against a white backdrop. Locals love the village of Ōhara (p131) in the dead of winter; the sight of the garden, branches sheathed in ice crystals, and the mountains beyond from the main hall at Hōsen-in is spectacular. Cold weather is of course conducive to onsen-soaking. Try Funaoka Onsen (p84) in town or Kurama Onsen (p130), which has outdoor baths, up in the hills above town. Though they're considered the first sign of spring, the plum blossoms start to bloom in February. They're heartier than the cherry blossoms, darker in hue and a little bigger, and can last through mid-March. See them at Kitano Tenman-gū (p115).

What to Eat & Drink

Chief among winter pleasures is *yudōfu* (tofu cooked in a pot) – a Kyoto specialty. Try it at Okutan (p110) or Yudōfu Sagano (p126). Another representative dish is *kabura-mushi,* a dumpling made of turnip – the vegetable of winter – and minced fish or fish paste (and maybe also chopped lily bulb and gingko nuts) served in a clear broth. Look for it at obanzai restaurants (p36). This is also the season for pickled vegetables, especially *senmaizuke* (pickled turnips): head to Nishiki Market (p65) and feast your eyes on the possibilities.

For sake fans, winter means *shiboritate* – the fresh-pressed, first sake of the season, served chilled and usually unpasteurised. Or go for a *tokkuri* (ceramic flask) of body-warming *atsukan* (sake heated to 50°C). At teahouses, look for *amazake,* a naturally sweet, fermented rice drink (with no alcohol content), served piping hot.

With Kids

Kyoto is great for kids. The usual worries aren't an issue in ultra-safe and spotless Japan. Your biggest challenge will be keeping your children entertained. The very things that many adults come to Kyoto to see (temples, gardens and shrines) can be a bit boring for little ones.

NAYOMEE / GETTY IMAGES ©

Okazaki-Kōen Area

On a sunny day in Kyoto, local parents of young children tend to congregate in the Okazaki-kōen area. This region of Northern Higashiyama features a park, playing fields, a zoo, a playground and two museums. Best of all, the area is completely flat and has wide pavements, perfect for those with strollers. It can also be accessed by subway (take the Tōzai subway line to Higashiyama Station and walk north along Shira-kawa Canal). Tip: the pond behind the Kyoto Municipal Museum of Art (p105) is perfect for picnics. The Kamo-gawa riverbank is also great for kids and on hot days they can wade in the river. The area around Demachiyanagi is one of the most popular spots for parents and children to play.

Parks & Gardens

The Imperial Palace Park (p81) is the Central Park of Kyoto, and the sprawling expanse of fields, trails, ponds and woods is perfect for a walk or bicycle ride with the kids. For a picnic, a stroll or a Frisbee toss, the Kyoto Botanical Gardens (p82) are just the ticket. And the cherry blossoms last longer here than almost anywhere in town. Further afield is Takara-ga-ike-kōen, (p83) where you can hire rowboats and paddleboats on the main pond during summer.

Museums

With vintage steam locomotives, one of which you can ride, the Kyoto Railway Museum (p58) is a must for train-crazy kids, young and old. It's a wonderful interactive museum and there's a giant diorama with miniature trains wooshing around that will keep them entertained. The Manga Museum (p66) is perfect for kids interested in Japanese comics, while the quirky Kaleidoscope Museum (p66) is a fun way to while away an hour or so.

Other Child-Friendly Attractions

Fushimi Inari-Taisha

Kids will be entranced by the hypnotic arcades of *torii* (entrance gates) at this sprawling Shintō shrine (p56). There's plenty of room to run and play and burn off some energy here.

Arashiyama Monkey Park Iwatayama

Both kids and adults will find the antics of the monkeys at this park (p124) fascinating, and it's easy to combine this with a trip to the sights of Arashiyama.

Kiyomizu-dera

With fortunes to take, holy water to drink and an incredible underground sanctuary, this hands-on temple (p90) will keep even the most hyper kids happy for an hour or two.

Eating with Kids

Food can be an issue in Japan if your child is a picky eater. Let's face it: even adults can be put off by some of the things found in Japanese cuisine – asking a kid to eat sea urchin might simply be too much.

If you're going to a *kaiseki* (Japanese haute cuisine) restaurant, have your lodgings call ahead to see if they can rustle up some kid-friendly dishes. Ditto if you'll be dining at your ryokan.

You'll find quite a few so-called 'family restaurants' in Kyoto, such as Royal Host

NEED TO KNOW

Changing facilities Located in department stores and some train stations.

Cots Available in hotels (book in advance) but not ryokan.

Kids' menus Usually only in 'family restaurants'.

Transport Comfortable and safe; child seats available in rental cars but not taxis.

Babysitting (www.babysitters.jp) Partners with select hotels in Kyoto, provides English-speaking babysitters.

and Saizeriya, and these usually serve something that even finicky kids can stomach (pizza, fried chicken, French fries etc). These places often have kids' menus, too.

In addition to family restaurants, you'll find many of the usual Western fast-food chains represented in Kyoto. And there are supermarkets and convenience stores everywhere where you can self-cater for kids who simply won't eat what's on offer in restaurants.

Some of our favourite restaurants for kids include the following:

Ganko (p71) Bustling eatery with children's set meals and plenty for adults to like.

Karafuneya Coffee Sanjō Honten (p68) Plastic food models and tempting sundaes.

Nishiki Warai (p68) Entertaining fare *(okonomiyaki)* good for slightly older children (hot griddles not safe for young ones).

Like a Local

In a relatively small city crammed with tourists, it can be difficult to seek out the 'real' Kyoto – but look and you'll find it. It's where discerning locals dine in intimate restaurants hidden behind noren, catch up over coffee in chic cafes, and pray at tucked-away local shrines and temples.

Eating Out

To eat like a local, head downtown to the streets surrounding Kiyamachi-dōri and into that tight warren of lanes that lie between Oike-dōri and Shijō-dōri (north–south, respectively) and Kawaramachi-dōri and Karasuma-dōri (east–west, respectively). Here you'll find hundreds of restaurants packed cheek by jowl, and hungry Kyotoites out prowling among them, searching for the new, the tasty and the innovative.

You'll also find crowds of in-the-know locals jostling for last-minute discounts on gourmet food and *bentō* boxes for dinner at Daimaru and Taskashimaya department stores right before closing time.

Join the Celebrations

Kyoto has a packed calendar of festivals year-round giving visitors the perfect chance to mingle with locals and gain a deeper understanding of Japanese culture. While there are the three most important *matsuri* (festivals) – Gion Matsuri (p24), Aoi Matsuri (p24) and Jidai Matsuri (p24) – there are also a number of other events, such as joining the locals on the banks of

Kamo-gawa to watch fires being lit on Daimonji-yama to bid farewell to ancestors on 16 August (p24), or witnessing the annual yabusame (horseback archery; p24) event at Shimogamo-jinja in May.

A great way to join in the fun with locals is by attending a *hanami* (p26; cherry-blossom viewing party). They take place all over Kyoto during the blossom season.

Local Experiences

Biking Bicycles are a popular means of transport for Kyoto residents. Visitors can rent bicycles all over town; unlike in other cities around the world, Kyoto's rental bikes aren't brightly painted to stand out but are indistinguishable from locals' bikes.

Bathing Public bathhouses (*sentō*) are dotted around Kyoto's streets where locals come to socialise with neighbours as they soak away. Follow the lead of locals – strip off, wash yourself before entering the bath, slink into the hot water and enjoy. Check out www.japanbaths.com for more info.

Strolling Make like a local and hit the paths along the banks of the Kamo-gawa for an evening stroll, or head to Takara-ga-ike-kōen for a walk along the 1.8km path that loops around the main pond.

Local Temples & Shrines

Head to these locals' favourite temples and shrines to escape the tourist crowds.

Honen-in (p105) Duck around the corner from crowded Ginkaku-ji to this peaceful temple.

Enkō-ji (p107) Most people head to popular Shisen-dō while in this area, but this small temple nearby has gardens well loved by locals.

Ninna-ji (p115) This sprawling temple complex has pleasant grounds for wandering and attracts locals during cherry-blossom season.

Entoku-in (圓徳院; Map p218, C3; ☑075-525-0101; 530 Shimokawara-chō, Kōdai-ji, Higashiyama-ku; adult/child ¥500/200; ⊗10am-5.30pm; ⬛Kyoto City bus 206 to Yasui, Ⓢ Tōzai line to Higashiyama) This subtemple of Kodai-ji is often overlooked by tourists but locals know it has a beautiful small Zen garden for quiet meditation.

Okazaki-jinja (岡崎神社; Map p214, E5; ☑075-771-1963; 51 Okazaki Higashitennochō, Sakyō-ku; ⊗9am-5pm; ⬛Kyoto City bus 32, 93 or 100 to Okazakijinja-mae) Small quiet shrine with the rabbit as its spirit animal where locals pray for fertility.

For Free

You may think that the cost of sightseeing in Kyoto is going to require taking a second mortgage on your home. Luckily there's plenty you can do for free – you could fill at least a week with activities that won't cost a penny. Here are just a few.

Heian-jingū (p107)

Temples

The general rule is that you can tour most of the temple grounds for free, but you pay to enter the gardens and the main hall. There are exceptions to this, so if you see a temple, don't hesitate to march in and check it out. If the main hall is open, remove your shoes and enter. If you have to pay, rest assured that someone will let you know. Following are some temples with spacious grounds that can be toured free of charge.

Nanzen-ji (p103) The sprawling grounds of this superb Northern Higashiyama temple make it a favourite temple for a stroll.

Chion-in (p88) You can tour the grounds at this immense temple complex for free.

Tōfuku-ji (p57) At the south end of the Higashiyama Mountains, this fine Zen temple has expansive grounds.

Hōnen-in (p105) This tiny Pure Land paradise is a must-see. There is a gallery in one of the halls that often has free art exhibits.

Higashi Hongan-ji (p57) Close to Kyoto Station, you can take a tour of the awesome structures and shiny interiors at this temple for free.

Shrines

Like temples, you can usually tour the grounds of Shintō shrines completely free of charge. Of course, some faithful believers pay a special fee to enter the *haiden* (prayer hall) to be blessed, but this is unlikely to concern the tourist. If there is a treasure hall or garden, you may have to pay to enter, but otherwise, shrines are free.

Fushimi Inari-Taisha (p56) One of Kyoto's top sights, the only money you're likely to drop here is to buy a drink after climbing the mountain.

Heian-jingū (p107) This vast popular Northern Higashiyama shrine has a huge gravel-strewn courtyard that you can explore for free. Note that you must pay a fee to enter the gardens.

Shimogamo-jinja (p81) Take a stroll through the magnificent Tadasu-no-Mori (Forest of Truth) that leads to the main hall at this shrine.

Yasaka-jinja (p92) Overlooking Gion both physically and spiritually, this popular shrine is highly recommended in both the daytime and evening, when the lanterns make it magical.

Kamigamo-jinja (p82) Check out one of Japan's oldest shrines and a Unesco World Heritage Site, north of the botanical gardens.

Parks

Kyoto is studded with parks, ranging from the huge Imperial Palace Park to tiny pockets in residential neighbourhoods where local kids gather to play. All of Kyoto's parks are free.

Kyoto Imperial Palace Park (p81) Kyoto's Central Park is a treasure that many visitors to the city overlook. It has everything from baseball diamonds to carp ponds.

Maruyama-kōen (p92) Above Yasaka-jinja and smack on the main Southern Higashiyama sightseeing route, this lovely park is a great spot for a picnic. It also happens to be Kyoto's most popular *hanami* (cherry-blossom viewing) spot.

Takara-ga-ike-kōen (p83) This expansive park with a large main pond and walking trail makes for the perfect escape from the city.

Imperial Properties

All of Kyoto's imperial properties can be toured for free – Kyoto Imperial Palace (p81), Sentō Imperial Palace (p81), Shūgaku-in Rikyū Imperial Villa (p107) and Katsura Rikyū Imperial Villa (p125). Keep in mind, however, that only the main one, the Kyoto Imperial Palace, allows children to enter (as long as they are accompanied by adults). Children below the age of 18 are not permitted at the other three.

Other Attractions

Kamo-gawa (p63) Popular with locals, the riverside is a great place to spend a relaxing afternoon strolling and picnicking.

Nishiki Market (p65) It costs nothing to wander through this wonderful market. Of course, you might find something that you just *have* to buy...

Department stores Have a look at the fabulous variety of goods for sale in Kyoto's department stores. While you're there, stop by the food floor and snag some free food samples.

Kyoto Station (p57) Kyoto's station building is pretty impressive and the view from the rooftop observatory is the best you'll get – short of paying to ascend Kyoto Tower or expending the energy to climb Daimonji-yama.

Festivals There's nothing like a colourful Kyoto festival, and they're always free. If you're lucky, you might even be asked to participate.

Arashiyama Bamboo Grove (p121) It costs nothing to take a magical stroll around one of the most popular sights in Kyoto.

Saving Money

Sleep cheap You can find private rooms in guesthouses and budget ryokan for as low as ¥4000 per person if you look around. If you're willing to shack up in a dorm at guesthouses or hostels, you can find beds for as low as ¥2500 per person.

Fine dine in the daytime Many of Kyoto's finest restaurants serve pared-down versions of their dinnertime fare at lunch. A *kaiseki* (Japanese haute cuisine) restaurant that can cost ¥20,000 a head at dinner might serve a lunchtime set for as little as ¥4000.

Rent a cycle Kyoto is largely flat and drivers are generally safe and courteous, making Kyoto a great city to explore by bicycle. Bike hire starts from as little as ¥700 for the day.

Buy a bus, train or subway pass Some great ticket deals are available for Kyoto and the surrounding areas. The all-day city bus pass at ¥600 is excellent value.

Cheap eats *Konbini* (convenience stores), supermarkets and the basement floors of department stores are all good places to pick up cheap *bentō* box lunches and takeaway snacks, such as *onigiri* (rice-ball snack).

NORIKKO / SHUTTERSTOCK ©

Selection of pickles

 # Eating

Kyoto is one of the world's great food cities. When you consider atmosphere, service and quality, it's hard to think of a city where you get more bang for your dining buck. You can pretty much find a great dining option in any neighbourhood but most of the best spots are clustered downtown.

A History of Excellence

Kyoto punches way above its weight in the culinary arena. Among the reasons for this is that Kyoto was the centre of the country for most of its history, and its chefs had to please the fussiest of palates in the realm: the imperial court, the nobility and the heads of the main religious sects.

Another reason for Kyoto's excellent cuisine is the surrounding natural resources. The city sits atop very good groundwater (essential for making good tofu, sake and tea), and has very fertile soil for growing vegetables in the city and surrounding areas. In fact, you can still find several distinct subspecies of vegetables in the city's markets known as *kyō-yasai* (Kyoto vegetables).

The result is a relatively small city packed with fine restaurants.

Kyoto's Food Scene

Many of Kyoto's restaurants focus on local specialities, known as *kyō-ryōri* (Kyoto cuisine). In this style of cooking, the preparation of dishes makes ingenious use of fresh seasonal vegetables and emphasises subtle flavours, revealing the natural taste of the ingredients. *Kyō-ryōri* is selected according to the mood and hues of the ever-changing seasons, and the presentation and atmosphere in which it's enjoyed are as important as the flavour. Different types of *kyō-ryōri* include *kaiseki* (Japanese haute cuisine), *obanzai* (Kyoto home-style cooking) and *shojin-ryōri* (Buddhist vegetarian cuisine).

NEED TO KNOW

Opening Hours

Most restaurants open 11.30am to 2pm for lunch and 6pm to around 10pm for dinner, although some places (especially cafes) stay open all afternoon. Most places close one day a week (Monday or Tuesday being the most common). Last order is usually 30 minutes before closing.

Price Ranges

The following price ranges refer to the cost of a meal for one, not including a drink.

¥ less than ¥2000

¥¥ ¥2000–5000

¥¥¥ more than ¥5000

Tipping

There is no tipping in restaurants or cafes.

Credit Cards

Credit cards can be used at some mid-range and high-end places, especially those in department stores. Credit cards cannot be used in most small local eateries. To be safe, bring cash.

Reservations

Many popular restaurants require advance bookings, usually a day or two. At traditional high-end restaurants a reservation is essential, sometimes a month in advance. If you don't speak Japanese, the easiest thing to do is ask someone at the place you're staying to call for you.

Dress Code

For casual restaurants, you can wear whatever is comfortable. For nicer places, smart casual is usually fine.

All the other major Japanese favourites – including sushi, ramen, tempura and *okonomiyaki* (savoury pancake; batter and cabbage cakes cooked on a griddle) – can also be found in Kyoto, as can a range of international restaurants. European cuisine – particularly French, Italian and Spanish – is popular, and there are a number of Indian and Chinese restaurants. There are also some decent burger places opening up – aside from the usual fast-food chains – that offer inventive fillings, brioche buns and top-quality Wagyu beef, which are proving popular with Kyotoites and expats.

Kyoto Specialities

KAISEKI

Kaiseki is the pinnacle of refined dining, where ingredients, preparation, setting and presentation come together to create a dining experience quite unlike any other. Born as an adjunct to the tea ceremony, *kaiseki* is a largely vegetarian affair (though fish is often served) and it's usually eaten in the private room of a *ryōtei* (traditional, high-class Japanese restaurant) or ryokan. The meal is served in several small courses, giving the opportunity to admire the plates and bowls, which are carefully chosen to complement the food and seasons. Rice is eaten last (usually with an assortment of pickles) and the drink of choice is sake or beer. The Kyoto version of *kaiseki* is known as *kyō-kaiseki* and it features a variety of *kyō-yasai.*

A good *kaiseki* dinner costs upwards of ¥10,000 per person. A cheaper way to sample its delights is to visit a *kaiseki* restaurant for lunch. Most places offer lunch menus featuring a sample of the food for around ¥4000. An easy way to sample *kaiseki* is by booking a night in a 1st-class Kyoto ryokan and asking for the breakfast/dinner option.

TOFU-RYŌRI

Kyoto is famed for its tofu (soybean curd), a result of the city's excellent water and large population of (theoretically) vegetarian Buddhist monks. There are numerous exquisite *yudōfu* (tofu cooked in a pot) restaurants scattered throughout the city – many are concentrated in Northern Higashiyama along the roads around Nanzen-ji and in the Arashiyama area. One typical Kyoto tofu by-product is called *yuba,* sheets of the chewy, thin film that settles on the surface of vats of simmering soy milk. This turns up in many ryokan meals and *kaiseki* restaurants.

OBANZAI

On the flip side to Kyoto's refined *kaiseki* cuisine for the nobility, *obanzai* is the traditional home-style cooking for the everyday person – it's food for the soul. *Obanzai* cuisine features multiple dishes prepared simply, yet still packing a flavour punch through local seasonal ingredients. Fresh Kyoto vegetables, *kyo-yasai,* are at the heart of *obanzai* to provide a nourishing and affordable meal. The atmosphere of *obanzai* restaurants is usually relaxed and welcoming – and as well as seasonal vegetables, you can expect dishes such as miso soup, pickles, tofu and stews. Places to try *obanzai* include Menami (p69) in the downtown area and

Usagi no Ippo (p109) in the Okazaki-kōen area in Northern Higashiyama.

SHOJIN-RYŌRI

With over 1000 Buddhist temples, Kyoto is *the* city to sample *shojin-ryōri*. A number of temples in the city have attached simple restaurants serving *shojin-ryōri*. A typical meal involves several dishes prepared without meat and fish and centred on ingredients like tofu and seasonal vegetables. Many places also omit other animal products, such as dairy, so it can be a great choice for vegans – just be sure to ask ahead to confirm.

KYO-GASHI

If you're something of a sweet tooth, Kyoto will more than satisfy your cravings with its traditional confectionary, *kyo-gashi*. *Wagashi* is a name given to a variety of sweets and cakes that is available throughout Japan but Kyoto, in particular, is the perfect spot to sample these sugary temptations, thanks to its long tradition rooted in tea ceremony and *wagashi* making. The sweets are tied closely to the *matcha* (powdered green tea) tea ceremony and served to temper the bitterness of the tea. They are also tied into the seasons and enjoyed at celebrations throughout the year, with *wagashi* makers coming up with different designs such as cherry blossoms for summer and maple leaves to represent autumn. These delicate pieces of colourful treats are exquisite and almost too good to eat. *Namagashi* (raw sweets) are the most delicate and are made daily, so they must be eaten immediately.

One of the most famous places to try tea and *wagashi* is the family-run centuries-old Kagizen Yoshifusa (p94) in Gion or the *wagashi* institution Toraya Karyō Kyoto Ichijō (p84). Types of everyday *wagashi* include *dango* (soft rice-flour balls), *daifuku* (sticky rice cakes filled with red bean paste) and *mochi* (pounded rice made into cakes). Pick up some of these at Demachi Futaba (p84) or Tsukimochiya Naomasa (p77).

Eating in a Japanese Restaurant

When you enter a restaurant, you'll be greeted with a hearty *irasshaimase* (Welcome!). In all but the most casual places the waiter will next ask you *nan-mei sama* (How many people?). Answer with your fingers, which is what the Japanese do. You will then be led to a table, a place at the counter or a tatami room. Once seated you will be given an *o-shibori* (hot towel), a cup of tea or water (this is free) and a menu.

Many restaurants in Kyoto have English menus but you don't want to restrict yourself to only those places. While a menu in Japanese can seem daunting if you don't read the language, there are two phrases that may help: *o-susume wa nan desu ka* (What do you recommend?) and *o-makase shimasu* (Please decide for me).

When you've finished eating, signal for the bill by crossing one index finger over the other to form an 'x'. This is the standard sign for 'bill please'. You can also say *o-kanjō kudasai*. There is no tipping in Japan, though higher-end restaurants often tack on a 10% service fee. Usually you will be given a bill to take to the cashier at the front of the restaurant, but some places allow you to pay while seated at your table. Only the bigger and more international places take credit cards, so cash is always the surer option.

Special Diets
VEGETARIAN & VEGAN

Travellers who eat fish should have almost no trouble dining in Kyoto: almost all *shokudō*, *izakaya* and other common places offer a set meal with fish as the main dish. Vegans and vegetarians who don't eat fish will have options like tofu and other bean products. *Shōjin-ryōri* restaurants are a good choice and there is a growing number of vegetarian and vegan restaurants in the city. Note that the stock (*dashi*) used to make most *misoshiru* (miso soup) and some vegetable dishes contains fish, so if you want to avoid fish, check with staff if *dashi* has been used and avoid *misoshiru*.

Look for a copy of the *Kyoto Vege Map* at guesthouses and veg restaurants – it's a handy map listing many of the city's best vegetarian and vegan restaurants.

GLUTEN-FREE

Those with a gluten intolerance will find it a little tricky, though not impossible, to eat well. Rice, sushi, tofu and soba noodles made from buckwheat are all good options, though beware of *shōyu* (soy sauce), which might be added to a lot of dishes. There are a few cafes and restaurants in the city offering a small selection of gluten-free meals – try Choice (p94) close to Sanjō Station.

HALAL

There are a number of halal restaurants in Kyoto and others offering a separate halal menu. See Halal Gourmet Japan (www.halalgourmet.jp) for a list of restaurants that can accommodate halal diners.

Eating Etiquette

When it comes to eating in Japan, there are a number of implicit rules, but they're fairly easy to remember. If you're worried about putting your foot in it, relax – the Japanese don't expect you to know what to do, and they are unlikely to be offended as long as you follow the standard rules of politeness from your own country. Here are a few major points to keep in mind:

Chopsticks in rice Do not stick your *hashi* (chopsticks) upright in a bowl of rice. This is how rice is offered to the dead in Buddhist rituals. Similarly, do not pass food from your chopsticks to someone else's. This is another funeral ritual.

Slurp When you eat noodles in Japan, it's perfectly OK, even expected, to slurp them. Aficionados claim that slurping brings out the full flavour of the broth.

Polite expressions Before digging in, it is customary in Japan to say *itadakimasu* (literally 'I will receive' but closer to 'bon appétit' in meaning). Similarly, at the end of the meal, thanks is given to the host or cook with the phrase *gochisō-sama deshita*, which means 'It was a real feast'.

What to Eat

SUSHI

There are two main types of sushi: *nigiri-zushi* (served on a small bed of rice – the most common variety originating in Tokyo) and *maki-zushi* (served in a seaweed roll). Sushi without rice is known as sashimi or *tsukuri* (or, politely, *o-tsukuri*).

Sushi styles vary from region to region and Kyoto has its own different styles of sushi. As the city is located inland and fresh seafood was hard to come by back in the day, Kyoto had to come up with a different way of preparing fish. Kyoto-style sushi involves using fish that is cooked or cured, rather than raw as in the typical *nigiri-zushi*. *Saba-zushi* is made using pickled mackerel, *hamo-zushi* uses pike conger eel, and *temari-zushi* is prepared by rolling sushi into balls and placing an ingredient on top. Most sushi restaurants in Kyoto that you'll come across serve *nigiri-zushi* and *maki-zushi*, but if you're keen to try Kyoto-style sushi, one of Kyoto's oldest sushi restaurants, Izuju in Gion, is your best bet.

The beauty about sushi is that it's easy to order. If you sit at the counter of a sushi restaurant, you can simply point at what you want, as most of the selections are visible in a refrigerated glass case between you

and the sushi chef. *Kaiten-zushi* (conveyor-belt sushi restaurants) make it even easier; simply pick off what you want from the belt as it moves past you. Before popping the sushi into your mouth, dip it very lightly in *shōyu* (soy sauce), which you pour from a small decanter into a low dish specially provided for the purpose.

RAMEN

The Japanese imported this dish from China and put their own spin on it to make what is one of the world's most delicious fast foods. Ramen restaurants are easily distinguished by their long counters lined with customers hunched over steaming bowls. Dishes are big bowls of noodles in a meat broth, served with a variety of toppings, such as sliced pork, bean sprouts and leeks. In some restaurants you may be asked if you'd prefer *kotteri* (thick and fatty) or *assari* (thin and light) soup.

There are a couple of classic Kyoto-style ramen – one is made with a *shōyu* (soy sauce) and chicken-stock base, a thick soup and straight noodles, while the other popular style involves chunks of pork fat in the soup for extra richness.

Don't be afraid to do as the locals do and slurp up a storm as you eat ramen.

SOBA & UDON

Soba (thin, brown buckwheat noodles) and udon (thick, white wheat noodles) are Japan's answer to Chinese-style ramen. Many noodle restaurants offer both udon and soba prepared in a variety of ways.

Noodles are usually served in a bowl containing a light, bonito (a tuna-like fish)-flavoured broth, but you can also order them served cold and piled on a bamboo screen with a cold broth for dipping (this is called *zaru soba*). If you order *zaru soba*, you'll receive a small plate of wasabi and sliced spring onions – put these into the cup of broth and eat the noodles by dipping them in this mixture. At the end of your meal, the waiter will give you some hot broth to mix with the leftover sauce, which you drink like a kind of tea. As with ramen, feel free to slurp as loudly as you please.

OKONOMIYAKI

Okonomiyaki are thick, savoury pancakes, stuffed with pork, squid, cabbage, cheese – anything really (*okonomi* means 'as you like'; *yaki* means fry). *Okonomiyaki* is commonly associated with the Kansai region, specifically Osaka, and Hiroshima, both offering their own style of the dish quite different from the other. In Kyoto, you'll mostly find the Kansai style where the batter and ingredients are mixed together before frying. Hiroshima style involves layering the ingredients before frying.

At an *okonomiyaki* restaurant you sit around a *teppan* (iron hotplate), armed with a spatula and chopsticks to cook your choice of meat, seafood and vegetables in a cabbage and vegetable batter.

Some restaurants will do most of the cooking and bring the nearly finished product over to your hotplate for you to season with *katsuo bushi* (bonito flakes), *shōyu*, *ao-nori* (an ingredient similar to parsley), Japanese Worcestershire-style sauce and mayonnaise. Cheaper places will simply hand you a bowl filled with the ingredients and expect you to cook it for yourself. If this happens, don't panic. First, mix the batter and filling thoroughly, then place it on the hotplate, flattening it into a pancake shape. After five minutes or so, use the spatula to flip it and cook for another five minutes.

Most *okonomiyaki* places also serve *yaki-soba* (fried noodles with meat and vegetables) and *yasai-itame* (stir-fried vegetables). All of this is washed down with mugs of draught beer.

Where to Eat
SHOKUDŌ
This is the most common type of restaurant in Japan, and is found near train stations, tourist spots and just about any other place people congregate. Easily distinguished by the presence of plastic food displays in the window, these inexpensive places usually serve a variety of *washoku* (Japanese dishes) and *yōshoku* (Western dishes).

At lunch, and sometimes dinner, the easiest meal to order at a *shokudō* is a *teishoku* (set-course meal). This usually includes a main dish of meat or fish, a bowl of rice, *misoshiru* (miso soup), shredded cabbage and some *tsukemono* (Japanese pickles). In addition, most *shokudō* serve a fairly standard selection of *donburi-mono* (rice dishes) and *menrui* (noodle dishes). When you order noodles, you can choose between soba and udon, both of which are served with a variety of toppings. Expect to spend ¥600 to ¥1000 for a meal at a *shokudō*.

IZAKAYA
Izakaya is the Japanese equivalent of a pub, where you'll find a boisterous atmosphere and a range of dishes on offer, usually ordered tapas-style to share – though it's also perfectly suitable for solo diners to sit at the counter. The food is generally a mix of deep-fried dishes, sushi and sashimi, and grilled seafood and meat, paired with loads of beer, sake or *shōchū* (a strong distilled alcohol often made from potatoes). If you don't want alcohol, it's fine to order a soft drink instead, but it would be strange not to order a drink.

Cooking Courses
If you want to learn how to cook some of the delightful foods you've tried in Kyoto, we recommend **Uzuki** (www.kyotouzuki.com; 2hr class per person from ¥4500), a small cooking class conducted in a Japanese home for groups of two to four people. You will learn how to cook a variety of dishes and then sit down and enjoy the fruits of your labour. You can consult beforehand if you have particular dishes you'd like to cook. The fee includes all ingredients. Reserve via the website.

Another great cooking school in Kyoto is Haru Cooking Class (p85), a friendly one-man operation located a little bit north of Demachiyanagi. Haru speaks great English and can teach both vegetarian and non-vegetarian cooking. He also offers tours of Nishiki Market. Reserve by email.

Eating by Neighbourhood
•••

➜ **Kyoto Station & South Kyoto** (p59) There are eateries scattered all around the Kyoto Station building and a handful of *izakaya* and local spots further south.

➜ **Downtown Kyoto** (p67) The centre of Kyoto's dining scene, it has the thickest concentration of restaurants in the city.

➜ **Imperial Palace & Around** (p83) Not the best place for dining out but there are plenty of cafes perfect for a light lunch.

➜ **Gion & Southern Higashiyama** (p94) Offerings fall into two categories: tourist eateries near the temples and refined places in Gion.

➜ **Northern Higashiyama** (p108) Not a dining centre, but plenty of eateries can be found, including cheap places near Kyoto University.

➜ **Northwest Kyoto** (p117) Great eating options are a bit hard to come by in this spread-out area but there are some good choices a short walk from Kinkaku-ji.

➜ **Arashiyama & Sagano** (p124) Cheap eateries for tourists cram the main drag, with a few high-end spots further out and along the river.

Lonely Planet's Top Choices

Kikunoi (p95) One of the best places to try *kaiseki*. Dine in private rooms.

Omen (p108) Slurp delicious udon noodles at this favourite restaurant close to Ginkaku-ji.

Giro Giro Hitoshina (p69) Creative *kaiseki* stripped of formalities and easy on the wallet.

Yoshikawa (p71) Watch chefs prepare exceptionally tasty tempura from your counter seat.

Honke Owariya (p67) Tuck into homemade soba with the locals downtown.

Goya (p108) Superb Okinawan cuisine at a bright and stylish place in Northern Higashiyama.

Best By Budget

¥

Musashi Sushi (p69) Conveyor-belt sushi at its best.

Ippūdō (p67) Delectable ramen in the heart of downtown.

Honke Owariya (p67) Delicious soba and udon in a traditional old confectionery store.

Omen (p108) Udon and fresh vegetables beautifully presented in an atmospheric restaurant near Ginkaku-ji.

¥¥

Tsukiji Sushisei (p70) Really good Tokyo-style sushi at reasonable rates.

Shunsai Tempura Arima (p70) Friendly and approachable tempura in a family-run restaurant.

Giro Giro Hitoshina (p69) Exellent and affordable modern *kaiseki*.

Menami (p69) Welcoming local favourite downtown for *obanzai*.

¥¥¥

Kikunoi (p95) Arguably one of the best restaurants in Kyoto.

Yoshikawa (p71) Tempura specialist with counter seating attached to a lovely ryokan.

Kitcho Arashiyama (p127) One of the city's most reputable *kaiseki* restaurants.

Mishima-tei (p71) High-quality sukiyaki downtown.

Best For Atmosphere & Views

Kitcho Arashiyama (p127) Stunning garden views from your private dining room.

Hyōtei (p110) Atmosphere in bucketloads at this tucked-away traditional *kaiseki* restaurant.

Kyōgoku Kane-yo (p67) Dine on *unagi* in this old-world atmosphere.

Tōsuirō (p70) Excellent tofu dishes on the riverside.

Best Kaiseki

Kitcho Arashiyama (p127) No-holds-barred *kaiseki* served in superb private rooms.

Kikunoi (p95) Wonderful *kaiseki* in a classic setting.

Giro Giro Hitoshina (p69) Affordable *kaiseki* minus the pomp and formality.

Best Sushi

Musashi Sushi (p69) Convenient and cheap downtown sushi-belt restaurant.

Tsukiji Sushisei (p70) High-quality sushi in an approachable setting.

Ganko (p71) Big, touristy and bright, with very good à la carte sushi.

Best Ramen

Ippūdō (p67) Tasty Kyushu-style ramen and crispy *gyōza*.

Karako (p109) Delicious thick meaty soup and tender pork.

Kyoto Rāmen Kōji (p59) Choice of nine ramen joints in Kyoto Station.

Best Soba & Udon

Honke Owariya (p67) Filling soba and udon in a quiet downtown spot.

Hinode Udon (p109) Delicious noodles near Nanzen-ji.

Omen Kodai-ji (p94) Wonderful noodles in a smart setting in Southern Higashiyama.

Best Teahouses & Sweets

Kagizen Yoshifusa (p94) Grab a tea and sweet at this Gion institution.

Papa Jon's (p83) Delicious NYC cheesecake and light lunches.

Saryo Suisen (p67) Sky-high sundaes in a cosy teahouse.

Toraya Karyō Kyoto Ichijō (p84) Classic teahouse near the Imperial Palace Park with delicious traditional sweets.

Best Vegetarian & Vegan

Biotei (p69) High-quality vegetarian cafe right downtown.

mumokuteki cafe (p68) Casual vegan and vegetarian food in a cafe downtown.

Shigetsu (p126) A great place to try *shōjin-ryōri*.

Vegans Cafe & Restaurant (p59) Tasty vegan fare convenient when sightseeing around Fushimi Inari-Taisha.

Drinking & Nightlife

Kyoto is a city with endless options for drinking, whether it's an expertly crafted single-origin coffee in a hipster cafe, a rich matcha (powdered green tea) at a traditional tearoom, carefully crafted cocktails and single malts in a sophisticated six-seater bar, or Japanese craft beer in a brewery.

Where to Drink

Kyoto has a much deeper nightlife scene than what might first appear on the surface. Many bars are tucked away, hard to find and not obvious when wandering down streets and laneways. One exception is the city's main nightlife strip, Kiyamachi-dōri, where there's no shortage of watering holes on offer – everything from rough-and-ready student hang-outs to impossibly chic spots.

There are a few student bars and *izakaya* (Japanese pub-eateries) around the Kyoto University area, including the popular cocktail spot Bar Tantei (p110), and a smattering of pubs and *izakaya* around Gion, close to Gion-Shijō Station.

If in doubt of where to go, seeking out *izakaya* is a good bet. They serve a variety of sake and beer and Japanese food to go with it.

What to Drink

BEER

Beer is the overwhelming favourite drink to have with dinner, but gone are the days of simply having the well-known brands, Asahi, Sapporo, Kirin etc, on the menu. Craft beer is changing the beer landscape in Kyoto, with breweries like Kyoto Brewing Company (p60) and bars specialising in craft beer, such as Tadg's Gastro Pub (p72), Beer Komachi (p95) and Bungalow (p71), to name a few.

SAKE

While beer is the popular choice, sake *(nihonshū)* is making a comeback in the Old Capital. It's especially popular with sushi, *kaiseki* (Japanese haute cuisine) and at *izakayas*. Sake is usually consumed cold in Japan, especially the good stuff, but some people order it hot (the Japanese word for this is *atsukan*) at more casual places like *izakaya* and *yakitori* restaurants.

TEA

Kyoto is traditionally known for its high-quality green tea and the art of the ancient tea ceremony (p179). *Matcha* is high in caffeine and is served at tea ceremonies and in teahouses at many temples in the city. Other types of popular tea include sencha, which is a medium-grade green tea with some sharpness to the taste; *gyokuro*, which is a smoother tea with a rich umami taste; *mugicha,* a roasted barley tea; and *hōjicha,* a roasted green tea with the least amount of caffeine.

A favourite traditional tea among Kyotoites is *iribancha,* which has a distinct smoky aroma and taste, and can sometimes be smelled wafting from shops or homes around the city.

COFFEE

Coffee is moving into town in a big way. Alongside the quaint old tearooms and old-school *kissaten* (coffee shops), you'll now find almost as many modern cafes taking

NEED TO KNOW

Opening Hours

➡ Bars and *izakaya:* around 6pm to midnight or later

➡ Clubs: around 9pm to 2am or later

Cover Charge

Many bars in Japan have a 'seat charge', effectively a charge to rent a seat. The is typically around ¥500, though you'll only come across this at a handful of places in Kyoto since many foreigner-friendly bars don't impose a charge.

Resources

Kansai Scene (www.kansaiscene.com) Magazine with listings of foreigner-friendly bars and details of upcoming events. Available at major bookshops and foreigner-friendly businesses. See website for places where you can grab a copy.

Deep Kyoto (www.deepkyoto.com) This website has listings on little-known Kyoto bars, cafes and restaurants, as well as some event information.

Door Policy

Most bars have no door policy per se, but some places may be uncomfortable if you just walk in (Kyoto bars are famous for requiring guests to be introduced by an established patron). Clubs usually admit all comers, as long as you aren't obviously addled or inappropriately dressed.

Drinking Etiquette

It is bad form to fill your own glass. Fill the glass of the person next to you and wait for them to reciprocate; as they pour, raise your glass slightly with two hands. Once all glasses are filled, the usual starting signal is a chorus of *kampai* (cheers!).

coffee very seriously and attracting not only expats and tourists but young Kyotoites. Downtown has a number of top-notch hip cafes that are sourcing single-origin beans from South America and Africa and doing their own roasting, such as the excellent Weekenders Coffee Tominoko-ji (p71) and Kamogawa Cafe (p84).

SHŌCHŪ

Shōchū is popular throughout Japan and is a clear spirit typically made from potato and barley. At around an average alcohol content of 30%, it's a drink that packs a potent punch. It's usually served diluted with hot water *(oyu-wari)* or in a *chūhai* cocktail mixed with soft drinks. It's on the menu at *izakaya* and you can buy *chūhai* cans in supermarkets and *konbini* (convenience stores).

Drinking & Nightlife by Neighbourhood

➡ **Kyoto Station & South Kyoto** (p60) Not much of a nightlife destination, but plenty of bars and *izakaya* about if you need them.

➡ **Downtown Kyoto** (p71) Home to raucous bars around Kiyamachi, refined and traditional Ponto-chō spots, and cocktail bars hidden in backstreets.

➡ **Imperial Palace & Around** (p84) While this isn't party central and the options are limited, you can get a drink at many of the cafes spread around.

➡ **Gion & Southern Higashiyama** (p95) A mix of high-end (hard to enter) traditional spots, hostess bars and approachable nightspots.

➡ **Northern Higashiyama** (p110) Your best bet in this area is to seek out bars and clubs close to Keage and Jingū-Marutamachi stations.

➡ **Northwest Kyoto** (p117) This spread-out neighbourhood doesn't offer much for those looking for a night out.

➡ **Arashiyama & Sagano** (p127) The only real options for a drink here are restaurants and a few cafes.

Lonely Planet's Top Choices

World (p73) Kyoto's coolest club.

Bar K6 (p72) A slick spot for a civilised drink near the river.

Sake Bar Yoramu (p72) A sake-lover's paradise.

Bungalow (p71) Great spot for craft beer downtown.

Nokishita 711 (p71) Tiny bar hidden away mixing up inventive gin cocktails.

Best Craft Beer

Bungalow (p71) Cool industrial downtown bar with great beer.

Kyoto Brewing Company (p60) Great little standing-room-only tasting room.

Beer Komachi (p95) Japanese and imported bottled craft beer and excellent bar food to match.

Best Coffee

Weekenders Coffee Tominoko-ji (p71) Standing-room-only spot downtown brewing some of the city's best coffee.

% Arabica (p127) Top location and excellent coffee in Arashiyama.

Vermillion Espresso Bar (p60) Melbourne-inspired cafe near Fushimi Inari-Taisha.

Kiln (p72) Pretty canal-side location and excellent speciality coffee.

Kamogawa Cafe (p84) Coffee is roasted by the owner at this inviting cafe near the Imperial Palace Park.

Best For Tea

Shōren-in (p92) One of the loveliest spots to sip *matcha* while admiring the superb garden at this off-the-beaten path temple.

Ōkōchi Sansō (p120) Don't miss enjoying a cup of green tea at the traditional teahouse here in Arashiyama.

Kagizen Yoshifusa (p94) Nowhere better to sit down with some *matcha* than at this historic Gion teahouse.

Toraya Karyō Kyoto Ichijō (p84) Close to Imperial Palace Park is the long-standing Toraya sweet shop and cafe with excellent tea on offer.

Hiranoya (p127) After traipsing around the temples in Arashiyama, this atmospheric thatched teahouse is the perfect rest stop.

Best Pubs & Izakaya

Tadg's Gastro Pub (p72) Both expats and Japanese frequent this welcoming spot near downtown.

Rocking Bar ING (p73) Dark hole-in-the-wall bar with a legendary owner and dedicated local clientele.

Best Upmarket Bars

Bar K6 (p72) Single malts and expertly mixed cocktails are the draw at this smart local gathering spot.

Tōzan Bar (p95) The basement bar at the Hyatt Regency Kyoto is worth a trip for the design alone.

Gion Finlandia Bar (p96) Sophisticated Gion den with bow-tied bartenders.

Bar Rocking Chair (p72) Swanky secret cocktail bar in the backstreets of downtown.

Best Clubs

Metro (p110) Attracts a mix of creative types for disco events and live music.

World (p73) The city's hottest club hosting big-name events and DJs.

Butterfly (p73) Smaller scale club popular on weekends.

Entertainment

If you've never seen the otherworldly spectacle of kabuki (stylised Japanese theatre) or the colourful extravagance of a geisha dance, you've come to the right place: Kyoto is the best city in Japan to enjoy traditional Japanese performing arts. In addition, you'll find a lively music scene, plenty of cinemas and modern performances of all sorts.

Traditional Performing Arts

KABUKI

Performances of kabuki, Japan's most colourful and popular traditional form of performance art, are regularly held at the Minami-za theatre (p96). If renovations there are still ongoing the famous Kaomise (Face Showing) performance will be shown at ROHM Theatre Kyoto (p110). The best place to check for upcoming events is in the *Kyoto Visitor's Guide,* which is available at bookshops and foreigner-friendly accommodation around town. Tour companies can also help with tickets.

GEISHA & MAIKO PERFORMANCES

Each year Kyoto's geisha (or, properly speaking, *geiko* and *maiko* – fully fledged and trainee geisha respectively) perform fantastic dances (known as *odori*), usually on seasonal themes. Three of the geisha districts perform their dance in April, to coincide with the cherry blossoms, one performs in May, and the final one performs its dance in November, to coincide with the autumn foliage. For a small additional fee, you can participate in a brief tea ceremony before the show.

We highly recommend seeing one of these dances if you are in town when they are being held. Ask at the Kyoto Tourist Information Center (p189) or at your lodgings for help with ticket purchase. Tour companies can also help with tickets.

Another way to experience geisha and *maiko* entertainment is to join a regularly scheduled performance held at venues across town. One of the best is put on by Gion Hatanaka (p149), but if you're on a budget you can get a taster at the event organised by the JTB Kansai Tourist Information Office (p192) in Kyoto

Tower. It hosts a basic 45-minute *maiko* performance and Q&A every Monday, Wednesday and Saturday from 3.45pm (¥3000).

Live Music

Kyoto's large music venues usually specialise in classical music or touring Japanese acts (for a lot of big international acts, it's necessary to travel to Osaka). Smaller venues host a variety of Japanese acts, traditional and modern, as well as independent international acts. Small specialised live-music venues in Japan are known as 'live houses' and Kyoto's Taku-Taku (p73) is a great live house to see local bands. Also check out what's on at Metro (p110) at Jingū-Marutamachi Station and Jittoku (p85). For info on upcoming traditional music events, check the *Kyoto Visitor's Guide* or Deep Kyoto (www.deepkyoto.com). For modern acts, check *Kansai Scene* magazine.

Entertainment by Neighbourhood

Lonely Planet's Top Choices

Miyako Odori (p96) Kyoto's most dazzling geisha dance.

ROHM Theatre Kyoto (p110) For everything from ballet and opera to hosting the annual Kaomise kabuki performance.

Kyoto Cuisine & Maiko Evening (p96) One of the best ways to actually meet a geisha is at Gion Hatanaka.

Best Geisha Dances

Kyō Odori (p96) Held between first and third Sunday in April.

Miyako Odori (p96) Held throughout April.

Kitano Odori (p117) Held between 15 and 25 April.

Kamogawa Odori (p73) Held between 1 and 24 May.

Gion Odori (p96) Held between 1 and 10 November.

Best Maiko Performances

Maiko Theatre (p98) New modern theatre hosting *maiko* performance for small groups.

Maiko Dinner Show Yasakadori Enraku (p96) Dinner shows at a traditional restaurant.

Kyoto Cuisine & Maiko Evening (p96) Reputable event with dances by geisha and *maiko* at Gion Hatanaka ryokan.

Best Live-Music Venues

Taku-Taku (p73) A downtown 'live house' with a storied history.

Jittoku (p85) An atmospheric 'live house' in an old sake warehouse.

Best Classical-Music Venues

Kyoto Concert Hall (p85) Kyoto's premier classical-music venue.

ALTI (p85) A great classical-music spot located alongside the Kyoto Gosho.

ROHM Theatre Kyoto (p110) Hosts classical-music concerts with first-rate acoustics.

NEED TO KNOW

Resources

Kansai Scene (www.kansaiscene.com) This magazine has listings of what's on in the city. You can grab a copy at major bookshops and foreigner-friendly businesses.

Kyoto Guide (www.kyotoguide.com) For a month-by-month run-down on events from festivals to geisha dances.

Buying Tickets

To get your hands on tickets to most of Kyoto's traditional performing arts, such as geisha dances, kabuki and *nō* performances, your best is to enquire at your hotel or ryokan. Most business hotels and top-tier ryokan should be able to assist. Otherwise, enquire at the Kyoto Tourist Information Center (p189).

 Shopping

Kyoto has a fantastic variety of both traditional and modern shops. Most are located in the Downtown Kyoto area, making the city a very convenient place to shop. Whether you're looking for fans, kimono and tea, or the latest electronics, hip fashion and ingenuous gadgets, Kyoto has plenty to offer.

Traditional Arts & Crafts

Kyoto has a long history as Japan's artistic and cultural workshop: it's the place where the country's finest artisans produced the goods used in tea ceremonies, calligraphy, flower arrangement and religious ceremonies, as well as in kimono fabrics and other textiles. Indeed, Kyoto is the best place to find traditional arts and crafts in all of Japan.

Where to Shop

Shopping neighbourhoods in Kyoto tend to be organised by specialities, which makes things easier if you're after specific items. Here are some of Kyoto's most important shopping streets and what you'll find there:

Teramachi-dōri, north of Oike-dōri Japanese crafts, tea-ceremony goods, green tea and antiques.

Teramachi-dōri, south of Shijō-dōri Electronics and computers.

Shijō-dōri, between Kawaramachi-dōri and Karasuma-dōri Department stores, fashion boutiques and traditional arts and crafts.

Shinmonzen-dōri Antiques.

Gojō-zaka Pottery.

Shopping by Neighbourhood

➡ **Kyoto Station & South Kyoto** (p61) Big electronics and camera shops surround Kyoto Station, while there are a few crafts shops further out.

➡ **Downtown Kyoto** (p73) The entire downtown area is one giant shopping district.

➡ **Imperial Palace & Around** (p85) Head to Nishijin for handcrafted textiles.

➡ **Gion & Southern Higashiyama** (p98) Ceramics and traditional crafts.

➡ **Northern Higashiyama** (p111) Great traditional craft shops.

➡ **Northwest Kyoto** (p117) Hosts one of the city's best monthly flea markets.

➡ **Arashiyama & Sagano** (p127) Good for bamboo craft products.

MUST-SEE FLEA MARKETS

Many travellers plan their trips around the cherry blossoms or one of Kyoto's great festivals. Few, however, plan their trips around Kyoto's brilliant markets. This is a shame because Kyoto's two monthly markets are among the best flea markets in the country. You can find everything from vintage kimonos and antique lacquerware to ceramic sake sets and *testubin* (Japanese cast-iron teapots). The dates to keep in mind are the 21st of the month for the Kōbō-san Market at Tō-ji, and the 25th of the month for the Tenjin-san Market at Kitano Tenman-gū.

Lonely Planet's Top Choices

Ippodō Tea (p74) This is *the* tea shop to buy green tea, both *matcha* (powdered tea) and leaf.

Kyūkyo-dō (p74) Traditional shop in the Teramachi arcade selling an excellent selection of arts and crafts.

Wagami no Mise (p74) The selection of *washi* is just mind-boggling here.

Takashimaya (p73) The city's best department store.

Aritsugu (p74) Pick up one of Japan's most renowned brands of chef's knives.

Tokyu Hands (p76) A great range of gadgets, homewares, cosmetics and more.

Best Department Stores

Daimaru (p77) A sumptuous selection at this vast downtown store.

Takashimaya (p73) An elegant and rich assortment of shops, along with great restaurants and a food floor to boggle the mind.

BAL (p76) For high-end fashion, and books on the basement floors.

Best Traditional Crafts

Wagami no Mise (p74) A beautiful selection of *washi*

(Japanese handmade paper) at this downtown shop.

Zōhiko (p73) A wonderland for the lover of lacquerware.

Nijūsan-ya (p77) Boxwood combs and other geisha accoutrements.

Takashimaya (p73) The 6th floor of this department store has great lacquerware, pottery, wood crafts and so on.

Tsujikura (p77) Exquisite collection of colourful *wagasa* (waxed-paper umbrellas).

Best Markets

Kōbō-san Market (p61) From used kimonos to ceramics and antiques, this market has it all.

Tenjin-san Market (p117) You'll find everything from junk to treasures at this monthly market.

Nishiki Market (p65) Food is only the start of the offerings at Kyoto's most famous market.

Best Electronics

Bic Camera (p61) A mammoth retailer of electronics, computers, cameras and much more.

Yodobashi Camera (p61) All the gizmos you could ever want, and a great restaurant floor.

NEED TO KNOW

Opening Hours

➡ Department stores: 10am to 8pm or 9pm

➡ Smaller shops: 9am to 5pm, may be closed Sunday

Payment

Departments stores, modern stores, boutiques etc accept credit cards. Some small traditional shops only accept cash.

Best Food & Kitchenware

Nishiki Market (p65) Head here for traditional food-related gifts, including cooking implements, tea, sweets and sake.

Takashimaya (p73) The food floor is superb and the selection of kitchenware and dining ware on the 6th floor is not to be missed.

Aritsugu (p74) Pick up one of the best chef's knives in the world.

Kaikadō (p61) Gorgeous high-quality handcrafted *chazutsu* (tea canisters).

Best Fashion

Kyoto Marui (p76) A department store with a dedicated fashionista following.

BAL (p76) For the hottest high-end designers.

Temples & Shrines

Kyoto's temples and shrines are the main draw for many visitors to the city, and for good reason: they are among the best examples of religious architecture on earth. Moreover, temples are where you will find Japan's most superb gardens. With over 1600 Buddhist temples and more than 400 Shintō shrines, exploring these wonders is the work of a lifetime.

What to Do at a Temple

There are no steadfast rituals you must follow when visiting a Buddhist temple. Many temples require that you remove your shoes before climbing the steps into the main hall (wearing a pair of slip-on shoes will make this a lot easier). If there is a low slatted board *(sunoko)* on the ground, step out of your shoes onto this.

At many temples, you can pay a small fee (usually ¥500) for a cup of *matcha* (powdered green tea) and a Japanese sweet, which you can enjoy while looking over the garden. This is a wonderful way to enjoy a temple.

What to Do at a Shrine

There is a distinct ritual to visiting a shrine, but as long as you behave in a respectful manner, you do not have to follow it closely. If you want to do as the locals do, here is the basic drill: rinse your mouth and hands with pure water at a *temizuya* (small pavilion), using the stone ablution *chōzuya* (basin) and *hishaku* (bamboo ladle) provided for this purpose. Rinse both hands before pouring water into a cupped hand to rinse the mouth. Do not spit the water into the basin; rather, spit it onto the gravel that surrounds the basin.

Next, proceed to the *haiden* (worshippers' hall), which stands before the main hall of the shrine. Here, you will find an offering box over which a bell hangs with a long rope attached. Visitors toss a coin into the box, then grab and shake the rope to 'wake the gods', bow twice, clap loudly twice, bow again twice (once deeply, once lightly), and then step back and to the side.

Amulets are popular at shrines. *O-mamori* (special talismans) are purchased to ensure good luck or ward off evil. *O-mikuji* (fortunes) are chosen by drawing a numbered rod from a box and taking the corresponding fortune slip.

See p178 for a guide to the differences between temples and shrines.

Temples & Shrines by Neighbourhood

➡ **Kyoto Station & South Kyoto** (p56) Kyoto's most famous shrine, Fushimi Inari-Taisha, can be found here, along with a couple of the city's biggest temples.

➡ **Downtown Kyoto** (p66) Not a hotspot but there are a few local shrines and temples squeezed in between shops and restaurants.

➡ **Imperial Palace & Around** (p80) Home to important Shintō shrines and the superb Daitoku-ji Buddhist temple complex with its Zen gardens.

➡ **Gion & Southern Higashiyama** (p88) Superb temples are thick on the ground, including Kiyomizu-dera, Chion-in and Shōren-in, and colourful Yasaka-jinja.

➡ **Northern Higashiyama** (p102) A green area rich in temples and shrines, including Nanzen-ji, Ginkaku-ji and Heian-jingū.

➡ **Northwest Kyoto** (p114) Three Unesco World Heritage sites head the list: Kinkaku-ji, Ryōan-ji and Ninna-ji.

➡ **Arashiyama & Sagano** (p121) Tenryū-ji leads the procession of fine temples here.

Lonely Planet's Top Choices

Nanzen-ji (p103) The one temple that has it all: expansive grounds, a fine *kare-sansui* (dry landscape) garden, intimate subtemples and soaring halls.

Ginkaku-ji (p102) The famed 'Silver Pavilion' boasts one of Kyoto's finest gardens.

Kinkaku-ji (p114) A golden apparition rises above a tranquil reflecting pond; it's arguably Kyoto's most impressive sight.

Fushimi Inari-Taisha (p56) A mountain covered with hypnotic arcades of *torii* (shrine gates).

Shōren-in (p92) A rarely visited retreat on the main Southern Higashiyama tourist route with a superb garden.

Shimogamo-jinja (p81) A historic and lovely shrine approached by a soothing tree-lined arcade.

Best for Fewer Crowds

Shōren-in (p92) An overlooked beauty in Southern Higashiyama.

Hōnen-in (p105) Peace and quiet just a stone's throw from the Path of Philosophy.

Tōfuku-ji (p57) Outside of autumn-foliage season, you might have the place to yourself.

Enkō-ji (p107) Small temple with stunning gardens overlooked by most tourists.

Best Temple Gardens

Ryōan-ji (p115) Fifteen mystical rocks against a sea of white gravel – what could it all mean?

Tōfuku-ji (p57) A modern masterpiece in moss, gravel and stone.

Saihō-ji (p125) They don't call it Moss Temple (Kokedera) for nothing – it's a green wonderland.

Tenryū-ji (p121) The 14th-century Zen garden is one of the most superb temple gardens in the city.

Ginkaku-ji (p102) Walkways, a waterfall and carefully raked cones of white sand.

Daitoku-ji (p80) A must-see for anyone with a fondness for Zen gardens.

Best for Children

Kiyomizu-dera (p90) There's a lot to do at this 'interactive temple'. Older kids will enjoy getting spooked in the Tainai-meguri.

Fushimi Inari-Taisha (p56) Children are mesmerised by the shrine gates here.

Nanzen-ji (p103) Plenty of room to spread out and kids can enjoy taking photos and nagivating under the aqueduct arches.

Best for Meditation

Myōshin-ji (p115) Introductory classes are held at Shunkō-in, one of the subtemples at this complex in Northwest Kyoto.

Tōfuku-ji (p57) This is the real deal in Zen meditation classes.

Best for Views

Tenryū-ji (p121) The view of the Arashiyama mountains over the pond here is sublime.

Ginkaku-ji (p102) Climb the path behind the garden for a classic view over the city.

Kiyomizu-dera (p90) The view across the Kyoto basin here is worth the walk up the hill.

PLAN YOUR TRIP TEMPLES & SHRINES

NEED TO KNOW

Admission Fees

Most shrines and some temple grounds have free entry, though some shrines have treasure houses that require an admission fee, and most temples charge an entry fee for the buildings and gardens – usually ¥400 to ¥600. There may be separate entry fees for the buildings and the garden.

Opening Hours

Most shrines are open 24 hours daily and most temples are open 9am to 5pm, seven days a week. Hours sometimes vary seasonally, with longer hours in summer and reduced hours in winter.

Dress Code

There's no strict dress code for temples and shrines in Japan but it still pays to be respectful. Most sights require you to take off your shoes before entering the temple. Either wear your best socks or prepare to flaunt your bare feet, or use the (sometimes sweaty!) slippers provided.

Best for Cherry Blossoms

Tenryū-ji (p121) The gardens at this temple in Arashiyama are even more spectacular come cherry-blossom season.

Ninna-ji (p115) This temple's famous grove Omuro-no-Sakura attracts huge crowds for the cherry trees in bloom.

Heian-jingū (p107) The beautiful gardens behind this shrine feature lovely cherry trees.

Explore Kyoto

KYOTO'S TOP SIGHTS

Neighbourhoods at a Glance

❶ Kyoto Station & South Kyoto p54

Dominated by the eponymous Kyoto Station, this neighbourhood serves as the gateway to Kyoto. There are a couple of worthwhile temples within walking distance of the station, and the excellent Kyoto Railway Museum is a short bus ride away. Venture further south and you'll come to one of the city's most stunning attractions, the Shintō shrine complex Fushimi Inari-Taisha, as well as the superb Tōfuku-ji temple and garden.

❷ Downtown Kyoto p62

If all you're interested in on your Kyoto trip is dining on great cuisine, knocking back sake and craft beer at bars, boutique shopping and staying in some of the finest ryokan, you may

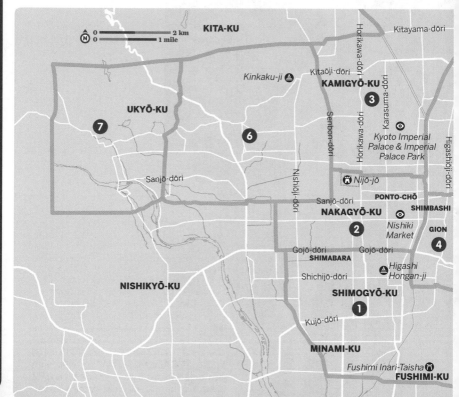

just never leave Downtown Kyoto (which is, naturally, smack bang in the middle of the city). And you wouldn't need to sacrifice culture or sightseeing, with heavyweight attractions such as Nijō-jō, the famed Nishiki Market and a smattering of small temples, shrines and museums.

❸ Imperial Palace & Around p78

Kyoto's Imperial Palace neighbourhood is the greenest area in the city centre; perfect if you're looking to take a break from pounding the pavement. Dominating the area is the expansive grounds of the Imperial Palace and its park, while to the northwest sits Daitoku-ji – a self-contained world of Zen temples, lovely gardens and lanes. Head north where the greenery continues at the Kyoto Botanical Gardens and the forest setting of the Shimogamo-jinja. This area is also home to Kyoto's traditional textile district, Nishijin.

❹ Gion & Southern Higashiyama p86

Southern Higashiyama, at the base of the Higashiyama (Eastern Mountains), is Kyoto's richest area for sightseeing. Thick with temples, shrines, museums and traditional shops, it's great to explore on foot, with some pedestrian-only walkways plus parks and expansive temple grounds. It's also home to the Gion entertainment district and some of the city's finest ryokan.

❺ Northern Higashiyama p100

At the northern end of the Higashiyama Mountains, this area is packed with first-rate attractions and soothing greenery, making it one of the best parts of the city for relaxed sightseeing. The main area stretches from Nanzen-ji in the south to Ginkaku-ji in the north, two temples linked by the lovely Path of Philosophy (Tetsugaku-no-Michi). Other attractions include Hōnen-in, a quiet temple overlooked by the crowds, the superb Eikan-dō temple with city views, and the museums around Okazaki-kōen.

❻ Northwest Kyoto p112

Northwest Kyoto contains two of Kyoto's most important temples: Kinkaku-ji (the Golden Pavilion) and Ryōan-ji, home of Japan's most famous Zen garden. Other noteworthy sights include the enclosed world of Myōshin-ji and the atmospheric Kitano Tenman-gū Shintō shrine. Further afield are the mountaintop temples of Takao.

❼ Arashiyama & Sagano p118

Arashiyama and Sagano, two adjoining neighbourhoods at the base of Kyoto's western mountains, form the city's second-most-popular sightseeing district after Southern Higashiyama. Foreign and domestic tourists flock here to see Tenryū-ji, a temple with a stunning mountain backdrop, and the famous Arashiyama Bamboo Grove. There are also several small temples scattered around and a not-to-be-missed hilltop villa with gardens – Ōkōchi-Sansō – making it a great place to escape the city and simply wander.

NEIGHBOURHOODS AT A GLANCE

Shirakawa-dōri

SAKYŌ-KU
❺
⛩ Ginkaku-ji

⛩ Nanzen-ji

⛩ Chion-in

HIGASHIYAMA-KU

⛩ Kiyomizu-dera

Kyoto Station & South Kyoto

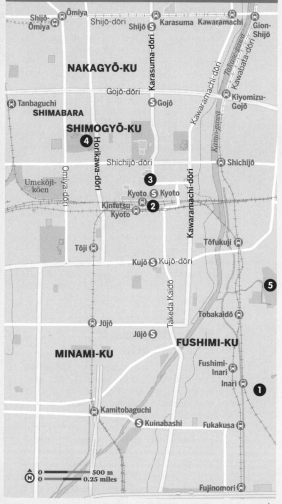

Neighbourhood Top Five

1 **Fushimi Inari-Taisha** (p56) Wandering through the hypnotic arcades of *torii* (entrance gates to a Shintō shrine).

2 **Kyoto Station** (p57) Gazing up at the striking architecture and taking in views from the Sky Garden.

3 **Kyoto Tower** (p57) Whisking up to the top of the tower for great views over the city.

4 **Nishi Hongan-ji** (p57) Immersing yourself in the grandeur of this temple.

5 **Tōfuku-ji** (p57) Strolling through the expansive grounds of this beautiful temple complex.

For more detail of this area see Map p216 ➡

Explore Kyoto Station & South Kyoto

For most travellers to Kyoto, the Kyoto Station area serves as the entry point to the city. Odds are, your first step in Kyoto will be onto one of the train platforms in Kyoto Station. This being the case, be warned that your first glimpse of the city is likely to be an anticlimax at best, a rude shock at worst: the area around the station is mainly concrete, hotels and billboards with the retro Kyoto Tower dominating the landscape. But, rest assured, there is good stuff (and the more traditional landscape you probably came here for) in every direction.

The station building itself is packed with restaurants and shops, as are the streets surrounding the buildings, though the better options lie elsewhere outside of this area. You will still find some great-value hotels here and it does make a convenient base for exploring. There are also a couple of worthwhile temples within a very easy walk from the station: Nishi Hongan-ji and Higashi Hongan-ji.

The area south of the station is undergoing a bit of a regeneration with some great design hotels, hip hostels and cafes starting to sprout up. And a short train ride or leisurely walk further southeast will have you exploring a couple of the city's top sights: Fushimi Inari-Taisha and Tōfuku-ji.

Local Life

→ **Hang-out** On weekends you'll find locals sipping some of the finest craft beer at the Kyoto Brewing Company (p60).

→ **Eating out** Get stuck into *okonomiyaki* at neighbourhood bar-restaurant Arata (p59), hidden away in a street south of the station.

Getting There & Away

→ **Train** The JR lines, including the *shinkansen* (bullet train), and the private Kintetsu line operate to/from Kyoto Station.

→ **Bus** Many city buses, JR buses and other bus lines operate to/from the Kyoto Station Bus Terminal (on the north side of the station).

→ **Subway** The Karasuma subway line stops directly underneath Kyoto Station (the Kyoto Station stop is called simply 'Kyoto').

Lonely Planet's Top Tip

During high seasons for tourism (cherry-blossom season in April and autumn-foliage season in November), the taxi ranks on the south and north side of Kyoto Station can be very long. If you're in a hurry, walk a few blocks north of the station and hail a cab off the street.

✗ Best Places to Eat

→ Vegans Cafe & Restaurant (p59)
→ Cube (p59)
→ Eat Paradise (p59)
→ Kyoto Rāmen Kōji (p59)

For reviews, see p59. ➡

♒ Best Places to Drink

→ Kyoto Brewing Company (p60)
→ Roots of all Evil (p60)
→ Kurasu (p60)

For reviews, see p60. ➡

🔒 Best Places to Shop

→ Bic Camera (p61)
→ Yodobashi Camera (p61)
→ Kaikadō (p61)
→ JR Isetan Department Store (p61)

For reviews, see p61. ➡

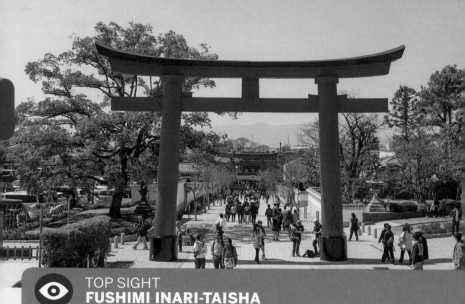

TOP SIGHT
FUSHIMI INARI-TAISHA

With seemingly endless arcades of vermilion *torii* (shrine gates) spread across a thickly wooded mountain, this vast shrine complex is a world unto its own. It is, quite simply, one of the most impressive and memorable sights in all of Kyoto. A pathway wanders 4km up the mountain and is lined with dozens of atmospheric sub-shrines.

From 8th-Century Beginnings

Fushimi Inari was dedicated to the gods of rice and sake by the Hata family in the 8th century. As the role of agriculture diminished, deities were enrolled to ensure prosperity in business. Nowadays the shrine is one of Japan's most popular, and is the head shrine for some 40,000 Inari shrines scattered the length and breadth of the country.

The Messenger of Inari

As you explore the shrine, you will come across hundreds of stone foxes. The fox is considered the messenger of Inari, the god of cereals, and the stone foxes, too, are often referred to as Inari. The key often seen in the fox's mouth is for the rice granary. On an incidental note, the Japanese traditionally see the fox as a sacred, somewhat mysterious figure capable of 'possessing' humans – the favoured point of entry is under the fingernails.

Hiking

The walk around the upper precincts of the shrine is a pleasant day hike. It also makes for a very eerie stroll in the late afternoon and early evening, when the various graveyards and miniature shrines along the path take on a mysterious air. It's best to go with a friend at this time.

DON'T MISS

➜ View of Kyoto from the upper trails
➜ The fox-shaped prayer plaques hanging everywhere
➜ Photo opportunities inside the seemingly endless *torii*

PRACTICALITIES

➜ 伏見稲荷大社
➜ 68 Yabunouchi-chō, Fukakusa, Fushimi-ku
➜ admission free
➜ ◷dawn-dusk
➜ ℝJR Nara line to Inari or Keihan line to Fushimi-Inari

◉ SIGHTS

HIGASHI HONGAN-JI   BUDDHIST TEMPLE
Map p216 (東本願寺, Eastern Temple of the True
Vow; www.higashihonganji.or.jp; Karasuma-dōri,
Shichijō-agaru, Shimogyō-ku; audio guide at information centre ¥500; ⊙5.50am-5.30pm Mar-
Oct, 6.20am-4.30pm Nov-Feb; ⬛Kyoto Station)
FREE A short walk north of Kyoto Station,
Higashi Hongan-ji is the last word in all
things grand and gaudy. Considering its
proximity to the station, the free admission,
the awesome structures and the dazzling
interiors, this temple is the obvious spot to
visit when near the station. The temple is
dominated by the vast **Goei-dō** (Main Hall),
said to be the second-largest wooden structure in Japan, standing 38m high, 76m long
and 58m wide. The refurbished hall contains an image of Shinran, the founder of
the sect, although the image is often hidden
behind sumptuous gilded doors.

There's a tremendous **coil of rope** made
from human hair on display in the passageway to the adjoining refurbished **Amida-dō**
hall, where the Amida Buddha is enshrined
on the central altar. Following the destruction of the temple in the 1880s, a group of
female temple devotees donated their locks
to make the ropes that hauled the massive
timbers used for reconstruction.

Higashi Hongan-ji was established in
1602 by Shogun Tokugawa Ieyasu in a 'di-
vide and conquer' attempt to weaken the
power of the enormously popular Jōdo
Shin-shū (True Pure Land) school of Buddhism. The temple is now the headquarters
of the Ōtani branch of Jōdo Shin-shū.

SHŌSEI-EN   GARDENS
Map p216 (渉成園; ☑075-371-9210; Karasuma-
dōri, Shichijō-agaru, Shimogyō-ku; adult/child
¥500/250; ⊙9am-5pm Mar-Oct, to 4pm Nov-Feb;
⬛Kyoto Station) About five minutes' walk
east of Higashi Hongan-ji, this garden is a
peaceful green island in a vast expanse of
concrete. While it's not on par with many
other gardens in Kyoto, it's worth a visit if
you find yourself in need of something to
do near Kyoto Station, perhaps paired with
a visit to the temple. The lovely grounds,
incorporating the **Kikoku-tei** villa, were
completed in 1657.

NISHI HONGAN-JI   BUDDHIST TEMPLE
Map p216 (西本願寺; Horikawa-dōri, Hanayachō-
sagaru, Shimogyō-ku; ⊙5.30am-5pm; ⬛Kyoto
Station) **FREE** A vast temple complex

located about 15 minutes' walk northwest
of Kyoto Station, Nishi Hongan-ji comprises
several buildings that feature some of the
finest examples of architecture and artistic
achievement from the Azuchi-Momoyama
period (1568–1603). The **Goei-dō** is a mar-
vellous sight. Another must-see building is
the **Daisho-in** hall, which has sumptuous
paintings, carvings and metal ornamenta-
tion. A small garden and two *nō* (stylised
Japanese dance-drama) stages are connected with the hall. The dazzling **Kara-mon**
has intricate ornamental carvings.

KYOTO STATION   NOTABLE BUILDING
Map p216 (京都駅; www.kyoto-station-building.
co.jp; Karasuma-dōri, Higashishiokōji-chō,
Shiokōji-sagaru, Shimogyō-ku; ⬛Kyoto Station)
The Kyoto Station building is a striking
steel-and-glass structure – a kind of futuristic cathedral for the transport age – with
a tremendous space that arches above you
as you enter the main concourse. Be sure
to take the escalator from the 7th floor on
the east side of the building up to the 11th-
floor glass corridor, Skyway (open 10am to
10pm), that runs high above the main concourse of the station, and catch some views
from the 15th-floor Sky Garden terrace.

The station building contains several
food courts, a foreign currency exchange
shop, as well as the JR Isetan Department
Store and the Kyoto Tourist Information
Center (p192).

**KYOTO TOWER
OBSERVATION DECK**   VIEWPOINT
Map p216 (京都タワー; Karasuma-dōri, Shichijō-
sagaru, Shimogyō-ku; adult ¥770, child ¥150-520;
⊙9am-9pm, last entry 8.40pm; ⬛Kyoto Station)
Located right outside the Karasuma (north)
gate of Kyoto Station, this retro tower looks
like a rocket perched atop the Kyoto Tower
Hotel. The observation deck on the tower
provides excellent views in all directions
and you can really get a sense for the Kyoto
bonchi (flat basin). It's a great place to get
orientated to the city upon arrival. There
are free mounted binoculars to use and a
cool touchscreen panel showing what the
view looks like both day and night.

★TŌFUKU-JI   BUDDHIST TEMPLE
(東福寺; ☑075-561-0087; 15-778 Honmahi,
Higashiyama-ku; Hōjō garden ¥400, Tsūten-kyō
bridge¥400; ⊙9am-4pm; ⬛Keihan line to Tōfukuji
or JR Nara line to Tōfukuji) Home to a spectacular garden, several superb structures

and beautiful precincts, Tōfuku-ji is one of the best temples in Kyoto. It's well worth a visit and can easily be paired with a trip to Fushimi Inari-Taisha (the temples are linked by the Keihan and JR train lines). The present temple complex includes 24 subtemples. The huge **San-mon** is the oldest Zen main gate in Japan, the **Hōjō** (Abbot's Hall) was reconstructed in 1890, and the gardens were laid out in 1938.

The northern garden has stones and moss neatly arranged in a chequerboard pattern. From a viewing platform at the back of the gardens you can observe the **Tsūten-kyō** (Bridge to Heaven), which spans a valley filled with maples.

Founded in 1236 by the priest Enni, Tōfuku-ji belongs to the Rinzai sect of Zen Buddhism. As this temple was intended to compare with Tōdai-ji and Kōfuku-ji in Nara, it was given a name combining characters from the names of each of these temples.

Tōfuku-ji offers regular Zen meditation sessions for beginners, but don't expect coddling or English-language explanations: this is the real deal. Get a Japanese speaker to enquire at the temple about the next session (it holds about four a month for beginners).

Note that Tōfuku-ji is one of Kyoto's most famous autumn-foliage spots, and it is invariably packed during the peak of colours in November. Otherwise, it's often very quiet.

TŌ-JI
BUDDHIST TEMPLE

Map p216 (東寺; 1 Kujō-chō, Minami-ku; admission to grounds free, Kondō & Kōdō each ¥500, pagoda, Kondō & Kōdō ¥800; ◎8.30am-5.30pm 20 Mar-19 Sep, to 4.30pm 20 Sep-19 Mar; 🚌Kyoto City bus 205 from Kyoto Station, 🚊Kintetsu Kyoto line to Tōji) One of the sights south of Kyoto Station, Tō-ji is an appealing complex of halls and a fantastic pagoda that makes a fine backdrop for the monthly flea market held on the grounds. The temple was established in 794 by imperial decree to protect the city. In 823 the emperor handed it over to Kūkai (known posthumously as Kōbō Daishi), the founder of the Shingon school of Buddhism.

Many of the temple buildings were destroyed by fire or fighting during the 15th century, and most of the remaining buildings were destroyed in the Momoyama period.

The **Nandai-mon** (Main Gate) was transported here in 1894 from Sanjūsangen-dō in Southern Higashiyama. The **Kōdō** (Lecture Hall) dates from the 1600s and contains 21 images representing a Mikkyō (esoteric Buddhist) mandala. The **Kondō** (Main Hall), which was rebuilt in 1606, combines Chinese, Indian and Japanese architectural styles and contains statues depicting the Yakushi (Healing Buddha) trinity.

In the southern part of the garden stands the **Gojū-no-tō**, a five-storey pagoda that, despite having burnt down five times, was doggedly rebuilt in 1643. Standing at 57m, it is now the highest pagoda in Japan.

The Kōbō-san market fair is held here on the 21st of each month. There is also a regular market that runs on the first Sunday of each month.

KYOTO RAILWAY MUSEUM
MUSEUM

Map p216 (梅小路蒸気機関車館; www.kyoto railwaymuseum.jp; Kankiji-chō, Shimogyō-ku; adult ¥1200, child ¥200-500, train ride ¥300/100; ◎10am-5.30pm Thu-Tue; 🚻; 🚌Kyoto City bus 103, 104 or 110 from Kyoto Station to Umekōji-kōen/Kyoto Railway Museum-mae) The Umekoji Steam Locomotive Museum underwent a massive expansion in 2016 to reopen as the Kyoto Railway Museum. This superb museum is spread over three floors showcasing 53 trains, from vintage steam locomotives in the outside Roundhouse Shed to commuter trains and the first *shinkansen* (bullet train) from 1964. Kids will love the interactive displays and impressive railroad diorama with miniature trains zipping through the intricate landscape. You can also take a 10-minute ride on one of the smoke-spewing choo-choos.

Several of the exhibits have come from Osaka's Modern Transportation Museum, which has now closed. Displays walk visitors through the history of Japanese railway innovation and delve into a new level of detail from railway uniforms and tools to a working level crossing and the inner workings of the ticket machine – buy your ticket, feed it into the machine and watch through the transparent cover! The museum has an open passageway layout so you can peer down on the displays and trains from the upper levels, as well as see city views from the 3rd-floor Skydeck.

SUMIYA PLEASURE HOUSE
NOTABLE BUILDING

Map p216 (角屋もてなしの文化美術館; ☑075-351-0024; Nishishinyashikiageya-chō 32,

Shimogyō-ku; adult/child ¥1000/500; ⊙10am-4pm Tue-Sun; 🚌Kyoto City bus 205 from Kyoto Station, 🚇JR line to Tanbaguchi) Sumiya Pleasure House is the last remaining *ageya* (pleasure house) in the old Shimabara pleasure quarter. Built in 1641, this stately two-storey, 20-room structure allows a rare glimpse into Edo-era nirvana. With its delicate latticework exterior, Sumiya has a huge open kitchen and an extensive series of rooms (including one extravagantly decorated with mother-of-pearl inlay). To visit the 2nd storey, you need to join one of the 30-minute tours in Japanese (¥800).

Shimabara, a district northwest of Kyoto Station, was Kyoto's original pleasure quarters. At its peak during the Edo period (1603–1868) the area flourished, with more than 20 enormous *ageya* – magnificent banquet halls where artists, writers and statesmen gathered in a 'floating world' ambience of conversation, art and fornication. Geisha were often sent from their *okiya* (living quarters) to entertain patrons at these restaurant-cum-brothels. By the start of the Meiji period, however, such activities had drifted north to the Gion district and Shimabara had lost its prominence.

There is an English leaflet available and captions throughout.

EATING

★VEGANS CAFE & RESTAURANT
VEGAN, JAPANESE ¥

(☏075-643-3922; www.veganscafe.com; 4-88 Nishiura-chō, Fukakusa, Fushimi-ku; meals ¥540-2500; ⊙11.30am-5pm Thu-Tue, to 9pm Sat; 🚗🌱; 🚉Keihan line to Fujinomori) 🌿 Who needs meat and dairy when food can taste this good without it? This light-filled cafe is a haven for vegans and vegetarians with a range of meals from healthy salad, rice and miso sets, to huge bowls of soy-milk miso ramen and deep-fried tofu pizza. There's organic beer, wine and coffee, too. It's a convenient detour when sightseeing around Fushimi-Inari.

KYOTO TOWER SANDO
FOOD HALL ¥

Map p216 (Kyoto Tower, B1 Karasuma-dōri, Shichijō-sagaru, Shimogyō-ku; ⊙11am-11pm; 🚉Kyoto Station) Head to the basement floor of the Kyoto Tower building for a range of food stalls to feast on. There's everything from a Mexican taco stand and ramen

to *yakiniku* (grilled meat) and *kaiten-sushi*. Seek out stand-up bar Roots of all Evil (p60) for a pre- or post-dinner gin cocktail.

ARATA
OKONOMIYAKI ¥

Map p216 (あらた; ☏075-661-5444; 24-4 Nishikujō Inmachi, Minami-ku; okonomiyaki from ¥530; ⊙5-11pm Mon-Sat; 🚉Kyoto Station) This small neighbourhood *okonomiyaki* (savoury pancake) restaurant is a great place to grab dinner if you're in the Kyoto Station area. It's cheap and cheerful with a local friendly atmosphere.

KYOTO RĀMEN KŌJI
RAMEN ¥

Map p216 (京都拉麺小路; ☏075-361-4401; www.kyoto-ramen-koji.com; 10F Kyoto Station Bldg, Karasuma-dōri, Shiokōji-sagaru, Shimogyō-ku; ramen ¥730-1150; ⊙11am-10pm; 🚉Kyoto Station) If you love your noodles, do not miss this collection of nine ramen restaurants on the 10th floor of the Kyoto Station building (on the west end, take the escalators that start in the main concourse or access via the JR Isetan Department Store south elevator to the 11th floor). Buy tickets from the machines (in English, with pictures) before queuing.

EAT PARADISE
JAPANESE ¥

Map p216 (イートパラダイス; ☏075-352-1111; 10F Kyoto Station Bldg, Karasuma-dōri, Shiokōji-sagaru, Shimogyō-ku; ⊙11am-10pm; 🚉Kyoto Station) On the 10th floor of the Kyoto Station building, you'll find this collection of decent restaurants. Among the choices here are Tonkatsu Wako for *tonkatsu* (deep-fried breaded pork cutlet), Tenichi for sublime tempura, and Wakuden for approachable *kaiseki* (Japanese haute cuisine).

Take the west escalators from the main concourse to get here – Eat Paradise is in front of you when you get to the 10th floor. Alternatively, take the north elevator in the JR Isetan Department store to the 11th floor. Note that the restaurants here can be crowded, especially at lunchtimes on weekends.

CUBE
JAPANESE ¥

Map p216 (ザ キューブ; ☏075-371-2134; 10F Kyoto Station Bldg, Karasuma-dōri, Shiokōji-sagaru, Shimogyō-ku; ⊙11am-10pm; 🚉Kyoto Station) This is a great collection of restaurants located on the 10th floor of the Kyoto Station building; otherwise it can be accessed by the JR Isetan Department Store south elevator

WORTH A DETOUR

FUSHIMI SAKE DISTRICT

Fushimi, home to 37 sake breweries, is one of Japan's most famous sake-producing regions. Its location on the Uji-gawa made it perfect for sake production, as fresh, high-quality rice was readily available from the fields of neighbouring Shiga-ken and the final product could be easily loaded onto boats for export downriver to Osaka.

Despite its fame, Fushimi is one of Kyoto's least-attractive areas. It's also a hard area to navigate due to a lack of English signage. It's probably only worth a visit if you have a real interest in sake and sake production.

To get to Fushimi, take the Keihan line train from Sanjō Station to Chūshojima Station (¥270, 15 minutes).

The largest of Fushimi's sake breweries is **Gekkeikan Sake Ōkura Museum** (月桂冠大倉記念館; ☑075-623-2056; www.gekkeikan.co.jp; 247 Minamihama-chō, Fushimi-ku; adult/child ¥300/100; ⏰9.30am-4.30pm; ☒Keihan line to Chūshojima), the world's leading producer of sake. Although most of the sake is now made in Osaka, a limited amount is still handmade in a Meiji-era *sakagura* (sake brewery) here in Fushimi. The museum is home to a collection of artefacts and memorabilia tracing the 350-year history of Gekkeikan and the sake-brewing process.

Kizakura Kappa Country (キザクラカッパカントリー; ☑075-611-9919; 228 Shioya-chō, Fushimi-ku; ⏰11.30am-2.30pm & 5-10pm; ☒Keihan line to Chūshojima) FREE is a short walk from Gekkeikan. The vast complex houses both sake and beer breweries (not open to the public), courtyard gardens and a small gallery dedicated to the mythical (and sneaky) creature Kappa. The restaurant-bar is an appealing option for a bite and a bit of fresh-brewed ale.

Another lunch option is the tasty *yakitori* (chicken grilled on skewers) at **Torisei** (鳥せい; ☑075-622-5533; 186 Kamiaburagake-chō, Fushimi-ku; yakitori pieces from ¥140, lunch sets from ¥750; ⏰11.30am-11pm Tue-Fri, from 11am Sat & Sun; ☒Keihan line to Chūshojima), washed down with sake. It's run by the owner of the Yamamoto Honke sake brewery). Head straight up the street from Gekkeikan away from the canal, past the second street on the right and look for the sake barrels out the front.

(11th floor). Most of the restaurants here serve Japanese food and some come with views. Note the restaurants can get crowded with queues, especially on weekends.

🍷 DRINKING & NIGHTLIFE

KURASU   COFFEE
Map p216 (☑075-744-0804; www.kurasu.kyoto; 552 Higashiaburano-koji chō, Shimogyō-ku; coffee from ¥330; ⏰8am-6pm; ☎; ☒Kyoto Station) Finally there's good coffee to be found near Kyoto Station! This minimalist cafe has a menu of monthly rotating coffee from specialty roasters in Japan, and offers filter coffee and espresso along with a *matcha* latte and Prana chai.

ROOTS OF ALL EVIL   BAR
Map p216 (www.nokishita.net; Kyoto Tower, B1 Karasuma-dōri, Shichijō-sagaru, Shimogyō-ku; ⏰11am-11pm; ☒Kyoto Station) 🍷 Stop by this standing bar in the Kyoto Tower Sando food basement for creative gin cocktails. It's run by the owner of Nokishita 711 (p71) and offers interesting herbal, spicy, floral gin infusions. Cocktails from ¥800.

VERMILLION ESPRESSO BAR   CAFE
(バーミリオン; 85 Onmae-chō, Fukakusa-inari, Fushimi-ku; ⏰9am-5pm Mon-Fri, 10am-5pm Sat & Sun, closed irregularly; ☎; ☒JR Nara line to Inari or Keihan line to Fushimi-Inari) A Melbourne-inspired cafe, tiny Vermillion takes its name from the colour of the *torii* (gates) of the nearby Fushimi Inari-Taisha shrine. It does standout coffee as well as a small selection of cakes, which can be taken away or sit in at the one communal table. It's on the main street, just a short hop from Inari Station.

KYOTO BREWING COMPANY   BREWERY
(京都醸造株式会社; ☑075-574-7820; www.kyotobrewing.com; 25-1 Takahata-chō, Nishikujō, Minami-ku; ⏰1-6pm Sat & Sun; ☒Kintetsu line to Jūjō) You'll find its beer in many of Kyoto's bars but it's worth a trip out to this small

tasting room to sample it in a friendly local setting in South Kyoto. Check out the brewery vats as you sip on a selection of six beers on tap, including a few limited releases. Open most weekends from 1pm to 6pm; check the website.

 SHOPPING

KAIKADŌ HOMEWARES

(開化堂; ☎075-351-5788; www.kaikado.jp; 84-1 Umeminato-chō, Shimogyō-ku; ❍noon-6pm Mon-Sat; ᏰKeihan line to Kiyomizu-Gojō) Stop by this tiny tucked-away store to covet the beautiful tin, copper and brass *chazutsu* (tea canisters) handcrafted by a family of artisans for over 130 years. They may not come cheap, but if they are looked after carefully, they will last a lifetime.

YODOBASHI CAMERA ELECTRONICS

Map p216 (ヨドバシカメラ; ☎075-351-1010; 590-2 Higashi Shiokōji-chō, Shimogyō-ku; ❍9.30am-10pm; ᏰKyoto Station) This mammoth shop sells a range of electronics, camera and computer goods, and also has a restaurant floor, a branch of popular Uniqlo budget clothing store, a supermarket, a bookshop, a cafe and, well, the list goes on. It's a few minutes' walk north of Kyoto Station.

BIC CAMERA ELECTRONICS

Map p216 (ビックカメラ; ☎075-353-1111; 927 Higashi Shiokōji-chō, Shimogyō-ku; ❍10am-9pm; ᏰKyoto Station) The sheer amount of gadgets and goods this store has on display is amazing. Just be sure that an English operating manual is available for your purchases. It's also a good place to pick up a prepaid Japanese SIM card. It's directly connected to Kyoto Station via the Nishinotō-in gate; otherwise, it's accessed by leaving the north (Karasuma) gate and walking west.

KUNGYOKU-DŌ ARTS & CRAFTS

Map p216 (薫玉堂; ☎075-371-0162; www.kungyokudo.co.jp; Horikawa-dōri, Nishihonganji-mae, Shimogyō-ku; ❍9am-5.30pm, closed 1st & 3rd Sun of month; ᏰKyoto Station) A haven for the olfactory sense, this shop has sold incense and aromatic woods (for burning, similar to incense) for four centuries. This is a great place to pick up some distinctively

Japanese souvenirs and gifts that are easy to carry home.

KŌBŌ-SAN MARKET MARKET

Map p216 (弘法さん, 東寺露天市; 1 Kujō-chō, Tō-ji, Minami-ku; ❍dawn-dusk, 21st of each month; ᏰKyoto City bus 205 from Kyoto Station, ᏰKintetsu Kyoto line to Tōji) This market is held at Tō-ji each month to commemorate the death of Kōbō Daishi, who in 823 was appointed abbot of the temple. If you're after used kimonos, pottery, bric-a-brac, plants, tools and general Japanalia, this is the place.

JR ISETAN DEPARTMENT STORE DEPARTMENT STORE

Map p216 (ジェイアール京都伊勢丹; ☎075-352-1111; Kyoto Station Bldg, Karasuma-dōri, Shiokōji-sagaru, Shimogyō-ku; ❍10am-8pm; ᏰKyoto Station) Isetan is an elegant department store located inside the Kyoto Station building, making it perfect for a last-minute spot of shopping before hopping on the train to the airport. Don't miss the B1 and B2 food floors.

POPONDETTA ÆON MALL KYOTO SHOP TOYS

Map p216 (ポポンデッタ イオンモールKYOTO 店; ☎075-644-9220; 4th fl, Æon Mall Kyoto, 1 Nishikujō, Turiiguchi-chō, Minami-ku; ❍10am-9pm; ᏰKyoto Station) If you've got a child who likes trains, don't miss this excellent toy train shop. In addition to a wide range of toy trains, you'll find a great model railroad layout to keep the kids entertained.

KYŌSEN-DŌ ARTS & CRAFTS

Map p216 (京扇堂; ☎075-371-4151; www.kyosendo.co.jp; Tsutsugane-chō 46, Higashinotōin-dōri, Shōmen-agaru, Shimogyō-ku; ❍9am-5pm; ᏰKyoto Station) Kyōsen-dō sells a colourful variety of paper fans starting at reasonable prices.

KŌJITSU SANSŌ SPORTS & OUTDOORS

Map p216 (好日山荘; ☎075-708-5178; 5th fl, Kyoto Yodobashi Camera, 590-2 Higashi Shiokōji-chō, Shimogyō-ku; ❍9.30am-10pm; ᏰKyoto Station) On the 5th floor of the Yodobashi Camera building, this is one of Kyoto's biggest outdoor goods shops. If you're heading up to the Japan Alps to do some hiking, you might want to stop here before getting on the train.

Downtown Kyoto

Neighbourhood Top Five

❶ **Nijō-jō** (p64) Treading lightly over squeaking 'nightingale' floors while exploring the castle.

❷ **Nishiki Market** (p65) Marvelling at all the weird and wonderful ingredients that go into Kyoto cuisine.

❸ **Ponto-chō** (p66) Strolling this atmospheric street in the evening lantern light.

❹ **Takashimaya** (p73) Drooling over gourmet goods on display in this department store's basement food floor.

❺ **Tawaraya** (p146) Experiencing a night at one of the world's finest places to stay in this centuries-old ryokan.

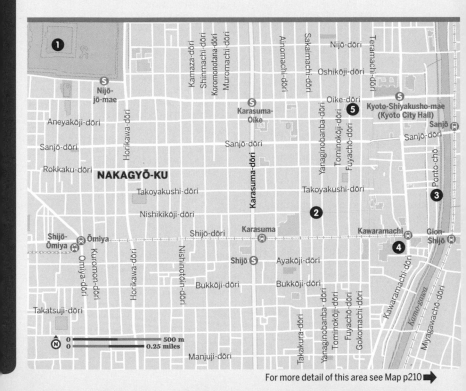

For more detail of this area see Map p210 ➡

Explore Downtown Kyoto

Downtown Kyoto is bounded by the Kamo-gawa (the river) to the east, Karasuma-dōri to the west, Oike-dōri to the north and Shijō-dōri to the south. In this relatively small square area, you will find the thickest selection of restaurants, shops, hotels and businesses in all of Kyoto.

The main streets of Shijō and Kawaramachi hold some of the best department stores and a few eating options, but you'll also find a huge selection of shops and restaurants in the area's four covered shopping streets (known as *shōtengai*): Sanjō (good for restaurants), Teramachi (a mix of art, souvenirs and clothing), Shinkyōgoku (mostly tacky souvenirs for kids) and Nishiki Market (the city's main food market). But don't just explore these main shopping streets: also head into the maze of smaller streets west of Teramachi, where you'll find a great array of interesting boutiques, cafes, a couple of museums and restaurants.

Local Life

➡ **Shopping** It might be a tourist hotspot but Nishiki Market (p65) is still a gourmet food shopping favourite for locals.

➡ **Hang-out** Locals linger for hours at Café Bibliotec Hello! (p67) sipping coffee, chatting and reading novels.

➡ **Romantic spot** Paris has the Seine and Kyoto has the Kamo-gawa. This is where local couples go for a bit of 'quality time'.

Getting There & Away

➡ **Subway** The Karasuma subway line stops at Shijō and Karasuma-Oike stations. The Tōzai line also stops at Karasuma-Oike Station and Kyoto-Shiyakusho-mae Station.

➡ **Train** The Hankyū line stops at Karasuma and Kawaramachi stations.

➡ **Bus** Many city buses stop in Downtown Kyoto.

 ## Lonely Planet's Top Tip

Finding a good place to eat in Downtown Kyoto can be confusing (there are almost *too many* places to choose from). If you want a lot of choice in a small area, hit one of the *resutoran-gai* (restaurant floors) at Takashimaya or Daimaru.

DOWNTOWN KYOTO

 ### Best Places to Eat

➡ Ippūdō (p67)
➡ Giro Giro Hitoshina (p69)
➡ Yoshikawa (p71)
➡ Honke Owariya (p67)
➡ Roan Kikunoi (p71)
➡ Menami (p69)

For reviews, see p67.

 ### Best Places to Drink

➡ Nokishita 711 (p71)
➡ Bar Rocking Chair (p72)
➡ Bungalow (p71)
➡ Sake Bar Yoramu (p72)
➡ Bar K6 (p72)
➡ World (p73)

For reviews, see p71.

Best Places to Shop

➡ Takashimaya (p73)
➡ Wagami no Mise (p74)
➡ Ippōdō Tea (p74)
➡ Aritsugu (p74)
➡ Zōhiko (p73)
➡ Kyūkyo-dō (p74)

For reviews, see p73.

TOP SIGHT
NIJŌ-JŌ

Standing like a direct challenge to the might of the emperor in the nearby Imperial Palace, the shogun castle of Nijō-jō is a stunning monument to the power of the warlords who effectively ruled Japan for centuries. It's a fascinating destination, with superb (almost rococo) interiors, and the grounds contain expansive gardens that are perfect for a stroll.

Background

In 1868 the last Tokugawa shogun, Yoshinobu, surrendered his power to the newly restored Emperor Meiji inside Nijō-jō.

Nijō-jō is built on land that was originally occupied by the 8th-century Imperial Palace, which was abandoned in 1227. The castle was constructed in 1603 as the official Kyoto residence of the first Tokugawa shogun, Ieyasu. To safeguard against treachery, Ieyasu had the interior fitted with 'nightingale' floors (intruders were detected by the squeaking boards) and concealed chambers where bodyguards could keep watch and spring out at a moment's notice.

The Shinsen-en Garden, just south of the castle, is all that remains of the original palace. This forlorn garden has small shrines and a pond.

Highlights

The **Momoyama-era Kara-mon gate**, originally part of Hideyoshi's Fushimi-jō in the south of the city, features lavish, masterful woodcarving and metalwork. After passing through the gate, you enter the **Ninomaru palace**, which is divided into five buildings with numerous chambers. Access to the buildings used to depend on rank – only those of highest rank were permitted into the inner buildings. The **Ōhiroma Yon-no-Ma** (Fourth Chamber) has spectacular screen paintings, though these are reproductions. Original paintings are stored in the **Nijo Castle 400th Anniversary Gallery** on the northeast side of the palace. The exhibitions change quarterly and are on display during scheduled periods throughout the year. Check the website for the schedule.

The neighbouring **Honmaru palace** dates from the mid-19th century. After the Meiji Restoration in 1868, the castle became a detached palace of the imperial household and in 1939 it was given to Kyoto City. These days it's only open for a special autumn viewing.

Ninomaru Palace Garden, the garden that surrounds the inner castle buildings, is a must-see. This superb garden was designed by Kobori Enshū, Japan's most celebrated garden designer. This vast garden comprises three separate islets spanned by stone bridges and is meticulously maintained. The Ninomaru palace and garden take about an hour to walk through. A detailed fact sheet in English is provided.

DON'T MISS

➡ Ninomaru Palace Garden
➡ Ōhiroma Yon-no-Ma
➡ Original screen paintings in the Nijō-jō 400th Anniversary Gallery

PRACTICALITIES

➡ 二条城
➡ Map p210, A1
➡ 541 Nijōjō-chō, Nijō-dōri, Horikawa nishi-iru, Nakagyō-ku
➡ adult/child ¥600/200
➡ ⊗8.45am-5pm, last entry 4pm, closed Tue Dec, Jan, Jul & Aug
➡ ⑤Tōzai line to Nijō-jō-mae, ⑧JR line to Nijō

TOP SIGHT
NISHIKI MARKET

Nishiki Market (Nishiki-kōji Ichiba) is one of Kyoto's real highlights, especially if you have an interest in cooking and eating. Commonly known as Kyoto no daidokoro (Kyoto's kitchen) by locals, it's where most of Kyoto's high-end restaurateurs and wealthy individuals do their food shopping. This is the place to see the weird and wonderful foods that go into Kyoto cuisine.

History

The pedestrian-only, covered Nishiki Market is right in the centre of town, one block north of Shijō-dōri, running from Teramachi *shōtengai* (market streets) to Takakura-dōri (ending almost behind Daimaru department store). It's said that there were stores here as early as the 14th century, and it's known for sure that the street was a wholesale fish market in the Edo period (1603–1868). After the end of Edo, as Japan entered the modern era, the market became a retail market, which it remains today.

The Wares

The emphasis is on locally produced Japanese food items like *tsukemono* (Japanese pickles), tea, beans, rice, seaweed and fish. In recent years the market has been evolving from a strictly local food market into a tourist attraction, and you'll now find several souvenir shops selling Kyoto-style souvenirs mixed in among the food stalls.

Shopping Highlight

Aritsugu (p74) turns out some of the most exquisite knives on earth. Take time to pick the perfect one for your needs, then watch as the craftsmen carefully put a final edge on the knife with the giant round sharpening stone – the end product will be so sharp it will scare you.

DON'T MISS

➡ Aritsugu

➡ Trying some of the 'unique' street food, such as *takotamago* (small octopus head stuffed with a quail egg on a stick)

PRACTICALITIES

➡ 錦市場

➡ Map p210, F4

➡ Nishikikōji-dōri, btwn Teramachi & Takakura, Nakagyō-ku

➡ ⏰9am-5pm

➡ ⑤Karasuma line to Shijō, ㋹Hankyū line to Karasuma or Kawaramachi

⊙ SIGHTS

KYOTO UKIYO-E MUSEUM MUSEUM

Map p210 (京都浮世絵美術館; ☑075-223-3003; www.kyoto-ukiyoe-museum.com; 2nd fl, Kirihata Bldg, Shijō-dōri, Teramachi Nishiiri, Shimogyō-ku; adult/child ¥600/300; ⊙10.30am-6.30pm; ℞Hankyū line to Kawaramachi) Opened in 2017, this one-room museum displays a selection of *ukiyo-e* (woodblock prints) by some of Japan's most well-known artists, including Hiroshige Utagawa, Utamaro Kitagawa and Hokusai Katsushika. *Ukiyo-e* is said to have originated in the 16th century with prints showing the lives of common people in Kyoto, and most of the works shown here are of scenes from Kyoto. The exhibitions change every few months but Japan's most famous *ukiyo-e* work, Hokusai's *The Great Wave off Kanagawa,* is permanently on display.

PONTO-CHŌ AREA

Map p210 (先斗町; Ponto-chō, Nakagyō-ku; ⑤Tōzai line to Sanjo-Keihan or Kyoto-Shiyakusho-mae, ℞Keihan line to Sanjo, Hankyū line to Kawaramachi) There are few streets in Asia that rival this narrow pedestrian-only walkway for atmosphere. Not much to look at by day, the street comes alive at night, with wonderful lanterns, traditional wooden exteriors, and elegant Kyotoites disappearing into the doorways of elite old restaurants and bars. Ponto-chō is also a great place to spot *geiko* (geisha) and *maiko* (apprentice geisha) making their way between appointments, especially on weekend evenings at the Shijō-dōri end of the street. Many of the restaurants and teahouses can be difficult to enter, but several reasonably priced, accessible places can be found. Even if you have no intention of patronising one of the businesses here, it makes a nice stroll in the evening, perhaps combined with a walk in nearby Gion.

KYOTO INTERNATIONAL MANGA MUSEUM MUSEUM

Map p210 (京都国際マンガミュージアム; www.kyotomm.jp; Karasuma-dōri, Oike-agaru, Nakagyō-ku; adult/child ¥800/100; ⊙10am-6pm Thu-Tue; 🚻; ⑤Karasuma or Tōzai lines to Karasuma-Oike) Located in an old elementary school building, this museum is the perfect introduction to the art of manga (Japanese comics). It has 300,000 manga in its collection, 50,000 of which are on display in the *Wall of Manga* exhibit. While most of the manga and displays are in Japanese, the collection of translated works is growing. In addition to the galleries that show both the historical development of manga and original artwork done in manga style, there are beginners' workshops and portrait drawings on weekends.

Visitors with children will appreciate the children's library and the occasional performances of *kami-shibai* (humorous traditional Japanese sliding-picture shows), not to mention the artificial lawn where the kids can run free. The museum hosts six-month-long special exhibits yearly: check the website for details.

MUSEUM OF KYOTO MUSEUM

Map p210 (京都文化博物館; ☑075-222-0888; www.bunpaku.or.jp; Takakura-dōri, Sanjō-agaru, Nakagyō-ku; ¥500, extra for special exhibitions; ⊙10am-7.30pm Tue-Sun; ⑤Karasuma or Tōzai lines to Karasuma-Oike) This museum is worth visiting if a special exhibition is on (the regular exhibits are not particularly interesting and don't have much in the way of English explanations). On the 1st floor, the Roji Tempō is a reconstruction of a typical merchant area in Kyoto during the Edo period (this section can be entered free; some of the shops sell souvenirs and serve local dishes). Check the *Kyoto Visitor's Guide* for upcoming special exhibitions.

KALEIDOSCOPE MUSEUM OF KYOTO MUSEUM

Map p210 (京都万華鏡ミュージアム; ☑075-254-7902; 706-3 Dongeinmae-chō, Aneykōji-dōri, Higashinotōin higashi-iru, Nakagyō-ku; adult/child ¥300/200, special exhibits extra; ⊙10am-6pm Tue-Sun; ⑤Karasuma or Tōzai lines to Karasuma-Oike) This one-room museum is filled with unexpected wonders in a wide variety of kaleidoscopes. Not sure who will enjoy this more, children or the adults trying to keep them entertained. It's right behind the Museum of Kyoto.

SHIORI-AN MUSEUM

Map p210 (紫織庵; ☑075-241-0215; Shinmachi-dōri, Sanjō-dōri, Rokkaku-agaru, Nakagyō-ku; ¥800; ⊙10am-5pm; ⑤Karasuma or Tōzai lines to Karasuma-Oike) Located in a large merchant's house, this kimono-shop-museum walks visitors through the architecture of a traditional building built in the *daibeizukuri* style. You can also see the back part of the house that was converted into a Western-style building around the turn of last century (when Japan became fascinated with all things Western), as well as kimonos on display. There is an English brochure available.

ATMOSPHERIC STROLLS IN KYOTO

Kyoto is one of the world's great walking cities, especially after dark. The soft glow of paper lanterns hung from *machiya* (traditional Japanese townhouses) turn the already pretty streets into something out of a movie set.

Ponto-chō Take a short but sweet stroll through one of the most atmospheric lanes in all of Japan. Expect crowds in the evening.

Kiyamachi The section of Kiyamachi-dōri between Oike and Gojō is incredibly beautiful after dark, especially during cherry-blossom season. The section between Sanjō and Shijō is not as romantic as it's home to a lot of the city's clubs and nightlife.

Kiyomizu to Yasaka While it's clogged with tourists during the day, the main tourist route from Kiyomizu-dera down to Yasaka-jinja is usually almost deserted after dark. It's truly magical at this time.

Path of Philosophy (p105) The crowds are usually gone by 5pm here, leaving this scenic pathway to locals and savvy travellers.

Gion (p89) A brief stroll along Hanami-kōji, across Shijō, and over to Shimbashi, is well off the beaten path but it can't detract from the beauty of this historic area.

EATING

★**HONKE OWARIYA**　　　　NOODLES ¥
Map p210 (本家尾張屋; ☑075-231-3446; www.
honke-owariya.co.jp; 322 Kurumaya-chō, Nijō,
Nakagyō-ku; soba from ¥760; ⊘11am-7pm; ⑤Karasuma or Tōzai lines to Karasuma-Oike) Set in an old sweets shop in a traditional building on a quiet downtown street, this is where locals come for excellent soba (buckwheat noodle) dishes. The highly recommended house speciality, *hourai soba* (¥2160), comes with a stack of five small plates of soba with a selection of toppings, including shiitake mushrooms, shrimp tempura, thin slices of omelette and sesame seeds.

★**CAFÉ BIBLIOTEC HELLO!**　　　CAFE ¥
Map p210 (カフェビブリオティックハロー!;
☑075-231-8625; 650 Seimei-chō, Nijō-dōri, Yanaginobanba higashi-iru, Nakagyō-ku; meals from ¥850, coffee ¥450; ⊘11.30am-midnight; ❋☏;
⑤Tōzai line to Kyoto-Shiyakusho-mae) As the name suggests, books line the walls of this cool cafe located in a converted *machiya* (traditional Japanese townhouse) attracting a mix of locals and tourists. It's a great place to relax with a book or to tap away at your laptop over a coffee or light lunch. Look for the huge banana plants out the front.

KYŌGOKU KANE-YO　　　JAPANESE ¥
Map p210 (京極かねよ; ☑075-221-0669;
456 Matsugaechō, Rokkaku, Shinkyōgoku
higashi-iru, Nakagyō-ku; unagi over rice from ¥1400; ⊘11.30am-9pm; ⑤Tōzai line to Kyoto-Shiyakusho-mae) This is a good place to try *unagi* (eel). You can choose to either sit downstairs with a nice view of the water-

fall, or upstairs on the tatami. The *kane-yo donburi* (eel over rice) set is excellent value. Look for the barrels of live eels outside and the wooden facade.

IPPŪDŌ　　　RAMEN ¥
Map p210 (一風堂; ☑075-213-8800; Higashinotōin, Nishikikōji higashi-iru, Nakagyō-ku; ramen from ¥790; ⊘11am-3am, to 2am Sun; ⑤Karasuma line to Shijō) There's a reason that there's usually a line outside this place at lunchtime: the ramen is fantastic and the bite-sized *gyōza* (dumplings) are to die for. The *gyōza* set meal (from ¥1440) is great value.

SARYO SUISEN　　　SWEETS, CAFE ¥
Map p210 (茶寮翠泉; ☑075-278-0111; 521
Takatsuji-chō, Shimogyō-ku; matcha parfait ¥1480; ⊘10.30am-6pm; ⑤Karasuma line to Shijō) There are countless places in Kyoto to be restrained with your *matcha* (powdered green tea) and sweets...this teahouse isn't one of them. Roll up your sleeves, loosen your belt and get ready for a sugar high – it's all about the *matcha* parfaits here, piled as high as Kyoto Tower with sponge cake, *matcha* ice cream, sweet red-bean paste, *dango* (soft rice-flour balls) and more.

GYOZA CHAO CHAO　　　DUMPLINGS ¥
Map p210 (☑075-251-0056; Kiyamachi-dōri, Sanjō-sagaru, Nakagyō-ku; 3 pieces from ¥300; ⊘5pm-2am Mon-Fri, 2pm-2am Sat, 2pm-midnight Sun; ⑤Tōzai line to Kyoto-Shiyakusho-mae) Smack bang in the heart of Kyoto's bar scene, it's no wonder Chao Chao draws long queues for its crispy *gyōza* (dumplings) – great as a predrink dinner, even better as a late-night drunken snack. Grab a counter

seat or squish beside a table and try to stop chao chao chowing down plates of shrimp, boiled ginger, garlic kimchi or pork *gyōza*.

Vegetarians aren't forgotten – try the excellent *yuba gyōza* made with freeze-dried tofu wrapped in a soy milk skin. Cash only.

PAPA JON'S
CAFE ¥

Map p210 (パパジョンズカフェ　本店; ☎075-211-1600; cnr Rokkaku-dōri & Sakaimachi-dōri higashi-iru, Nakagyō-ku; cake from ¥500, lunch from ¥850; ◷9.30am-9pm, closed 3rd Tue of month; ☎; Ⓢ Karasuma or Tōzai lines to Karasuma-Oike) This convenient downtown branch of the original favourite Papa Jon's (p83) serves its excellent New York cheesecake, as well as breakfast sets, quiche, soup and salads. It also does a range of gluten-free cakes, including the cheesecake.

CAFE PHALAM
CAFE ¥

(カフェパラン; ☎075-496-4843; www.phalam. jp; Shin Nijyo Bldg, 24 Hokusei-chō, Nishinokyo, Nakagyō-ku; meals from ¥850, coffee ¥330; ◷9am-8pm Mon-Fri, to 7pm Sat & Sun; ☎🖊; Ⓢ Tōzai line to Nijō, ⒭ JR line to Nijō) A short walk from Nijō-jō, this homey cafe is a great spot to lunch on mainly vegan and vegetarian homemade food, from veggie burgers with salad to vegan cakes. The excellent coffee served in large cups is made from beans sourced from Africa and South America, and the kids will be happy with the selection of toys.

MUMOKUTEKI CAFE
VEGETARIAN ¥

Map p210 (ムモクテキカフェ; ☎075-213-7733; www.mumokuteki.com; 2nd fl, Human Forum Bldg, 351 Iseya-chō, Gokomachi-dōri, Rokkaku-sagaru, Nakagyō-ku; meals from ¥1000; ◷11.30am-10pm; 🖊; ⒭ Hankyū line to Kawaramachi) Above the mumokuteki shop in the middle of the downtown area, this popular cafe is a lifesaver for vegetarians. The food is tasty, varied and served in casual homey surroundings. Try the tofu and avocado burger paired with a fresh vegetable juice. Most of the food served is vegan, but non-vegan options are clearly marked on the picture menu.

LE BOUCHON
FRENCH ¥

Map p210 (ブション; ☎075-211-5220; www.bel lecour.co.jp; 71 Enoki-chō, Nijo-dōri, Teramachi higashi-iru, Nakagyo-ku; set lunch from ¥1340, mains from ¥1650; ◷11.30am-2.30pm & 5.30-9.30pm Fri-Wed; Ⓢ Tōzai line to Kyoto-Shiyakusho-mae) For casual French fare at reasonable prices, Le Bouchon is a great choice. Like a good Parisian bistro, it's got old-school charm and tends to be boisterous, crowded

and approachable. The set meals are the way to go and the fish dishes usually outshine the meat dishes.

OMEN NIPPON
JAPANESE, NOODLES ¥

Map p210 (おめんNippon; ☎075-253-0377; 171 Kashiwaya-chō, Shijō-dōri, Ponto-chō nishi-iru, Nakagyo-ku; udon from ¥1150; ◷11.30am-3pm & 5-10pm Fri-Wed; ☎; ⒭ Hankyū line to Kawaramachi) This is the downtown branch of the famous Ginkaku-ji noodle restaurant. It serves a variety of healthy set meals and, of course, the signature omen udon noodles served in a broth with a side of fresh vegetables. It's a small place that's a nice oasis amid the downtown mayhem. Look for the word 'Nippon' on the sign.

MEW'Z CAFE
ASIAN ¥

Map p210 (ミューズカフェ; ☎075-212-2911; 717-1 Yōhōjimae-chō, Teramachi-dōri, Nijō-agaru, Nakagyo-ku; lunch/dinner sets from ¥820/1100; ◷11.30am-10pm Mon-Fri, to 10.30pm Sat & Sun; ☎; Ⓢ Tōzai line to Kyoto-Shiyakusho-mae) With its relaxed bohemian feel and Pan-Asian menu, Mew'z cafe-restaurant is a great place to break up bouts of shopping on Teramachi-dōri. Drop in for a Vietnamese coffee, a glass of wine or a Tsingtao beer, otherwise dine on nasi goreng, Thai curries, satay skewers or a *bánh mì* (Vietnamese baguette) with avocado and shrimp.

KARAFUNEYA COFFEE
SANJŌ HONTEN
CAFE ¥

Map p210 (からふねや珈琲三条本店; ☎075-254-8774; 39 Daikoku-chō, Kawaramachi-dōri, Sanjō-sagaru, Nakagyō-ku; parfait from ¥780; ◷9am-11pm, to 1am Fri & Sat; Ⓢ Tōzai line to Kyoto-Shiyakusho-mae, ⒭ Keihan line to Sanjō) This coffee and dessert cafe is smack in the middle of Kyoto's main shopping district. In a country famous for its plastic food models, Karafuneya takes them to a whole new level – check out the centrepiece as you enter: the mother of all sundaes goes for ¥50,000! Lesser mortals can try the tasty *matcha* parfait (¥870).

NISHIKI WARAI
OKONOMIYAKI ¥

Map p210 (錦わらい; ☎075-257-5966; www. nishikiwarai.com; 1st fl, Mizukōto Bldg, 597 Nishiuoya-chō, Nishikikōji-dōri, Takakura nishi-iru, Nakagyo-ku; okonomiyaki from ¥700; ◷11.30am-midnight; Ⓢ Karasuma line to Shijō, ⒭ Hankyū line to Karasuma) Nishiki Warai is a great place to try *okonomiyaki* (savoury pancakes) in casual surroundings. It can get a little smoky, but it's a fun spot to eat. Your *okonomiyaki* will be served ready-made to the hotplate at your table. It's about 20m west of the west end of Nishiki Market; look for the English sign in the window.

RĀMEN KAIRIKIYA
RAMEN ¥

Map p210 (ラーメン魁力屋; ☑075-251-0303; 1st fl, Hijikata Bldg, 435-2 Ebisu-chō, Kawaramachi-dōri, Sanjō-agaru, Nakagyō-ku; ramen from ¥650; ⓧ11am-3am; ⓢTōzai line to Kyoto-Shiyakusho-mae) Not far from the Sanjō and Kawaramachi intersection, this popular ramen specialist welcomes foreigners with an English menu and friendly staff. It's got several types of ramen to choose from and tasty sets that include items like fried rice, fried chicken or *gyōza*, all for about ¥880. It's pretty easy to spot: look for the red-and-white signage.

MUSASHI SUSHI
SUSHI ¥

Map p210 (寿しのむさし; ☑075-222-0634; www.sushinomusashi.com; Kawaramachi-dōri, Sanjō-agaru, Nakagyō-ku; plates from ¥146; ⓧ11am-10pm; ⓢTōzai line to Kyoto-Shiyakusho-mae, ⓡKeihan line to Sanjō) If you've never tried a *kaiten-sushi* (conveyor-belt sushi restaurant), don't miss this place – most dishes are a mere ¥146. Not the best sushi in the world, but it's cheap, reliable and fun. It's also easy to eat here: you just grab what you want off the conveyor belt. If you don't see what you want, there's also an English menu to order from. Musashi is just outside the entrance to the Sanjō covered arcade; look for the miniature sushi conveyor belt in the window.

BIOTEI
VEGETARIAN ¥

Map p210 (びお亭; ☑075-255-0086; 2nd fl, M&I Bldg, 28 Umetada-chō, Sanjō-dōri, Higashinotōin nishi-iru, Nakagyō-ku; lunch/dinner sets from ¥870/1295; ⓧ11.30am-2pm & 5-8.30pm, closed Sun, Mon, lunch Sat & dinner Thu; ◢; ⓢTōzai or Karasuma lines to Karasuma-Oike) Located diagonally across from Nakagyō post office, this is a favourite of Kyoto vegetarians, serving daily sets of Japanese food with dishes such as deep-fried crumbed tofu and black seaweed salad with rice, miso and pickles. The seating is rather cramped but the food is excellent, beautifully presented and carefully made from quality ingredients.

CAFÉ INDEPENDANTS
CAFE ¥

Map p210 (カフェ アンデパンダン; ☑075-255-4312; www.cafe-independants.com; Basement, 1928 Bldg, Sanjō-Gokomachi kado, Nakagyō-ku; meals from ¥600; ⓧ11.30am-midnight; ◢) ⓢTōzai line to Kyoto-Shiyakusho-mae) Located beneath a gallery, this cool subterranean cafe offers a range of snacks, meals and drinks, including craft beer, coffee and cocktails, in a bohemian atmosphere (after you eat, check out the gallery space upstairs). A lot of the food offerings are displayed for you to choose from. Take the stairs on your left before the gallery.

APPRIVOISER WHOLEFOOD CAFE
CAFE ¥

Map p210 (☑075-351-6251; http://vegecafe.org; 716 Matsubara-dōri, Matsubara-sagaru, Shimogyō-ku; meals from ¥500; ⓧ8am-7pm Tue-Sun; ◢◢; ⓡHankyū line to Kawaramachi or Keihan line to Kiyomizu-Gojō) This simple cosy cafe is a great spot to grab a healthy breakfast – it opens early (a rarity in Kyoto) and serves a tasty cheap Japanese breakfast set, a good morning curry and homemade granola with yoghurt, along with organic coffee and a delicious house-made chai.

★GIRO GIRO HITOSHINA
KAISEKI ¥¥

Map p210 (☑075-343-7070; 420-7 Nanba-chō, Nishi-kiyamachi-dōri, Matsubara-sagaru, Shimogyō-ku; kaiseki from ¥4100; ⓧ5.30pm-midnight; ⓡHankyū line to Kawaramachi or Keihan line to Kiyomizu-Gojō) Often referred to as 'punk *kaiseki*', Giro Giro takes traditional *kaiseki* and strips any formality so you're left with great food but in a boisterous atmosphere and with thousands more yen left in your pocket. In a quiet lane near Kiyamachi-dōri, things liven up inside with patrons sitting at the counter around the open kitchen chatting it up with chefs preparing inventive dishes. There are two sittings per night and the seasonal menu consists of eight courses. There are upstairs tables, too, but if you want a counter seat, book well in advance; for a Friday or Saturday night you'll need to allow a couple of months in advance. Cash only.

★MENAMI
JAPANESE ¥¥

Map p210 (めなみ; ☑075-231-1095; www.menami.jp; Kiyamachi-dōri, Sanjō-agaru, Nakagyō-ku; dishes ¥400-1000; ⓧ5-11pm Mon-Sat; ⓢTōzai line to Kyoto-Shiyakusho-mae, ⓡKeihan line to Sanjō) This welcoming neighbourhood favourite specialises in *obanzai ryōri* – a type of Kyoto home-style cooking using seasonal ingredients – done creatively and served as tapas-size plates. Don't miss the delicious spring rolls wrapped with *yuba* (tofu skin; 生ゆば春巻). Try to book a counter seat where you can eye off bowls filled with dishes to choose from while watching the chefs in action. Otherwise, start with the *obanzai* taster plate (¥1200) and go from there. Book ahead.

SHUNSAI TEMPURA ARIMA　TEMPURA ¥¥

Map p210 (旬菜天ぷら　有馬; ☑075-344-0111; 572 Sanno-chō, Muromachi-dōri, Takatsuji-agaru, Shimogyō-ku; lunch/dinner sets from ¥1080/4860; ☺11.30am-2pm & 5.30-10.30pm Fri-Wed; Ⓢ Karasuma line to Shijō) Tempura is one of Japan's tastiest dishes and this friendly downtown restaurant is a great place to try it. It's a tiny family-run joint with a welcoming atmosphere. The English-language menus and set meals make ordering easy. It's on a corner with a small English sign.

SHI-SHIN SAMURAI CAFE AND BAR　CAFE ¥¥

Map p210 (士心; ☑075-231-5155; http://univer salpeace.co.jp/shishin; 230-1 Kamimyōkakuji-chō, Koromonotana-dōri, Oshikōji-agaru, Nakagyō-ku; dishes from ¥700, set dinner course ¥5000; ☺5.30-11pm Tue-Sun; ☑; Ⓢ Karasuma or Tōzai lines to Karasuma-Oike) Decked out in replica swords and armour, this restaurant might not strike you as a place dedicated to world peace, yet the young owner here is passionate about it and doing his bit by bringing people together through food. The meals are tasty, with plenty of vegetarian options, and the friendly staff will give you a history lesson on samurai. The link between world peace and the samurai theme is *bushidō* – a mixture of Shintoism, Buddhism, and Confucianism religions and a samurai code of conduct focusing on Zen and inner strength rather than violence.

TŌSUIRŌ　TOFU ¥¥

Map p210 (豆水楼; ☑075-251-1600; www.tou suiro.com; Kiyamachi-dōri, Sanjō-agaru, Nakagyō-ku; lunch/dinner from ¥2835/4536; ☺11.30am-2.30pm & 5-10pm Mon-Sat, noon-3.30pm & 5-9.30pm Sun; Ⓢ Tōzai line to Kyoto-Shiyakusho-mae) You will be amazed by the variety of dishes that can be created with tofu at this specialist tofu restaurant. It's got traditional Japanese decor and in summer you can sit on the *yuka* (dining platform) outside and take in a view of the river (¥1000 seat charge). You'll find it at the end of an alley on the north side off Kiyamachi-dōri. At lunch the *machiya-zen* tofu set (¥2494) is highly recommended, while for dinner the Higashiyama tofu set (¥3969) is excellent.

FUJINO-YA　JAPANESE ¥¥

Map p210 (藤の家; ☑075-221-2446; Ponto-chō, Shijō-agaru, Nakagyō-ku; tempura sets from ¥1300, dishes from ¥450; ☺5-10.30pm, closed Wed Oct-Apr; Ⓡ Hankyū line to Kawaramachi) This is one of the easiest places for non-Japanese to enter on Ponto-chō, a street where many of the other restaurants turn down even unfamiliar Japanese diners. Here you can feast on tempura and *kushi-katsu* (deep-fried skewers of meat, seafood and vegetables) in tatami rooms overlooking the Kamo-gawa. Cash only.

TSUKIJI SUSHISEI　SUSHI ¥¥

Map p210 (築地寿司清; ☑075-252-1537; 581 Obiya-chō, Takakura-dōri, Nishikikōji-sagaru, Nakagyō-ku; sushi sets from ¥1512, per piece from ¥162; ☺11.30am-3pm & 5-10pm Mon-Fri, 11.30am-10pm Sat & Sun; Ⓢ Karasuma line to Shijō) On the basement floor, next to Daimaru department store, this simple sushi restaurant serves excellent sushi. You can order a set or just point at what looks good. You can see inside the restaurant from street level, so it should be easy to spot.

TAGOTO HONTEN　KAISEKI ¥¥

Map p210 (田ごと本店; ☑075-221-1811; www. kyoto-tagoto.co.jp; 34 Otabi-chō, Shijō-dōri, Kawaramachi nishi-iru, Nakagyō-ku; lunch/dinner from ¥1850/4000; ☺11am-8.30pm; Ⓡ Keihan line to Shijō or Hankyū line to Kawaramachi) Across from Takashimaya department store, this long-standing Kyoto restaurant serves approachable *kaiseki* fare in a variety of rooms, both private and common. Its *kiku* set (¥1890) includes some sashimi, tempura and a variety of other nibblies. *Kaiseki* dinner courses start at ¥7000 and you must make reservations in advance. Otherwise try the cheaper mini *kaiseki* lunch (¥4000).

DEN SHICHI　SUSHI ¥¥

(傳七; ☑075-323-0700; Saiin, 4-1 Tatsumi-chō, Ukyō-ku; lunch/dinner from ¥550/2700; ☺11.30am-2pm & 5-10.30pm; Ⓡ Hankyū line to Saiin) One of the best reasonably priced sushi restaurants in Kyoto. It's a classic: long counter, bellowing sushi chefs and great fresh fish. The lunch sets are unbelievable value and the glass sushi cases make ordering a little easier than at some other places. Look for the black-and-white sign about 100m west of Saiin Station on Shijō-dōri.

KERALA　INDIAN ¥¥

Map p210 (ケララ; ☑075-251-0141; 2nd fl, KUS Bldg, Kawaramachi-dōri, Sanjō-agaru, Nakagyō-ku; lunch/dinner from ¥900/2600; ☺11.30am-2pm & 5-9pm; ☑; Ⓢ Tōzai line to Kyoto-Shiyakusho-mae, Ⓡ Keihan line to Sanjō) Kyoto's best Indian restaurant is a narrow upstairs spot on Kawaramachi-dōri. The ¥900 lunch set menu is an excellent deal, as is the vegetarian lunch (¥1200). Dinners run closer to

¥2600 per head and are of very high quality. Finish off the meal with the incredibly rich and creamy coconut ice cream.

GANKO
SUSHI ¥¥

Map p210 (がんこ; ☏075-255-1128; www.gankofood.co.jp; 101 Nakajima-chō, Sanjō-dōri, Kawaramachi higashi-iru, Nakagyō-ku; meals ¥842-3326; ☺11am-11pm; ⚡; Ⓢ Tōzai line to Kyoto-Shiyakusho-mae or Sanjō Keihan, ⓇKeihan line to Sanjō) This giant four-storey dining hall is part of Kansai's biggest sushi chain. The ground floor is the sushi area, with a long sushi counter and plenty of tables. It's very popular with both tourists and locals. There's an extensive English/picture menu and good-value set meals. It may have the most plastic-looking food models of any restaurant window in Kyoto. Near Sanjō-Ōhashi bridge. They have a more upmarket branch with a garden nearby.

★ROAN KIKUNOI
KAISEKI ¥¥¥

Map p210 (露庵菊乃井; ☏075-361-5580; www.kikunoi.jp; 118 Saito-chō, Kiyamachi-dōri, Shijō-sagaru, Shimogyō-ku; lunch/dinner from ¥4000/13,000; ☺11.30am-1.30pm & 5-8.30pm Thu-Tue; Ⓡ Hankyū line to Kawaramachi or Keihan line to Gion-Shijō) A fantastic place to experience the wonders of *kaiseki*. It's a lovely intimate space located right downtown. The chef takes an experimental and creative approach to *kaiseki* and the results are a wonder for the eyes and palate. Highly recommended. Reserve through your hotel or ryokan or at least a few days in advance.

★YOSHIKAWA
TEMPURA ¥¥¥

Map p210 (吉川; ☏075-221-5544; www.kyoto-yoshikawa.co.jp; 135 Matsushita-chō, Tominokōji, Oike-sagaru, Nakagyō-ku; lunch ¥3000-25,000, dinner ¥8000-25,000; ☺11am-1.45pm & 5-8pm; Ⓢ Tōzai line to Karasuma-Oike or Kyoto-Shiyakusho-mae) This is the place to go for delectable tempura with a daily changing menu. Attached to the Yoshikawa ryokan (p146), it offers table seating, but it's much more interesting to sit and eat around the small intimate counter and observe the chefs at work. Reservation is required for tatami room, and counter bar for dinner. Note: counter bar is closed Sunday.

KIYAMACHI SAKURAGAWA
KAISEKI ¥¥¥

Map p210 (木屋町　櫻川; ☏075-255-4477; Kiyamachi-dōri, Nijō-sagaru, Nakagyō-ku; lunch/dinner sets from ¥5000/12,000; ☺11.30am-2pm & 5-9pm Mon-Sat; Ⓢ Tōzai line to Kyoto-Shiyakusho-mae) This elegant restaurant on a scenic stretch of Kiyamachi-dōri is an excellent

place to try *kaiseki*. The modest but fully satisfying food is beautifully presented and it's a joy to watch the chef in action. The warmth of the reception adds to the quality of the food. Reservations are recommended and smart casual is the way to go here.

MISHIMA-TEI
JAPANESE ¥¥¥

Map p210 (三嶋亭; ☏075-221-0003; 405 Sakurano-chō, Teramachi-dōri, Sanjō-sagaru, Nakagyō-ku; sukiyaki lunch/dinner from ¥7722/14,850; ☺11.30am-9pm; Ⓢ Tōzai line to Kyoto-Shiyakusho-mae) Mishima-tei is a good place to sample sukiyaki (thin slices of beef cooked in sake, soy and vinegar broth, and dipped in raw egg) as the quality of the meat is very high, which is hardly surprising when there is a butcher downstairs. It's at the intersection of the Sanjō and Teramachi covered arcades.

Note that you'll need your hotel to make a booking for you as it doesn't accept reservations without a Japanese telephone number.

🍷🍸 DRINKING & NIGHTLIFE

★BUNGALOW
CRAFT BEER

Map p210 (バンガロー; ☏075-256-8205; www.bungalow.jp; 15 Kashiwaya-chō, Shijō dōri, Shimogyō-ku; ☺3pm-2am Mon-Sat; Ⓡ Hankyū line to Ōmiya) Spread over two floors with an open-air downstairs bar, Bungalow serves a great range of Japanese craft beer along with natural wines in a cool industrial space. The regularly changing menu features 10 beers on tap from all over Japan and it also serves excellent food.

NOKISHITA 711
COCKTAIL BAR

Map p210 (☏075-741-6564; www.nokishita.net; 235 Atsumari-B, Sendo-chō, Shimogyō-ku; ☺6pm-2am, to midnight Sun; ⚡; Ⓡ Hankyū line to Kawaramachi) The sign inside says 'Kyoto Loves Gin' and if you do too, you won't want to miss this quirky little bar. Owner Tomo infuses gin with interesting ingredients, such as bamboo and smoked tea, and mixes up delicious cocktails with unique flavours – black sesame, yuzu pepper and truffle honey. There's a great range of gins from around the world.

WEEKENDERS COFFEE
COFFEE

Map p210 (ウィークエンダーズ　コーヒー; ☏075-746-2206; www.weekenderscoffee.com; 560 Honeyana-chō, Nakagyō-ku; coffee from ¥430; ☺7.30am-6pm Thu-Tue; Ⓡ Hankyū line to Kawaramachi) A standing-room-only coffee bar tucked away in a traditional building at the back of a parking lot in Downtown Kyoto. Sure, it's a strange location but it's where you'll find some of the city's best coffee being brewed by roaster-owner Masahiro Kaneko.

BAR ROCKING CHAIR
COCKTAIL BAR

Map p210 (http://bar-rockingchair.jp; 432-2 Tachibana-chō, Gokomachi-dōri, Bukkoji-sagaru, Shimogyō-ku; cover ¥500; ⊙5pm-2am Wed-Mon; ⓇHankyū line to Kawaramachi) Tucked away in the quiet backstreets of Downtown Kyoto, this dimly lit, dark-wood cocktail bar is a good choice for an upscale drink (though at upscale prices). Set up in an converted *machiya* (traditional Japanese townhouse), there's no menu here but the smartly dressed bartenders speak a little English and will try to customise something to your taste.

KILN
COFFEE

Map p210 (☑075-353-3555; 194 Sendo-chō, Kiyamachi-dori, Shimogyō-ku; ⊙11am-11pm Thu-Tue; ⓢ; ⓇHankyū line to Kawaramachi) On a pretty stretch of canal, Kiln's big windows frame the view and make it the perfect spot to stare lazily while waiting for your caffeine to kick in. The brew is made with single-origin beans and there's a selection of cakes and toasted sandwiches. If your stomach is rumbling for more, the upstairs restaurant does a decent dry-aged Wagyu burger for lunch.

KABOKU TEAROOM
TEAHOUSE

Map p210 (喫茶室嘉木; Teramachi-dōri, Nijō-agaru, Nakagyō-ku; ⊙10am-6pm; ⓢTōzai line to Kyoto-Shiyakusho-mae) A casual tearoom attached to the Ippōdō Tea (p74) store, Kaboku serves a range of tea, including *sencha, genmaicha* and *matcha,* and provides a great break while exploring the shops around the Teramachi covered arcade. Try the thicker *koicha*-style *matcha* and grab a counter seat to watch it being prepared.

SAKE BAR YORAMU
BAR

Map p210 (酒バー よらむ; ☑075-213-1512; www.sakebar-yoramu.com; 35-1 Matsuya-chō, Nijō-dōri, Higashinotoin higashi-iru, Nakagyō-ku; ⊙6pm-midnight Wed-Sat; ⓢKarasuma or Tōzai lines to Karasuma-Oike) Named for Yoramu, the Israeli sake expert who runs Sake Bar Yoramu, this bar is highly recommended for anyone after an education in sake. It's very small and can only accommodate a handful of people. If you're not sure what you like, go for a sake tasting set of three. By day, it's a soba restaurant called Toru Soba.

TADG'S GASTRO PUB
PUB

Map p210 (ダイグ ガストロ パブ; ☑075-213-0214; www.tadgs.com; 1st fl, 498 Kamikoriki-chō, Nakagyō-ku; ⊙11.30am-11pm; ⓢ; ⓢTōzai line to Kyoto-Shiyakusho-mae) Looking out on a scenic stretch of Kiyamachi-dōri, Tadg's is a great place for a drink in the evening. Choose from an extensive selection of craft beers (including nine rotating Japanese beers on tap), along with a variety of wines, sake and spirits. Seating is available, including an enclosed garden out the back for smokers.

BAR K6
BAR

Map p210 (バーK6; ☑075-255-5009; 2nd fl, Le Valls Bldg, Nijō-dōri, Kiyamachi higashi-iru, Nakagyō-ku; ⊙6pm-3am, to 5am Fri & Sat; ⓢTōzai line to Kyoto-Shiyakusho-mae, ⓇKeihan line to Jingu-Marutamachi) Overlooking one of the prettiest stretches of Kiyamachi-dōri, this upscale modern Japanese bar has a great selection of single malts and some of the best cocktails in town. It's popular with well-heeled locals and travellers staying at some of the top-flight hotels nearby.

ZEN KASHOIN
CAFE

Map p210 (茶寮「然」カフェ; ☑075-241-3300; Zenkashoin Kyoto Muromachi Store, 271-1 Takoyakushi-chō, Muromachi-dōri, Nijō-sagaru, Nakagyō-ku; matcha tea from ¥800; ⊙10am-7pm, closed 2nd & 4th Mon of month; ⓢKarasuma or Tōzai line to Karasuma-Oike) The modern tearoom here is a great place for a break in a quiet spot in Downtown Kyoto. You can enjoy a nice cup of *matcha* served with a delicious Kyoto sweet, all in extremely comfortable surroundings. There's also an attached gallery shop for browsing afterwards.

ATLANTIS
BAR

Map p210 (アトランティス; ☑075-241-1621; 161 Matsumoto-chō, Ponto-chō-Shijō-agaru, Nakagyō-ku; ⊙6pm-2am, to 1am Sun; ⓇHankyū line to Kawaramachi) This is a slick Ponto-chō bar that welcomes foreigners and draws a fair smattering of Kyoto's beautiful people, and wannabe beautiful people. In summer you can sit outside on a platform looking over the Kamo-gawa (terrace closes at 11pm). It's often crowded so you may have to wait a bit to get in, especially if you want to sit outside.

INODA COFFEE
CAFE

Map p210 (イノダコーヒー; ☑075-221-0507; Sakaimachi-dōri, Sanjō-sagaru, Nakagyō-ku; coffee from ¥560; ⊙7am-7pm; ⓢKarasuma or Tōzai lines to Karasuma-Oike) This chain is a Kyoto institution and has branches across the city.

Though slightly expensive, the old-Japan atmosphere makes it worth a try, especially if you want to try a Japanese, rather than international, coffee chain. Big windows look out to a garden view and it's popular with the older local crowd.

BAR BUNKYU

BAR

Map p210 (バー 文久; ☑075-211-1982; http://bar bunkyu.jimdo.com; 534 Ebisu-chō, Kawaramachi, Sanjō-agaru, Futasujime higashi-iru, Nakagyō-ku; drinks from ¥1000; ☺6pm-late Fri-Wed; ⑤Tōzai line to Kyoto-Shiyakusho-mae) This intimate whiskey bar is a good place to go for a quiet drink when downtown. It can only seat a handful of guests around the small wooden counter. The friendly bartender will be happy to help you choose a tipple. If you're coming from Kawaramachi, turn at the Catholic church and look for it on your right.

WORLD

CLUB

Map p210 (ワールド; ☑075-213-4119; www.world-kyoto.com; Basement, Imagium Bldg, 97 Shin-chō, Nishikiyamachi, Shijō-agaru, Shimogyō-ku; cover ¥2000-3000; ☺8pm-late; ⑧Hankyū line to Kawaramachi) Kyoto's largest club hosts some of the biggest events. It has two floors, a dance floor and lockers where you can leave your stuff while you dance the night away. Events include everything from deep soul to reggae and techno to salsa.

SAMA SAMA

BAR

Map p210 (サマサマ; ☑075-241-4100; 532-16 Kamiōsaka-chō, Kiyamachi, Sanjō-agaru, Nakagyō-ku; ☺6pm-2am Tue-Thu & Sun, to 3am Fri & Sat; ☎; ⑤Tōzai line to Kyoto-Shiyakusho-mae) An Indonesian-owned bar that feels like a very comfortable cave somewhere near the Mediterranean. Grab a seat at the counter or make yourself at home on the floor cushions and enjoy a wide variety of drinks paired with food, including Indonesian classics like nasi goreng (¥850). It's down an alley just north of Sanjō; look for the signboard.

ROCKING BAR ING

BAR

Map p210 (ロック居酒屋ING; ☑075-255-5087; www.kyotoingbar.com; 2nd fl, Royal Bldg, 288 Minamikurayama-chō, Nishikiyamachi-dōri, Takoyakushi-agaru, Nakagyō-ku; drinks from ¥550; ☺7pm-2am Sun-Thu, to 5am Fri & Sat; ⑧Hankyū line to Kawaramachi) This izakaya-cum-bar on Kiyamachi-dōri is a great choice for a drink in Kyoto and attracts a mix of locals and foreigners. It offers cheap bar snacks (¥300 to ¥750) and drinks, good music and friendly staff. It's in the Royal building.

BUTTERFLY

CLUB

Map p210 (☑075-211-5025; http://butterfly-kyo to.com; B1 Forum Bldg, 67-3 Daikoku-chō, Nishi-kiyamachi, Nakagyō-ku; cover incl a drink ¥1000; ☺10pm-3am Sun-Thu, to 5am Fri & Sat; ⑧Keihan line to Gion-Shijō or Hankyū line to Kawaramachi) If you prefer your clubs on the smaller scale, Butterfly's a good choice. It's on the quiet side during the week but on weekends it gets jumping with a good mix of locals, expats and tourists sidling up to the island bar and sweatin' it out to DJs.

☆ ENTERTAINMENT

TAKU-TAKU

LIVE MUSIC

Map p210 (磔磔; ☑075-351-1321; Tominokōji-dōri-Bukkōji, Shimogyō-ku; ¥1500-3500; ☺7-9pm; ⑧Hankyū line to Kawaramachi) One of Kyoto's most atmospheric live-music clubs, with a long history of hosting some great local and international acts. Check the Kyoto Visitor's Guide and flyers in local coffee shops for details on upcoming events. It's rather hard to spot: the sign is only in Japanese. Look for the wooden sign with black kanji on it and go through the gate.

KAMOGAWA ODORI

DANCE

Map p210 (鴨川をどり; ☑075-221-2025; Ponto-chō, Sanjō-sagaru, Nakagyō-ku; normal/special seat ¥2300/4200, special seat with tea ¥4800; ☺shows 12.30pm, 2.20pm & 4.10pm; ⑤Tōzai line to Kyoto-Shiyakusho-mae) Geisha dances from 1 to 24 May at Ponto-chō Kaburen-jō Theatre in Ponto-chō.

🛍 SHOPPING

★ZŌHIKO

ARTS & CRAFTS

Map p210 (象彦; ☑075-229-6625; www.zohiko.co.jp; 719-1 Yohojimae-chō, Teramachi-dōri, Nijō-agaru, Nakagyō-ku; ☺10am-6pm; ⑤Tōzai line to Kyoto-Shiyakusho-mae) Zōhiko is the best place in Kyoto to buy one of Japan's most beguiling art and craft forms: lacquerware. If you aren't familiar with just how beautiful these products can be, you owe it to yourself to make the pilgrimage to Zōhiko. You'll find a great selection of cups, bowls, trays and various kinds of boxes.

★TAKASHIMAYA

DEPARTMENT STORE

Map p210 (高島屋; ☑075-221-8811; Shijō-Kawaramachi Kado, Shimogyō-ku; ☺10am-8pm, restaurants to 9.30pm; ⑧Hankyū line to

Kawaramachi) The *grande dame* of Kyoto department stores, Takashimaya is almost a tourist attraction in its own right, from the mind-boggling riches of the basement food floor to the wonderful selection of lacquerware and ceramics on the 6th floor. And don't miss the kimono display.

★ARITSUGU
HOMEWARES

Map p210 (有次; ☑075-221-1091; 219 Kajiya-chō, Nishikikōji-dōri, Gokomachi nishi-iru, Nakagyō-ku; ⊙9am-5.30pm; ⑧Hankyū line to Kawaramachi) While you're in Nishiki Market, have a look at this shop – it has some of the best kitchen knives in the world. Choose your knife – all-rounder, sushi, vegetable – and the staff will show you how to care for it before sharpening and boxing it up. You can also have your name engraved in English or Japanese. Knives start at around ¥10,000.

Founded in 1560, Aritsugu was originally involved in the production of swords and the blacksmith skills have been passed down over the years through generation after generation. It also carries a selection of excellent and unique Japanese kitchenware and whetstones for knife sharpening.

★IPPŌDŌ TEA
TEA

Map p210 (一保堂茶舗; ☑075-211-3421; www.ippodo-tea.co.jp; Teramachi-dōri, Nijō-agaru, Nakagyō-ku; ⊙9am-6pm; ⑤Tōzai line to Kyoto-Shiyakusho-mae) This old-style tea shop sells some of the best Japanese tea in Kyoto, and you'll be given an English leaflet with prices and descriptions of each one. Its *matcha* makes an excellent and lightweight souvenir; 40g containers start at ¥500. Ippōdō is north of the city hall, on Teramachi-dōri. It has an adjoining teahouse, Kaboku Tearoom (p72); last order 5.30pm.

KYŪKYO-DŌ
ARTS & CRAFTS

Map p210 (鳩居堂; ☑075-231-0510; 520 Shimo-honnōjimae-chō, Teramachi-dōri, Aneyakōji-agaru, Nakagyō-ku; ⊙10am-6pm Mon-Sat; ⑤Tōzai line to Kyoto-Shiyakusho-mae) This old shop in the Teramachi covered arcade sells a selection of incense, *shodō* (calligraphy) goods, tea-ceremony supplies and *washi*. Prices are on the high side but the quality is good. Overall, this is your best one-stop shop for distinctively Japanese souvenirs.

★WAGAMI NO MISE
ARTS & CRAFTS

Map p210 (倭紙の店; ☑075-341-1419; 1st fl, Kajinoha Bldg, 298 Ōgisakaya-chō, Higashinotōin-dōri, Bukkōji-agaru, Shimogyō-ku; ⊙9.30am-5.30pm Mon-Fri, to 4.30pm Sat; ⑤Karasuma line

🏃 Local Life
An Afternoon of Shopping

This area is Kyoto's beating heart of consumerism, where locals head to shop at the best boutiques and departments stores, pick up gourmet goods from the Nishiki Market to cook at home, and to drop in for a casual lunch and coffee in between.

❶ Nishiki Market
Arrive early to beat the crowds at the wonderful Nishiki Market (p65), home to a bounty of ingredients that go into Kyoto's cuisine. Wander from stall to stall inspecting the gourmet goods, duck into shops selling spices and sweets, and grab a snack to go.

❷ Daimaru
You can really while away the hours at Daimaru (p77), perhaps the best-known department store, a short walk from the Nishiki Market. Most of that time could be spent just checking out what's on offer in the basement food section, where locals head to pick up bentō boxes, sweets, tempura and sushi.

❸ Takashimaya
From one department store to the next: Takashimaya (p73) is a favourite for its wide variety of quality goods on offer. Take your time here moving from floor to floor, browsing everything from pottery, kimonos and lacquerware to fashion, homewares and the fantastic basement food floors.

❹ Tagoto Honten
Take a break at Tagoto Honten (p70), just across the street from Takashimaya, which is a magnet for shoppers in need of a feed. It's a great spot to sample affordable *kaiseki* (Japanese haute cuisine) in a lovely, quiet setting that has you forgetting the hustle of the main streets outside. Save room for dessert, though.

❺ Karakuneya Coffee Sanjo Honten
Hopefully your delicate *kaiseki* meal has left you just satisfied with room for more. Karafuneya Coffee Sanjō Honten (p68)

NAKAGYŌ-KU

is a local's favourite for light lunches and coffee but the real temptation is the huge selection of sundaes on the menu. Tuck into a *matcha* parfait or *azuki* (sweet red bean) with black sesame.

6 Kaboku Tearoom

Walk off the dessert and make your way to lovely Kaboku Tearoom (p72) to refresh yourself with a cup of tea. Choose from a range of green teas, including high-quality *matcha*, *sencha* and *genmaicha*. You can watch the *matcha* being whisked up at the counter.

7 Ippōdō Tea

Once you've sipped your tea and know what you like, head next door to Ippōdō Tea to stock up on tea to take home. Bags and small containers make the perfect lightweight souvenir of your shopping day.

MATTHIAS TUNGER / GETTY IMAGES ©

Ippōdō Tea

to Shijō) This place sells a fabulous variety of *washi* (Japanese handmade paper) for reasonable prices and is a great spot to pick up a gift or souvenir. Look for the Morita Japanese Paper Company sign on the wall out the front.

KYOTO DESIGN HOUSE
ARTS & CRAFTS

Map p210 (☏075-221-0200; www.kyoto-dh.com; 1st fl, Nikawa Bldg, Tominokōji-dōri, 105 Fukanaga-chō, Nakagyō-ku; ◐11am-8pm, closed last weekday of each month; ⑤Karasuma or Tōzai lines to Karasuma-Oike) The Tadao Ando–designed Nikawa building is the perfect home for this design store, which stocks arts and crafts mainly designed by local Kyoto artists melding traditional with modern design. From handmade ceramics and *ohako* candy boxes to beautiful cushions using silk from the Nishijin textile district, this is the best place to pick up great gifts and souvenirs.

MARUZEN
BOOKS

Map p210 (丸善; Basement, BAL, 251 Yamazaki-chō, Kawaramachi-sanjo sagaru, Nakagyō-ku; ◐11am-9pm; ⑭Hankyū line to Kawaramachi) Occupying two basement floors of the BAL department store (p76), this excellent bookshop has a massive range of English-language books across all subjects on basement level 2, plenty of titles on Kyoto and Japan, a great selection of Japanese literature, magazines from around the globe and travel guides.

TOKYU HANDS
DEPARTMENT STORE

Map p210 (東急ハンズ京都店; ☏075-254-3109; http://kyoto.tokyu-hands.co.jp; Shijō-dōri, Karasuma higashi-iru, Shimogyō-ku; ◐10am-8.30pm; ⑤Karasuma line to Shijō) While the Kyoto branch doesn't have the selection of bigger branches in places like Tokyo, it's still well worth a browse for fans of gadgets and unique homewares. It's a good place for an interesting gift or souvenir, from Hario coffee equipment and lacquerware *bentō* boxes to stationery and cosmetics.

KAMIJI KAKIMOTO
ARTS & CRAFTS

Map p210 (紙司柿本; ☏075-211-3481; 54 Tokiwagi-chō, Teramachi-dōri, Nijō-agaru, Nakagyō-ku; ◐9am-6pm; ⑤Tōzai line to Kyoto-Shiyakusho-mae) This is one of the best places to buy *washi* (Japanese handmade paper) in Kyoto. It's got such unusual items as *washi* computer printer paper and *washi* wallpaper, along with great letter writing and wrapping paper. Look for the hanging white *noren* (curtain) out the front.

FUNAHASHI-YA
FOOD

Map p210 (船はしや; 112 Nakajima-chō, Sanjō-dōri, Kawaramachi higashi-iru, Nakagyō-ku; ◐10am-8pm; ⑤Tōzai line to Kyoto-Shiyakusho-mae or Sanjō Keihan, ⑭Keihan line to Sanjō) Around since 1885, Funahashi-ya has long been a popular stop to pick up Japanese rice crackers (known as *o-kaki* in Kyoto) and its signature *go-shiki-mame* 'five coloured beans' – dried green pea sweets coated in sugar flavours from plum to cinnamon. The traditional wooden shop is on the west bank of the Kamo-gawa at the end of the Sanjō bridge next to Starbucks.

JOE'S GARAGE
MUSIC

Map p210 (2nd fl, Tomishaya Bldg, 572 Takakura-dōri, Nagakyō-ku; ◐noon-9pm Sun-Fri, from 5pm Sat; ⑤Karasuma line to Shijō) Named after a Frank Zappa album, the music selection here is as genre-spanning as the musician himself, with jazz and rock to obscure Japanese albums available. There's a good range of vinyl, too.

BAL
DEPARTMENT STORE

Map p210 (バル; www.bal-bldg.com; 251 Yamazaki-chō, Kawaramachi-sanjo sagaru, Nakagyō-ku; ◐11am-8pm; ⑭Hankyū line to Kawaramachi) For all your high-end fashion and homeware needs, the chic and elegant BAL department store is the place to go. You'll find designer fashion, botanical skincare from Neal's Yard, great souvenirs and gifts at Today's Special, and the ever popular Muji. The two basement floors house the huge Maruzen (p76) bookstore.

ERIZEN
TEXTILES

Map p210 (ゑり善; ☏075-221-1618; Shijō-Kawaramachi, Otabi-chō, Shimogyō-ku; ◐10am-8pm Tue-Sun; ⑭Hankyū line to Kawaramachi) Roughly opposite Takashimaya department store, Erizen is one of the best places in Kyoto to buy a kimono or kimono fabric. It has a great selection of *kyō-yūzen* (Kyoto dyed fabrics) and other kimono fabrics. Prices are not cheap but the service is of a high level. Staff can measure you for a kimono and post it to your home later.

KYOTO MARUI
DEPARTMENT STORE

Map p210 (京都マルイ; ☏075-257-0101; 68 Shin-chō, Shijō-dōri, Kawaramachi higashi-iru, Shimogyō-ku; ◐10.30am-8.30pm, restaurants to

10pm; ⒭Hankyū line to Kawaramachi) This new youth-oriented department store hails from Tokyo and brings some of that fashion sense with it. It's a good place to see what's hot with the local fashionistas, plus there's an international supermarket on the basement floor (8am to 10pm). It's on the intersection of Shijō-dōri and Kawaramachi-dōri; the building is marked with the sign OIOI.

TSUKIMOCHIYA NAOMASA — SWEETS
Map p210 (月餅家 直正; ☑075-231-0175; 530 Kamiōsaka-chō, Kiyamachi-dōri, Sanjō-agaru, Nakagyō-ku; ¥160; ◷10am-8pm Wed-Mon; ⒭Keihan line to Sanjō) This classic old sweet shop, about 50m north of Sanjō-dōri on Kiyamachi-dōri, is a great place to get acquainted with traditional Kyoto sweets. Just point at what looks good and the friendly staff will wrap it up nicely for you. There's no English sign; look for the traditional Kyoto exterior and the sweets in the window.

NISHIHARU — ARTS & CRAFTS
Map p210 (西春; ☑075-211-2849; http://nishi-haru-kyoto.com; 1 Ishibashi-cho, Teramachi-Sanjō Kado, Nakagyō-ku; ◷11am-7pm, closed irregularly; ⒮Tōzai line to Kyoto-Shiyakusho-mae, ⒭Keihan line to Sanjō) This is an attractive shop dealing in wood-block prints. All prints are accompanied by English explanations and the owner is happy to take the time to find something you really like. Prices start at around ¥10,000. It's located at the intersection of the Sanjō and Teramachi covered arcades.

TSUJIKURA — ARTS & CRAFTS
Map p210 (辻倉; ☑075-221-4396; www.kyoto tsujikura.com; 7th fl, Tsujikura Bldg, Kawaramachi-dōri, Nakagyō-ku; ◷11am-7pm Thu-Tue; ⒭Hankyū line to Kawaramachi) Tsujikura is a small store stocking the beautiful *wagasa* (waxed-paper umbrellas) the company has been manufacturing since the 17th century, which come in a mix of colours with traditional and modern design. It also has a small selection of Isamu Noguchi's famous Akari paper lamps.

MINA — SHOPPING CENTRE
Map p210 (ミーナ京都; ☑075-222-8470; Kawaramachi-dōri, Shijō-agaru, Nakagyō-ku; ◷11am-9pm; ⒭Keihan line to Gion-Shijō or Hankyū line to Kawaramachi) Mina has branches of two of Japan's most popular chains: Uniqlo, a budget clothing brand that has spread overseas, and Loft, a fashionable

department store that stocks all manner of gadgets and gift items.

RAKUSHIKAN — ARTS & CRAFTS
Map p210 (楽紙館; ☑075-251-0078; http://raku shikan.com; 1st fl, Museum of Kyoto, Takakura-dōri, Sanjō-agaru, Nakagyō-ku; ◷10am-7pm Tue-Sun; ⒮Karasuma or Tōzai lines to Karasuma-Oike) This small shop on the east side of the Museum of Kyoto is a great place to buy *washi* (Japanese handmade paper) and interesting cards and paper craft products.

FUJII DAIMARU
DEPARTMENT STORE — DEPARTMENT STORE
Map p210 (フジイダイマル; ☑075-221-8181; Shijō-dōri, Teramachi nishi-iru; ◷10.30am-8pm; ⒮Hankyū line to Kawaramachi) This smallish department store on Shijō-dōri is very popular with young locals who flock here to peruse the interesting selection of up-to-the-minute fashions, including the well-known Japanese store Beams. There's a branch of ％ Arabica coffee on the 1st floor and a good selection of food in the basement Tavelt supermarket, as well as organic groceries.

DAIMARU — DEPARTMENT STORE
Map p210 (大丸; ☑075-211-8111; Tachiuri Nishi-machi 79, Shijō-dōri, Takakura nishi-iru, Shimogyō-ku; ◷10am-8pm, restaurants 11am-8pm; ⒮Karasuma line to Shijō, ⒭Hankyū line to Karasuma) Daimaru has fantastic service, a brilliant selection of goods and a basement food floor that will make you want to move to Kyoto.

NIJŪSAN-YA — FASHION & ACCESSORIES
Map p210 (二十三や; ☑075-221-2371; Shijō-dōri, Kawaramachi higashi-iru, Shimogyō-ku; ◷10am-8pm, closed irregularly on a Wed; ⒭Hankyū line to Kawaramachi) Boxwood combs and hair clips are one of Kyoto's most famous traditional crafts, and they are still used in the elaborate hairstyles of the city's geisha and *maiko*. This tiny hole-in-the-wall shop has a fine selection for you to choose from (and if you don't like what's on view, you can ask if it has other choices in stock – it usually does).

MEIDI-YA — FOOD
Map p210 (明治屋; ☑075-221-7661; Sanjō-dōri, Kawaramachi higashi-iru, Nakagyō-ku; ◷10am-9pm; ⒭Keihan line to Sanjō) Gourmet supermarket on Sanjō-dōri with a good selection of imported food and an excellent selection of wine.

Imperial Palace & Around

Neighbourhood Top Five

❶ Daitoku-ji (p80) Exploring the many temples and admiring the Zen garden at Kōtō-in.

❷ Sentō Imperial Palace (p81) Strolling around the superb gardens here de-

signed by renowned landscape artist Kobori Enshū.

❸ Shimogamo-jinja (p81) Taking a stroll through the long tree-lined approach to this lovely temple.

❹ Funaoka Onsen (p84) Taking a dip in the outdoor bath at this iconic old onsen.

❺ Kazariya (p83) Enjoying a traditional sweet of *aburimochi* and a pot of tea at this 300-year-old establishment.

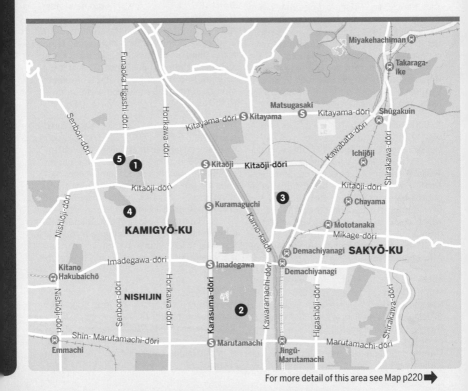

For more detail of this area see Map p220 ➡

Explore Imperial Palace & Around

The Imperial Palace area stretches from near the southern boundary of the Imperial Palace Park up north to the Takara-ga-ike-koen and one of Japan's oldest shrines, Kamigamo-jinja. In between, the vast Imperial Palace Park is home to the Imperial Palace itself, as well as the Sentō Imperial Palace. Just northeast of the park's boundary is Shimogamo-jinja, while the complex of Daitoku-ji lies on the west side directly north from the traditional textile district of Nishijin. If you head further north in a straight line from the park, you'll come to the Kyoto Botanical Gardens.

It's possible to explore a lot of this area in one day and it lends itself well to being explored by bicycle. You'll find many tourists zipping around on bicycles along the park's boundaries and up to Daitoku-ji. A nice route is to explore the park and palace and then pick up a bicycle at the rental shop at Demachiyanagi Station, a short walk from the park's northeast boundary. It's then possible to cycle to Shimogama-jinja and up to the Botanical Gardens, most of it along the riverside bike path. You can then head over to Daitoku-ji and back to the station via the Nishijin district.

Most sights are also easily accessible by subway as they are linked on the Karasuma subway line, which runs up the west boundary of the park. The Botanical Gardens are just a couple of stops away at Kitayama Station and Daitoku-ji is a short walk from the Kitaoji Station.

Local Life

➡ **Hang-out** Kyoto families with children gather on sunny weekends along the banks of the Kamo-gawa, just north of Kamo-Ōhashi.

➡ **Jogging route** Local runners favour the many paths of the Kyoto Imperial Palace Park (p81).

➡ **Picnic spot** Spread a blanket and eat al fresco in the expansive fields of the Kyoto Botanical Gardens (p82).

Getting There & Away

➡ **Subway** Take the Karasuma line to access most of the sights, including the Imperial Palace Park and Daitoku-ji.

➡ **Bus** Buses are the most convenient way to visit sights in the far north.

Lonely Planet's Top Tip

During cherry-blossom season (early April), the city's main tourist sites will be mobbed. If you want to enjoy the blossoms without the crowds, head to the banks of the Kamo-gawa or Takano-gawa, north of Imadegawa-dōri.

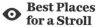 ## Best Place to Eat

➡ Kanei (p83)

➡ Toraya Karyō Kyoto Ichijō (p84)

➡ Sarasa Nishijin (p84)

➡ Papa Jon's (p83)

➡ Grand Burger (p83)

For reviews, see p83. ➡

Best Places for a Stroll

➡ Kyoto Botanical Gardens (p82)

➡ Shimogamo-jinja (p81)

➡ Takara-ga-ike-kōen (p83)

➡ Kyoto Imperial Palace Park (p81)

For reviews, see p81.

TOP SIGHT
DAITOKU-JI

Daitoku-ji is a separate world within Kyoto – a world of Zen temples, perfectly raked *kare-sansui* (dry landscape) gardens and wandering lanes. It's one of the most rewarding destinations in this part of the city, particularly for those with an interest in Japanese gardens. Daitoku-ji itself is not usually open to the public but there are several subtemples dotted around the grounds that you can enter.

Main Temple
The eponymous Daitoku-ji is the main temple here (on the eastern side of the grounds) and serves as the headquarters for the Rinzai Daitoku-ji school of Zen Buddhism. It was founded in 1319, burnt down in the next century, and rebuilt in the 16th century. The **San-mon** gate (1589) has a self-carved statue of its erector, the famous tea master Sen no Rikyū, on its 2nd storey.

Daisen-in
The two small Zen gardens at popular **Daisen-in** (大仙院; adult/child ¥400/270; ◷9am-5pm Mar-Nov, to 4.30pm Dec-Feb) subtemple are elegant examples of 17th-century *kare-sansui* style. Here the trees, rocks and sand are said to represent and express various spectacles of nature, from waterfalls and valleys to mountain lakes.

Zuihō-in
Subtemple **Zuihō-in** (瑞峯院; adult/child ¥400/300; ◷9am-5pm) enshrines the 16th-century Christian *daimyō* (domain lord) Ōtomo Sōrin. In the early 1960s, a landscape architect named Shigemori Misuzu rearranged the stones in the back rock garden into the shape of a crucifix. More interesting is the main rock garden, raked into appealing patterns reminiscent of water ripples. It's roughly in the middle of the complex; you may have to ask for directions.

Ōbai-in
If you are lucky enough to be in Kyoto during autumn, one of the two periods **Ōbai-in** (黄梅院; ¥600; ◷end Mar-early May & early Oct-early Dec) is opened to the public, you should make an effort to visit to see the changing colours. This subtemple is a world of interlinked gardens, including an incredibly rich moss garden and a starkly simple *kare-sansui*. When you enter the Daitoku-ji complex via the east (main) gate, it's on the left.

Ryōgen-in
Ryōgen-in (龍源院; adult/child ¥350/200; ◷9am-4.30pm) has two pleasing gardens, one moss and one *kare-sansui*. The *kare-sansui* has an interesting island in its midst that invites lazy contemplation. When you enter the Daitoku-ji complex via the east (main) gate, it's on the left, just before Ōbai-in.

Kōtō-in
On the far western edge of the Daitoku-ji complex, the sublime garden of **Kōtō-in** (高桐院; ¥400; ◷9am-4.30pm) is one of the best in all Kyoto and it's worth a special trip, though has been closed for renovations (re-opening March 2019). It's located within a fine bamboo grove that you traverse via a moss-lined path. Once inside there is a small stroll garden that leads to the centrepiece: a rectangle of moss and maple trees, backed by bamboo. Take some time on the verandah here to soak it all up.

👁 SIGHTS

RAKU MUSEUM   MUSEUM

Map p220 (樂美術館; ☎075-414-0304; http://raku-yaki.or.jp; 84 Aburanokōji, Nakadachi-uri agaru, Kamigyō-ku; admission varies; ☺10am-4.30pm Tue-Sun; 🚌Kyoto City bus 9 or 12 to Ichijō Modoribashi, ⓢKarasuma line to Imadegawa) Hidden in a residential area in the Nishijin district, this fine museum is dedicated to the art of Raku pottery, a technique involving hand building and low firing, and has strong roots in the tea ceremony. Raku Chōjirō founded Raku ware in the late 16th century when he began making tea bowls, and the family continues to produce Raku pottery today. Exhibitions here display pieces from the family's exquisite collection and change every few months. There are English captions throughout.

SENTŌ IMPERIAL PALACE   HISTORIC BUILDING

Map p220 (仙洞御所, Sentō Gosho; ☎075-211-1215; www.kunaicho.go.jp; Kyoto Gyōen, Kamigyō-ku; ☺tours 9.30am, 11am, 1.30pm, 2.30pm & 3.30pm Tue-Sun; ⓢKarasuma line to Marutamachi or Imadegawa) 𝗙𝗥𝗘𝗘 The Sentō Gosho is the second imperial property located within the Kyoto Imperial Palace Park (the other one is the Imperial Palace itself). The structures are not particularly grand, but the gardens, laid out in 1630 by renowned landscape designer Kobori Enshū, are excellent. Admission is by one-hour tour only (in Japanese; English audio guides are free). You must be over 18 years old and you will need to bring your passport. Your ticket can be printed or shown on a smartphone.

The palace was originally constructed in 1630 during the reign of Emperor Go-Mizunō as a residence for retired emperors. It was repeatedly destroyed by fire and reconstructed; and continued to serve its purpose until a final blaze in 1854, after which it was never rebuilt. Today only two original structures, the **Seika-tei** and **Yūshin-tei** teahouses, remain.

You can book tickets in advance at the Imperial Household Agency office (p82) or online for morning tours; for afternoon tours tickets go on sale at the palace from 11am and are on a first-come, first-served basis until capacity is sold.

KYOTO IMPERIAL PALACE   HISTORIC BUILDING

Map p220 (京都御所, Kyoto Gosho; ☎075-211-1215; www.kunaicho.go.jp; Kyoto Gyōen, Kamigyō-ku; ☺9am-5pm Apr-Aug, 9am-4.30pm Sep & Mar, 9am-4pm Oct-Feb, last entry 40min before closing, closed Mon; ⓢKarasuma line to Marutamachi or Imadegawa) 𝗙𝗥𝗘𝗘 The Kyoto Imperial Palace, known as the Gosho in Japanese, is a walled complex that sits in the middle of the Kyoto Imperial Palace Park. While no longer the official residence of the Japanese emperor, it's still a grand edifice, though it doesn't rate highly in comparison with other attractions in Kyoto. Visitors can wander around the marked route in the grounds where English signs explain the history of the buildings. Entrance is via the main Seishomon Gate where you'll be given a map.

The original imperial palace was built in 794 and was replaced numerous times after destruction by fire. The present building, on a different site and smaller than the original, was constructed in 1855. Enthronement of a new emperor and other state ceremonies are still held here, so at times the palace is closed to the public. Take note: the grounds are covered in gravel stones so wear shoes that are easy to walk in.

Free English guided tours run at 10am and 2pm.

SHIMOGAMO-JINJA   SHINTO SHRINE

Map p220 (下鴨神社; www.shimogamo-jinja.or.jp; 59 Izumigawa-chō, Shimogamo, Sakyō-ku; ☺6.30am-5pm, 🚌Kyoto City bus 205 to Shimogamo-jinja-mae, 🚃Keihan line to Demachiyanagi) 𝗙𝗥𝗘𝗘 This shrine, dating from the 8th century, is a Unesco World Heritage Site. It is nestled in the fork of the Kamo-gawa and Takano-gawa, and is approached along a shady path through the lovely Tadasu-no-mori. This wooded area is said to be a place where lies cannot be concealed and is considered a prime location to sort out disputes. The trees here are mostly broadleaf (a rarity in Kyoto) and they are gorgeous in the springtime.

The shrine is dedicated to the god of harvest. Traditionally, pure water was drawn from the nearby rivers for purification and agricultural ceremonies. The **Hondō** (Main Hall) dates from 1863 and, like the **Haiden** hall at its sister shrine, Kamigamo-jinja, is an excellent example of *nagare*-style shrine architecture. The annual *yabusame* (horseback archery) event here is spectacular. It happens on 3 May in Tadasu-no-mori.

KYOTO IMPERIAL PALACE PARK   PARK

Map p220 (京都御苑; Kyoto Gyōen, Kamigyō-ku; ☺dawn-dusk; ⓢKarasuma line to Marutamachi

RESERVATION & ADMISSION TO KYOTO'S IMPERIAL PROPERTIES

Visitors no longer have to apply for permission to visit the Kyoto Imperial Palace (p81). The palace, situated inside the Imperial Palace Park, is open to the public from Tuesday to Sunday and you just need to go straight to the main gate for entry. Children are permitted with an accompanying adult.

Permission to visit the Sentō Imperial Palace (p81), Katsura Rikyū (p125) and Shūgaku-in Rikyū (p107) is granted by the Kunaichō, the **Imperial Household Agency** (宮内庁京都事務所; Map p220; ☎075-211-1215; www.kunaicho.go.jp; Imperial Palace Park, Kyoto Gyōen, Kamigyō-ku; ⊗8.45am-5pm Tue-Sun; ⑤Karasuma line to Imadegawa), which is inside the Imperial Palace Park. For morning tours you have to book in advance at the Imperial Household Agency office or by filling out the application form on its website. You must be over 18 years to enter each property. For afternoon tours, you can book tickets on the same day at the properties themselves from 11am. Only a certain number of tickets are issued each day, so it's first-come, first-served. Tours run for 60 minutes and you are required to arrive at least 20 minutes beforehand. All tours are free and are in Japanese with English audio guides available.

or Imadegawa) **FREE** The Kyoto Imperial Palace (Kyoto Gosho) and Sentō Imperial Palace (Sentō Gosho) are surrounded by the spacious Kyoto Imperial Palace Park, which is planted with a huge variety of flowering trees and open fields. It's perfect for picnics, strolls and just about any sport you can think of. Take some time to visit the pond at the park's southern end, which contains gorgeous carp. The park is most beautiful in the plum- and cherry-blossom seasons (late February and late March, respectively).

The plum arbour is located about midway along the park on the west side. There are several large *shidareze-zakura* ('weeping' cherry trees) at the north end of the park, making it a great cherry-blossom destination. The park is between Teramachi-dōri and Karasuma-dōri (to the east and west) and Imadegawa-dōri and Marutamachi-dōri (to the north and south).

KYOTO BOTANICAL GARDENS   GARDENS
Map p220 (京都府立植物園; Shimogamohangichō, Sakyō-ku; adult/child gardens ¥200/free, greenhouse ¥200/free; ⊗9am-5pm, greenhouse 10am-4pm; ⑤Karasuma line to Kitayama) The Kyoto Botanical Gardens occupy 24 hectares and feature over 12,000 plants, flowers and trees. It is pleasant to stroll through the rose, cherry and herb gardens or see the rows of camphor trees and the large tropical **greenhouse**. This is a good spot for a picnic. It's also the perfect location for a *hanami* (cherry-blossom viewing) party,

and the blossoms here tend to hold on a little longer than those elsewhere in the city.

KAMIGAMO-JINJA   SHINTO SHRINE
Map p220 (上賀茂神社; ☎075-781-0011; www.kamigamojinja.jp; 339 Motoyama, Kamigamo, Kita-ku; ⊗6am-5pm; ☐Kyoto City bus 9 to Kamigamo-misonobashi) **FREE** Around 2km north of the Botanical Gardens is Kamigamo-jinja, one of Japan's oldest shrines, which predates the founding of Kyoto. Established in 679, it is dedicated to Raijin, the god of thunder, and is one of Kyoto's 17 Unesco World Heritage Sites. The present buildings (more than 40 in all), including the impressive Haiden hall, are exact reproductions of the originals, dating from the 17th to 19th centuries.

KYOTO STATE GUEST HOUSE   NOTABLE BUILDING
Map p220 (www8.cao.go.jp/geihinkan/kyoto/kyoto-e.html; Kyoto Gyōen, Kamigyō-ku; ¥1500; ⊗tours at noon Thu-Tue; ⑤Karasuma line to Imadegawa) Built in 2005 to welcome foreign dignitaries, the Kyoto State Guest House is not a must-see sight, unless you have a real interest in architecture. English guided 60-minute tours are a bit painfully slow-moving, taking visitors through room by room of the building, which was designed as a modern interpretation of traditional Japanese architecture. The central garden and koi-filled pond is quite lovely and you do get an insight into the incredible craftmanship that has gone into every detail.

TAKARA-GA-IKE-KŌEN   PARK

Map p220 (宝ヶ池公園; Iwakura, Matsugasaki, Sakyō-ku; §Karasuma line to Kokusaikaikan Station) This expansive park is an excellent place for a stroll or picnic in natural surroundings. Far from the throngs in the city centre, it is a popular place for birdwatching and has spacious gardens. There is a 1.8km loop around the main pond, where rowboats can be hired for ¥1000 per hour and paddleboats are ¥1000 per 30 minutes.

NISHIJIN TEXTILE CENTER   MUSEUM

Map p220 (西陣織会館; ☑075-451-9231; www. nishijinori.jp; Horikawa-dōri, Imadegawa-sagaru, Kamigyō-ku; ⊙10am-6pm; ⊒Kyoto City bus 9 or 12 to Horikawa-Imadegawa) **FREE** In the heart of the Nishijin textile district, this is worth a peek before starting a walk around the area. There are displays of completed fabrics and kimonos, as well as weaving demonstrations, plus a shop selling items on the 2nd floor. Unfortunately, it's often overrun by large tour groups. It's on the southwest corner of the Horikawa-dōri and Imadegawa-dōri intersection.

Free 10-minute kimono fashion shows are held daily at 10.30am, 11.30am, 1pm, 2pm, 3pm and 4pm. You can also try your hand at weaving (40 minutes, ¥1200).

NISHIJIN   AREA

Map p220 (西陣, Nishijin, Kamigyō-ku; ⊒Kyoto City bus 9 or 12 to Horikawa-Imadegawa) Nishijin is Kyoto's traditional textile centre, the source of all those dazzling kimono fabrics and obi (kimono sashes) that you see being paraded about town. The area is famous for Nishijin-ori (Nishijin weaving) and the main attraction is the Nishijin Textile Center. There are quite a few *machiya* (traditional Japanese townhouses) in this district, so it can be a good place simply to wander, particularly around Jofukuji-dōri. Be sure to stop by traditional indigo dye workshop and store, Aizen Kōbō (p85).

ORINASU-KAN   MUSEUM

Map p220 (織成舘; 693 Daikoku-chō, Kamigyō-ku; adult/child ¥500/350; ⊙10am-4pm, closed Mon; ⊒Kyoto City bus 9 or 12 to Horikawa-Imadegawa) This atmospheric, and usually quiet, museum, housed in a Nishijin weaving factory, has impressive exhibits of Nishijin textiles.

✗ EATING

★KANEI   NOODLES ¥

Map p220 (かね井; ☑075-441-8283; 11-1 Murasakino Higashifujinomori-chō, Kita-ku; noodles from ¥950; ⊙11.30am-2.30pm Tue-Sun; ⊒Kyoto City bus 206 to Daitoku-ji-mae) A small traditional place not far from Funaoka Onsen, Kanei is for soba (buckwheat noodles) connoisseurs – the noodles are made by hand here and are delicious. The owners don't speak much English, so here's what to order: *zaru soba* (¥950) or *kake soba* (soba in a broth; ¥1000). Prepare to queue and note that noodles often sell out early.

★KAZARIYA   SWEETS ¥

Map p220 (かざりや; ☑075-491-9402; Murasakino Imamiya-chō, Kita-ku; sweets ¥500; ⊙10am-5pm Thu-Tue; ⊒Kyoto City bus 46 to Imamiya-jinja) There are two restaurants at the eastern entrance to Imamiya-jinja specialising in *aburi-mochi* (grilled rice cakes coated with soya-bean flour) served with *miso-dare* (sweet-bean paste). Kazariya is on the left side when facing the shrine gate. For over 300 years it has been serving plates of the skewered treats with a pot of tea to enjoy in its traditional teahouse.

It's a lovely place to take a break after exploring the grounds of nearby Daitoku-ji.

★PAPA JON'S   CAFE ¥

Map p220 (パパジョンズカフェ　本店; ☑075-415-2655; 642-4 Shokokuji-chō, Karasuma-dōri, Kamidachiuri higashi-iru, Kamigyō-ku; lunch from ¥850; ⊙9.30am-9pm; 🛜; §Karasuma line to Imadegawa) A short walk from the north border of the Kyoto Imperial Palace Park, this light-filled cafe serves brilliant New York cheesecake and hot drinks. Other menu items include breakfast sets, homemade quiche, soup and tasty salads, as well as gluten-free cakes. There are a few branches around town, including a convenient downtown cafe (p68).

GRAND BURGER   BURGERS ¥

Map p220 (☑075-256-7317; http://grand-burger.com; 107 Shinnyodomae-chō, Teramachi-dōri, Imadegawa-sagaru, Kamigyō-ku; burger sets ¥980-1280; ⊙11am-9pm; 🛜; ⊒Keihan line to Demachiyanagi) A short walk from the northeast gate of Imperial Palace Park, this burger cafe is a great spot for a break while sightseeing. Prop up at the counter or grab a table and bite into juicy burgers with toppings such as avocado and bacon. Sets come with fries and coleslaw. There's a range of international beers, too. No veg option.

DEMACHI FUTABA
SWEETS ¥

Map p220 (出町ふたば; ☑075-231-1658; 236 Seiryu-cho, Imadegawa-agaru, Kawaramachi-dori, Kamigyō-ku; mame-mochi from ¥180; ⊘8.30am-5.30pm, closed Tue & 4th Wed of month; ☒Keihan line to Demachiyanagi) Join the queue of locals here for some of the city's tastiest sweets, with the *mame-mochi* (glutinous rice sweet with black beans) being the standout star. There's no English menu so just point to what takes your fancy. Look for the hanging paper signs and sweets on display.

SARASA NISHIJIN
CAFE ¥

Map p220 (さらさ西陣; ☑075-432-5075; 11-1 Murasakino Higashifujinomori-chō, Kita-ku; lunch from ¥840; ⊘noon-11pm Thu-Tue; ☎; ☒Kyoto City bus 206 to Daitoku-ji-mae) This is one of Kyoto's most interesting cafes – it's built inside an old *sentō* (public bathhouse) and the original tiles have been preserved. Light meals and coffee are the staples here. Service can be slow, but it's worth a stop for the ambience. Lines out the door are not uncommon. It's near Funaoka Onsen.

★TORAYA KARYŌ KYOTO ICHIJŌ
CAFE ¥¥

Map p220 (虎屋菓寮　京都一条店; ☑075-441-3113; 400 Hirohashidono-chō, Ichijō-dōri, Karasuma-nishi-iru, Kamigyō-ku; tea & sweets from ¥1296; ⊘10am-6pm; ⑤Karasuma line to Imadegawa) This gorgeous tearoom-cafe is a stone's throw from the west side of the Imperial Palace Park. It's fantastic for a break from sightseeing in this part of town. The menu has some pictures and simple English. You can enjoy a nice cup of *matcha* (powdered green tea) and its signature *yokan* jelly sweet.

MANZARA HONTEN
JAPANESE ¥¥

Map p220 (まんざら本店; ☑075-253-1558; Kawaramachi-dori, Ebisugawa-agaru, Nakagyō-ku; omakase ¥5500; ⊘5pm-midnight; ⑤Keihan line to Jingū-Marutamachi) Located in a converted *machiya*, Manzara represents a pleasing fusion of traditional and modern Japanese culture. The fare is creative modern Japanese and the surroundings are decidedly stylish. The *omakase* (chef's recommendation) course is good value, and à la carte dishes are available from ¥500.

🍺 DRINKING & NIGHTLIFE

KAMOGAWA CAFE
COFFEE

Map p220 (かもがわカフェ; ☑075-211-4757; Kamiikesu-chō, Kamigyō-ku; coffee from ¥500; ⊘noon-11pm Fri-Wed; ☒Keihan line to Jingū-Marutamachi) If you're looking for great coffee while sightseeing near Imperial Palace Park, head to this lovely cafe with its coloured stained-glass windows, inviting loft space and soft jazz tunes. Single-origin beans are roasted by the owner and brewed almost any way you like. There's no English menu but the friendly owner will happily talk you through it.

PUBLIC BATHS

After a day spent marching from temple to temple, nothing feels better than a good hot bath. Kyoto is full of *sentō* (public baths), ranging from small neighbourhood baths with one or two tubs to massive complexes offering saunas, mineral baths and even electric baths. The **Funaoka Onsen** (船岡温泉; Map p220; https://funaokaonsen.info; 82-1 Minami-Funaoka-chō-Murasakino, Kita-ku; ¥430; ⊘3pm-1am Mon-Sat, 8am-1am Sun & holidays; ☒Kyoto City bus 206 to Senbon Kuramaguchi) is one of the best in Kyoto and could even double as an evening's entertainment.

This old bath boasts outdoor bathing and a sauna, as well as some museum-quality woodcarvings in the changing room (apparently carved during Japan's invasion of Manchuria). Bring your own bath supplies (soap, shampoo, a towel to dry yourself and another small towel for washing); if you forget, you can buy toiletries and rent towels at the front desk.

To find it, head west from Horikawa-dōri along Kuramaguchi-dōri. It's on the left, not far past the Lawson convenience store. Look for the large rocks out the front.

 ENTERTAINMENT

KYOTO CONCERT HALL — CONCERT VENUE
Map p220 (京都コンサートホール; ☎075-711-2980, ticket counter 075-711-3231; www.kyoto-ongeibun.jp/kyotoconcerthall; Shimogamo, 1-26 Hangi-chō, Sakyō-ku; ☺box office 10am-5pm; Ⓢ Karasuma line to Kitayama) This is Kyoto's main classical-music venue, along with ROHM Theatre (p110). It's a lovely hall with excellent acoustics and it never fails to draw an appreciative crowd of knowledgeable Kyotoites. Check *Kyoto Visitor's Guide* or the website for upcoming concerts.

JITTOKU — LIVE MUSIC
Map p220 (拾得; ☎075-841-1691; 815 Hishiya-chō, Kamigyō-ku; ☺5.30pm-midnight, live music 7-9pm; ⓈTōzai line to Nijōjō-mae) Jittoku is located in an atmospheric old *sakagura* (sake brewery). It plays host to a variety of shows – check *Kansai Scene* to see what's on. It also serves food.

ALTI — CONCERT VENUE
Map p220 (京都府立府民ホール　アルティ; ☎075-441-1414; Karasuma-dōri, Ichijō-sagaru, Kamigyō-ku; ⓈKarasuma line to Imadegawa) Occasional classical-music and dance performances are held at this midtown concert hall. Check *Kyoto Visitor's Guide* for upcoming concerts.

🛍 SHOPPING

AIZEN KŌBŌ — CLOTHING
Map p220 (愛染工房; ☎075-441-0355; www.aizenkobo.jp; 215 Yoko Omiya-chō, Nakasuji-dōri, Omiya Nishi-iru, Kamigyō-ku; ☺10am-5.30pm; ⬛Kyoto City bus 9 to Horikawa-Imadegawa) In the heart of the Nishijin textile district in a beautifully restored *machiya*, Aizen Kōbō has been producing its indigo-dyed hand-woven textiles for three generations using traditional methods known as *aizome*. Products are hand dyed using natural fermenting indigo and vegetable dye sourced from the Tade plant, native to Japan.

You can purchase high-quality textiles, from shirts and *noren* (curtains that hang in the entry of Japanese restaurants) to tablecloths and *samu-e* (traditional garments worn by Zen Buddhist priests), or have something custom-made. It's best to call ahead on weekends to make sure it's open.

NISHIJIN TEXTILE CENTER — FASHION & ACCESSORIES
Map p220 (西陣織会館; ☎075-451-9231; Horikawa-dōri, Imadegawa-sagaru, Kamigyō-ku; ☺10am-6pm; ⬛Kyoto City bus 9 to Horikawa-Imadegawa) The Nishijin Textile Center sells a variety of goods fashioned from the textiles for which this part of Kyoto is famous. Goods on offer range from inexpensive change purses and neckties to proper obi.

 ACTIVITIES

HARU COOKING CLASS — COOKING
Map p220 (料理教室はる; www.kyoto-cooking-class.com; 166-32 Shimogamo Miyazaki-chō, Sakyō-ku; veg/non-veg per person from ¥5900/7900; ☺classes from 2pm, reservation required) Haru Cooking Class is a friendly one-man cooking school located in a private home a little bit north of Demachiyanagi. The school's teacher, Taro, speaks English and can teach both vegetarian (though fish stock may be used) and non-vegetarian cooking in classes that run for three to four hours. Reserve by email.

Taro also offers tours of Nishiki Market once a week at noon (¥4000 per person).

CLUB ŌKITSU KYOTO — TEA CEREMONY
Map p220 (京都桜橘倶楽部「桜橘庵」; ☎075-411-8585; www.okitsu-kyoto.com; 524-1 Mototsuchimikado chō, Kamichōjamachi-dōri, Shinmachi higashi-iru, Kamigyō-ku; ⓈKarasuma line to Imadegawa) Ōkitsu provides an upmarket introduction to various aspects of Japanese culture, including tea ceremony and the incense ceremony. The introduction is performed in an exquisite Japanese villa near the Kyoto Imperial Palace, and participants get a real sense of the elegance and refinement of traditional Japanese culture.

URASENKE CHADŌ RESEARCH CENTER — TEA CEREMONY
Map p220 (茶道資料館; ☎075-431-6474; Horikawa-dōri, Teranouchi-aguru, Kamigyō-ku; tea ceremony ¥700; ☺9am-4.30pm; ⓈKarasuma line to Kuramaguchi) Anyone interested in tea ceremony should make their first stop the Urasenke Chadō Research Center. Urasenke is Japan's largest tea school and hosts hundreds of students annually who come from branch schools worldwide to further their studies in 'the way of tea'.

Gion & Southern Higashiyama

Neighbourhood Top Five

1 **Kiyomizu-dera** (p90) Climbing to the top of the Southern Higashiyama district to visit one of Kyoto's most colourful temples.

2 **Chion-in** (p88) Letting your soul be soothed by the chanting monks.

3 **Shōren-in** (p92) Sipping a cup of green tea while admiring the sublime garden.

4 **Yasaka-jinja** (p92) Clapping your hands to awaken the gods at this shrine near Maruyama-kōen.

5 Gion district (p89) Taking an evening stroll through the world of geisha.

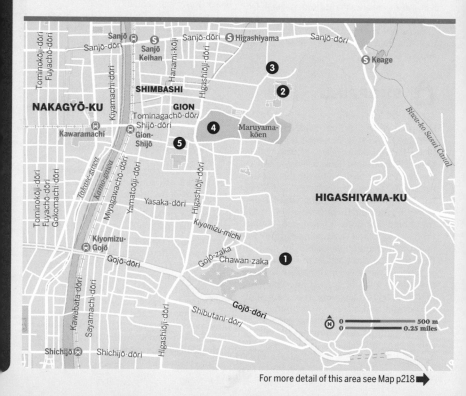

For more detail of this area see Map p218 ➡

Explore Southern Higashiyama

Stretching along the base of the Higashiyama (Eastern Mountains) from the top of Shichijō-dōri to the top of Sanjō-dōri, Southern Higashiyama comprises the thickest concentration of sights in all of Kyoto. This area is home to some of Kyoto's best temples, including Kiyomizu-dera, Chion-in and Kōdai-ji, the green sanctuary of Maruyama-kōen, and several of the city's loveliest lanes: Ishibei-koji, Shimbashi and Nene-no-Michi. Needless to say, this is where you should begin your exploration of Kyoto.

There is a well-established sightseeing route through this district that starts at Kiyomizu-dera and finishes up on Sanjō-dōri. It's best to walk this from south (Kiyomizu) to north (Sanjō), since you'll be going slowly downhill most of the way, but it's perfectly possible to do it from north to south. Keep in mind that this walking route does not cover some of the sights at the southern end of this district, like Sanjūsangen-dō, a fine temple, and the Kyoto National Museum.

With so many sights crammed in to one area, you could easily spend a full day here.

Downhill from the main sightseeing route, you'll find Gion, Kyoto's high-end entertainment and geisha district. This area is most scenic in the evening, which is also when you stand the best chance of spotting geisha.

Local Life

➡ **Hang-outs** Maruyama-kōen (p92), a green oasis in the middle of Southern Higashiyama, is popular with locals for picnics, strolls and dates.

➡ **Eating** The scenic lanes of Ninen-zaka and Sannen-zaka (p91) are lined with tea shops and restaurants.

➡ **Tea** Locals have been sipping *matcha* (powdered green tea) and tucking into sweets at the Gion institution Kagizen Yoshifusa (p94) for many years.

Getting There & Away

➡ **Train** The private Keihan line provides access to Southern Higashiyama. Get off at Gion-shijō or Shichijō stations and walk uphill (east).

➡ **Bus** Kyoto City buses serve various stops in the district and are a good way to access Kiyomizu-dera.

➡ **Subway** The Tōzai subway line's Higashiyama Station offers easy access to the northern end of the district.

Lonely Planet's Top Tip

This is Kyoto's most popular sightseeing district, so it will be crowded during peak seasons. Walking or taking the train/subway is the way to go as traffic comes to a standstill and buses are slow and overcrowded.

✖ Best Places to Eat

➡ Kagizen Yoshifusa (p94)
➡ Omen Kodai-ji (p94)
➡ Kikunoi (p95)
➡ Gion Karyō (p95)

For reviews, see p94.

☕ Best Places to Drink

➡ Beer Komachi (p95)
➡ Gion Finlandia Bar (p96)
➡ Tōzan Bar (p95)

For reviews, see p95. ➡

🛍 Best Places to Shop

➡ Ichizawa Shinzaburo Hanpu (p98)
➡ Asahi-dō (p98)
➡ Miura Shōmei (p98)

For reviews, see p98. ➡

GION & SOUTHERN HIGASHIYAMA

TOP SIGHT
CHION-IN

A collection of soaring buildings and spacious courtyards, Chion-in serves as the headquarters of the Jōdo sect, the largest sect of Buddhism in Japan. It's the most popular pilgrimage temple in Kyoto and it's always a hive of religious activity. For visitors with a taste for the grand, this temple is sure to satisfy.

Jōdo Buddhism HQ

Chion-in was established in 1234 on the site where Hōnen, one of the most famous figures in Japanese Buddhism, taught his brand of Buddhism (Jōdo, or Pure Land, Buddhism) and eventually fasted to death. Today it's still the headquarters of the Jōdo school, founded by Hōnen.

Impressive Temple Structures

The oldest of the present buildings date from the 17th century. The two-storey **San-mon** temple gate is the largest in Japan. The immense **Miei-dō Hall**, which measures 35m wide and 45m long, houses an image of Hōnen and is connected with the **Dai Hōjō** hall by a 'nightingale' floor that squeaks as one walks over it. Miei-dō Hall is under restoration and closed to the public. It's expected to be finished in 2020.

Temple Bell

Chion-in's temple bell was cast in 1633. It is the largest temple bell in Japan. It's up a flight of steps at the southeastern corner of the temple precincts. The bell is rung by the temple's monks 108 times on New Year's Eve each year.

Gardens

Walk around the back of the main hall to see the temple's gardens. On the way, you'll pass a darkened hall with a small statue of Amida Buddha glowing eerily. It's a nice contrast to the splendour of the main hall.

DON'T MISS

→ The temple bell
→ Chanting monks in the Miei-dō Hall

PRACTICALITIES

→ 知恩院
→ Map p218, D2
→ www.chion-in.or.jp
→ 400 Rinka-chō, Higashiyama-ku
→ inner buildings & garden adult/child ¥500/250, grounds free
→ ⊙9am-4.30pm
→ Ⓢ Tōzai line to Higashiyama

TOP SIGHT
GION

Gion is the famous entertainment and geisha quarter on the eastern bank of the Kamo-gawa. While Gion's true origins were in teahouses catering to weary visitors to the nearby shrine Yasaka-jinja, by the mid 18th century the area was Kyoto's largest pleasure district. The best way to experience Gion these days is with an evening stroll around the atmospheric streets lined with 17th-century traditional restaurants and teahouses.

Start off on the main street **Hanami-kōji**, which runs north–south and bisects Shijō-dōri. Hanami-kōji does get very crowded with tourists at this time, so be sure to duck off into the backstreets and lanes running off it to explore some quieter areas.

If you walk from Shijō-dōri along the northern section of Hanami-kōji and take your third left, you will find yourself on **Shimbashi** (sometimes called Shirakawa Minami-dōri), which is one of Kyoto's most beautiful streets, especially in the evening and during cherry-blossom season.

A bit further north lie **Shinmonzen-dōri** and **Furumonzen-dōri**, running east–west. Wander in either direction along these streets, which are packed with old houses, art galleries and shops specialising in antiques.

DON'T MISS

➡ Geisha scurrying to appointments in the early evening

➡ *Machiya* (traditional Japanese townhouses) in lanes off the main streets

PRACTICALITIES

➡ 祇園周辺

➡ Map p218, D3

➡ Higashiyama-ku

➡ ⑤Tōzai line to Sanjō, ®Keihan line to Gion-Shijō

TOP SIGHT
KIYOMIZU-DERA

Kiyomizu-dera is one of the city's most popular temples. Built around a holy spring (*kiyomizu* means 'pure water'), the temple has attracted pilgrims since the 8th century AD. In addition to halls holding fine Buddhist images, the complex includes a Shintō shrine that is associated with matters of the heart – buy a prayer plaque here to assure success in romance.

A Kyoto Icon

This ancient temple was first built in 798, but the present buildings are reconstructions dating from 1633. As an affiliate of the Hossō school of Buddhism, which originated in Nara, it has successfully survived the many intrigues of local Kyoto schools of Buddhism through the centuries and is now one of the most famous landmarks of the city (the reason it can get very crowded during spring and autumn).

The Hondō (Main Hall)

The Hondō, which houses a Jūichi-men (11-headed) Kannon figure, has a huge verandah that juts out over the hillside, supported by 139 15m-high wooden pillars. Below this is Otowa-no-taki spring, where visitors drink sacred water believed to bestow health and long life. The main hall is being renovated and may be covered, though is still accessible.

Jishu-jinja

After exiting the verandah, up to your left you will find Jishu-jinja, where visitors try to ensure success in love by closing their eyes and walking between a pair of 'Love Stones'.

Tainai-meguri

Before you enter the actual temple precincts, visit one of the oddest sights in Japan: the Tainai-meguri. By entering the hall, you are figuratively entering the womb of Daizuigu Bosatsu, a female Bodhisattva who has the power to grant any human wish.

DON'T MISS

➡ Cherry-blossom, autumn and O-Bon light-ups
➡ Tainai-meguri

PRACTICALITIES

➡ 清水寺
➡ Map p218, D5
➡ ☎075-551-1234
➡ www.kiyomizudera.or.jp
➡ 1-294 Kiyomizu, Higashiyama-ku
➡ adult/child ¥400/200
➡ ⊙6am-6pm, closing times vary seasonally
➡ 🚌Kyoto City bus 206 to Kiyōmizu-michi or Gojō-zaka, 🚉Keihan line to Kiyomizu-Gojō

◉ SIGHTS

SANJŪSANGEN-DŌ TEMPLE
BUDDHIST TEMPLE

Map p218 (三十三間堂; ☑075-561-0467; 657 Sanjūsangendōma wari-chō, Higashiyama-ku; adult/child ¥600/300; ⊗8am-5pm Apr–mid-Nov, 9am-4pm mid-Nov–Mar; ⬛Kyoto City bus 206 or 208 to Sanjūsangen-dō-mae, ⬛Keihan line to Shichijō) This superb temple's name refers to the 33 *sanjūsan* (bays) between the pillars of this long, narrow edifice. The building houses 1001 wooden statues of Kannon (the Buddhist goddess of mercy); the chief image, the 1000-armed Senjū-Kannon, was carved by the celebrated sculptor Tankei in 1254. It is flanked by 500 smaller Kannon images, neatly lined in rows. The visual effect is stunning, making this a must-see in Southern Higashiyama and a good starting point for exploration of the area.

The original temple, called Rengeō-in, was built in 1164 at the request of the retired emperor Go-shirakawa. After it burnt to the ground in 1249, a faithful copy was constructed in 1266.

If you look closely, you might notice that the supposedly 1000-armed statues don't have the required number. Just keep in mind that a nifty Buddhist mathematical formula holds that 40 arms are the equivalent of 1000 because each saves 25 worlds.

At the back of the hall are 28 guardian statues in a variety of expressive poses. The gallery at the western side of the hall is famous for the annual **Tōshiya festival**, held on 15 January, when archers shoot arrows along the length of the hall. The ceremony dates from the Edo period, when an annual contest was held to see how many arrows could be shot from the southern to northern end in 24 hours. The all-time record was set in 1686, when an archer successfully landed more than 8000 arrows at the northern end.

KYOTO NATIONAL MUSEUM
MUSEUM

Map p218 (京都国立博物館; www.kyohaku.go.jp; 527 Chaya-machi, Higashiyama-ku; admission varies; ⊗9.30am-5pm, to 8pm Fri & Sat, closed Mon; ⬛Kyoto City bus 206 or 208 to Sanjūsangen-dō-mae, ⬛Keihan line to Shichijō) The Kyoto National Museum is the city's premier art museum and plays host to the highest-level exhibitions in the city. It was founded in 1895 as an imperial repository for art and treasures from local temples and shrines.

The **Heisei Chishinkan**, designed by Taniguchi Yoshio and opened in 2014, is a brilliant modern counterpoint to the original red-brick **main hall** building, which was closed and undergoing structural work at the time of research. Check the *Kyoto Visitor's Guide* to see what's on while you're in town.

KAWAI KANJIRŌ MEMORIAL HALL
MUSEUM

Map p218 (河井寛治郎記念館; ☑075-561-3585; 569 Kanei-chō, Gojō-zaka, Higashiyama-ku; adult/child ¥900/300; ⊗10am-5pm Tue-Sun; ⬛Kyoto City bus 206 or 207 to Umamachi) This small memorial hall is one of Kyoto's most commonly overlooked little gems. The hall was the home and workshop of one of Japan's most famous potters, Kawai Kanjirō (1890–1966). The 1937 house is built in rural style and contains examples of Kanjirō's work, his collection of folk art and ceramics, his workshop and a fascinating *nobori-gama* (stepped kiln). The museum is near the intersection of Gojō-dōri and Higashiōji-dōri.

KENNIN-JI
BUDDHIST TEMPLE

Map p218 (建仁寺; www.kenninji.jp; 584 Komatsu-chō, Yamatoōji-dōri, Shijo-sagaru, Higashiyama-ku; ¥500; ⊗10am-5pm Mar-Oct, to 4.30pm Nov-Feb; ⬛Keihan line to Gion-Shijō) Founded in 1202 by the monk Eisai, Kennin-ji is the oldest Zen temple in Kyoto. It is an island of peace and calm on the border of the boisterous Gion nightlife district and it makes a fine counterpoint to the worldly pleasures of that area. The highlight at Kennin-ji is the fine and expansive *kare-sansui* (dry landscape). The painting of the twin dragons on the roof of the **Hōdō** hall is also fantastic.

NINEN-ZAKA & SANNEN-ZAKA AREA
AREA

Map p218 (二年坂・三年坂; Higashiyama-ku; ⬛Kyoto City bus 206 to Kiyomizu-michi or Gojō-zaka, ⬛Keihan line to Kiyomizu-Gojō) Just downhill from and slightly to the north of Kiyomizu-dera, you will find one of Kyoto's loveliest restored neighbourhoods, the Ninen-zaka–Sannen-zaka area. The name refers to the two main streets of the area: Ninen-zaka and Sannen-zaka, literally 'Two-Year Hill' and 'Three-Year Hill' (the years referring to the ancient imperial years when they were first laid out). These two charming streets are lined with old wooden houses, traditional shops and restaurants.

KŌDAI-JI
BUDDHIST TEMPLE

Map p218 (高台寺; ☏075-561-9966; www. kodaiji.com; 526 Shimokawara-chō, Kōdai-ji, Higashiyama-ku; ¥600; ⊙9am-5.30pm; ☐Kyoto City bus 206 to Yasui, ⑤Tōzai line to Higashiyama) This exquisite temple was founded in 1605 by Kita-no-Mandokoro in memory of her late husband, Toyotomi Hideyoshi. The extensive grounds include gardens designed by the famed landscape architect Kobori Enshū, and teahouses designed by the renowned master of the tea ceremony, Sen no Rikyū. The ticket also allows entry to the small Sho museum across the road from the entrance to Kōdai-ji.

The temple holds three annual special night-time illuminations, when the gardens are lit by multicoloured spotlights. The illuminations are held from mid-March to early May, 1 to 18 August, and late October to early December.

MARUYAMA-KŌEN
PARK

Map p218 (円山公園; Maruyama-chō, Higashiyama-ku; ⑤Tōzai line to Higashiyama) Maruyama-kōen is a favourite of locals and visitors alike. This park is the place to come to escape the bustle of the city centre and amble around gardens, ponds, souvenir shops and restaurants. Peaceful paths meander through the trees, and carp glide through the waters of a small pond in the park's centre.

For two weeks in early April, when the park's cherry trees come into bloom, the calm atmosphere is shattered by hordes of drunken revellers having *hanami* (cherry-blossom viewing) parties under the trees. The centrepiece is a massive *shidare-zakura* cherry tree; this is one of the most beautiful sights in Kyoto, particularly the *yozakura* (night cherry blossoms) when lit up from below at night. For those who don't mind crowds, this is a good place to observe the Japanese at their most uninhibited. Arrive early and claim a good spot high on the east side of the park, from where you can peer down on the mayhem below.

YASAKA-JINJA
SHINTO SHRINE

Map p218 (八坂神社; ☏075-561-6155; www. yasaka-jinja.or.jp; 625 Gion-machi, Kita-gawa, Higashiyama-ku; ⊙24hr; ⑤Tōzai line to Higashiyama) **FREE** This colourful and spacious shrine is considered the guardian shrine of the Gion entertainment district. It's a bustling place that is well worth a visit while exploring Southern Higashiyama; it can

easily be paired with Maruyama-kōen, the park just up the hill.

The present buildings, with the exception of the older, two-storey west gate, date from 1654. The granite *torii* (shrine gate) on the south side was erected in 1666 and stands 9.5m high, making it one of the tallest in Japan. The roof of the main shrine is covered with cypress shingles. Among the treasures here are a pair of carved wooden *koma-inu* (guardian lion-dogs) attributed to the renowned sculptor Unkei.

This shrine is particularly popular as a spot for *hatsu-mōde* (first shrine visit of the New Year). If you don't mind a stampede, come here around midnight on New Year's Eve or on any of the days following. Surviving the crush is proof that you're blessed by the gods!

YASUI KONPIRA-GŪ
SHINTO SHRINE

Map p218 (安井金比羅宮; www.yasui-konpiragu. or.jp; 70 Simobenten-chō, Higashiyama-ku; ⊙24hr; ☐Kyoto City bus 204 to Higashiyama-Yasui) This interesting little Shintō shrine on the edge of Gion contains one of the most peculiar objects we've encountered anywhere in Japan: the **enkiri/enmusubi ishi**. Resembling some kind of shaggy igloo, this is a stone that is thought to bind good relationships tighter and sever bad relationships.

If you'd like to take advantage of the stone's powers, here's the drill: purchase a special piece of paper from the counter next to the stone and write your name and wish on it. If you want to bind your love tighter (figuratively, of course), grasp the paper and crawl through the tunnel in the stone from front to back. If you want out of your present relationship, crawl through from back to front. Then, use the glue provided and stick your wishing paper to the ever-huge collection of wishes decorating the stone.

★SHŌREN-IN
BUDDHIST TEMPLE

Map p218 (青蓮院; 69-1 Sanjōbō-chō, Awataguchi, Higashiyama-ku; ¥500; ⊙9am-5pm; ⑤Tōzai line to Higashiyama) This temple is hard to miss, with its giant camphor trees growing just outside the walls. Fortunately, most tourists march right on past, heading to the area's more famous temples. That is their loss, because this intimate little sanctuary contains a superb landscape garden, which you can enjoy while drinking a cup of green tea (¥500, 9am to 3.30pm; ask at the reception office).

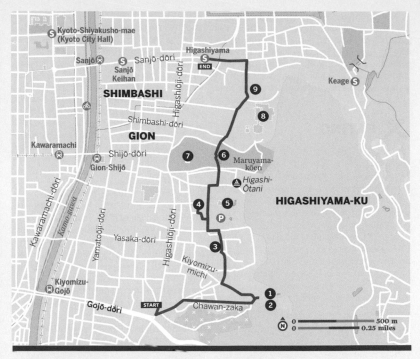

🏃 Neighbourhood Walk
Southern Higashlyama Highlights

START GOJŌ-ZAKA BUS STOP
END HIGASHIYAMA STATION
LENGTH 5KM; FOUR HOURS

From the starting point at Gojō-zaka bus stop on Higashiōji-dōri (bus 100, 110, 206 or 207), walk up Gojō-zaka slope. Head uphill until you reach the first fork in the road; bear right and continue up Chawan-zaka (Teapot Lane). At the top of the hill, you'll come to Kiyomizu-dera. Before you enter the temple, we recommend that you pay ¥100 to descend into the **❶ Tainai-meguri**, the entrance to which is just to the left of the main temple entrance. Next, enter **❷ Kiyomizu-dera** (p90).

After touring Kiyomizu-dera, exit along Kiyomizu-michi. Continue down the hill and take a right at the four-way intersection down stone-paved steps. This is Sannen-zaka, where you will find tiny little **❸ Kasagi-ya** (p94), which has been serving tea and Japanese-style sweets for as long as anyone can remember. It's on the left, just below a vending machine and a few doors before Starbucks. Halfway down Sannen-zaka, the road curves to the left, Follow it a short distance, then go right down a flight of steps into Ninen-zaka. At the end of Ninen-zaka zigzag left (at the vending machines) then right (just past the car park) and continue north. Very soon, on your left, you'll come to the entrance to **❹ Ishibei-kōji** – perhaps the most beautiful street in Kyoto. Take a detour to explore this, then retrace your steps and continue north, passing almost immediately the entrance to **❺ Kōdai-ji** (p92) on the right up a long flight of stairs.

After Kōdai-ji continue north to the T-junction; turn right here then take a quick left. You'll cross the wide pedestrian arcade that leads to Higashi Ōtani cemetery and then descend into **❻ Maruyama-kōen** (p92). In the centre of the park, you'll see the giant Gion *shidare-zakura*, Kyoto's most famous cherry tree. From the park, head west into the grounds of **❼ Yasaka-jinja** (p92). Then return to the park and head north to tour the grounds of the impressive **❽ Chion-in** (p88). From here it's a quick walk to **❾ Shōren-in** (p92). From Shōren-in walk down to Sanjō-dōri to Higashiyama Station.

Shōren-in, commonly called Awata Palace after the neighbourhood in which it is located, was originally the residence of the chief abbot of the Tendai school. Founded in 1150, the present building dates from 1895 and the main hall has sliding screens with paintings from the 16th and 17th centuries.

✖ EATING

★ OMEN KODAI-JI   NOODLES ¥
Map p218 (おめん 高台寺店; ☑ 075-541-5007; 362 Masuya-chō, Kōdaiji-dōri, Shimokawara higashi-iru, Higashiyama-ku; noodles from ¥1150; ⏱ 11am-9pm; ☐ Kyoto City bus 206 to Higashi-yama-Yasui) Housed in a remodelled Japanese building with a light, airy feeling, this branch of Kyoto's famed Omen noodle chain is the best place to stop while exploring the Southern Higashiyama district. Upstairs has fine views over the area. The signature udon (thick, white wheat noodles) served in broth with a selection of fresh vegetables is delicious.

★ KAGIZEN YOSHIFUSA   TEAHOUSE ¥
Map p218 (鍵善良房; ☑ 075-561-1818; www. kagizen.co.jp; 264 Gion machi, Kita-gawa, Higashiyama-ku; kuzukiri ¥1000, matcha & sweet ¥880; ⏱ 9.30am-6pm Tue-Sun; ☐ Hankyū line to Kawaramachi, Keihan line to Gion-Shijō) This Gion institution is one of Kyoto's oldest and best-known okashi-ya (sweet shops). It sells a variety of traditional sweets and has a lovely tearoom out the back where you can sample cold kuzukiri (transparent arrowroot noodles) served with a kuro-mitsu (sweet black sugar) dipping sauce, or just a nice cup of matcha and a sweet.

All in all, this is one of the best spots in Gion for a rest. Look for the sweets in the window, the wide front and the black-and-white noren curtains.

SARYO TSUJIRI   SWEETS, CAFE ¥
Map p218 (茶寮都路里; http://giontsujiri.co.jp; 2nd fl, 573 Gion-machi, Minamigawa, Higashiyama-ku; matcha & sweet ¥880, parfait from ¥1100; ⏱ 10am-10pm; ☐ Hankyū line to Kawaramachi, Keihan line to Gion-Shijō) Take a break from the crowds and head upstairs to this bright cafe serving a range of matcha sweets and treats, from overloaded parfaits to matcha soba noodles. The ground-floor shop sells a good range of high-quality tea from the tea-growing area of Uji.

GION YUKI   IZAKAYA ¥
Map p218 (遊亀 祇園; ☑ 075-525-2666; 111-1 Tominaga-chō, Higashiyama-ku; dishes ¥380-680; ⏱ 5-11pm Mon-Fri, to midnight Sat; ☐ Keihan line to Gion-Shijō) Squeeze in at the counter elbow-to-elbow with tourists and locals for front-row seats to watch the chefs do their thing at this lively izakaya. Seafood is big on the menu, from sashimi plates and grilled fish to tasty tempura, and sake is the drink of choice – no surprise considering the owner is a sake brewer. Look for the short hanging red curtains.

EFISH CAFE   CAFE ¥
Map p218 (エフィッシュ; ☑ 075-361-3069; www. shinproducts.com; 798-1 Nishihashizume-chō, Gojō-sagaru, Shimogyo-ku; meals from ¥820, coffee from ¥480; ⏱ 10am-10pm; 🛜; ☐ Keihan line to Kiyomizu-Gojō) Hidden in a quiet riverside spot, Efish is a small modern cafe serving tasty fresh juices, good coffee and light lunches, such as sandwiches, soups and healthy salads. The dinner menu offers more substantial meals along the lines of vegetarian taco sets and curries. It also sells a range of handmade ceramics and design products.

CHOICE   CAFE ¥
Map p218 (チョイス; ☑ 075-762-1233; www. choice-hs.net; 89-1 Sanjō-dōri, Ohashi-chō, Higashiyama-ku; meals from ¥1100; ⏱ 9am-9pm, closed Sun; 🛜🍽; ⬓ Tōzai line to Sanjō Keihan, ☐ Keihan line to Sanjō) 🌱 Choice is a spacious comfortable cafe with a great, well, choice of gluten-free and vegan fare. Drop in for breakfast pancakes, vegan cheese plates, coffee or a glass of organic wine.

RAKUSHŌ   CAFE ¥
Map p218 (洛匠; ☑ 075-561-6892; 516 Washio-chō, Kodaijikitamon-dōri, Shimogawara higashi-iru, Higashiyama-ku; tea from ¥620; ⏱ 9.30am-6pm, closed irregularly; ☐ Kyoto City bus 204 to Higashiyama-Yasui) This casual Japanese-style tearoom on Nene-no-Michi in the heart of the Southern Higashiyama sightseeing district is well placed for a break while doing the main tourist route in this area. The real attraction is the small koi (Japanese carp) pond adjoining the tearoom. The owner is a champion koi breeder and his fish are superb!

KASAGI-YA   TEAHOUSE ¥
Map p218 (かさぎ屋; ☑ 075-561-9562; 349 Masuya-chō, Kōdai-ji, Higashiyama-ku; tea &

sweets from ¥650; ⊙11am-6pm Wed-Mon; 🚌Kyoto City bus 206 to Higashiyama-Yasui) At Kasagi-ya, on Sannen-zaka near Kiyomizudera, you can enjoy a nice cup of *matcha* and a variety of sweets. This old wooden shop has atmosphere to boot and friendly staff – which makes it worth the wait if there's a queue. It's hard to spot; it's a few doors up from Starbucks up the stairs on the same side.

HISAGO   NOODLES ¥

Map p218 (ひさご; 📞075-561-2109; 484 Shimokawara-chō, Higashiyama-ku; meals from ¥950; ⊙11.30am-7.30pm Tue-Sun; 🚌Kyoto City bus 206 to Higashiyama-Yasui) If you need a quick meal while in the main Southern Higashiyama sightseeing district, this simple noodle and rice restaurant is a good bet. It's within easy walking distance of Kiyomizudera and Maruyama-kōen. *Oyako-donburi* (chicken and egg over rice; ¥1010) is the speciality of the house.

There is no English sign; look for the traditional front and the small collection of food models on display. In the busy seasons, there's almost always a queue outside.

YAGURA   NOODLES ¥¥

Map p218 (やぐ羅; 📞075-561-1035; Shijō-dōri, Yamatoōji nishi-iru, Higashiyama-ku; soba ¥1150; ⊙11.30am 9pm, closed irregularly; 🚃Keihan line to Gion-Shijō) Across from Minami-za theatre, this noodle specialist is an unassuming and casual spot for a filling lunch or dinner while exploring Gion. Choose from a range of *donburi*, soba and udon noodle dishes, or opt for the *omakase* – a set of three dishes from the daily specials. Look for the bowls of noodles on display in the window.

BAMBOO   IZAKAYA ¥¥

Map p218 (晩boo; 📞075-771-5559; Minami gawa, 1st fl, Higashiyama-Sanjō higashi-iru, Higashiyama-ku; dishes from ¥500; ⊙5.30pm-midnight; 🚇Tōzai line to Higashiyama) Bamboo is one of Kyoto's more approachable *izakaya* (Japanese pub-eatery). It's on Sanjō-dōri, near the mouth of a traditional, old shopping arcade. You can sit at the counter here and order a variety of typical *izakaya* dishes, watching the chefs do their thing.

★KIKUNOI   KAISEKI ¥¥¥

Map p218 (菊乃井; 📞075-561-0015; www.kikunoi.jp; 459 Shimokawara-chō, Yasakatoriimaesagaru, Shimokawara-dōri, Higashiyama-ku; lunch/dinner from ¥10,000/16,000; ⊙noon-1pm & 5-8pm; 🚃Keihan line to Gion-Shijō) One of Kyoto's true culinary temples, serving some of the finest *kaiseki* (Japanese haute cuisine) in the city by famous Michelin-starred chef Mutara. Located in a hidden nook near Maruyama-kōen, this restaurant has everything necessary for the full over-the-top *kaiseki* experience, from setting to service to exquisitely executed cuisine, often with a creative twist. Reserve through your hotel at least a month in advance.

GION KARYŌ   KAISEKI ¥¥¥

Map p218 (祇園迦陵; 📞075-532-0025; 570-235 Gion-machi, Minamigawa, Higashiyama-ku; lunch/dinner courses from ¥5000/10,000; ⊙11.30am-3.30pm & 6-10.30pm Thu-Tue; 🚃Keihan line to Gion-Shijō) Take an old Kyoto house, renovate it to make it comfortable for modern diners, serve reasonably priced and excellent *kaiseki* and you have Karyō's recipe for success. The chef and servers are welcoming and an English menu makes ordering a snap. There are counter seats where you can watch the chef working and rooms with *hori-kotatsu* (sunken floors) for groups.

DRINKING & NIGHTLIFE

BEER KOMACHI   CRAFT BEER

Map p218 (ビア小町; 📞075-746-6152; www.beerkomachi.com; 444 Hachiken-chō, Higashiyama-ku; ⊙5-11pm Mon & Wed-Fri, 3-11pm Sat & Sun; 🛜; 🚇Tōzai line to Higashiyama) Located in the Furokawa-chō covered shopping arcade close to Higashiyama Station, this tiny casual bar is dedicated to promoting Japanese craft beer. There are usually seven Japanese beers on tap, which rotate on an almost daily basis. There's a great bar-food menu and a list of sake if you're not much of a beer drinker.

TŌZAN BAR   BAR

Map p218 (📞075-541-3201; www.kyoto.regency.hyatt.com; Hyatt Regency Kyoto, 644-2 Sanjūsangendō-mawari, Higashiyama-ku; ⊙5pm-midnight; 🚃Keihan line to Shichijō) Even if you're not spending the night at the Hyatt Regency, drop by the cool and cosy underground bar for a tipple or two. Kitted out by renowned design firm Super Potato, the dimly lit atmospheric space features interesting touches, such as old locks, wooden beams, an antique-book library space and a wall feature made from traditional wooden sweet moulds.

% ARABICA
COFFEE

Map p218 (📞075-746-3669; 87 Hoshino-chō, Higashiyama-ku; coffee from ¥300; ⏰8am-6pm; 🚍Kyoto City bus 206 to Higashiyama-Yasui) This branch of % Arabica sits in the shadow of nearby Yasaka Pagoda on an atmospheric stone paved street. Grab a takeaway single-origin brew and continue strolling and sightseeing in the area. There's usually a queue out the front of Kyoto's pretty young things taking Instagrammable selfies as they wait.

GION FINLANDIA BAR
BAR

Map p218 (ぎをん フィンランディアバー; 📞075-541-3482; www.finlandiabar.com; 570-123 Gion-machi, Minamigawa, Higashiyama-ku; cover ¥500; ⏰6pm-3am; 🚉Keihan line to Gion-Shijō) This stylish, minimalist Gion bar in an old geisha house is a great place for a civilised drink. There's no menu, so just prop up at the bar and let the bow-tied bartender know what you like, whether it's an expertly crafted cocktail or a high-end Japanese single malt. Friday and Saturday nights can get busy, so you may have to queue.

☆ ENTERTAINMENT

★ MIYAKO ODORI
DANCE

Map p218 (都をどり; 📞075-541-3391; www.miyako-odori.jp/english; Gion Kōbu Kaburen-jō Theatre, 570-2 Gion-machi, Minamigawa, Higashiyama-ku; with/without tea ¥4600/¥3500; ⏰shows 12.30pm, 2.20pm & 4.10pm; 🚍Kyoto City bus 206 to Gion, 🚉Keihan line to Gion-Shijō) This 45-minute dance is a wonderful geisha performance. It's a real stunner and the colourful images are mesmerising. It's held throughout April, usually at Gion Kōbu Kaburen-jō Theatre, on Hanami-kōji, just south of Shijō-dōri. The building was under renovation at the time of research, and performances were being held at Kyoto Art Theater Shunjuza; check the website for details.

★ MINAMI-ZA
THEATRE

Map p218 (南座; www.kabukiweb.net; Shijō-Ōhashi, Higashiyama-ku; 🚉Keihan line to Gion-Shijō) This theatre in Gion is the oldest kabuki theatre in Japan. The major event of the year is the **Kaomise festival** in December,

which features Japan's finest kabuki actors. If the theatre is still closed for renovations, Kaomise will be held at ROHM Theatre Kyoto (p110).

KYŌ ODORI
DANCE

Map p218 (京おどり; 📞075-561-1151; Miyagawachō Kaburenjo, 4-306 Miyagawasuji, Higashiyama-ku; with/without tea nonreserved seat ¥2800/2200, reserved seat ¥4800/4200; ⏰shows 1pm, 2.45pm & 4.30pm; 🚉Keihan line to Gion-Shijō) Put on by the Miyagawa-chō geisha district, this wonderful geisha dance is among the most picturesque performances of the Kyoto year. It's held from the first to the third Sunday in April at the **Miyagawa-chō Kaburen-jō Theatre** (宮川町歌舞練場), east of the Kamo-gawa between Shijō-dōri and Gojō-dōri.

GION ODORI
DANCE

Map p218 (祇園をどり; 📞075-561-0224; Gion, Higashiyama-ku; admission with/without tea ¥4500/4000; ⏰shows 1.30pm & 4pm; 🚍Kyoto City bus 206 to Gion) This is a quaint and charming geisha dance put on by the geisha of the Gion Higashi geisha district. It's held from 1 to 10 November at the **Gion Kaikan Theatre** (祇園会館), near Yasaka-jinja.

MAIKO DINNER SHOW YASAKADORI ENRAKU
DANCE

Map p218 (八坂通り燕楽; 📞075-741-8727; www.travel-kyoto-maiko.com; 594-3 Komatsu-chō, Higashiyama-ku; show incl dinner & drinks adult/child/under 6yr ¥19,000/13,000/free; ⏰6-8pm Tue & Thu; 🚉Keihan line to Kiyomizu-Gojō) Traditional restaurant Yasadori Enraku started hosting intimate *maiko* (apprentice geisha) performances in early 2017. Guests are seated on tatami-mat floors at low tables for dinner and shows include a dance performance, as well as the chance to partake in *ozashiki* (party drinking games), have a chat to *maiko* and get your photo taken. The price includes all you can drink.

KYOTO CUISINE & MAIKO EVENING
DANCE

Map p218 (ぎおん畑中; 📞075-541-5315; www.kyoto-maiko.jp; 505 Gion-machi, Minami-gawa, Higashiyama-ku; per person ¥19,000; ⏰6-8pm Mon, Wed, Fri & Sat; 🚍Kyoto City bus 206 to Gion or Chionin-mae, 🚉Keihan line to Gion-Shijō) If you want to witness geisha perform and then actually speak with them, one of the best opportunities is at Gion Hatanaka (p149), a Gion ryokan that offers a regularly scheduled evening of elegant Kyoto *kaiseki*

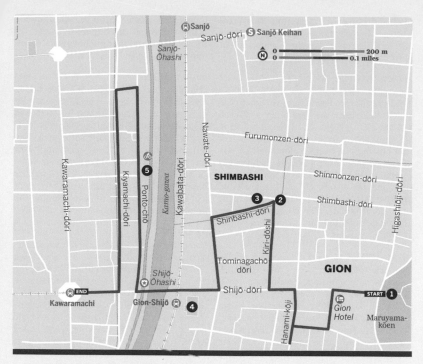

Neighbourhood Walk
Night Walk Through the Floating World

START YASAKA-JINJA
END KAWARAMACHI STATION
LENGTH 3KM; TWO HOURS

Start on the steps of ❶ **Yasaka-jinja** (p92; at the intersection of Shijō-dōri and Higashiōji-dōri), a 10-minute walk from Shijō (Keihan line) or Kawaramachi (Hankyū line) stations. Cross to the south side of Shijō-dōri and just after passing the APA Gion Hotel turn left. Walk 150m and take the second right. Another 100m brings you to Hanami-kōji, a picturesque street of *ryōtei* (traditional, high-class restaurants). Take a look then walk back north to Shijō-dōri.

Cross Shijō-dōri and go west for about 20m then turn right into Kiri-dōshi. As you continue along Kiri-dōshi, you'll cross Tominagachō-dōri, which is lined with buildings containing hundreds of hostess bars.

Kiri-dōshi crosses another street and then narrows to a tiny alley. You are now about to enter Gion's most lovely area, which lies just across ❷ **Tatsumi-bashi bridge**. This is the Shimbashi district, which features some of Kyoto's finest traditional architecture, most upmarket restaurants and exclusive hostess bars.

At the fork in the road you will find a small ❸ **Tatsumi shrine**. Take a left and walk west along the canal. Admire the views across the canal into some of the finest restaurants in Kyoto. You will occasionally spot geisha entertaining guests in some of these elite establishments.

At the end of Shimbashi, take a left onto gaudy Nawate-dōri. Head west on Shijō-dōri, passing ❹ **Minami-za** (p96), Kyoto's main kabuki theatre. Cross the Kamo-gawa on the north side of Shijō-Ōhashi and walk to the *kōban* (police box) on your right. You are now standing at the intersection of Shijō-dōri and ❺ **Ponto-chō**. Heading north brings you into an entirely different world of upmarket restaurants, bars, clubs and cafes.

At the north end of Ponto-chō at Sanjō-dōri, take a left and another left on Kiyamachi-dōri. This is a much more casual and inexpensive entertainment district.

food and personal entertainment by real Kyoto *geiko* (fully fledged geisha) as well as *maiko*. Children under seven years are not permitted.

MAIKO THEATRE · DANCE

Map p218 (舞妓シアター; ☎075-741-8258; 302-2 Daikoku-chō, Higashiyama-ku; adult/child ¥6800/2000, lunch show incl bentō adult/child ¥8800/3800; ⏱90min show 12pm, 2pm & 4pm; 🚃Keihan line to Kiyomizu-Gojō) This is a new spot hosting *maiko* shows for small groups in a modern building. It includes a bit of tea ceremony, two short dances, conversation time and photo ops. Drinks are available and there's a *bentō* box option for the lunchtime performance. There's some waiting around at times but this is one of the more affordable options.

GION CORNER · THEATRE

Map p218 (ギオンコーナー; ☎075-561-1119; www.kyoto-gioncorner.com; Yasaka Kaikan, 570-2 Gion-machi, Minamigawa, Higashiyama-ku; adult/child ¥3150/1900; ⏱performances 6pm & 7pm daily mid-Mar–Nov, Fri-Sun Dec–mid-Mar; 🚌Kyoto City bus 206 to Gion, 🚃Keihan line to Gion-Shijō) Gion Corner presents one-hour shows that include a bit of tea ceremony, koto (Japanese zither) music, ikebana (art of flower arranging), *gagaku* (court music), *kyōgen* (ancient comic plays), *kyōmai* (Kyoto-style dance) and *bunraku* (classical puppet theatre). It's a hugely touristy affair and fairly pricey for what you get. Tickets have been discounted from ¥3150 to ¥2500 for foreigners for quite some time.

🛍 SHOPPING

★ICHIZAWA
SHINZABURO HANPU · FASHION & ACCESSORIES

Map p218 (一澤信三郎帆布; ☎075-541-0436; www.ichizawa.co.jp; 602 Takabatake-chō, Higashiyama-ku; ⏱9am-6pm Wed-Mon; Ⓢ Tōzai line to Higashiyama) This company has been making its canvas bags for over 110 years and the store is often crammed with those in the know picking up a skillfully crafted Kyoto product. Originally designed as 'tool' bags for workers to carry sake bottles, milk and ice blocks, the current designs still reflect this idea. Choose from a range of styles and colours.

Pop upstairs to the workshop and you can usually get a look on weekends at how the bags are made. This is the one and only place where you can buy these bags – it's the sole store and they are not available online – making it the perfect souvenir.

MIURA SHŌMEI · HOMEWARES

Map p218 (三浦照明; ☎075-561-2816; http://miurashomei.co.jp; 284 Gion-machi, Kitagawa, Higashiyama-ku; ⏱10am-7pm Mon-Sat; 🚃Hankyū line to Kawaramachi, Keihan line to Gion-Shijō) If you've taken a shine to the soft warm glow of paper lanterns in your ryokan and want one to take home, this is the shop to get one. In business for over 120 years, each light is handcrafted using natural materials, such as bamboo and cedar. You can also find the famous Akari lamps by Isami Noguchi here.

ASAHI-DŌ · CERAMICS

Map p218 (朝日堂; ☎075-531-2181; www.asahi-do.co.jp/english; 1-280 Kiyomizu, Higashiyama-ku; ⏱9am-6pm; 🚌Kyoto City bus 206 to Kiyomizu-michi or Gojō-zaka, 🚃Keihan line to Kiyomizu-Gojō) Located in the heart of the Kiyomizu pottery area, Asahi-dō has been specialising in Kyōyaki-Kiyomizuyaki (Kyoto-style pottery) since 1870. The complex is called Asahi Touan and comprises the main store with the widest collection of Kyoto-style pottery in the city, as well as other stores selling a range of works, including some by the best up-and-coming ceramic artists in Japan.

YOJIYA · COSMETICS

Map p218 (よーじや; ☎075-541-0177; Shijō-dōri, Higashiyama-ku; ⏱10am-8pm; 🚃Keihan line to Gion-Shijō) Peruse the cosmetics and skincare here at one of Kyoto's most well-known brands. The famous oil-blotting facial papers make a great lightweight and cheap souvenir. There are a few branches around town – this one is on the corner of Shijō-dōri and Hanami-kōji; look for the logo of a face.

KAGOSHIN · ARTS & CRAFTS

Map p218 (籠新; ☎075-771-0209; 4 chō-me, Sanjō-dōri, Sanjō-Ōhashi-higashi, Higashiyama-ku; ⏱9am-6pm Tue-Sun; Ⓢ Tōzai line to Sanjō-Keihan) Kagoshin is a small semi-open traditional bamboo craft shop that has been around for generations on Sanjō-dōri, only a few minutes' walk east of the Kamo-gawa. It has a good selection of baskets, chopstick holders, bamboo vases, decorations and knick-knacks. The baskets make a lovely, light souvenir and look great in alcove displays.

DRESSING UP IN MAIKO COSTUME

If you ever wondered how *you* might look as a *maiko* (apprentice geisha), Kyoto has many organisations in town that offer the chance. **Maika** (舞香; Map p218; ☑075-551-1661; www.maica.tv; 297 Miyagawa suji 4-chōme, Higashiyama-ku; maiko/geisha from ¥6500/8000; ◷shop 9am-9pm; ◪Keihan line to Gion-Shijo or Kiyomizu-Gojo) is in the Gion district. Here you can be dressed up to live out your *maiko* fantasy. Prices begin at ¥6500 for the basic treatment, which includes full make-up and formal kimono. If you don't mind spending some extra yen, it's possible to head out in costume for a stroll through Gion (and be stared at like never before!). The process takes about an hour. Call to reserve at least one day in advance.

ACTIVITIES

★CAMELLIA TEA EXPERIENCE
TEA CEREMONY

Map p218 (茶道体験カメリア; ☑075-525-3238; www.tea-kyoto.com; 349 Masuya-chō, Higashi-yama-ku; per person ¥2000; ◪Kyoto City bus 206 to Yasui) Camellia is a superb place to try a simple Japanese tea ceremony. It's located in a beautiful old Japanese house just off Ninen-zaka. The host speaks fluent English and explains the ceremony simply and clearly to the group, while managing to perform an elegant ceremony. The price includes a bowl of *matcha* and a sweet. The website has an excellent map and explanation.

The 45-minute ceremonies are held on the hour from 10am to 5pm. Private tea ceremonies are held in a 100-year-old house with lovely gardens close to Ryōan-ji (p115) in northwest Kyoto (¥6000 per person).

EN
TEA CEREMONY

Map p218 (えん; ☑080-3782-2706; www.teacer emonyen.com; 272 Matsubara-chō, Higashiyama-ku; per person ¥2500; ◷ceremonies 2pm, 3pm, 4pm, 5pm & 6pm; ◪Kyoto City bus 206 to Gion or Chionin-mae) A small teahouse near Gion where you can experience a Japanese tea ceremony with a minimum of fuss or expense. Check the website for latest times, as these may change. English explanations are provided, and reservations recommended in high season. It's a bit tricky to find: it's down a little alley off Higashiōji-dōri – look for the sign south of Tenkaippin Rāmen.

Northern Higashiyama

Neighbourhood Top Five

❶ Nanzen-ji (p103) Immersing yourself in the wonderful gardens, intimate subtemples and a hidden grotto waiting in the woods.

❷ Ginkaku-ji (p102) Taking the bamboo-lined path to see Kyoto's famed 'Silver Pavilion'.

❸ Path of Philosophy (Tetsugaku-no-Michi) (p105) Getting lost in thought on this pretty flower-strewn path.

❹ Hōnen-in (p105) Escaping the crowds and finding yourself at this lovely Buddhist sanctuary.

❺ Eikan-dō (p104) Scaling up the steps to the Tahō-tō pagoda to peer down over the city.

For more detail of this area see Map p214 ➡

Explore Northern Higashiyama

Running along the base of the Higashiyama (Eastern Mountains) from Sanjō-dōri in the south to Imadegawa-dōri in the north, the Northern Higashiyama area is one of Kyoto's most important sightseeing districts. It contains a long strip of temples, including Nanzen-ji, Eikan-dō, Hōnen-in and Ginkaku-ji, all connected by the lovely Path of Philosophy, and temples further north: Manshu-in, Shisen-dō and Shugaku-in Rikyu. It's also home to museums, parks and a few interesting Shintō shrines.

Northern Higashiyama can be divided into two main sections: the strip of temples located directly at the base of the mountains, most of which are accessible from the Path of Philosophy; and the museums and shrine district known as Okazaki-kōen (Okazaki Park), which occupies a wide swathe of the area between the mountains and the river.

It's a fairly large area and can be explored on foot, mostly over car-free walkways, making it one of Kyoto's most pleasant areas for sightseeing. You can explore a fair bit of Northern Higashiyama in about half a day, but a full day allows a more leisurely pace.

Many people use Kyoto City bus 5 to access this area – convenient since this bus traverses the entire district – but this bus is often crowded and can be slow. If coming from Kyoto Station or downtown, it's better to take the subway here. Unfortunately, there are no trains or subways convenient to the northern end of this district. A variety of buses will take you to downtown and Kyoto Station. Otherwise, rent a bicycle; this is one of the best ways to explore Northern Higashiyama.

Local Life

→ **Temple** Tucked away off the main sightseeing trail, peaceful Enkō-ji (p107) is a favourite with locals, particularly for its autumn leaves.

→ **Eating** Much loved by Kyotoites, popular ramen joint Karako (p109) is not far from the Okazaki-kōen area.

Getting There & Away

→ **Train** The Keihan line stops at stations on the west side of the district.

→ **Bus** Kyoto City bus 5 traverses the district. Several other City buses stop here as well.

→ **Subway** The Tōzai subway line is the best way to access Northern Higashiyama.

Lonely Planet's Top Tip

Visit the big-name sights here (Ginkaku-ji, Eikan-dō and Nanzen-ji) early on a weekday morning to avoid the crowds. Alternatively, go right before closing.

 Best Places to Eat

→ Omen (p108)
→ Goya (p108)
→ Falafel Garden (p109)
→ Hinode Udon (p109)
→ Usagi no Ippo (p109)

For reviews, see p108. →

 Best Places to Drink

→ Kick Up (p110)
→ Metro (p110)
→ Bar Tantei (p110)

For reviews, see p110. →

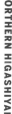

NORTHERN HIGASHIYAMA

TOP SIGHT
GINKAKU-JI

At the northern end of the Path of Philosophy, Kyoto's famed Silver Pavilion (Ginkaku-ji) is an enclosed paradise of ponds, thick moss, classical Japanese architecture and swaying bamboo groves. It is unquestionably one of the most luxurious gardens in the city and belongs near the top of any Kyoto sightseeing itinerary.

From Villa to Temple

In 1482 shogun Ashikaga Yoshimasa constructed a villa at this fine mountainside location, which he used as a genteel retreat from the turmoil of civil war. Although Ginkaku-ji translates as Silver Pavilion, this is simply a nickname to distinguish it from Kinkaku-ji (the Golden Pavilion on the other side of town).

The main hall, which overlooks the pond, was originally covered in black lacquer. After Yoshimasa's death it was converted to a temple. The temple belongs to the Shōkoku-ji sect of the Rinzai school of Zen.

Yoshimasa Effigy

In addition to the Buddha image in the main hall, the Tōgudō (residence of Yoshimasa) houses an effigy of Yoshimasa dressed in monk's garb. It also houses a tea ceremony room, which is thought to be the original that all tea ceremony rooms in future have been created from.

The Gardens

You will find walkways leading through the gardens, which were laid out by painter and garden designer Sōami. The gardens include meticulously raked cones of white sand known as *kōgetsudai,* designed to reflect moonlight and enhance the beauty of the garden at night.

DON'T MISS

➡ Footpath to views over Kyoto
➡ Small waterfall at back of garden (follow the path)

PRACTICALITIES

➡ 銀閣寺
➡ Map p214, G2
➡ 2 Ginkaku-ji-chō, Sakyō-ku
➡ adult/child ¥500/300
➡ ⏱8.30am-5pm Mar-Nov, 9am-4.30pm Dec-Feb
➡ 🚌Kyoto City bus 5 to Ginkakuji-michi stop

TOP SIGHT
NANZEN-JI

Nanzen-ji, a complex of Zen temples and subtemples tucked against the Higashiyama (Eastern Mountains), is the Platonic form of Japanese Buddhist temple. It's got it all: a fine little *kare-sansui* (dry landscape) garden, soaring main halls, great gardens and an incredibly scenic location.

Rinzai HQa

Nanzen-ji began its life as a retirement villa for Emperor Kameyama. Upon his passing in 1291, it was dedicated as a Zen temple. It operates now as the headquarters of the Rinzai school of Zen.

Highlights

At the entrance to the temple stands the **San-mon gate** (1628), its ceiling adorned with Tosa- and Kanō-school murals of birds and angels. Beyond the San-mon is the **Honden** (Main Hall) with a dragon painting on the ceiling.

Beyond the Honden, the **Hōjō** hall contains the Leaping Tiger Garden, a classical *kare-sansui* garden. Sadly, a tape loop in Japanese detracts from the experience of the garden.

After visiting the Honden and the Leaping Tiger Garden, walk under the aqueduct and take a hard left and walk up the hill. Climb the steps to **Kōtoku-an**, a fine subtemple nestled at the base of the mountains. It's free to enter and you will have the place to yourself about half the time.

Despite its popularity Nanzen-ji doesn't feel crowded, even during the autumn-foliage season (November), when the maples turn crimson and stand in beautiful contrast to the moss beneath their boughs.

DON'T MISS

➡ Kōtoku-an
➡ Hōjō (Leaping Tiger Garden)

PRACTICALITIES

➡ 南禅寺
➡ Map p214, F6
➡ www.nanzenji.com
➡ 86 Fukuchi-chō, Nanzen-ji, Sakyō-ku
➡ adult/child Nanzen-in ¥300/150, Hōjō garden ¥500/300, San-mon gate ¥500/300, grounds free
➡ ⊙8.40am-5pm Mar-Nov, to 4.30pm Dec-Feb
➡ 🚌Kyoto City bus 5 to Eikandō-michi, Ⓢ Tōzai line to Keage

◉ SIGHTS

NANZEN-IN
GARDENS

Map p214 (南禅院; ☎075-771-0365; Fukuchi-chō, Nanzen-ji, Sakyō-ku; ¥300; ◎8.40am-5pm; 🚌Kyoto City bus 5 to Eikandō-michi, Ⓢ Tōzai line to Keage) This subtemple of Nanzen-ji is up the steps after you pass under the aqueduct. It has an attractive garden designed around a heart-shaped pond. This garden is best seen in the morning or around noon, when sunlight shines directly into the pond and illuminates the colourful carp.

TENJU-AN
BUDDHIST TEMPLE

Map p214 (天授庵; 86-8 Fukuchi-chō, Nanzen-ji, Sakyō-ku; adult/child ¥500/300; ◎9am-5pm Mar–mid-Nov, to 4.30pm mid-Nov–Feb; 🚌Kyoto City bus 5 to Eikandō-michi, Ⓢ Tōzai line to Keage) A subtemple of Nanzen-ji, Tenju-an is located on the south side of San-mon, the main gate of Nanzen-ji. Constructed in 1337, Tenju-an has a splendid garden and a great collection of carp in its pond.

KONCHI-IN
BUDDHIST TEMPLE

Map p214 (金地院; 86-12 Fukuchi-chō, Nanzen-ji, Sakyō-ku; adult/child ¥400/200; ◎8.30am-5pm Mar-Nov, to 4.30pm Dec-Feb; 🚌Kyoto City bus 5 to Eikandō-michi, Ⓢ Tōzai line to Keage) Just southwest of the main precincts of Nanzen-ji, this fine subtemple has a wonderful garden designed by Kobori Enshū, known as the Crane and Tortoise garden. If you want to find a good example of the *shakkei* (borrowed scenery) technique, look no further.

NANZEN-JI OKU-NO-IN
BUDDHIST SHRINE

Map p214 (南禅寺奥の院; Fukuchi-chō, Nanzen-ji, Sakyō-ku; ◎dawn-dusk; 🚌Kyoto City bus 5 to Eikandō-michi, Ⓢ Tōzai line to Keage) FREE Perhaps the best part of Nanzen-ji is overlooked by most visitors: Nanzen-ji Oku-no-in, a small shrine hidden in a forested hollow behind the main precinct. It's here that pilgrims pray while standing under the falls, sometimes in the dead of winter.

To get here, walk up to the red-brick aqueduct in front of Nanzen-in. Follow the road that runs parallel to the aqueduct up into the hills, and walk past (or through) Kōtoku-an, a small subtemple on your left. Continue up the steps into the woods until you reach a waterfall in a beautiful mountain glen.

NOMURA MUSEUM
MUSEUM

Map p214 (野村美術館; ☎075-751-0374; Nanzen-ji, Shimokawara-chō 61, Sakyō-ku; ¥700; ◎10am-4.30pm Tue-Sun early Mar-early Jun & early Sep-early Dec; 🚌Kyoto City bus 5 to Eikandō-michi, Ⓢ Tōzai line to Keage) This museum is a 10-minute walk north of Nanzen-ji. Exhibits include scrolls, paintings, implements used in tea ceremonies and ceramics that were bequeathed by business magnate Nomura Tokushiki. If you have an abiding interest in the tea ceremony or in Japanese decorative techniques such as lacquer and *maki-e* (decorative lacquer technique using silver and gold powders), this museum makes an interesting break from temple hopping.

MURIN-AN
GARDENS

Map p214 (無鄰菴; ☎075-771-3909; https://murin-an.jp/en; Nanzen-ji, Kusakawa-chō, Sakyō-ku; ¥410; ◎8.30am-6pm; Ⓢ Tōzai line to Keage) Often overlooked by the hordes that descend on the Higashiyama area, this elegant villa was the home of prominent statesman Yamagata Aritomo (1838–1922) and the site of a pivotal 1903 political conference as Japan was heading into the Russo-Japanese War. Built in 1896, the grounds contain well-preserved wooden buildings, including a fine Japanese tearoom. The Western-style annexe is characteristic of Meiji-period architecture and the serene garden features small streams that draw water from the Biwa-ko Sosui canal.

For ¥600 you can savour a bowl of frothy *matcha* (powdered green tea) with a sweet while viewing the *shakkei* backdrop of the Higashiyama Mountains. It's particularly beautiful in the maple-leaf season of November.

★EIKAN-DŌ
BUDDHIST TEMPLE

Map p214 (永観堂; ☎075-761-0007; www.eikando.or.jp; 48 Eikandō-chō, Sakyō-ku; adult/child ¥600/400; ◎9am-5pm; 🚌Kyoto City bus 5 to Eikandō-michi, Ⓢ Tōzai line to Keage) Perhaps Kyoto's most famous (and most crowded) autumn-foliage destination, Eikan-dō is a superb temple just a short walk south of the famous Path of Philosophy. Eikan-dō is made interesting by its varied architecture, its gardens and its works of art. It was founded as Zenrin-ji in 855 by the priest Shinshō, but the name was changed to Eikan-dō in the 11th century to honour the philanthropic priest Eikan.

In the **Amida-dō** hall at the southern end of the complex is a famous statue of Mikaeri Amida Buddha glancing backwards.

From Amida-dō, head north to the end of the curving covered **garyūrō** (walkway). Change into the sandals provided, then climb the steep steps up the mountainside to the **Tahō-tō** pagoda, from where there's a fine view across the city.

For most of November, the admission fee increases to ¥1000 to visit during the day for the autumn leaves, and the temple stays open to 8.30pm for the autumn nighttime illumination (¥600).

PATH OF PHILOSOPHY
(TETSUGAKU-NO-MICHI) AREA

Map p214 (哲学の道; Sakyō-ku; 🚌Kyoto City bus 5 to Eikandō-michi or Ginkakuji-michi, ⓢTōzai line to Keage) The Tetsugaku-no-Michi is one of the most pleasant walks in all of Kyoto. Lined with a great variety of flowering plants, bushes and trees, it is a corridor of colour throughout most of the year. Follow the traffic-free route along a canal lined with cherry trees that come into spectacular bloom in early April. It only takes 30 minutes to do the walk, which starts at Nyakuōji-bashi, above Eikan-dō, and leads to Ginkaku-ji.

The path takes its name from one of its most famous strollers: 20th-century philosopher Nishida Kitarō, who is said to have meandered lost in thought along the path.

During the day in the cherry-blossom season, you should be prepared for crowds; a night stroll will definitely be quieter.

REIKAN-JI BUDDHIST TEMPLE

Map p214 (霊鑑寺; 📞075-771-4040; 12 Shishigatani goshonodan-chō, Sakyō-ku; ¥600; ⏰10am-4pm spring & autumn; 🚌Kyoto City bus 5 or 17 to Ginkakuji-michi) Only open to the public in spring and autumn, Reikan-ji is one of Kyoto's great lesser-visited attractions. During the spring opening, you will find the grounds positively rioting with camellia. In autumn, the brilliant reds of the maples will dazzle the eye. The small collection of artworks in the main building is almost as good as the colours outside. Check with the Kyoto Tourist Information Center for exact opening dates, as they vary by year.

HŌNEN-IN BUDDHIST TEMPLE

Map p214 (法然院; 30 Goshonodan-chō, Shishigatani, Sakyō-ku; ⏰6am-4pm; 🚌Kyoto City bus 5 to Ginkakuji-michi) FREE Founded in 1680 to honour the priest Hōnen, this is a lovely, secluded temple with carefully raked gardens set back in the woods. The temple buildings include a small gallery where frequent exhibitions featuring local and international artists are held. If you need to escape the crowds that positively plague nearby Ginkaku-ji, come to this serene refuge.

Hōnen-in is a 12-minute walk from Ginkaku-ji, on a side street above the Path of Philosophy (Tetsugaku-no-Michi); there are wooden signposts pointing the way.

OKAZAKI-KŌEN AREA AREA

Map p214 (岡崎公園; Okazaki, Sakyō-ku; 🚌Kyoto City bus 5 to Okazakikoen Bijutsukan/Heianjingu-mae, ⓢTōzai line to Higashiyama) Okazaki-kōen is an expanse of parks and canals that lies between Niōmon-dōri and Heian-jingū. Two of Kyoto's significant museums can be found here – the National Museum of Modern Art and Kyoto Municipal Museum of Art – as well as two smaller museums. If you find yourself in Kyoto on a rainy day, there's enough indoor sightseeing here to keep you dry.

NATIONAL MUSEUM
OF MODERN ART MUSEUM

Map p214 (京都国立近代美術館; www.momak. go.jp; Enshōji-chō, Okazaki, Sakyō-ku; ¥430, special exhibitions extra; ⏰9.30am-5pm, to 8pm Fri, closed Mon; 🚌Kyoto City bus 5 to Okazakikoen Bijutsukan/Heianjingu-mae, ⓢTōzai line to Higashiyama) This museum is renowned for its Japanese ceramics and paintings. There is an outstanding permanent collection, which includes many pottery pieces by Kawai Kanjirō. The coffee shop here is a nice place for a break and overlooks a picturesque canal. The museum also hosts regular special exhibitions, so check the website for what's on.

KYOTO MUNICIPAL
MUSEUM OF ART MUSEUM

Map p214 (京都市美術館; 124 Enshōji-chō, Okazaki, Sakyō-ku; admission varies; ⏰9am-5pm, closed Mon; 🚌Kyoto City bus 5 to Okazakikoen Bijutsukan/Heianjingu-mae, ⓢTōzai line to Higashiyama) This fine museum holds several major exhibitions a year, as well as a variety

Neighbourhood Walk
A Philosophical Meander

START KEAGE STATION
END GINKAKU-JI-MICHI BUS STOP
LENGTH ABOUT 6KM; FOUR HOURS

Start at Keage Station on the Tōzai subway line, walk downhill, cross the pedestrian overpass, head back uphill and go through the tunnel under the old funicular tracks. This leads to a narrow street that winds towards **1** **Konchi-in** (p104).

Just past Konchi-in, take a right on the main road and walk up through the gate into **2** **Nanzen-ji** (p103). Continue east, up the slope and you'll soon see the brick Sōsui aqueduct on your right; cross under this, take a quick left and walk up the hill towards the mountains. You'll come first to the lovely **3** **Kōtoku-an** subtemple. Beyond this, the trail enters the woods. Follow it up to the secluded **4** **Nanzen-ji Oku-no-in** (p104), a tiny shrine built around a waterfall.

Return the way you came and exit the north side of Nanzen-ji, following the road through a gate. You'll soon come to

5 **Eikan-dō** (p104), a large temple famous for its artworks and pagoda. At the corner just beyond Eikan-dō, a sign in English and Japanese points up the hill to the Path of Philosophy. If you're hungry, take a short detour north to **6** **Hinode Udon** (p109), a fine noodle restaurant. Otherwise, head up the hill to the **7** **Path of Philosophy (Tetsugaku-no-michi)** (p105), which is the pedestrian path that heads north along the canal.

It's then a straight shot up the lovely tree-lined canal for about 800m until you reach a small sign in English and Japanese pointing up the hill to **8** **Hōnen-in** (p105). Follow the sign, take a left at the top of the hill, walk past a small park and you'll see the picturesque thatched gate of Hōnen-in. After checking out the temple (free), exit via the thatched gate and take a quick right downhill.

From here, follow the narrow side streets north to **9** **Ginkaku-ji** (p102), the famed Silver Pavilion.

of free shows. It's always worth stopping by to see if something is on while you are in town. The pond behind the museum is a great place for a picnic.

This museum's main building will be closed for renovations until 2019; some exhibitions are being held in the nearby annex.

FUREAI-KAN KYOTO MUSEUM OF TRADITIONAL CRAFTS
MUSEUM

Map p214 (みやこめっせ・京都伝統産業ふれあい館; ☑075-762-2670; https://kmtc.jp/en; 9-1 Seishōji-chō, Okazaki, Sakyō-ku; ⊙9am-5pm, closed 29 Dec-3 Jan; ⑤Tōzai line to Higashiyama) FREE Well worth a visit for anyone interested in traditional Kyoto arts and crafts, Fureai-Kan has excellent exhibits, including woodblock prints, lacquerware, bamboo goods and gold-leaf work, with information panels in English. You can also see a 15-minute *maiko* or *geiko* performance, each held one Sunday a month at 2pm, 2.30pm and 3pm. Check the website for details. It's located in the basement of Miyako Messe (Kyoto International Exhibition Hall). The attached shop sells a good range of gifts and souvenirs.

HEIAN-JINGŪ
SHINTO SHRINE

Map p214 (平安神宮; ☑075-761-0221; Nishitennō-chō, Okazaki, Sakyō-ku; garden adult/child ¥600/300; ⊙6am-5pm Nov-Feb, 6am-6pm Mar-Oct, garden 8.30am-4.30pm; ☐Kyoto City bus 5 to Okazakikoen Bijutsukan/Heianjingu-mae, ⑤Tōzai line to Higashiyama) One of Kyoto's more popular sights, this shrine was built in 1895 to commemorate the 1100th anniversary of the founding of the city. The shrine buildings are colourful replicas, reduced to a two-thirds scale, of the Imperial Court Palace of the Heian period (794–1185). About 500m in front of the shrine is a massive steel **torii** (shrine gate). Although it appears to be entirely separate, this is actually considered the main entrance to the shrine itself.

The vast **garden** here, behind the shrine, is a fine place for a wander and particularly lovely during the cherry-blossom season. With its large pond, water lilies and Chinese-inspired bridge, the garden is a tribute to the style that was popular in the Heian period. It is well known for its wisteria, irises and *beni-shidare-zakura* (red weeping cherry blossoms).

One of Kyoto's biggest festivals, the **Jidai Matsuri**, is held here on 22 October. On 2 and 3 June, **Takigi nō** is also held here. Takigi nō is a picturesque form of *nō* (stylised dance-drama performed on a bare stage) staged in the light of blazing fires. Tickets cost ¥3000 if you pay in advance (ask at the Kyoto Tourist Information Center for the location of ticket agencies) or you can pay ¥4000 at the entrance gate.

SHŪGAKU-IN RIKYŪ IMPERIAL VILLA
NOTABLE BUILDING

(修学院離宮; ☑075-211-1215; www.kunaicho.go.jp; Shūgaku-in, Yabusoe, Sakyō-ku; ⊙tours 9am, 10am, 11am, 1.30pm & 3pm Tue-Sun; ☐Kyoto City bus 5 from Kyoto Station to Shūgakuinrikyū-michi) FREE One of the highlights of northeast Kyoto, this superb imperial villa was designed as a lavish summer retreat for the imperial family. Its gardens, with their views down over the city, are worth the trouble it takes to visit. The one-hour tours are held in Japanese, with English audio guides free of charge. You must be over 18 years to enter and you will need to bring your passport for ID.

Construction of the villa was begun in the 1650s by Emperor Go-Mizunō, following his abdication. Work was continued by his daughter Akeno-miya after his death in 1680.

The villa grounds are divided into three enormous garden areas on a hillside – lower, middle and upper. Each has superb tea-ceremony houses: the upper, **Kami-no-chaya**, and lower, **Shimo-no-chaya**, were completed in 1659, and the middle teahouse, **Naka-no-chaya**, was completed in 1682. The gardens' reputation rests on their ponds, pathways and impressive use of *shakkei* (borrowed scenery) in the form of the surrounding hills. The view from Kami-no-chaya is particularly impressive.

You can book tickets in advance at the Imperial Household Agency (p82) office or online for morning tours, but for afternoon tours tickets go on sale at the villa from 11am and are available on a first-come, first-served basis until capacity is sold.

ENKŌ-JI
BUDDHIST TEMPLE

(圓光寺; ☑075-781-8025; www.enkouji.jp; 13 Ichijoji Kotani-chō, Sakyō-ku; adult/child ¥500/300; ⊙9am-5pm; ☐Kyoto City bus 5 from Kyoto Station to Ichijōji-sagarimatsu-cho) It might be best known for its autumn maple leaves, but this small temple is well worth a visit any time of the year. It has two stunning gardens – the first is an incredible *kare-sansui* garden called Honryu-tei (Dragon Garden) and as you pass through the gate you'll come to the second, a very pretty stroll garden. Take your time wandering around; there's a pond, a small bamboo forest and breathtaking views from the small hill behind the temple.

SHISEN-DŌ
BUDDHIST TEMPLE

(詩仙堂; ☎075-781-2954; www.kyoto-shisendo. com; Ichijōji, 27 Monguchi-chō, Sakyō-ku; adult/child ¥500/200; ☻9am-5pm; ☐Kyoto City bus 5 from Kyoto Station to Ichijōji-sagarimatsu-cho) A highlight of the far northern Higashiyama area, Shisen-dō (House of Poet-Hermits) was built in 1641 by Ishikawa Jōzan, a scholar of Chinese classics and a landscape architect who wanted a place to retire. The hermitage is noted for its display of poems and portraits of 36 ancient Chinese poets, which can be found in the **Shisen-no-ma** room. The white-sand *kare-sansui* (dry landscape) garden is lined with azaleas, which are said to represent islands in the sea. It's a tranquil place to relax.

In the garden, water flows from a small waterfall to the *shishi-odoshi*, or *sōzu*, a device designed to scare away wild boar and deer. It's made from a bamboo pipe into which water slowly trickles, fills up and swings down to empty. On the upswing to its original position the bamboo strikes a stone with a 'thwack' – just loud enough to interrupt your snooze – before starting to refill.

EATING

★GOYA
OKINAWAN ¥

Map p214 (ゴーヤ; ☎075-752-1158; http:// goya-asia.com; 114-6 Nishida-chō, Jōdo-ji, Sakyō-ku; dishes from ¥680; ☻11.30am-3.30pm & 5.30pm-midnight Thu-Tue; ✍; ☐Kyoto City bus 5 to Ginkakuji-michi) This Okinawan-style restaurant has tasty food (with plenty of vegetarian options), a plant-filled stylish interior and comfortable upstairs seating. It's perfect for lunch while exploring Northern Higashiyama and just a short walk from Ginkaku-ji. Choose from simple dishes, such as taco rice and *gōya champurū* (bitter melon stir-fry), or try the delicious *nasi champurū* – a plate of daily changing dishes.

★OMEN
NOODLES ¥

Map p214 (おめん; ☎075-771-8994; www.omen. co.jp; 74 Jōdo-ji Ishibashi-chō, Sakyō-ku; noodles from ¥1150; ☻11am-9pm; ☐Kyoto City bus 5 to Ginkakuji-michi) This elegant noodle shop is named after the thick white noodles that are served in broth with a selection of seven fresh vegetables. Just say *omen* and you'll be given your choice of hot or cold noodles, a bowl of soup to dip them in and a plate of vegetables (put these into the soup along with the sesame seeds).

There's also an extensive à la carte menu. You can get a tasty salad here, brilliant *tori sansho yaki* (chicken cooked with Japanese mountain spice), good tempura and occasionally a nice plate of sashimi. Best of all, there's an English menu. It's about five minutes' walk from Ginkaku-ji in a traditional

---

DAIMONJI-YAMA CLIMB

Length 5km; 1½ hours

Located directly behind Ginkaku-ji, Daimonji-yama is the main site of the Daimon-ji Gozan Okuribi. From almost anywhere in town the Chinese character for 'great' (大; *dai*) is visible in the middle of a bare patch on the face of this mountain. On 16 August this character is set ablaze to guide the spirits of the dead on their journey home. The view of Kyoto from the top is unparalleled.

Take Kyoto City bus 5 to the Ginkaku-ji Michi stop and walk up to Ginkaku-ji (p102). Here, you have the option of visiting the temple or starting the hike immediately. To find the trailhead, turn left in front of the temple and head north for about 50m towards a stone *torii* (shrine gate). Just before the *torii*, turn right up the hill.

The trail proper starts just after a small car park on the right. It's a broad avenue through the trees. You'll see a signboard and then a bridge after it. Cross the bridge to the right, then continue up a smaller, switchback trail. When the trail reaches a saddle not far from the top, go to the left. You'll climb a long flight of steps before coming out at the top of the bald patch. The sunset from here is great, but bring a torch.

apanese house with a lantern outside. Highly recommended.

USAGI NO IPPO
JAPANESE ¥

Map p214 (卯サギの一歩; ☏075-201-6497; 91-23 Okazaki Enshōji-chō, Sakyō-ku; meals from ¥1300; ⏱11am-5pm, group bookings only after 5pm; ⓢTōzai line to Higashiyama) Perfectly located for a break when museum-hopping in the Okazaki-kōen area, this delightful restaurant is set in an old *machiya* (traditional Japanese townhouse) with tatami-mat floors, a small pleasant garden and a cute rabbit theme. The delicious *obanzai* (Kyoto home-style cooking) sets are great value and might include tasty dishes such as chicken tenderloin wrapped in shiso.

OMURAYA
JAPANESE ¥

Map p214 (おむら家; ☏075-712-1337; www.omurahouse.com/omuraya; 28 Tanaka Monzen-chō, Sakyō-ku; meals from ¥1500; ⏱5pm-midnight; ⓡKyoto City bus 206 to Hyakumanben) In a converted *machiya* close to Kyoto University you'll find this friendly local *obanzai* restaurant with an *izakaya* (Japanese pub-eatery) atmosphere. The food is rustic and cooked from mostly seasonal and local ingredients.

SUJATA
VEGETARIAN ¥

Map p214 (スジャータ; ☏075-721-0789; www.sujata-cafe.com; 96-2 Tanaka Monzen-chō, Sakyō-ku; meals from ¥850; ⏱noon-6.30pm; 🖉; ⓡKyoto City bus 206 to Hyakumanben) Opposite Kyoto University, this humble cafe is a godsend for vegetarians. The menu is limited but the food is fresh, tasty, mostly organic and nutritious, including Indian curries or a Japanese set. There's a few counter seats and tables downstairs and tatami-mat seating upstairs. Sip on authentic homemade chai and relax to the soothing background music. Ask about the free meditation classes.

KIRAKU
OKONOMIYAKI ¥

Map p214 (きらく三条本店; ☏075-761-5780; 208 Nakanochō, Sanjō-Shirakawa, Higashiyama-ku; okonomiyaki from ¥700; ⏱11.30am-2pm & 5pm-midnight Tue-Sun; ⓢTōzai line to Higashiyama or Keage) This approachable and friendly *okonomiyaki* (savoury pancake) restaurant on Sanjō, close to Nanzen-ji and other popular Northern Higashiyama sights, is a good place to stop for lunch while exploring the area or for dinner after a long day of sightseeing. In addition to the usual *okonomiyaki* favourites, you'll find dishes such as *gyōza* (dumplings) and *yaki-soba* (soba noodle stir-fry).

PRINZ
CAFE ¥

(プリンツ; ☏075-712-3900; www.prinz.jp; 5 Tanakatakahara-chō, Sakyō-ku; lunch from ¥1000, sets from ¥1650; ⏱11am-4pm & 6-10pm, lunch only Thu; ⓡEizan line to Chayama) Behind the blank white facade of Prinz, you'll find an inviting modern cafe-restaurant, gallery and garden – a chic island of coolness in an otherwise bland residential neighbourhood. The menu features light lunches, such as soup and salad, along with homemade pasta. It also has two stylish self-contained apartments upstairs (from ¥16,750 for two people).

FALAFEL GARDEN
ISRAELI ¥

Map p214 (ファラフェルガーデン; ☏075-712-1856; www.falafelgarden.com; 15-2 Kamiyanagi-chō, Tanaka, Sakyō-ku; falafel from ¥450; ⏱11am-10pm; 🖉; ⓡKeihan line to Demachiyanagi) If you're in need of a break from Japanese food, head to this casual spot near Demachiyanagi Station for excellent and filling falafel pita sandwiches or plates with generous dollops of homemade hummus, or a side of green chilli sauce for more of a kick. There's a small garden courtyard for sunny days.

KARAKO
RAMEN ¥

Map p214 (からこ; ☏075-752-8234; 12-3 Tokusei-chō, Okazaki, Sakyō-ku; ramen from ¥650; ⏱11.30am-2pm & 5pm-midnight; ⓡKyoto City bus 206 to Higashiyama-Nijō) Karako is a favourite ramen restaurant in Kyoto. While there's not much atmosphere, the ramen is excellent – the soup is thick and rich and the *chashū* (pork slices) melt in your mouth. The *kotteri* (thick soup) ramen is highly recommended. It also does a vegetarian version. Look for the lantern outside.

HINODE UDON
NOODLES ¥

Map p214 (日の出うどん; ☏075-751-9251; 36 Kitanobō-chō, Nanzenji, Sakyō-ku; noodles from ¥750; ⏱11am-3pm, closed Sun & occasionally Mon; ⓡKyoto City bus 5 to Eikandō-michi) Filling noodle and rice dishes are served at this pleasant shop with an English menu – the *nabeyaki udon* (pot-baked udon in broth) for ¥950 is a great choice. This is a good lunch spot when temple-hopping in the Northern Higashiyama area. It's popular so you'll probably have to queue. Cash only.

OKUTAN
TOFU ¥¥

Map p214 (奥丹; ☑075-771-8709; 86-30 Fukuchi-chō, Nanzen-ji, Sakyō-ku; set meals ¥3000; ⊙11am-4pm Mon-Wed & Fri, to 4.30pm Sat & Sun; ☑; Ⓢ Tōzai line to Keage) Just outside the precincts of Nanzen-ji, you'll find Okutan, a restaurant sited within the luxurious garden of Chōshō-in. This is a popular place that has specialised in vegetarian temple food for hundreds of years. Try a course of *yudōfu* (tofu cooked in a pot) together with vegetable side dishes (¥3000).

TORITO
YAKITORI ¥¥

Map p214 (とりと; ☑075-752-4144; 9-5 Marutamachi-dōri, Higashi Marutamachi, Kawabata higashi-iru, Sakyō-ku; yakitori from ¥162; ⊙5.30pm-midnight; Ⓡ Keihan line to Jingū-Marutamachi) This is part of the new wave of *yakitori* (skewers of chicken, and other meats or vegetables) restaurants in Kyoto that are updating the old standards in interesting and tasty ways. The food is very good and will likely appeal to non-Japanese palates. Dishes include *negima* (long onions and chicken) and *tsukune* (chicken meatballs). Best to book ahead.

HYŌTEI
KAISEKI ¥¥¥

Map p214 (瓢亭; ☑075-771-4116; 35 Kusagawa-chō, Nanzen-ji, Sakyō-ku; kaiseki lunch/dinner from ¥23,000/27,000, shōkadō bentō lunch ¥5400; ⊙11am-7.30pm, closed 2nd & 4th Tue of month; Ⓢ Tōzai line to Keage) The Hyōtei is considered one of Kyoto's oldest and most picturesque traditional restaurants. In the main building you can sample exquisite *kaiseki* (Japanese haute cuisine) courses in private tea rooms; book months ahead for weekend evenings. If you wish to sample the cuisine on a tighter budget, the annexe building offers breakfast and *shōkadō bentō* box lunches (8am to 3pm, closed Thursday).

🍷 DRINKING & NIGHTLIFE

BAR TANTEI
BAR

(BAR探偵; 26 Tanaka Satōnchi-chō, Sakyō-ku; cover ¥400; ⊙7pm-2am Mon-Sat; Ⓡ Eizan main line to Mototanaka) Paying homage to hard-boiled detective movies, lively Bar Tant (detective) is popular with Kyoto Universit. students and is a great place for a drink in the area. Look out for the secret bookshelf doorway.

ZAC BARAN
CAFE, JAZZ

Map p214 (ザックバラン; ☑075-751-9748; 18 Sannō-chō, Shōgoin, Sakyō-ku; ⊙6pm-2am; Ⓡ Kyoto City bus 206 to Kumanojinja-mae) Near the Kyoto Handicraft Center, this is a good spot to listen to some jazz tunes over a light meal or a drink. It serves a variety of spaghetti dishes (meals from ¥700) as well as a good lunch special.

KICK UP
BAR

Map p214 (キックアップ; ☑075-761-5604; 331 Higashikomonoza-chō, Higashiyama-ku; ⊙7pm-midnight, closed Wed; Ⓢ Tōzai line to Keage) Located just across the street from the Westin Miyako Kyoto, this wonderful bar attracts a regular crowd of Kyoto expats, local Japanese and guests from the Westin. It's subdued, relaxing and friendly.

METRO
CLUB

Map p214 (メトロ; ☑075-752-4765; www.metro. ne.jp; BF Ebisu Bldg, Kawabata-dōri, Marutamachi-sagaru, Sakyō-ku; ⊙about 8pm-3am; Ⓡ Keihan line to Jingū-Marutamachi) Metro is part disco, part live house and it even hosts the occasional art exhibition. It attracts an eclectic mix of creative types and has a different theme nightly, so check ahead in *Kansai Scene* to see what's going on. Metro is inside exit 2 of the Jingū-Marutamachi Station on the Keihan line.

☆ ENTERTAINMENT

ROHM THEATRE KYOTO
THEATRE

Map p214 (京都観世会館; ☑075-771-6051; www.rohmtheatrekyoto.jp; 44 Okazaki Enshōji-chō, Sakyō-ku; tickets from ¥3000; ⊙box office 10am-7pm; Ⓢ Tōzai line to Higashiyama) The Kyoto Kaikan Theatre underwent a renovation early in 2016 and transformed into the ROHM Theatre Kyoto. Housed in a striking modernist building, it holds three multipurpose halls with a 2000-seat main hall hosting everything from international ballet and opera performances to comedy shows, music concerts and *nō* (stylised dance-drama peformed on a bare stage).

SHOPPING

KYOTO HANDICRAFT CENTER ARTS & CRAFTS
Map p214 (京都ハンディクラフトセンター;
☑075-761-8001; www.kyotohandicraftcenter.
com; 17 Entomi-chō, Shōgoin, Sakyō-ku; ⊘10am-
7pm; ☐Kyoto City bus 206 to Kumano-jinja-mae)
Split between two buildings, East and
West, the Kyoto Handicraft Center sells
a good range of Japanese arts and crafts,
such as Hokusai woodblock prints (reproductions from ¥5000), Japanese dolls,
pearls, clothing, and a great selection
of books on Japanese culture and travel
guides. English-speaking staff are on hand
and currency exchange is available. Within
walking distance of the main Higashiyama
sightseeing route.

TŌZANDŌ GIFTS & SOUVENIRS
Map p214 (東山堂; ☑075-762-1341; 24 Entomi-
chō, Shōgoin, Sakyō-ku; ⊘10am-7pm; ☐Kyoto
City bus 206 to Kumano-jinja-mae) If you're a
fan of Japanese swords and armour, you
have to visit this wonderful shop on Marutamachi (diagonally opposite the Kyoto
Handicraft Center). It has authentic swords,
newly made Japanese armour, martial arts
goods etc, and there's usually someone on
hand who can speak English.

Northwest Kyoto

Neighbourhood Top Five

1 Kinkaku-ji (p114) Being dazzled by the single most impressive sight in all of Kyoto: the gold-plated main hall of the famed 'Golden Pavilion'.

2 Ryōan-ji (p115) Meditating on the 15 magical rocks in the Zen garden.

3 Myōshin-ji (p115) Taking a stroll through the enclosed world of Zen temples.

4 Kitano Tenman-gū (p115) Exploring the atmospheric shrine and shopping at Tenjin-san Market.

5 Jingo-ji (p116) Exploring the atmospheric mountaintop temples of Takao.

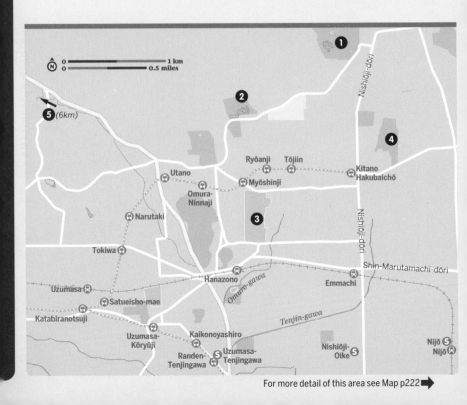

For more detail of this area see Map p222 ➡

Explore Northwest Kyoto

Northwest Kyoto comprises the section of the city that runs from roughly the boundary of the JR Nijō station all the way to the base of the mountains in the northwest corner of the city. This large area contains some of Kyoto's most celebrated temples such as Kinkaku-ji (Golden Pavilion) and Ryōan-ji (with its mystical rock garden).

The sights here are quite spread out. Many people visit Kinkaku-ji and Ryōan-ji in the morning, then continue by taxi down to the Arashiyama and Sagano area, which is also on the west side of the city.

It's a bit time-consuming to see the sights in Northwest Kyoto. Most sights are best accessed by city bus. Myōshin-ji and nearby attractions are also served by the Japan Railways (JR) line and by the private Randen Kitano line. If you're a keen cyclist, you can also explore the area on a bicycle, but keep in mind that there are some hills around Kinkaku-ji and Ryōan-ji, so you'll work up quite a sweat in summer.

Local Life

➡ **Market meeting** Tenjin-san Market (p117) is a popular meeting place for local expats and Kyoto residents.

➡ **Cherry-blossom spot** During late March to early April the Randen Kitano line between Narutaki and Utano stations passes through a tunnel of blooming cherry trees and there are also nighttime illuminations.

Getting There & Away

➡ **Train** JR Sagano (San-in) line stops near Myōshin-ji.

➡ **Tram** The private Randen Kitano line stops near Ninna-ji.

➡ **Bus** Kyoto City buses serve all the sights in this district.

Lonely Planet's Top Tip

Since Ryōan-ji and Kinkaku-ji (the two most famous sights in Northwest Kyoto) and Arashiyama are all on the west side of town, it is possible to visit these in one full day. Take a taxi between Arashiyama and Kinkaku-ji or Ryōan-ji (or vice versa).

 Best Parks & Gardens

➡ Myōshin-ji (p115)

➡ Taizō-in (p116)

➡ Ryōan-ji (p115)

For reviews, see p115. ➡

NORTHWEST KYOTO

TOP SIGHT
KINKAKU-JI

Kyoto's famed 'Golden Pavilion', Kinkaku-ji is one of the world's most impressive religious monuments. The image of the gold-plated pavilion rising over its reflecting pool is the kind that burns itself into your memory. But there's more to this temple than its shiny main hall. The grounds are spacious and include another pond, a tea arbour and some lovely greenery.

A Shogun's Villa

Originally built in 1397 as a retirement villa for shogun Ashikaga Yoshi-mitsu, Kinkaku-ji was converted into a Buddhist temple by his son, in compliance with his wishes. Also known as Rokuon-ji, Kinkaku-ji belongs to the Shōkokuji school of Buddhism.

In 1950 a young monk consummated his obsession with the temple by burning it to the ground. The monk's story is fictionalised in Mishima Yukio's 1956 novel *The Temple of the Golden Pavilion*.

The Pavilion & Grounds

The three-storey pavilion is covered in bright gold leaf and features a bronze phoenix on top of the roof. The mirror-like reflection of the temple in the Kyō-ko pond is extremely photogenic, especially when the maples are ablaze in autumn. In 1955 a full reconstruction was completed, following the original design exactly, but the gold-foil covering was extended to the lower floors.

After visiting the gold-plated pavilion, check out the Ryūmon-taki waterfall and Rigyo-seki stone, which looks like a carp attempting to swim up the falls. Nearby, there is a small gathering of stone Jizō figures onto which people throw coins and make wishes.

Sekka-tei Teahouse

The teahouse Sekka-tei embodies the spirit of *wabi sabi* (rustic simplicity) that defines the Japanese tea-ceremony ethic. It's at the top of the hill shortly before the temple exit.

DON'T MISS

➡ Sekka-tei

➡ Ryūmon-taki waterfall, Rigyo-seki stone

PRACTICALITIES

➡ 金閣寺

➡ Map p222, D1

➡ 1 Kinkakuji-chō, Kita-ku

➡ adult/child ¥400/200

➡ ⊙9am-5pm

➡ 🚌Kyoto City bus 205 from Kyoto Station to Kinkakuji-michi, 🚌Kyoto City bus 12 from Sanjō-Keihan to Kinkakuji-michi

◎ SIGHTS

KITANO TENMAN-GŪ
SHINTO SHRINE

Map p222 (北野天満宮; www.kitanotenmangu. or.jp; Bakuro-chō, Kamigyō-ku; ◎5am-6pm Apr-Sep, 5.30am-5.30pm Oct-Mar; ☐Kyoto City bus 50 from Kyoto Station to Kitano-Tenmangū-mae) **FREE** The most atmospheric Shintō shrine in Northwest Kyoto, Kitano Tenman-gū is also the site of Tenjin-San Market, one of Kyoto's most popular flea markets. It's a pleasant spot for a lazy stroll and the shrine buildings themselves are beautiful. The present buildings were built in 1607 by Toyotomi Hideyori; the grounds contain an extensive grove of plum trees, which burst into bloom in early March.

Kitano Tenman-gū was established in 947 to honour Sugawara Michizane (845–903), a noted Heian-era statesman and scholar. It is said that, having been defied by his political adversary Fujiwara Tokihira, Sugawara was exiled to Kyūshū for the rest of his life. Following his death in 903, earthquakes and storms hit Kyoto, and the Imperial Palace was repeatedly struck by lightning. Fearing that Sugawara, reincarnated as Raijin (God of Thunder), had returned from beyond to avenge his rivals, locals erected and dedicated this shrine to him.

Unless you are trying to avoid crowds, the best time to visit is during the **Tenjin-san** market fair, held on the 25th of each month – December and January are particularly colourful.

RYŌAN-JI
BUDDHIST TEMPLE

Map p222 (龍安寺; 13 Goryōnoshitamachi, Ryōan-ji, Ukyō-ku; adult/child ¥500/300; ◎8am-5pm Mar-Nov, 8.30am-4.30pm Dec-Feb; ☐Kyoto City bus 59 from Sanjō-Keihan to Ryoanji-mae) You've probably seen a picture of the rock garden here – it's one of the symbols of Kyoto and one of Japan's better-known sights. Ryōan-ji belongs to the Rinzai school and was founded in 1450. The garden, an oblong of sand with an austere collection of 15 carefully placed rocks, apparently adrift in a sea of sand, is enclosed by an earthen wall. The designer, who remains unknown to this day, provided no explanation.

Although many historians believe the garden was arranged by Sōami during the Muromachi period (1333–1568), some contend that it is a much later product of the Edo period. It is Japan's most famous **hiraniwa** (flat garden void of hills or ponds) and reveals the stunning simplicity and harmony of the principles of Zen meditation.

There is no doubt that it's a mesmerising and attractive sight, but it's hard to enjoy amid the mobs who come to check it off their 'must-see list'. An early-morning visit on a weekday is probably your best hope of seeing the garden under contemplative conditions. If you go when it's crowded, you'll find the less-famous garden around the corner of the stone garden a nice escape.

NINNA-JI
BUDDHIST TEMPLE

Map p222 (仁和寺; ☐075-461-1155; www.ninnaji.jp; 33 Omuroōuchi, Ukyō-ku; temple & garden adult/child ¥500/300; ◎9am-5pm Mar-Nov, to 4.30pm Dec-Feb; ☐Kyoto City bus 59 from Sanjo-Keihan to Omuro Ninna-ji, Kyoto City bus 26 from Kyoto Station to Omuro Ninna-ji) Few travellers make the journey all the way out to this sprawling temple complex, but most who do find it a pleasant spot. It's certainly a good counterpoint to the crowded and more famous temples nearby.

Originally containing more than 60 structures, Ninna-ji was built in 888 and is the head temple of the Omuro branch of the Shingon school. The present temple buildings, including a **five-storey pagoda**, date from the 17th century.

On the extensive grounds you'll find a peculiar grove of short-trunked, multi-petalled cherry trees called Omuro-no-Sakura, which draw large crowds in April. A separate fee (¥500) is charged to enter during blooming season.

Separate admission fees (an additional ¥500 each) are charged for both the **Kondō** (Main Hall) and **Reihōkan** (Treasure House), which are only open April to May and October to November.

MYŌSHIN-JI
BUDDHIST TEMPLE

Map p222 (妙心寺; www.myoshinji.or.jp; 1 Myoshin-ji-chō, Hanazono, Ukyō-ku; main temple free, other areas of complex adult/child ¥500/100; ◎9.10-11.40am & 1-4.40pm, to 3.40pm Nov-Feb; ☐Kyoto City bus 10 from Sanjo-Keihan to Myōshin-ji Kita-mon-mae) Myōshin-ji is a separate world within Kyoto, a walled-off complex of temples and subtemples that invites lazy strolling. The subtemple of **Taizō-in** here contains one of the city's more interesting gardens. Myōshin-ji dates from 1342 and belongs to the Rinzai school. There are 47 subtemples, but only a few are open to the public.

From the north gate, follow the broad stone avenue flanked by rows of temples to the southern part of the complex. The

WORTH A DETOUR

WORTH A DETOUR: TAKAO TEMPLES

The Takao area is tucked far away in the northwestern part of Kyoto. It is famed for autumn foliage and a trio of temples.

Down the river from the Takao bus stop, **Jingo-ji** (神護寺; 5 Takao-chō, Umegahata, Ukyō-ku; ¥600; ⊙9am-4pm; ▣Kyoto City bus 8 from Shijō Station to Takao, ▣JR bus from Kyoto Station to Yamashiro-Takao) is a mountaintop temple at the summit of a long flight of stairs. The **Kondō** (Gold Hall) is the most impressive of the temple's structures, located roughly in the middle of the grounds at the top of another flight of stairs. Be prepared for a somewhat strenuous climb, but it will be worth it.

After visiting the Kondō, head in the opposite direction along a wooded path to an open area overlooking the valley. Here you'll see people tossing small discs over the railing into the chasm below. These are *kawarakenage*, light clay discs that people throw like a Frisbee in order to rid themselves of their bad karma.

About five minutes' walk upstream from the base of the steps that lead to Jingo-ji, **Saimyō-ji** (西明寺; 2 Makino-chō, Umegahata, Ukyō-ku; ¥500; ⊙9am-5pm; ▣JR bus from Kyoto Station to Yamashiro-Takao) is a fine little temple worth stopping at. The approach over a red wooden bridge is very atmospheric; see if you can find your way round to the small waterfall at the side of the temple. The grotto here is pure magic.

Kōzan-ji (高山寺; 8 Toganoo-chō, Umegahata, Ukyō-ku; to see scroll ¥800; ⊙8.30am-5pm; ▣JR bus from Kyoto Station to Yamashiro-Takao or Toga-no-O), hidden amid a grove of towering cedar trees, is famous for the *chuju giga* scroll in its collection. It's an ink-brush depiction of frolicking animals that is considered by many to be the precursor of today's ubiquitous manga (Japanese comics). The temple is reached by following the main road north from the Yamashiro-Takao bus stop or, more conveniently, by getting off the JR bus at the Toga-no-O bus stop, right outside the temple. Note that there is an extra fee of ¥500 to visit the temple's gardens during the autumn-foliage season.

To reach Takao, take bus 8 from Nijō Station to the last stop, Takao (¥520, 40 minutes). From Kyoto Station, take the hourly JR bus to the Yamashiro-Takao stop (¥520, 50 minutes).

eponymous Myōshin-ji temple is roughly in the middle of the complex. Your entry fee entitles you to a tour of several of the buildings of the temple. The ceiling of the **Hattō** (Lecture Hall) here features Tanyū Kanō's unnerving painting *Unryūzu* (meaning 'Dragon glaring in eight directions'). Your guide will invite you to stand directly beneath the dragon; doing so makes it appear that it's spiralling up or down.

Shunkō-in, a subtemple of Myōshin-ji, offers regular 60-minute *zazen* (seated Zen meditation) sessions for foreigners with English explanations for ¥1500, or 90 minutes for ¥2500, including *matcha* (powdered green tea) and a sweet. This is highly recommended.

TAIZŌ-IN
BUDDHIST TEMPLE

Map p222 (退蔵院; www.taizoin.com; Myoshin-ji-chō, Hanazono, Ukyō-ku; adult/child ¥500/300; ⊙9am-5pm; ▣Kyoto City bus 10 from Sanjo-Keihan to Myōshin-ji Kita-mon-mae, ▣Kyoto City bus 8 from Shijō Station to Takao) This subtemple is in the southwestern corner of the grounds

of Myōshin-ji. The *kare-sansui* (dry landscape) depicting a waterfall and islands is well worth a visit, and there is a tatami-mat tearoom where you can enjoy a cup of *matcha* (¥500). It's a very peaceful spot.

KŌRYŪ-JI
BUDDHIST TEMPLE

Map p222 (広隆寺; ☎075-861-1461; 32 Hachioka-chō, Uzumasa, Ukyō-ku; adult ¥700, child ¥400-500; ⊙9am-5pm Mar-Nov, to 4.30pm Dec-Feb; ▣Keifuku line to Uzumasa) Kōryū-ji, one of the oldest temples in Japan, was founded in 622 to honour Prince Shōtoku, who was an enthusiastic promoter of Buddhism. It's notable mostly for its collection of Buddhist statuary; a visit with a knowledgeable guide is a good way to learn about the different levels of beings in the Buddhist pantheon. It's a bit out of the way, but it can be paired with nearby Myōshin-ji to form a half-day tour for those with an interest in Japanese Buddhism.

The **Hattō** (Lecture Hall) to the right of the main gate houses a magnificent trio of 9th-century statues: Buddha, flanked by manifestations of Kannon. The **Reihōkan** (Treasure House) contains numerous fine Buddhist statues, including the *Naki Miroku* (Crying Miroku) and the renowned *Miroku Bosatsu* (Bodhisattva of the Future), which is extraordinarily expressive. A national upset occurred in 1960 when an enraptured university student embraced the statue in a fit of passion (at least, that was his excuse) and inadvertently snapped off its little finger.

TŌEI STUDIO PARK AMUSEMENT PARK
Map p222 (東映太秦映画村; Tōei Uzumasa Eiga Mura; ☑075-864-7716; www.toei-eigamura.com/en; 10 Uzumasa Higashi Hachigaoka-chō, Ukyō-ku; adult/child 6-18yr/under 6yr ¥2200/1300/1100; ⏱9am-5pm; ☒JR Sagano (San-in) line to Uzumasa) In the Uzumasa area, Tōei Studio Park is rather touristy. It does, however, have some re-creations of Edo-period street scenes that give a decent idea of what Kyoto must have looked like before the advent of concrete.

 EATING

⭐**TOYOUKE-JAYA** TOFU ¥
Map p222 (とようけ茶屋; ☑075-462-3662; Imadegawa-dōri-Onmae nishi-iru, Kamigyō-ku; daily set meals from ¥1100; ⏱11am-3pm; ☒Kyoto City bus 101 to Kitano Tenmangū-mae) Locals line up for the tofu lunch sets at this famous restaurant across from Kitano Tenman-gū. Set meals usually include tofu, rice and miso soup. The problem is that it gets very crowded, especially when a market is on at the shrine. If you can get here when there's no queue, pop in for a healthy meal.

GONTARO NOODLES ¥
Map p222 (権太呂; ☑075-463-1039; http://gontaro.co.jp/index.html; 26 Hirano Miyazaki-chō, Kita-ku; meals from ¥850; ⏱10am-9pm Thu-Tue; ☒Kyoto City bus 205 or 12 to Kinkakuji-michi) This is a great choice for a spot of lunch when visiting Kinkaku-ji and the temples in the area. The setting is traditional and relaxed and it serves filling noodle meals, such as the tempura prawn and soba noodle set or the popular *kitsune udon* (udon with fried tofu).

RAMEN KAZU RAMEN ¥
Map p222 (ラーメンKAZU; ☑075-467-8282; http://kazu-no1.seesaa.net; 10-3 Kinugasa Sōmon-chō, Kita-ku; ramen from ¥600; ⏱11am-4pm; ☒Kyoto City bus 205 or 12 to Kinkakuji-michi) Convenient for lunch near Kinkaku-ji, this diner-style ramen eatery is decked out in black and white with checked tiles and bar stools. It does Kyoto-style ramen served with a thick broth.

⭐ **ENTERTAINMENT**

KITANO ODORI DANCE
Map p222 (北野をどり; ☑075-461-0148; Imadegawa-dōri, Nishihonmatsu nishi iru, Kamigyō-ku; admission/incl tea ¥4300/4800; ⏱shows 1.30pm & 4pm; ☒Kyoto City bus 50 to Kitano Tenmangu-mae) Performances by *maiko* (apprentice geisha) and *geiko* (the Kyoto word for geisha; a fully fledged *maiko*) of the Kamishichiken district are held in early April at Kamishichiken Kaburen-jō Theatre (上七軒歌舞練場), east of Kitano-Tenman-gū.

🛍 **SHOPPING**

TENJIN-SAN MARKET MARKET
Map p222 (天神さん, 北野天満宮露天市; Kitano Tenman-gū, Bakuro-chō, Kamigyō-ku; ⏱6am-9pm, 25th of each month; ☒Kyoto City bus 50 or 101 to Kitano Tenmangū-mae) This sprawling flea market is held on the 25th of each month at Kitano Tenman-gū and marks the birthday (and coincidentally the death) of the Heian-era statesman Sugawara Michizane (845–903). It's pleasant to explore the shrine before or after you do your shopping. You'll find loads of ceramics, second-hand kimonos, antiques and food stalls.

🏃 **ACTIVITIES**

SHUNKŌ-IN MEDITATION
Map p222 (春光院; ☑075-462-5488; www.shunkoin.com; Myōshin-ji, 42 Myoshin-ji-chō, Hanazono, Ukyō-ku; meditation class ¥2000, class & guided tour ¥2500; ☒JR Sagano (San-in) line to Hanazono) A subtemple of Myōshin-ji (p115), Shunkō-in is run by a monk who has studied abroad and made it his mission to introduce foreigners to his temple and Zen Buddhism. Regular introductory meditation classes are held in English and there is the option of a guided tour of the temple; check website for class schedule. You can also stay overnight in the accommodation (p150) here.

Arashiyama & Sagano

Neighbourhood Top Five

❶ Ōkōchi Sansō (p120) Meandering the trails through the villa's stunning garden and admiring the hilltop views.

❷ Arashiyama Bamboo Grove (p121) Entering a magical green world of swaying bamboo stalks.

❸ Tenryū-ji (p121) Meditating at the temple's sublime Zen garden to a backdrop of the Arashiyama mountains.

❹ Giō-ji (p123) Pausing at the beautiful lush moss garden at this quaint temple.

❺ Arashiyama Monkey Park Iwatayama (p124) Visiting our simian cousins while getting a panoramic view of Kyoto.

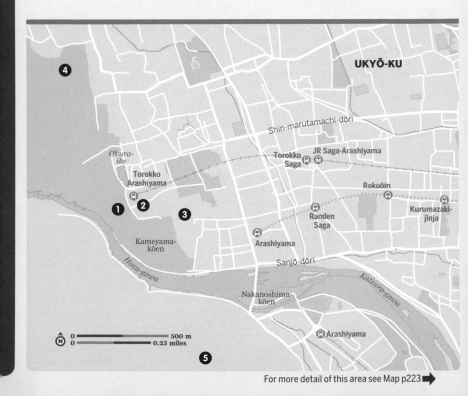

For more detail of this area see Map p223 ➡

Explore Arashiyama & Sagano

A half day is sufficient to do a quick visit of the main tourist track through Arashiyama and Sagano, which usually starts at the Tenryū-ji temple off the main street and heads north to end at Adashino Nenbutsu-ji (or whenever you get tired). It's best not to rush here, though, as this is the perfect place to take it slow wandering around the temples, strolling along the river or hiring a bicycle and exploring it on a slow ride, so a full day is preferable. Keep in mind that getting out to this area from Downtown Kyoto will take close to an hour if you take the bus, and about half an hour if you go by train or taxi.

Since some of the best sights in Northwest Kyoto, such as Kinkaku-ji and Ryōan-ji, are not too far from Arashiyama and Sagano, you can make a nice full-day tour of western Kyoto if you are willing to travel between these two areas by taxi and only spend half a day in Arashiyama.

Local Life

➡ **Hang-out** Kameyama-kōen (p121) is popular with locals for picnics.

➡ **Romantic stroll** The Hozu-gawa riverbank is favoured for romantic walks in the early evening.

➡ **Family favourite** Arashiyama Monkey Park Iwatayama (p124) is much loved by Kyoto's kids.

Getting There & Away

➡ **Train** The JR Sagano (San-in) line from Kyoto Station to Saga Arashiyama Station. The Hankyū line from downtown to Arashiyama (change en route at Katsura).

➡ **Tram** The Keifuku Randen Arashiyama line from Ōmiya Station to Keifuku Arashiyama Station.

➡ **Bus** From Marutamachi-dōri: bus 93; from Shijō-dōri: bus 11; from Kyoto Station: bus 28.

➡ **Subway** The Tōzai subway line stops at Uzumasa-Tenjin-gawa, where you can transfer to the Randen street tram.

Lonely Planet's Top Tip

The main drag of Arashiyama and Sagano is overdeveloped and not particularly appealing, aside from its few eating and shopping options. As soon as you can, head west into the hills to escape into nature (via Tenryū-ji or straight through the Arashiyama Bamboo Grove).

 **Best Places to Eat**

➡ Kitcho Arashiyama (p127)

➡ Shigetsu (p126)

➡ Yoshida-ya (p124)

For reviews, see p124.

 **Best Places to Enjoy Nature**

➡ Arashiyama Bamboo Grove (p121)

➡ Kameyama-kōen (p121)

➡ Ōkōchi Sansō (p120)

For reviews, see p120.➡

ARASHIYAMA & SAGANO

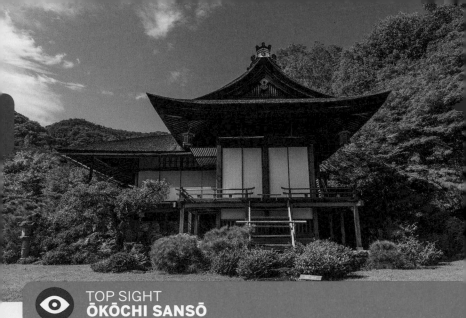

TOP SIGHT
ŌKŌCHI SANSŌ

Most visitors to Arashiyama are so enamoured with the swaying stalks of the famous Bamboo Forest that they overlook this stunning estate that sits at the western end of the grove. While the admission fee of ¥1000 might seem a bit hefty, it's certainly worth it and keep in mind that the price includes a bowl of *matcha* (green powdered tea) and a sweet.

The estate is the former villa and gardens of Ōkōchi Denjirō, a famous actor in the 1920s known for his *jid-aigeki* films, silent movie period dramas depicting the lives of samurais. The immaculate and carefully preserved gardens sprawl out over the property and up the slope of Ogura-san, from where there are extraordinary views over the city with the mountains on one side and the Hozu-gawa on the other.

Take your time exploring the trails through the garden, admiring the architecture of the villa and resting for a moment to contemplate the surrounding beauty and the sublime views. Afterwards, head to the delightful traditional teahouse with your ticket to enjoy that frothy bowl of *matcha* and Japanese sweet.

DON'T MISS

➡ Views over the city from the gardens

➡ Savouring *matcha* in the teahouse while gazing at the garden

PRACTICALITIES

➡ 大河内山荘

➡ Map p223, B3

➡ 8 Tabuchiyama-chō, Sagaogurayama, Ukyō-ku

➡ adult/child ¥1000/500

➡ ⊘9am-5pm

➡ ⊠Kyoto City bus 28 from Kyoto Station to Arashiyama-Tenryuji-mae, ⊠JR Sagano (San-in) line to Saga-Arashiyama or Hankyū line to Arashiyama, change at Katsura

⊙ SIGHTS

★TENRYŪ-JI
BUDDHIST TEMPLE

Map p223 (天龍寺; ☑075-881-1235; www.ten
ryuji.com; 68 Susukinobaba-chō, Saga-Tenryū-
ji, Ukyō-ku; adult/child garden only ¥500/300,
temple buildings & garden ¥800/600; ☺8.30am-
5.30pm, to 5pm mid-Oct–mid-Mar; ☐Kyoto City
bus 28 from Kyoto Station to Arashiyama-Tenryuji-
mae, ☒JR Sagano (San-in) line to Saga-Arashiyama
or Hankyū line to Arashiyama, change at Katsura)
A major temple of the Rinzai school,
Tenryū-ji has one of the most attractive gardens in all of Kyoto, particularly during the
spring cherry-blossom and autumn-foliage
seasons. The main 14th-century Zen garden, with its backdrop of the Arashiyama
mountains, is a good example of *shakkei*
(borrowed scenery). Unfortunately, it's no
secret that the garden here is world class,
so it pays to visit early in the morning or
on a weekday.

It was built in 1339 on the old site of Go-
Daigo's villa after a priest had a dream of
a dragon rising from the nearby river. The
dream was seen as a sign that the emperor's
spirit was uneasy and so the temple was
built as appeasement – hence the name
tenryū (heavenly dragon). The present
buildings date from 1900. You will find Arashiyama's famous bamboo grove situated
just outside the north gate of the temple.

NONOMIYA-JINJA
SHINTO SHRINE

Map p223 (野宮神社; Sagano Miyamachi, Ukyo-
ku; ☺6am-5pm; ☐Kyoto City bus 28 from Kyoto
Station to Arashiyama-Tenryuji-mae, ☒JR Sagano
(San-in) line to Saga-Arashiyama or Hankyū line to
Arashiyama, change at Katsura) 【FREE】This small
shrine is where imperial princesses were
sent for purification before serving at the Ise
shrine. It features in the famous Japanese
novel *The Tale of Genji*. These days people
come here to pray to Nonomiya Daikokuten
– the god of matchmaking and marriage.

★ARASHIYAMA BAMBOO GROVE
PARK

Map p223 (嵐山竹林; Ogurayama, Saga, Ukyō-
ku; ☺dawn-dusk; ☐Kyoto City bus 28 from Kyoto
Station to Arashiyama-Tenryuji-mae, ☒JR Sagano
(San-in) line to Saga-Arashiyama or Hankyū line to
Arashiyama, change at Katsura) 【FREE】The thick
green bamboo stalks seem to continue
endlessly in every direction and there's a
strange quality to the light at this famous
bamboo grove. It's most atmospheric on the
approach to Ōkōchi Sansō villa and you'll
be unable to resist trying to take a few

photos, but you might be disappointed with
the results: photos just can't capture the
magic of the place. The grove runs from
outside the north gate of Tenryū-ji to just
below Ōkōchi Sansō.

KAMEYAMA-KŌEN
PARK

Map p223 (亀山公園; Sagaogurayama, Ukyō-ku;
☺24hr; ☐Kyoto City bus 28 from Kyoto Station to
Arashiyama-Tenryuji-mae, ☒JR Sagano (San-in)
line to Saga-Arashiyama or Hankyū line to Arashiyama, change at Katsura) Just upstream from
Tōgetsu-kyō and behind Tenryū-ji, this
park is a nice place to escape the crowds
of Arashiyama. It's laced with trails, one of
which leads to a lookout over Katsura-gawa
and up into the Arashiyama mountains. It's
especially attractive during cherry-blossom
and autumn-foliage seasons. Keep an eye
out for monkeys, which occasionally descend from the nearby hills to pick fruit.

JŌJAKKŌ-JI
BUDDHIST TEMPLE

Map p223 (常寂光寺; 3 Ogura-chō, Sagaogurayama, Ukyō-ku; adult/child ¥500/200; ☺9am-
5pm; ☐Kyoto City bus 28 from Kyoto Station to Arashiyama-Tenryuji-mae, ☒JR Sagano (San-in) line
to Saga-Arashiyama or Hankyū line to Arashiyama,
change at Katsura) This temple is perched on
top of a mossy knoll and is famed for its
brilliant maple trees, which turn a lovely
crimson red in November, and its thatched-
roof Niō-mon gate. The *hondō* (main hall)
was constructed in the 16th century out of
wood sourced from Fushimi-jō.

RAKUSHISHA
HISTORIC BUILDING

Map p223 (落柿舎; 20 Hinomyōjin-chō, Sagaogurayama, Ukyō-ku; ¥250; ☺9am-5pm
Mar-Dec, 10am-4pm Jan & Feb, closed 31 Dec &
1 Jan; ☐Kyoto City bus 28 from Kyoto Station to
Arashiyama-Tenryuji-mae, ☒JR Sagano (San-in)
line to Saga-Arashiyama or Hankyū line to Arashiyama, change at Katsura) Formerly the building
here was the hut of Mukai Kyorai, the best-
known disciple of the illustrious haiku poet
Bashō. You can wander the small garden
where you'll find stones engraved with poems, including one with a haiku by Bashō,
and take a peek inside the rooms of the
cottage.

SEIRYŌ-JI
BUDDHIST TEMPLE

Map p223 (清涼寺; Saga Shaka-dō; ☑075-861-
0343; 46 Fujinoki-chō, Saga Shakado, Ukyō-ku;
adult/child ¥400/200; ☺9am-4pm, to 5pm Apr,
May, Oct & Nov; ☐Kyoto City bus 28 from Kyoto
Station to Arashiyama-Tenryuji-mae, ☒JR Sagano

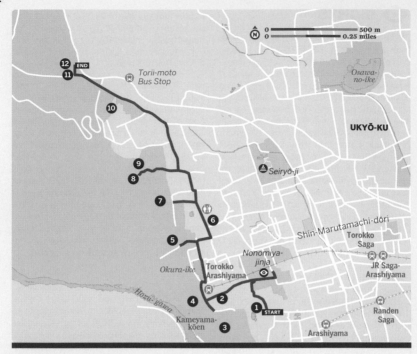

Neighbourhood Walk
Ambling Through Bamboo Groves & Temples

START TENRYŪ-JI
END TORII-MOTO BUS STOP
LENGTH ABOUT 4KM; FOUR HOURS

Start at ❶ **Tenryū-ji** (p121), where you can explore the temple and admire its stunning 14th-century Zen garden. After checking out the temple, exit via the north gate, turn left and enter the famous ❷ **Arashiyama Bamboo Grove** (p121).

At the top of the hill, you can take a quick detour to check out ❸ **Kameyama-kōen** (p121) or enter ❹ **Ōkōchi Sansō villa** (p120), the entrance to which is almost directly in front of you.

Continuing north from Ōkōchi Sansō, head downhill and past Okura-ike pond. Soon after passing the pond, you'll see the gate of ❺ **Jōjakkō-ji** (p121). After Jōjakkō-ji, walk straight east away from the temple gate, avoiding the temptation to take a left out of the gate and go north. About 100m east of the Jōjakkō-ji gate, take a left (just

before a cornfield) and you'll soon come to ❻ **Rakushisha** (p121), a charming poet's hut. After Rakushisha, continue north. About 150m further on brings you to the gate of ❼ **Nison-in** (p123).

Return to the main road from Nison-in and follow it gradually northwest for a few minutes. This will bring you to the turn-off for ❽ **Takiguchi-dera** (p123) and ❾ **Giō-ji** (p123), two wonderfully atmospheric little hillside temples (there is no English sign here; look for the four stone way markers). After visiting one or both of these temples, return to the main road and continue walking northwest. You'll soon see the stone steps that lead up to ❿ **Adashino Nenbutsu-ji** (p123) on your left. From here, it's a short walk onward to the huge orange ⓫ **Atago Torii**. A lovely spot to refresh yourself is the teahouse, ⓬ **Hiranoya** (p127), just north of the *torii*. You can take bus 62 or 72 back from the Torii-moto bus stop.

(San-in) line to Saga-Arashiyama or Hankyū line to Arashiyama, change at Katsura) This local temple and its peaceful gardens makes for a quiet change from the touristy temples along the main drag. It has an important standing wooden statue of Shaka, one of Japan's most famous Nyorai (historical term for Buddha), usually on display on the 8th of the month in April, May, October and November from 11am.

NISON-IN
BUDDHIST TEMPLE

Map p223 (二尊院; 27 Monzenchōjin-chō, Saganison-in, Ukyō-ku; ¥500; ⊙9am-4.30pm; 🚌Kyoto City bus 28 from Kyoto Station to Arashiyama-Tenryuji-mae, 🚃JR Sagano (San-in) line to Saga-Arashiyama or Hankyū line to Arashiyama, change at Katsura) This is a popular spot with maple-leaf watchers. Nison-in was originally built in the 9th century by Emperor Saga. It houses two important Kamakura-era Buddha statues side by side (Shaka on the right and Amida on the left). The temple features lacquered nightingale floors.

TAKIGUCHI-DERA
BUDDHIST TEMPLE

Map p223 (滝口寺; ☏075-871-3929; 10-4 Kameyama-chō, Saga, Ukyō-ku; adult/child ¥300/100; ⊙9am-5pm; 🚌Kyoto City bus 28 from Kyoto Station to Arashiyama-Tenryuji-mae, 🚃JR Sagano (San-in) line to Saga-Arashiyama or Hankyū line to Arashiyama, change at Katsura) Takiguchi-dera was founded by Heian-era nobleman Takiguchi Nyūdō, who entered the priesthood after being forbidden by his father to marry his peasant consort Yokobue. One day, Yokobue came to the temple with her flute to serenade Takiguchi, but was again refused by him; she wrote a farewell love sonnet on a stone (in her own blood) before throwing herself into the river to perish. The stone remains at the temple. Takiguchi-dera sits next to Gio-ji temple.

GIŌ-JI
BUDDHIST TEMPLE

Map p223 (祇王寺; www.giouji.or.jp; 32 Kozaka-chō, Sagatoriimoto, Ukyō-ku; adult/child ¥300/100; ⊙9am-5pm; 🚌Kyoto City bus 28 from Kyoto Station to Arashiyama-Tenryuji-mae, 🚃JR Sagano (San-in) line to Saga-Arashiyama or Hankyū line to Arashiyama, change at Katsura) This tiny temple near the north end of the main Arashiyama sightseeing route is one of Kyoto's hidden gems. Its main attraction is the lush moss garden outside the thatch-roofed hall of the temple. Giō-ji was named for the Heian-era *shirabyōshi* (traditional dancer) Giō, who committed herself here as a nun at age 21 after her romance ended with Taira-no-Kiyomori, the commander of the Heike clan.

She was usurped in Kiyomori's affections by a fellow entertainer, Hotoke Gozen (who later deserted Kiyomori to join Giō at the temple). Enshrined in the main hall are five wooden statues: these are Giō, Hotoke Gozen, Kiyomori, and Giō's mother and sister (who also served as nuns at the temple).

Giō-ji is also known for its autumn foliage displays.

ADASHINO NENBUTSU-JI
BUDDHIST TEMPLE

Map p223 (化野念仏寺; ☏075-861-2221; 17 Adashino-chō, Sagatoriimoto, Ukyō-ku; ¥500; ⊙9am-4.30pm, to 3.30pm Dec-Feb; 🚌Kyoto City bus 28 from Kyoto Station to Arashiyama-Tenryuji-mae, 🚃JR Sagano (San-in) line to Saga-Arashiyama or Hankyū line to Arashiyama, change at Katsura) This rather unusual temple is where the abandoned bones of paupers without kin were gathered. More than 8000 stone images are crammed into the temple grounds, dedicated to the repose of their spirits. The temple is not a must-see attraction, but it's certainly interesting and there's a small bamboo grove. Note: no photographs are allowed inside the stones area, only outside the stone walls.

The abandoned souls are remembered with candles each year in the Sentō Kuyō ceremony held here on the evenings of 23 and 24 August.

TOGETSU-KYŌ
BRIDGE

Map p223 (渡月橋; Saga Tenryū-ji, Susukinobaba-chō, Ukyō-ku; 🚌Kyoto City bus 28 from Kyoto Station to Arashiyama-Tenryuji-mae, 🚃JR Sagano (San-in) line to Saga-Arashiyama or Hankyū line to Arashiyama, change at Katsura) The dominant landmark in Arashiyama, this bridge is just a few minutes on foot from either the Keifuku line or Hankyū line Arashiyama stations. The original crossing, constructed in 1606, was about 100m upriver from the present bridge. From July to mid-September, Togetsu-kyō is a good spot from which to watch *ukai* (cormorant fishing) in the evening. To get close to the action you can pay ¥1800 to join a passenger boat. The Kyoto Tourist Information Center (p189) can provide more details.

On 13 April *jūsan-mairi,* an important rite of passage for local children aged 13, takes place here. Boys and girls (many in kimono), after paying respects at Hōrin-ji (a nearby temple) and receiving a blessing for wisdom, cross the bridge under strict parental order not to look back towards the temple until they've reached the northern side of the bridge. Not heeding this instruction is believed to bring bad luck for life!

You can rent boats from the **boat-rental stall** (Map p223; Hozu-gawa north bank; 1hr ¥1500) just upstream from the bridge. It's a nice way to spend some time in Arashiyama and kids love it.

ARASHIYAMA MONKEY PARK IWATAYAMA
PARK

Map p223 (嵐山モンキーパークいわたや ま; ☑075-872-0950; http://monkeypark.jp; 8 Genrokuzan-chō, Arashiyama, Ukyō-ku; adult/child ¥550/250; ⊙9am-5pm mid-Mar–Sep, to 4pm Oct–mid-Mar; ☑Kyoto City bus 28 from Kyoto Station to Arashiyama-Tenryuji-mae, ☑JR Sagano (San-in) line to Saga-Arashiyama or Hankyū line to Arashiyama, change at Katsura) Though it is common to spot wild monkeys in the nearby mountains, here you can encounter them at a close distance and enjoy watching the playful creatures frolic about. It makes for an excellent photo opportunity, not only of the monkeys but also of the panoramic view over Kyoto. Refreshingly, it is the animals who are free to roam while the humans who feed them are caged in a box!

You enter the park near the south side of Tōgetsu-kyō, through the orange *torii* (shrine gate) of Ichitani-jinja. Buy your tickets from the machine to the left of the shrine at the top of the steps. Just be warned: it's a steep climb up the hill to get to the monkeys. If it's a hot day, you're going to be drenched by the time you get to the spot where they gather.

DAIKAKU-JI
BUDDHIST TEMPLE

Map p223 (大覚寺; ☑075-871-0071; 4 Osawa-chō, Saga, Ukyō-ku; adult/child ¥500/300; ⊙9am-4.30pm; ☑JR Sagano (San-in) line to Saga-Arashiyama) After a 25-minute walk northeast of Nison-in you will find Daikaku-ji, one of Kyoto's less-commonly visited temples. It was built in the 9th century as a palace for Emperor Saga, who then converted it into a temple. The present buildings date from the 16th century and are palatial in style; they also contain some impressive paintings. The large Osawa-no-ike pond was once used by the emperor for boating and is a popular spot for viewing the harvest moon.

EATING

HAKKO SHOKUDO KAMOSHIKA
SHOKUDO ¥

Map p223 (発酵食堂カモシカ; ☑075-862-0106; 17-1 Saga-Tenryūji-Wakamiya-chō, Ukyō-ku; meals ¥900-2300; ⊙11am-3pm Tue-Sat; ☑; ☑Kyoto City bus 28 from Kyoto Station to Arashiyama-Tenryuji-mae, ☑JR Sagano (San-in) line to Saga-Arashiyama) This excellent restaurant on the north side of JR Saga-Arashiyama Station specialises in fermented Japanese foods, most of it vegetarian. The daily set, with about eight different fermented foods, is a delicious and healthy lunch option. There's an English menu and an English sign.

ARASHIYAMA YOSHIMURA
NOODLES ¥

Map p223 (嵐山よしむら; ☑075-863-5700; Togetsu-kyō kita, Saga-Tenryū-ji, Ukyō-ku; soba from ¥1000, meals from ¥1482; ⊙11am-5pm; ☑Kyoto City bus 28 from Kyoto Station to Arashiyama-Tenryuji-mae, ☑JR Sagano (San-in) line to Saga-Arashiyama or Hankyū line to Arashiyama, change at Katsura) For a tasty bowl of soba noodles and a million-dollar view over the Arashiyama mountains and the Togetsu-kyō bridge, head to this extremely popular eatery just north of the famous bridge, overlooking the Katsura-gawa. There's an English menu but no English sign; look out for the big glass windows and the stone wall.

YOSHIDA-YA
SHOKUDO ¥

Map p223 (よしだや; ☑075-861-0213; 20-24 Tsukurimichi-chō, Saga Tenryū-ji, Ukyō-ku; soba & udon from ¥650; ⊙10am-4pm Thu-Tue; ☑Kyoto City bus 28 from Kyoto Station to Arashiyama-Tenryuji-mae, ☑JR Sagano (San-in) line to Saga-Arashiyama or Hankyū line to Arashiyama, change at Katsura) This quaint and friendly little *teishoku-ya* (set-meal restaurant) is perfect for lunch while in Arashiyama. The standard *teishoku* favourites are on offer, including dishes like *oyakodon* (egg and chicken over a bowl of rice; ¥900) and filling bowls of udon and soba noodles. In summer, cool off with a refreshing *uji kintoki* (shaved ice with sweetened green tea; ¥600).

KAMEYAMA-YA
JAPANESE ¥

Map p223 (亀山家; ☑075-861-0759; Kamenoo-chō, Saga, Ukyō-ku; meals ¥550-1700; ⊙11.30am-3.30pm; ☑Kyoto City bus 28 from Kyoto Station to Arashiyama-Tenryuji-mae, ☑JR Sagano (San-in) line to Saga-Arashiyama or Hankyū line to Arashiyama, change at Katsura) On the banks of the

WORTH A DETOUR

OUTLYING SIGHTS
••

There are a few excellent sights in the southwest corner of Kyoto, lying to the south of the Arashiyama and Sagano area. A couple of them require advance planning, but as long as you're organised you could tack them onto a visit to Arashiyama, making it a full-day trip to the area.

Katsura Rikyū (桂離宮; ☑075-211-1215; http://sankan.kunaicho.go.jp; Katsura Detached Palace, Katsura Misono, Nishikyō-ku; ☉tours 9am, 10am, 11am, 1.30pm, 2.30pm, 3.30pm Tue-Sun; 🚌Kyoto City bus 33 to Katsura Rikyū-mae, 🚉Hankyū line to Katsura) FREE, one of Kyoto's imperial properties, is widely considered to be the pinnacle of Japanese traditional architecture and garden design. Set amid an otherwise drab neighbourhood, it is (very literally) an island of incredible beauty. The villa was built in 1624 for the emperor's brother, Prince Toshihito. Every conceivable detail of the villa – the teahouses, the large pond with islets and the surrounding garden – has been given meticulous attention.

One-hour tours are in Japanese, with English audio guides free of charge. You must be over 18 years and you will need to bring your passport for ID.

You can book tickets in advance at the Imperial Household Agency office (p82) or online for morning tours but for afternoon tours tickets go on sale at the palace from 11am and are on a first-come, first-served basis until capacity is sold.

It's a 15-minute walk from Katsura Station, on the Hankyū line. A taxi from the station to the villa will cost around ¥600. Alternatively, Kyoto bus 33 stops at Katsura Rikyū-mae stop, which is a five-minute walk from the villa.

Saihō-ji (西芳寺; 56 Jingatani-chō, Matsuo, Nishikyō-ku; ¥3000; 🚌Kyoto bus 73 from Kyoto Station or 63 from Sanjō-Keihan to Koke-dera) temple has one of Kyoto's best-known gardens and is famed for its superb moss garden, hence the temple's nickname: Koke-dera (Moss Temple). The heart-shaped garden, laid out in 1339 by Musō Kokushi, surrounds a tranquil pond and is simply stunning. In order to limit the number of visitors, you must apply to visit at least one week in advance, though the earlier the better to avoid disappointment.

To make a reservation to visit, you need to send a postcard and include your name, number of visitors, occupation, age (you must be over 18) and desired date (choice of alternative dates preferred), along with a self-addressed postcard for a reply to your address (in Japan or overseas). The address to send it to is: Saihō-ji, 56 Kamigaya-chō, Matsuo, Nishikyō-ku, Kyoto-shi 615-8286, JAPAN. Your return postcard will let you know the date and time of your visit.

When you arrive at Saihō-ji, visitors are required to copy a sutra with an ink brush. Foreigners are generally just required to write their name, address and a prayer, rather than attempt to copy the sutra. Once in the garden, you are free to explore on your own and at your own pace. The whole visit usually takes around one hour.

While the process might seem a little over-the-top, it's certainly worth the small effort to organise, particularly if you have a fondness for Japanese gardens. It's about a 30-minute walk from Katsura Rikyū, otherwise a taxi is the best option.

Jizō-in (☑075-381-3417; 23 Yamadakitano-chō, Nishikyō-ku; adult/child ¥500/300; ☉9am-4.30pm; 🚌Kyoto bus 63 from Sanjō-Keihan or 73 from Kyoto Station to Koke-dera) is a delightful little temple. It doesn't boast any spectacular buildings or treasures, but it has a lovely moss garden and is almost completely ignored by tourists, making it a great place to sit and contemplate. It's a five-minute walk from the car park and bus station near Saihō-ji; there is a stone staircase that climbs to the road leading to Jizō-in (it helps to ask someone to point the way, as it's not entirely clear).

Hozu-gawa sits this lovely semi-outdoor restaurant. The food is only pretty good, but the location is impossible to beat. Dishes include tempura over rice and noodles. There is no English sign but there are a couple of vending machines near the entrance.

SAGANO-YU
CAFE ¥

Map p223 (嵯峨野湯; ☑075-882-8985; www.sagano-yu.com; 4-3 Imahori-chō, Saga Tenryū-ji, Ukyō-ku; meals from ¥900; ☺11am-8pm; ☑Kyoto City bus 28 from Kyoto Station to Arashiyama-Tenryuji-mae, ☑JR Sagano (San-in) line to Saga-Arashiyama or Hankyū line to Arashiyama, change at Katsura) Located near the JR Saga-Arashiyama Station, this whitewashed chic cafe is set in an old public bathhouse complete with decorative tiles and taps still in place. It's a good spot to fill up on dishes such as cold sesame spicy pasta or curries, or to indulge in its *matcha azuki* (green tea and sweet red-bean paste) pancakes.

MUSUBI CAFE
CAFE ¥

Map p223 (むすび; ☑075-862-4195; www.musubi-cafe.jp; 1-8 Arashiyama Nakaoshita-chō, Nishikyō-ku; meals from ¥600; ☺10.30am-8pm; ☺☑; ☑Kyoto City bus 28 from Kyoto Station to Arashiyama-Tenryuji-mae, ☑Hankyū line to Arashiyama, change at Katsura) This cute light-filled cafe is a convenient stop close to Hankyū Arashiyama Station and a short walk from the Togetsu-kyō bridge. It offers a range of healthy dishes, and the lunch and dinner set meals are good value. Finish it off with something from the list of vegan cakes.

KOMICHI
CAFE ¥

Map p223 (こみち; ☑075-872-5313; 23 Ōjōin-chō, Nison-in Monzen, Saga, Ukyō-ku; matcha & sweet ¥650; ☺10am-5pm Thu-Tue; ☑Kyoto City bus 28 from Kyoto Station to Arashiyama-Tenryuji-ma☑ ☑JR Sagano (San-in) line to Saga-Arashiyama ☑ Hankyū line to Arashiyama, change at Katsura☑ This friendly little teahouse is perfectly located along the Arashiyama tourist trail. In addition to hot and cold tea and coffee, it serves *uji kintoki* (shaved ice with sweetened green tea) in summer and a variety of noodle dishes year-round. The picture menu helps with ordering.

★SHIGETSU
VEGETARIAN, JAPANESE ¥¥

Map p223 (篩月; ☑075-882-9725; 68 Susukinobaba-chō, Saga-Tenryū-ji, Ukyō-ku; lunch sets incl temple admission ¥3500, ¥5500 & ¥7500; ☺11am-2pm; ☑; ☑Kyoto City bus 28 from Kyoto Station to Arashiyama-Tenryuji-mae, ☑JR Sagano (San-in) line to Saga-Arashiyama or Hankyū line to Arashiyama, change at Katsura) To sample *shōjin-ryōri* (Buddhist vegetarian cuisine), try Shigetsu in the precincts of Tenryū-ji. This healthy fare has been sustaining monks for more than a thousand years in Japan, so it will probably get you through an afternoon of sightseeing, although carnivores may be left craving something more. Shigetsu has beautiful garden views.

YUDŌFU SAGANO
TOFU ¥¥

Map p223 (湯豆腐嵯峨野; ☑075-871-6946; 45 Susukinobaba-chō, Saga-Tenryū-ji, Ukyō-ku; lunch & dinner from ¥3800; ☺11am-7pm; ☑Kyoto City bus 28 from Kyoto Station to Arashiyama-Tenryuji-mae, ☑JR Sagano (San-in) line to Saga-

---

HOZU-GAWA RIVER TRIP

The **Hozu-gawa river trip** (☑0771-22-5846; www.hozugawakudari.jp; Hozu-chō, Kameoka-shi; adult/child 4-12yr ¥4100/2700; ☑JR Sagano (San-in) line from Kyoto Station to Kameoka) is a great way to enjoy the beauty of Kyoto's western mountains without any strain on the legs. With long bamboo poles, boatmen steer flat-bottom boats down the Hozu-gawa from Kameoka, 30km west of Kyoto Station, through steep, forested mountain canyons, before arriving at Arashiyama.

Between 10 March and 30 November there are seven trips daily leaving on the hour from 9am to 2pm, with the last trip at 3.30pm. During winter the number of trips is reduced to four per day (10am, 11.30am, 1pm and 2.30pm) and the boats are heated.

The ride lasts two hours and covers 16km through occasional sections of choppy water – a scenic jaunt with minimal danger. The scenery is especially breathtaking during cherry-blossom season in April and maple-foliage season in autumn.

The boats depart from a dock that is eight minutes' walk from Kameoka Station. Kameoka is accessible by rail from Kyoto Station or Nijō Station on the JR Sagano (San-in) line. The Kyoto Tourist Information Center (p189) provides an English-language leaflet and timetable for rail connections. The fare from Kyoto to Kameoka is ¥410 one way by regular train (don't spend the extra for the express; it makes little difference in travel time).

ashiyama or Hankyū line to Arashiyama, change t Katsura) This is a popular place to sample *yudōfu* (tofu cooked in a pot). It's fairly casual, with a spacious dining room. You can usually eat here without having to wait, and there's both indoor and outdoor seating. Look for the old cartwheels outside.

★KITCHO ARASHIYAMA   KAISEKI ¥¥¥
Map p223 (吉兆嵐山本店; ☑075-881-1101; www. kyoto-kitcho.com; 58 Susukinobaba-chō, Saga-Tenryūji, Ukyō-ku; lunch/dinner from ¥43,200/ 48,600; ☺11.30am-3pm & 5-10pm Thu-Tue; ⊙Kyoto City bus 28 from Kyoto Station to Arashiyama-Tenryuji-mae, ⊡JR Sagano (San-in) line to Saga-Arashiyama or Hankyū line to Arashiyama, change at Katsura) Considered one of the best *kaiseki* (Japanese haute cuisine) restaurants in Kyoto (and Japan, for that matter), Kitcho Arashiyama is the place to sample the full *kaiseki* experience. Meals are served in private rooms overlooking gardens. The food, service, explanations and atmosphere are all first rate. We suggest having a Japanese person call to reserve, or make a booking online via its website.

🍷 DRINKING & NIGHTLIFE

★HIRANOYA   TEAHOUSE
Map p223 (平野屋; ☑075-861-0359; 16 Sennō-chō, Saga-Toriimoto, Ukyō-ku; ☺11.30am-9pm; ⊙Kyoto City bus 72 from Kyoto Station to Otaginenbutsu-ji-mae) Located next to the Atago Torii (a large Shintō shrine gate), this thatched-roof restaurant is about as atmospheric as they get. It serves a simple cup of *matcha* for a relatively modest ¥840 (it comes with a traditional sweet). It's the perfect way to cool off after a long slog around the temples of Arashiyama and Sagano.

You can also sample full-course *kaiseki* meals here from ¥11,000 (by telephone reservation in Japanese only). Its speciality is *ayu* (sweetfish caught during cormorant fishing).

% ARABICA   COFFEE
Map p223 (☑075-748-0057; www.arabica.coffee; 3-47 Susukinobaba-chō, Saga-Tenryūji, Ukyō-ku; ☺8am-6pm; ⊙Kyoto City bus 28 from Kyoto Station to Arashiyama-Tenryuji-mae, ⊡JR

Sagano (San-in) line to Saga-Arashiyama) Peer through the floor-to-ceiling windows that look across the Hozu-gawa and mountain backdrop as you order your coffee at this tiny cafe bringing excellent brew to Arashiyama. Grab a takeaway and stroll along the river or nab a bench out the front to take in the views.

🛍 SHOPPING

ISHIKAWA TAKENOMISE   ARTS & CRAFTS
Map p223 (いしかわ竹乃店; ☑075-861-0076; www.takenomise.com; 35 Tsukurimici-chō, Saga Tenryū-ji, Ukyō-ku; ☺10am-6pm; ⊙Kyoto City bus 28 from Kyoto Station to Arashiyama-Tenryuji-mae, ⊡JR Sagano (San-in) line to Saga-Arashiyama or Hankyū line to Arashiyama, change at Katsura) After you've strolled through the Arashiyama Bamboo Grove, head to this souvenir store on the main street to peruse the packed shelves of handcrafted bamboo products, from flower baskets and chopsticks to rice scoops and sushi rolling mats.

PLATZ   ARTS & CRAFTS
Map p223 (プラッツ; ☑075-861-1721; www.kyoto-platz.jp; 5 Tsukurimici-chō, Saga Tenryū-ji, Ukyō-ku; ☺10am-7pm; ⊙Kyoto City bus 28 from Kyoto Station to Arashiyama-Tenryuji-mae, ⊡JR Sagano (San-in) line to Saga-Arashiyama or Hankyū line to Arashiyama, change at Katsura) Originally founded in the Nishijin textile district (p83) before moving the factory to Arashiyama, Platz is a delightful store selling beautiful handmade cushions along with bed linen and homewares.

🏃 ACTIVITIES

ARASHIYAMA STATION FOOT ONSEN   ONSEN
Map p223 (Keifuku Arashiyama Randen Station; ¥200; ☺9am-8pm, to 6pm in winter; ⊙Keifuku Randen line to Arashiyama, ⊡JR Sagano (San-in) line to Saga-Arashiyama or Hankyū line to Arashiyama, change at Katsura) Give your feet a soak after all the temple-hopping at this foot onsen located at the end of the Keifuku Arashiyama Randen Station platform. Price includes a souvenir towel.

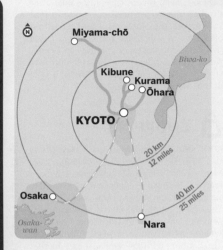

Day Trips from Kyoto

Kurama & Kibune p129

Escape to the hills for hiking and hot-spring soaking in these two charming valleys just 30 minutes from Kyoto. Kibune is an essential visit in summer for dining on platforms over the river.

Ōhara p131

Take a one-hour bus ride into the mountains for a glimpse of farming life along with temple strolling in this quiet town. Very popular for maple-leaf viewing in autumn.

Nara p134

Thirty minutes away from Kyoto by express train, Nara boasts a compact collection of truly first-rate sights. If you're in Kyoto for than five days, Nara is a must!

Osaka p136

A short train trip from Kyoto, Osaka is a great place to see modern Japan in all its hyperkinetic intensity. Sample the nightlife before catching the last train back to Kyoto.

Miyama-chō p139

If you want to see rural Japan (thatched-roof cottages etc), hire a car and head to these villages in the mountains north of the city.

Kurama & Kibune

both destinations by train from Kyoto costs ¥420/210 per adult/child and takes about 30 minutes to reach.

Explore

Roughly 30 minutes north of Kyoto, Kurama (鞍馬) and Kibune (貴船) are a pair of tranquil valleys that have been long favoured as places to escape the city. Kurama's main attractions are its mountain temple and onsen (hot spring). Kibune, a charming little hamlet just over the ridge, is a cluster of ryokan overlooking a mountain river. Kibune is best visited in summer, when the ryokan serve dinner on platforms built over the waters of Kibune-gawa.

The two valleys lend themselves to being explored together. In winter, start from Kibune, walk 30 minutes over the ridge, visit Kurama-dera, then soak in the onsen. In summer the reverse route is better: start from Kurama, walk up to the temple, then down the other side to Kibune to enjoy a meal suspended above the cool river.

The Best...

➜ **Sight** Kurama-dera
➜ **Activity** Kurama Onsen (p130)

Getting There & Away

➜ **Train** Take the Eizan line from Kyoto's Demachiyanagi Station. For Kibune, get off at the second-last stop, Kibune-guchi, take a right out of the station and walk about 20 minutes up the hill or jump on the shuttle bus (adult/child ¥160/80). For Kurama, go to the last stop, Kurama, and walk straight out of the station. To reach

◉ SIGHTS & ACTIVITIES

★**KURAMA-DERA**   BUDDHIST TEMPLE
(鞍馬寺; 1074 Kurama Honmachi, Sakyō-ku; ¥300; ⏱9am-4.30pm; 🚃Eizan line from Demachiyanagi to Kurama) Located high on a thickly wooded mountain, Kurama-dera is one of the few temples in modern Japan that still manages to retain an air of real spirituality. This is a magical place that gains much of its power from its brilliant natural setting. The entrance to the temple is just up the hill from Kurama Station. A cable car runs to/from the top (¥200 each way), or you can hike up in about 30 minutes (follow the path past the tram station).

The temple also has a fascinating history: in 770 the monk Gantei left Nara's Toshōdai-ji in search of a wilderness sanctuary in which to meditate. Wandering in the hills north of Kyoto, he came across a white horse that led him to the valley known today as Kurama. After seeing a vision of the deity Bishamon-ten, guardian of the northern quarter of the Buddhist heaven, Gantei established Kurama-dera just below the peak of Kurama-yama. Originally belonging to the Tendai school of Buddhism, Kurama has been independent since 1949, describing its own brand of Buddhism as Kurama-kyō.

It's worth walking up the trail from the main entrance (if it's not too hot); it winds through a forest of towering old-growth

DAY TRIPS FROM KYOTO KURAMA & KIBUNE

WORTH A DETOUR

MIHO MUSEUM

Around an hour from Kyoto, the architectural masterpiece that is the **Miho Museum** (ミホミュージアム; ☎0748-82-3411; www.miho.or.jp; 300 Tashiro Momodani; ¥1100; ⏱10am-5pm, closed some Mon & Tue & btwn exhibits) is a great day trip from the city. The glass-and-marble IM Pei–designed main building sits in a tranquil forested spot close to the town of Shigaraki and is integrated into the natural surroundings. From the ticket office, the museum is accessed by walking through a long tunnel that opens into a gorge. The Japanese, Egyptian, Middle Eastern, Chinese and South Asian artworks on display are from the Koyama family collection.

To get there, take the JR Tōkaido (Biwako) line from Kyoto Station to Ishiyama Station (¥240, 15 minutes), from where you take Teisan bus 150 to the museum (¥820, 50 minutes).

cryptomeria trees, passing by **Yuki-jinja**, a small Shintō shrine, on the way. Near the peak, there is a courtyard dominated by the **Honden** (Main Hall); behind this a trail leads off to the mountain's peak.

At the top, you can take a brief detour across the ridge to **Ōsugi-gongen**, a quiet shrine in a grove of trees. Those who want to continue to Kibune can take the trail down the other side. It's a 1.2km, 30-minute hike from the Honden to the valley floor of Kibune. On the way down are two mountain shrines, **Sōjō-ga-dani Fudō-dō** and **Okuno-in Maō-den**, which make pleasant rest stops.

KURAMA ONSEN　　　　　　　ONSEN
(鞍馬温泉; ☎075-741-2131; www.kurama-onsen.co.jp; 520 Kurama Honmachi, Sakyō-ku; adult/child outdoor bath only ¥1000/700, outdoor & indoor bath ¥2500/1600; ⏲10am-9pm; 🚋Eizan line from Demachiyanagi to Kurama) One of the few onsen within easy reach of Kyoto,

Kurama Onsen is a great place to relax after a hike. The outdoor bath (closes at 8pm in winter) has fine views of Kurama-yama, while the indoor bath area includes some relaxation areas in addition to the tubs.

✖ EATING

★YŌSHŪJI　　　　　　　VEGETARIAN ¥
(雍州路; ☎075-741-2848; 1074 Honmachi, Kurama, Sakyō-ku; meals from ¥1080; ⏲10am-6pm Wed-Mon; 🍴; 🚋Eizan line from Demachiyanagi to Kurama) Yōshūji serves superb *shōjin-ryōri* (Buddhist vegetarian cuisine) in a delightful old Japanese farmhouse with an *irori* (open hearth). The house special, a sumptuous selection of vegetarian dishes served in red lacquered bowls, is called *kurama-yama shōjin zen* (¥2700). Or if you just feel like a quick bite, try the *uzu-soba* (soba topped with mountain vegetables; ¥1080).

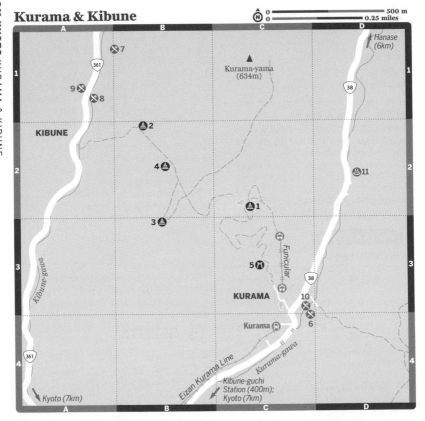

You'll find it halfway up the steps leading to the main gate of Kurama-dera; look for the orange lanterns out the front.

KIBUNE CLUB
CAFE ¥

(貴船倶楽部; ☑075-741-3039; 76 Kibune-chō, Kurama, Sakyō-ku; coffee from ¥500; ⊘11am-5pm, to 6pm Sat & Sun; ℝEizan line from Demachiyanagi to Kibune-guchi) The exposed wooden beams and open, airy feel of this rustic cafe make it a great spot to stop for a cuppa and cake (sets from ¥800) while exploring Kibune. In winter it sometimes cranks up the wood stove, which makes the place rather cosy. Cash only.

ABURAYA-SHOKUDŌ
SHOKUDŌ ¥

(鞍馬　油屋食堂; ☑075-741-2009; 252 Honmachi, Kurama, Sakyō-ku; udon & soba from ¥650; ⊘9am-4.30pm, closed irregularly; ℝEizan line from Demachiyanagi to Kurama) Just down the steps from the main gate of Kuramadera and on the street corner, this classic old-style *shokudō* (all-round restaurant) reminds us of what Japan was like before it got rich. Limited English is spoken but there's an English menu and the service is very friendly. It offers soba, udon and *donburi* (dishes served over rice) bowls at good prices.

HIROBUN
JAPANESE ¥¥

(ひろ文; ☑075-741-2147; 87 Kibune-chō, Kurama, Sakyō-ku; noodles from ¥1300, kaiseki courses from ¥8600; ⊘11am-9pm; ℝEizan line from Demachiyanagi to Kibune-guchi) This is a good place to sample *kawadoko* 'above-river' dining on platforms. A friendly crew of

ladies runs the show and the food is quite good; they are known for their Nagashi *somen* noodles in summer (11am to 4pm), which are served via flowing cold water down sliced bamboo pipes. Look for the black-and-white sign and the lantern. Reserve for dinner.

Note: it usually doesn't accept solo diners for the *kaiseki* (Japanese haute cuisine) courses.

Ōhara

Explore

Since ancient times Ōhara (大原), a quiet farming town about 15km north of Kyoto, has been regarded as a holy site by followers of the Jōdo (Pure Land) school of Buddhism. The region provides a charming glimpse of rural Japan, along with the picturesque Sanzen-in, Jakkō-in and several other fine temples, and is perfect for strolling. It's about a one-hour bus ride from Downtown Kyoto and makes for a pleasant day trip from the city. It's most popular in autumn, when the maple leaves change colour and the mountain views are spectacular.

The Best

➜ **Sight** Sanzen-in

➜ **Place to Eat** Seryō-Jaya (p133)

Getting There & Away

➜ **Bus** From Kyoto Station, Kyoto bus 17 or 18 runs to **Ōhara bus stop**. The ride takes about an hour and costs ¥550. From Keihan line's Sanjō Station, take Kyoto bus 16 or 17 (¥470, 45 minutes). Be careful to board a tan-coloured Kyoto bus, not a green Kyoto City bus of the same number. Note that the one-day bus pass can't be used for this trip as it's outside the zone.

◉ SIGHTS

★SANZEN-IN
BUDDHIST TEMPLE

(三千院; 540 Raikōin-chō, Ōhara, Sakyō-ku; ¥700; ⊘8.30am-5.30pm Mar-Nov, 9am-5pm Dec-Feb; ℝKyoto bus 17 or 18 from Kyoto Station to Ōhara) Famed for its autumn foliage,

Ōhara

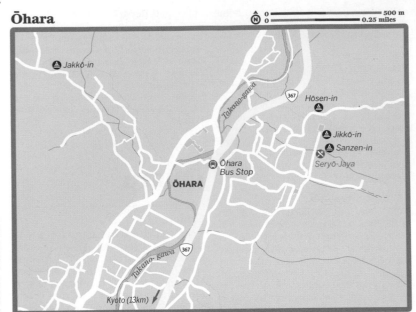

hydrangea garden and stunning Buddha images, this temple is deservedly popular with foreign and domestic tourists alike. The temple's garden, **Yūsei-en**, is one of the most photographed sights in Japan, and rightly so.

Take some time to sit on the steps of the **Shin-den** hall and admire the beauty of the Yūsei-en. Then head off to see **Ōjō-gokuraku-in** (Temple of Rebirth in Paradise), the hall in which stands the impressive Amitabha trinity, a large Amida image flanked by attendants Kannon (goddess of mercy) and Seishi (god of wisdom). After this, walk up to the garden at the back of the temple where, in late spring and summer, you can wander among hectares of blooming hydrangeas.

Sanzen-in was founded in 784 by the priest Saichō and belongs to the Tendai school. Saichō, considered one of the great patriarchs of Buddhism in Japan, also founded Enryaku-ji.

If you're keen for a short hike after leaving the temple, continue up the hill to see the rather oddly named **Soundless Waterfall** (Oto-nashi-no-taki; 音無の滝). Though, in fact, it sounds like any other waterfall, its resonance is believed to have inspired Shōmyō Buddhist chanting.

The approach to Sanzen-in is opposite the bus stop; there is no English sign but you can usually just follow the Japanese tourists. The temple is located about 600m up this walk on your left as you crest the hill.

JIKKŌ-IN
BUDDHIST TEMPLE

(実光院; ☎075-744-2537; 187 Shōrinin-chō, Ōhara, Sakyō-ku; ¥500; ⊗9am-4.30pm; 🚍Kyoto bus 17 or 18 from Kyoto Station to Ōhara) Only about 50m north of Sanzen-in, this small temple is often praised for its lovely garden and *fudan-zakura* cherry tree, which blossoms between October and March. You can enjoy *matcha* (powdered green tea) and a sweet here (¥200).

HŌSEN-IN
BUDDHIST TEMPLE

(宝泉院; ☎075-744-2409; 187 Shōrinin-chō, Ōhara, Sakyō-ku; adult ¥800, child ¥600-700; ⊗9am-5pm; 🚍Kyoto bus 17 or 18 from Kyoto Station to Ōhara) A quiet option, this temple is just down the path west of the entry gate to Shōrin-in. The main tatami room offers a view of a bamboo garden and the surrounding mountains, framed like a painting by the beams and posts of the building. There is also a fantastic 700-year-old pine tree in the garden. The blood-stained Chi Tenjō ceiling boards came from Fushimi-jō castle.

JAKKŌ-IN
BUDDHIST TEMPLE

(寂光院; 676 Kusao-chō, Ōhara, Sakyō-ku; adult/child ¥600/100; ⏱9am-5pm Mar-Nov, to 4.30pm Dec-Feb; 🚌Kyoto bus 17 or 18 from Kyoto Station to Ōhara) Jakkō-in is a small temple on the opposite side of Ōhara from Sanzen-in. It's reached by a pleasant 15-minute walk from the bus station through an 'old Japan' village. Walk out of the bus stop to the traffic lights on the main road, take the small road immediately to the left. Follow it over the bridge and across a road, then continue until you reach a T-intersection. Head left and then continue around to the right a few minutes up the hill.

EATING

SERYŌ-JAYA
SHOKUDO ¥

(芹生茶屋; ☎075-744-2301; 24 Shorinin-chō, Ōhara, Sakyō-ku; lunch sets from ¥1000; ⏱11am-5pm; 🚌Kyoto bus 17 or 18 from Kyoto Station to Ōhara) Seryō-Jaya serves tasty soba noodles and other fare incorporating produce from the area, such as mountain harvested mushrooms and pickled plum. There is outdoor seating in the warmer months. It's the first restaurant at the top of the stairs before the entrance to Sanzen-in. Look for the English menu and food models in the window.

DAY TRIPS FROM KYOTO ŌHARA

WORTH A DETOUR

HIEI-ZAN & ENRYAKU-JI
···

Located atop 848m-high **Hiei-zan** (the mountain that dominates the skyline in the northeast of Kyoto), the **Enryaku-ji** complex is an entire world of temples and dark forests that feels a long way from the hustle and bustle of the city below. A visit here is a good way to spend half a day hiking, poking around temples and enjoying the atmosphere of a key site in Japanese history. There are some incredible views of the mountains and Biwa-ko (Lake Biwa).

Enryaku-ji was founded in 788 by Saichō, also known as Dengyō-daishi, the priest who established the Tenzai school. At its height, Enryaku-ji possessed some 3000 buildings and an army of thousands of *sōhei* (warrior monks). In 1571 Oda Nobunaga saw the temple's power as a threat to his aims to unify the nation and he destroyed most of the buildings, along with the monks inside. Today only three pagodas and 120 minor temples remain.

The complex is divided into three sections: Tōtō, Saitō and Yokawa. The Tōtō (eastern pagoda section) contains the **Kompon Chū-dō** (Primary Central Hall), which is the most important building in the complex. The flames on the three dharma lamps in front of the altar have been kept lit for more than 1200 years.

The Saitō (western pagoda section) contains the **Shaka-dō**, which dates from 1595 and houses a rare Buddha sculpture of the Shaka Nyorai (Historical Buddha). The Saitō, with its stone paths winding through forests of tall trees, temples shrouded in mist and the sound of distant gongs, is the most atmospheric part of the temple. Hold on to your ticket from the Tōtō section, as you may need to show it here.

The **Yokawa** is of minimal interest and a 4km bus ride away from the Saitō area.

You can reach Hiei-zan and Enryaku-ji by train or bus. The most interesting way is the train/cable-car/funicular route starting on the Eizan line from Demachiyanagi Station to Yase Hieizanguchi. Note that this cable-car/funicular route does not operate in winter from early December to mid-March. You can also access Enryaku-ji by the JR Kosei line from Kyoto Station to Heizan Sakamoto Station and then a bus to the Sakamoto cable-car station, which runs year-round. If you're in a hurry or would like to save money, the best way is a direct bus from Sanjō Keihan or Kyoto stations.

Note that the Japanese word for funicular is ropeway. From the funicular station, you can hike through the wooded forest (2.2km) to the Tōtō section. Otherwise, it's a short walk to the bus station, from where you can board a bus to the Enryaku-ji Bus Center for the Tōtō section. You can hike between all three sections; otherwise the bus runs between them all quite frequently.

Nara

Explore

Nara is the most rewarding day trip from Kyoto and it's very easy to reach. By taking the Kintetsu limited express *(tokkyū)* from Kyoto Station to Kintetsu Nara Station, you're there in about 30 minutes – less time than it might take you to visit some of the more distant parts of Kyoto itself.

Whether you go by JR or Kintetsu, grab a map at the nearest tourist information centre (there's one at each station) and walk to Nara-kōen (Nara Park), which contains the thickest concentration of must-see sights in the city, including the awesome Daibutsu (Great Buddha) at Tōdai-ji. On the way, don't miss Isui-en, a compact stunner of a garden. With a 9am start, you can see the sights and be back in Kyoto in time for dinner.

The Best...

→ **Sight** Tōdai-ji

→ **Place to Eat** Kura (p136)

Getting There & Away

→ **Train** The Kintetsu Nara line is the fastest and most convenient connection between Kyoto (Kintetsu Kyoto Station, in Kyoto Station) and central Nara (Kintetsu Nara Station). Comfortable, all-reserved *tokkyū* trains (limited express; ¥1130, 35 minutes) run directly; *kyūkō* trains (express; ¥620, 45 minutes) usually require a change at Yamato-Saidaiji. For Japan Rail Pass holders, the JR Nara line connects JR Kyoto Station with JR Nara Station (*kaisoku,* rapid; ¥710, 45 minutes) with several departures per hour.

Need to Know

→ **Area Code** 🖉0742

→ **Location** 37km south of Kyoto

→ **Tourist Office JR Nara Station Information Centre** (🖉0742-27-2223; www.narashikanko.or.jp; ⊙9am-7pm; 🖀)

👁 SIGHTS

★**TŌDAI-JI**   BUDDHIST TEMPLE
(東大寺; www.todaiji.or.jp; 406-1 Zōshi-chō; adult/child Daibutsu-den ¥600/300, combination

Nara

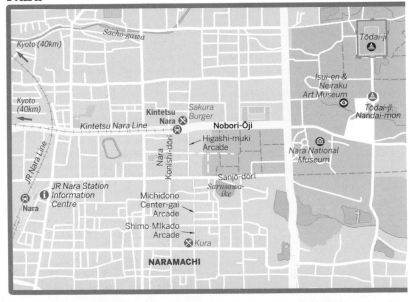

icket incl Tōdai-ji Museum ¥1000/400; ☺Daibut-su-den 8am-5pm Nov-Mar & Oct, 7.30am-5.30pm Apr-Oct) Nara's star attraction is the famous **Daibutsu (Great Buddha)**, centrepiece of this grand temple on the Unesco World Heritage List, with origins going back to AD 728. The Daibutsu statue itself is one of the largest bronze figures in the world and was originally cast in 746. The present statue, recast in the Edo period, stands just over 16m high and consists of 437 tonnes of bronze and 130kg of gold.

The Daibutsu is housed in Tōdai-ji's **Daibutsu-den** (大仏殿, Great Buddha Hall), which itself is the largest wooden building in the world. Incredibly, the present structure, rebuilt in 1709, is a mere two-thirds of the size of the original. Except for the Daibutsu-den, most of Tōdai-ji's grounds can be visited free of charge.

The Daibutsu is an image of Dainichi Nyorai (also known as Vairocana Buddha), the cosmic Buddha believed to give rise to all worlds and their respective Buddhas. Historians believe that Emperor Shōmu ordered the building of the Buddha as a charm against smallpox, which ravaged Japan in preceding years. Over the centuries the statue took quite a beating from earthquakes and fires, losing its head a couple of times (note the slight difference in colour between the head and the body).

As you circle the statue towards the back, you'll see a wooden column with a hole through its base. Popular belief maintains that those who can squeeze through the hole, which is exactly the same size as one of the Great Buddha's nostrils, are ensured of enlightenment. There's usually a line of children waiting to give it a try and parents waiting to snap their pictures. A hint for bigger 'kids': try going through with one or both arms above your head – someone on either end to push and pull helps too.

Though Tōdai-ji is often packed with tour groups and schoolchildren from across the country, it's big enough to absorb huge crowds and it belongs at the top of any Nara itinerary.

TŌDAI-JI NANDAI-MON BUDDHIST TEMPLE
(東大寺南大門, South Gate) The great south gate of Tōdai-ji (p134) contains two fierce-looking Niō guardians. These recently restored wooden images, carved in the 13th century by the famed sculptor Unkei, are some of the finest wooden statues in all of Japan, if not the world. They are truly dramatic works of art and seem ready to spring to life at any moment. The gate is about 200m south of the Tōdai-ji temple enclosure.

★KASUGA TAISHA SHINTO SHRINE
(春日大社; www.kasugataisha.or.jp; 160 Kasugano-chō; ☺6am-6pm Apr-Sep, 6.30am-5pm Oct-Mar) FREE Founded in the 8th century, this sprawling shrine, on the Unesco World Heritage List, lies at the foot of a deeply forested hill, where herds of sacred deer await handouts. Until the end of the 19th century, Kasuga Taisha was completely rebuilt every 20 years, according to Shintō tradition. Pathways are lined with hundreds of lanterns, with many hundreds more in the shrine itself. They're illuminated during the twice-yearly Mantōrō lantern festivals, held in early February and mid-August.

ISUI-EN & NEIRAKU ART MUSEUM GARDENS
(依水園・寧楽美術館; 74 Suimon-chō; museum & garden adult/child ¥900/300; ☺9.30am-4.30pm Wed-Mon, daily Apr, May, Oct & Nov) This exquisite, contemplative Meiji-era garden features abundant greenery, ponds and walkways with stepping stones designed

0 ────── 500 m
Ⓝ 0 ────── 0.25 miles

Nara-kōen

Kasuga Taisha 🏯

Mikasa-yama ▲
(293m)

for each to be observed as you walk, to appreciate their individual beauty. For ¥850 you can enjoy a cup of *matcha* and a Japanese sweet on tatami mats overlooking the garden. Admission covers the adjoining **Neiraku Art Museum**, displaying Chinese and Korean ceramics and bronzes in a quiet setting.

★**NARA NATIONAL MUSEUM**   MUSEUM
(奈良国立博物館, Nara Kokuritsu Hakubutsukan; ☑050-5542-8600; www.narahaku.go.jp; 50 Noboriōji-chō; ¥520, special exhibitions ¥1100-1420; ⏲9.30am-5pm, closed Mon) This world-class museum of Buddhist art is divided into two sections. Built in 1894 and strikingly renovated in 2016, the Nara Buddhist Sculpture Hall & Ritual Bronzes Gallery displays a rotating selection of about 100 *butsu-zō* (statues of Buddhas and bodhisattvas) at any one time, about half of which are national treasures or important cultural properties. Each image has detailed English explanations; the excellent booklet *Viewing Buddhist Sculptures* provides even more detail and is well worth the additional ¥500 donation.

 **EATING**

★**SAKURA BURGER**   BURGERS ¥
(さくらバーガー;   ☑0742-31-3813;   http://sakuraburger.com;   6   Higashimuki-kitamachi; burgers & sandwiches ¥840-1330; ⏲11am-4pm & 5-9pm Fri-Tue) This unassumingly gourmet burger joint is steps north of Kintetsu Nara Station. Expect a lunchtime queue for burgers, sandwiches and hot dogs with your choice of toppings. The namesake Sakura burger comes piled with veggies and a thick slice of house-smoked bacon. They even make their own ketchup. Dessert (while it lasts) is homemade apple pie or caramel walnut tart.

KURA   IZAKAYA ¥
(蔵; ☑0742-22-8771; 16 Kōmyōin-chō; dishes ¥100-1000; ⏲5-10pm) This friendly spot in Naramachi is styled like an old storehouse and has just 16 seats around a counter amid dark-wood panels and an old beer sign. Indulge in *mini-katsu* (mini pork cutlets), *yakitori* (grilled chicken skewers) and *oden* (fish cake and veggie hotpot). Order Nara's own Kazenomori sake (from ¥600), and everyone will think you're a sake sage.

Osaka

Explore

Less than an hour from Kyoto by train, Osaka is the perfect way to experience the energy of a big Japanese city without going all the way to Tokyo. Unlike Kyoto, which contains dozens of discrete tourist sights, Osaka is a city that you experience in its totality. Start with a visit to the castle, Osaka-jō, then head out to Osaka Aquarium (great for kids), and be sure to finish up in Minami (the city's southern hub) to experience the full neon madness that is Osaka after dark.

One day is usually enough to experience Osaka, and trains run late enough to get you back to your lodgings in Kyoto after dinner and a few drinks.

UJI & BYŌDŌ-IN

The small city of Uji is rich in Heian-period culture. Its main claims to fame are Byōdō-in and Ujigami-jinja (both Unesco World Heritage sites) and tea cultivation. Uji can be easily reached by rail from Kyoto on the Keihan Uji line (330, 30 minutes) from Sanjō Station (change at Chushojima) or the JR Nara line (240, 20 minutes) from Kyoto Station.

Byōdō-in (平等院; ☑0774-21-2861; www.byodoin.or.jp; 116 Uji-renge, Uji-shi; adult/child ¥600/300, Hōō-dō guided tour extra ¥300; ⏲gardens 8.30am-5.30pm, Hōō-dō 9.10am-4.10pm, Hoshokan Museum 9am-5pm; ⏏JR Nara line or Keihan line to Uji) is the star attraction in the suburb of Uji. It's home to one of the loveliest Buddhist structures in Japan: the Hōō-dō hall (Phoenix Hall), which is depicted on the back of the Japanese ¥10 coin. Perched overlooking a serene reflecting pond, this refurbished hall is a stunning sight. Paired with a stroll along the banks of the nearby Uji-gawa, this temple makes a good half-day trip out of Kyoto City.

Osaka (Minami Area)

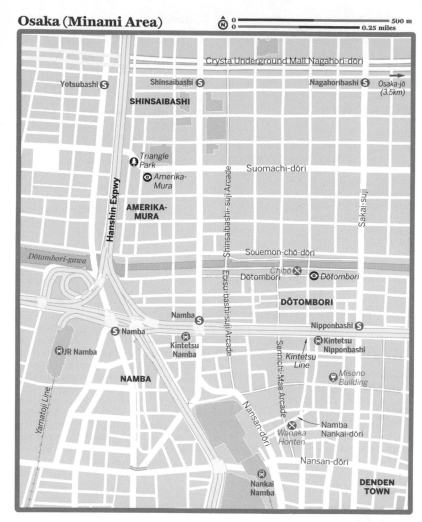

The Best
➡ **Sight** Osaka-jō (p138)
➡ **Place to Eat** Chibō (p139)
➡ **Place to Drink** Misono Building (p139)

Getting There & Away
➡ **Tōkaidō-Sanyō shinkansen** Run from Shin-Osaka Station one stop east to Kyoto Station (¥1420, 14 minutes), but from central Osaka it's easier to get the JR Kyoto line from Osaka Station to Kyoto (¥560, 30 minutes).

➡ **Hankyū Kyoto line** *Tokkyū* (limited express) trains run from Hankyū Umeda Station to Karasuma (¥400, 44 minutes) and Kawaramachi (¥400, 46 minutes) in Kyoto.

➡ **Keihan Main line** *Tokkyū* trains run from Osaka's Yodoyabashi Station, a stop on the Midō-suji subway line, to Gion-Shijō and Sanjō stations (¥410, 45 to 55 minutes) in Kyoto.

Need to Know
➡ **Area Code** ☑06
➡ **Location** 45km southwest of Kyoto

→**Tourist Office Osaka Visitors Information Center Umeda** (大阪市ビジタ ーズインフォメーションセンター・梅田; ☑06-6345-2189; www.osaka-info.jp; JR Osaka Station; ⊙7am-11pm; 🖳JR Osaka, north central exit)

⊙ SIGHTS

★**OSAKA-JŌ**   CASTLE
(大阪城; Osaka Castle; www.osakacastle.net; 1-1 Osaka-jō, Chūō-ku; grounds/castle keep free/¥600, combined with Osaka Museum of History ¥900; ⊙9am-5pm, to 7pm Aug; ⑤Chūō line to Tanimachi 4-chōme, exit 9, 🖳JR Loop line to Osaka-jō-kōen) After unifying Japan in the late 16th century, General Toyotomi Hideyoshi built this castle (1583) as a display of power, using, it's said, the labour of 100,000 workers. Although the present structure is a 1931 concrete reconstruction (refurbished in 1997), it's nonetheless quite a sight, looming dramatically over the surrounding park and moat. Inside is an excellent collection of art, armour, and day-to-day implements related to the castle, Hideyoshi and Osaka. An 8th-floor observation deck has 360-degree views.

★**AMERIKA-MURA**   AREA
(アメリカ村, America Village, Ame-Mura; http://americamura.jp; Nishi-Shinsaibashi, Chūō-ku; ⑤Midō-suji line to Shinsaibashi, exit 7) West of Midō-suji, Amerika-Mura is a compact enclave of hip, youth-focused and offbeat shops, plus cafes, bars, tattoo and piercing parlours, nightclubs, hair salons and a few discreet love hotels. In the middle is **Triangle Park** (三角公園, Sankaku-kōen; Nishi-Shinsaibashi, Chūō-ku; ⑤Midō-suji line to Shinsaibashi, exit 7), an all-concrete 'park' with benches for sitting and watching the fashion parade. Come night, it's a popular gathering spot.

★**DŌTOMBORI**   AREA
(道頓堀; www.dotonbori.or.jp; ⑤Midō-suji line to Namba, exit 14) Highly photogenic Dōtombori is the city's liveliest night spot and centre of the Minami (south) part of town. Its name comes from the 400-year-old canal, Dōtombori-gawa, now lined with pedestrian walkways and a riot of illuminated billboards glittering off its waters. Don't miss the famous **Glico running man** sign. South of the canal is a pedestrianised street that has dozens of restaurants vying for attention with the flashiest of signage.

OSAKA AQUARIUM KAIYŪKAN   AQUARIUM
(海遊館; ☑06-6576-5501; www.kaiyukan.com; 1-1-10 Kaigan-dōri, Minato-ku; adult/child ¥2300/1200; ⊙10am-8pm, closed irregularly; ⑤Chūō line to Osaka-kō, exit 1) Kaiyūkan is among Japan's best aquariums. An 800m-plus walkway winds past displays of sea life from around the Pacific 'ring of fire': Antarctic penguins, coral-reef butterflyfish, unreasonably cute Arctic otters, Monterey Bay seals and unearthly jellyfish. Most impressive is the ginormous central tank, housing a whale shark, manta and thousands of other fish. Note there are also captive dolphins here, which some visitors may not appreciate; there is growing evidence that keeping cetaceans in captivity is harmful for the animals.

WORTH A DETOUR

HIMEJI
....

Japan's most magnificent castle, **Himeji-jō** (姫路城, Himeji Castle; www.himejicastle.jp/en; 68 Honmachi; adult/child ¥1000/300, combination ticket with Kōko-en ¥1040/360; ⊙9am-5pm Sep-May, to 6pm May-Aug) is a Unesco World Heritage Site, national treasure and one of only a handful of original castles remaining (most are modern concrete reconstructions). It's nicknamed Shirasagi-jō (White Egret Castle) for its lustrous white plaster exterior and stately form on a hill rising from the plain. There's a five-storey main *tenshū* (keep) and three smaller keeps, all surrounded by moats and defensive walls punctuated with rectangular, circular and triangular openings for firing guns and shooting arrows.

If you've got a Japan Rail Pass, take the *shinkansen* (bullet train) from Kyoto (from ¥4750, 55 minutes). Otherwise, slower *shinkaisoku* trains on the JR Tōkaidō line run from Kyoto (¥2270, one hour).

 EATING

★WANAKA HONTEN
STREET FOOD ¥

(わなか本店; ☑06-6631-0127; http://takoyaki-wanaka.com; 11-19 Sennichi-mae, Chūō-ku; takoyaki per 8 from ¥450; ☺10am-11pm Mon-Fri, 8.30am-11pm Sat & Sun; ⑤Midō-suji line to Namba, exit 4) This famous *tako-yaki* (octopus dumplings) stand, just north of Dōguya-suji arcade, uses custom copper hotplates (instead of cast iron) to make dumplings that are crisper on the outside than usual (but still runny inside). There's a picture menu and tables and chairs in the back. One popular dish to try is *tako-sen* – two dumplings sandwiched between *sembei* (rice crackers).

★CHIBŌ
OKONOMIYAKI ¥¥

(千房; ☑06-6212-2211; www.chibo.com; 1-5-5 Dōtombori, Chūō-ku; mains ¥885-1675; ☺11am-1am Mon-Sat, to midnight Sun; ⑤Midō-suji line to Namba, exit 14) Chibō is one of Osaka's most famous *okonomiyaki* (savoury pancake) restaurants. It almost always has a line, but it moves fast because there is seating on multiple floors (though you might want to hold out for the coveted tables overlooking Dōtombori canal). Try the house special *Dōtombori yaki*, with pork, beef, squid, shrimp and cheese, and *tonpei-yaki* (omelette wrapped around fried pork).

YOSHINO SUSHI
SUSHI ¥¥

(吉野鮓; ☑06-6231-7181; www.yoshino-sushi.co.jp; 3-4-14 Awaji-machi, Chūō-ku; lunch from ¥3200; ☺11am-1.30pm Mon-Fri; ⑤Midō-suji line to Honmachi, exit 1) In business since 1841, Yoshino specialises in Osaka-style sushi, which is *hako-sushi* ('pressed sushi'). This older version of the dish (compared to the newer, hand-pressed Tokyo-style *nigiri-sushi*) is formed by a wooden mould, resulting in Mondrian-esque cubes of spongy omelette, soy-braised shiitake mushrooms, smokey eel and vinegar-marinated fish on rice. Reservations recommended

⬤ DRINKING & NIGHTLIFE

★MISONO BUILDING
BAR

(味園ビル; 2nd fl, Misono Bldg, 2-3-9 Sennichi-mae, Chūō-ku; ☺6pm-late; ⑤Sakai-suji line to Nipponbashi, exit 5) With a waterfall and grand, spiraling staircase out front, the Misono Building was once a symbol of the high life (c 1956). It's now fallen into a kind of decadent decay, making the building a lure for underground culture types, who have turned the 2nd floor into a strip of tiny, eccentric bars.

Miyama-chō

Explore

The antidote to the urban centres of Kyoto, Osaka and Nara is a visit to Miyama-chō, a collection of rural hamlets in the Kitayama (Northern Mountains) north of Kurama. Miyama-chō has two great sights: Ashiu, a hiker's paradise, and Kita (Kayabuki-noSato), a collection of thatched-roof houses. En route, you can stop at the temple of Bujō-ji. While you can reach all three by public transport, with a car you can hit them all and even do a quick hike in Ashiu in one long day.

The Best

➜ **Sight** Kayabuki-no-Sato (p140)
➜ **Place to Eat** Morishige (p140)

Getting There & Away

➜ **Train and Bus** Take the JR Sagano/San-in line from Kyoto Station to Hiyoshi Station (¥760, 50 minutes), then a bus from Hiyoshi to Kita (Kayabuki-no-Sato; ¥610, 50 minutes). Check this page for the bus schedules (scroll down for English): www.miyamanavi.net/access.

➜ **Car** The fastest road to Miyama-chō is Rte 162 (Shūzankaidō), but there is a lovely but longer (two-hour) option (routes 38/477) via Kurama and over Hanase-tōge and Sasari-tōge passes. This route is also good for getting to Bujō-ji.

➜ **Bus** You can also get to Bujō-ji and Ashū (but not Kita) via Kyoto bus 32 from Demachiyanagi Station in Kyoto. If you're only going to Bujō-ji, get off at Daihizan-guchi bus stop (¥930, 95 minutes) and walk 2km east on the narrow road. If you're going to Ashū, continue to Hirogawara (¥1100, 110 minutes) and hike over Sasari-tōge. From Hirogawara follow the road to the pass and then take the trail down to Ashū (use Shobunsha's Yama-to-Kogen series *Kitayama* map).

DAY TRIPS FROM KYOTO MIYAMA-CHŌ

⊙ SIGHTS

KAYABUKI-NO-SATO
VILLAGE

(かやぶきの里; ☑0771-77-0660; www.kayabuki nosato.com; Kita; ⊙shops & attractions 9am-5pm; ℗) **FREE** Along Rte 38 in the village of Kitamura, you'll find Miyama-chō's star attraction, a hamlet boasting a cluster of some 50 thatched-roof farmhouses, said to be the thickest concentration of these buildings in Japan. Many are now repurposed as museums – such as the Folk Museum (美山民俗資料館, Minzoku Shiryōkan) and Little Indigo Museum (ちいさな藍美術館, Chīsana Aibijutukan) – shops, cafes and inns, amid private homes and temples. Allow an hour or more for a good ramble.

BUJŌ-JI
TEMPLE

(峰定寺; Hanase-Harachi-chō; ¥500, children under 12yr not permitted; ⊙9am-3.30pm, closed on rainy/snowy days & Dec-Mar; ℗) Remote Bujō-ji is a *Shugendo* (mountain asceticism) temple that is also called 'the Northern Omine', a reference to Omine-san in Nara Prefecture, which is a centre for Japan's *yamabushi* (mountain mystics). It's a 430-step climb to the main hall.

First, you surrender your bags and cameras, and get a special pilgrim's bag and staff plus a printout of a mantra to chant as you climb. Only then can you pass through the gate and climb to the hall. Just before the hall, ring the bell, focus your thoughts and then climb to the verandah to soak up the views.

It's off Rte 38, 2km east of the Daihizanguchi bus stop.

✖ EATING

MORISHIGE
NOODLES ¥

(もりしげ; ☑0771-75-1086; Taninoshimo 15, Uchikubo, Miyama-chō; noodle dishes from ¥750; ⊙11am-3pm Wed-Sun) This thatched-roof place on the road to Kayabuki-no-Sato serves simple but tasty noodle dishes as well as *nabe* (hotpot) dishes. Look for it behind the cluster of shrubs and pines.

YURURI
JAPANESE ¥¥¥

(厨房　ゆるり; ☑0771-76-0741; http://youluly. umesao.com; 15 Sano-mae, Morisato; lunch/dinner sets from ¥3240/5400; ⊙closed Jan & Feb; ℗) A wonderfully elegant restaurant serving *kappō-ryōri* (gourmet set menus) in a fine thatched-roof house. It's about 30 minutes north of the Miyama-chō centre by car. Reservations are required (at least one day in advance).

 SLEEPING

MIYAMA HEIMAT YOUTH HOSTEL
HOSTEL ¥

(美山ハイマートユースホステル; ☑0771-75-0997; http://miyama-heimat.com; 57 Obuchi-nakasai, Miyama-chō, Nantan; dm members/nonmembers ¥3460/4100; ℗❀❄🅢) A real rarity, even in Japan: a youth hostel in a *kayabukiya* (thatched-roof house) – you can see some exposed beams built into the ceiling – with both Japanese- and Western-style bedding. Breakfast (¥700) and dinner (¥1240 to ¥4300) cost extra. It's in far western Miyama-chō, so you'll probably want your own transport as it's quite a distance to sights and activities and buses are infrequent.

ASIU YAMA-NO-IE
GUESTHOUSE ¥¥

(芦生山の家; ☑0771-77-0290; www.cans.zaq. ne.jp/asiuyamanoie; Ashū; r per person incl 2 meals ¥7560; ℗❄) Built in the early Aughts, this well-kept, spacious, eight-room wooden guesthouse is super convenient for hikers visiting the virgin forest of Ashū, which is practically next door. Rooms sleep up to four on Japanese-style futons or Western-style bunk beds. Have a Japanese speaker call to reserve.

🛏 Sleeping

You're spoiled for choice in Kyoto. Choose from ryokan (traditional Japanese inns), luxury hotels, business hotels, chic boutique hotels, guesthouses, hostels or capsule hotels. A huge range of hotels and budget guesthouses are clustered around the Kyoto Station area, while the city's best ryokan can be found downtown, spread out in Higashiyama, and in the hills of Arashiyama.

Ryokan

Ryokan are traditional Japanese inns, with tatami mats on the floor and futons instead of beds. The best places serve sublime Japanese cuisine, have extremely attentive service and beautiful rooms, often with garden views. Note that many places that call themselves ryokan are really just hotels with Japanese-style rooms. That isn't to say they aren't comfortable and they will generally cost substantially less than a ryokan. Also note that ryokan may not have private bathrooms, and at some places even toilets may be shared; inquire when you make a reservation. Many traditional ryokan also come without a TV. Finally, note that some simpler ryokan may not accept credit cards.

Business Hotels

'Business hotels' are budget or midrange hotels, usually with cramped but efficient rooms and small 'unit baths' (en suite tub/shower/toilet). In Kyoto, rooms generally cost ¥7000 to ¥12,000 and most accept credit cards. There is no room service but some of the nicer places have large shared baths and saunas on their premises. The front desk staff usually speak some English. These are often your best bet in terms of price versus performance, and there is none of the formality and confusion that you might encounter at a ryokan.

Luxury Hotels

There are several four- and five-star luxury hotels in Kyoto, including some of the top international brands. A number of them are located in the Higashiyama sightseeing district, in quieter spots downtown and in the popular day-trip area of Arashiyama and Sagano. Kyoto's luxury hotels are similar to their counterparts elsewhere in the world, but some have Japanese decorative touches and attentive Japanese service.

Hostels & Guesthouses

Kyoto's hostels have always had a reputation for being well maintained and clean, though they've taken a real step up in recent years. Design-savvy hostels are popping up all over the city, often with a cool cafe-bar in the lobby, and many hostels come with laundry and cooking facilities.

Guesthouses are similar to hostels, though most don't have the various perks thrown in, such as cafes and bars. However, the upside is that many of Kyoto's guesthouses are in traditional buildings, lending them a cosy atmosphere. Both hostels and guesthouses usually have a mix of dorms and private rooms. A bed in a shared dorm typically costs about ¥3000.

Capsule Hotels

A capsule hotel is a simple hotel where you sleep in a small coffin-sized 'capsule' and use shared bathing facilities. Many original capsule hotels simply serve as refuges for sozzled salarymen who've missed the last train home, but Kyoto has a range of capsule hotels geared to travellers, including foreign travellers. Some look like they are straight from the pages of an art and design magazine and feature modern conveniences, such as ambient light systems for waking up without an alarm, TVs with headphones and privacy shades. They're fun and great for a unique Japanese experience, but be prepared for noise.

NEED TO KNOW

Price Ranges

The following price ranges refer to a double room with private bathroom in high season. Ryokan often charge per person, but this is noted as necessary.

¥ less than ¥8000

¥¥ ¥8000–¥25,000

¥¥¥ more than ¥25,000

High Seasons

Kyoto's accommodation can be booked out months in advance in the late March to early April cherry-blossom season and the November autumn-foliage season. It can also be hard to find rooms during Golden Week (29 April to 5 May) and O-bon (mid-August).

Useful Websites

Lonely Planet (lonely planet.com/japan/hotels) Recommendations and bookings.

Japanese Guesthouses (www.japaneseguest houses.com) A site that specialises in ryokan bookings.

Jalan (www.jalan.net) Popular Japanese discount accommodation site, searchable in English.

Tipping

Tipping is not the done thing in Japan.

Tax

As of late 2018, visitors pay a lodging tax of ¥200 to ¥1000 per person per night, based on the room rate, to cope with the surge in the number of tourists visiting Kyoto.

Lonely Planet's Top Choices

Tawaraya (p146) One of the country's best ryokan where everything is exceptional, from the decor and cuisine to the service.

Ritz-Carlton Kyoto (p146) A winning downtown location, mountain views and stunning facilities at this top-notch hotel.

Four Seasons (p148) Outstanding new luxury digs around a beautiful garden and pond in a convenient sightseeing spot.

Lower East 9 Hostel (p144) Mid-century decor, hip cafe-bar and well-kitted-out dorms, south of Kyoto Station.

Shiraume Ryokan (p148) Excellent ryokan experience to be had on one of the city's prettiest streets.

Best By Budget: ¥

¥

Prime Pod (p145) Cool capsule-style hotel in an unbeatable downtown spot

Lower East 9 Hostel (p144) Mid-century furniture and spacious capsule dorms.

K's House Kyoto (p144) An international-style backpackers favourite.

¥¥

Royal Park Hotel The Kyoto (p145) Smart business hotel surrounded by restaurants, bars and shops.

Ibis Styles Kyoto Station (p144) Excellent-value business hotel right next to Kyoto Station.

Ryokan Uemura (p147) Charming ryokan in a perfect sightseeing location.

¥¥¥

Tawaraya (p146) One of the finest ryokan in Japan.

Ritz-Carlton Kyoto (p146) True luxury, incredible location and great views.

Four Seasons (p148) Brand-new luxury digs in the heart of Higashiyama.

Hoshinoya Kyoto (p150) Elegant villa-style accommodation surrounded by nature in Arashiyama – accessed by private boat!

Best Ryokan

Tawaraya (p146) A stay here will be the memory of a lifetime.

Hiiragiya Ryokan (p146) A true Kyoto classic.

Seikōrō (p148) A lovely ryokan that combines great value and elegant rooms.

Shiraume Ryokan (p148) Canal-side beauty with excellent service.

Best For Families

Sakara Kyoto (p149) Excellent apartment-style accommodation designed with families in mind.

Westin Miyako Kyoto (p149) An expansive hotel with all the grounds and facilities to keep everyone in the family occupied and happy.

Koto Inn (p149) Beautiful traditional house in a quiet spot close to many sights.

Best Value for Money

Royal Park Hotel The Kyoto (p145) Excellent-value boutique business hotel with spacious rooms.

Palace Side Hotel (p147) Great travellers' hotel with super-cheap rates.

Ryokan Uemura (p147) Charming ryokan with great rates in the heart of the Southern Higashiyama sightseeing district.

Yumiya Komachi (p147) Beautiful old building with good-value rooms close to the Gion action.

Where to Stay

NEIGHBOURHOOD	FOR	AGAINST
Kyoto Station & South Kyoto	Close to transport; plenty of department store shopping options; good location if you intend to explore the rest of Kansai.	Far from most sightseeing districts; not particularly attractive or astmospheric.
Downtown Kyoto	In the heart of everything – shops, restaurants and nightlife; some nice strolls in the area (eg Ponto-chō); great transport options.	Can feel a little busy; may be noisy; crowded pavements and the odd rowdy (but harmless) reveller on the street on weekend evenings.
Imperial Palace & Around	Relatively quiet and away from crowds. Near plenty of green spaces.	Can be far from most sights and a bit inconvenient; lacking in atmosphere; not too many options for dining, shopping etc.
Gion & Southern Higashiyama	In the heart of the city's main sightseeing district; beautiful walks in every direction, including fantastic evening strolls (eg Gion/Shimbashi, Ninen-zaka).	Fewer dining options than downtown; crowded at most times, particularly in the cherry-blossom season
Northern Higashiyama	Lots of sights nearby; peaceful and green; nice day and evening strolls.	Few negatives, unless you demand to be right in the heart of the shopping and dining district.
Northwest Kyoto	Peaceful and green with some interesting sights; away from the crowds.	Inconvenient and not well served by trains or subways; few dining or shopping options.
Arashiyama & Sagano	One of the main sightseeing districts; magical evening strolls along the river and among the bamboo grove.	On the far west side of town, so all sights except those nearby require a long trek; few good dining or shopping options.

SLEEPING

IF KYOTO IS FULLY BOOKED

Accommodation in Kyoto can get fully booked in the spring high season (late March to late April) and autumn high season (mid-October to the end of November). If you want to visit during these times and cannot find accommodation in Kyoto, don't give up. It's perfectly possible to stay in a nearby city and 'commute' into Kyoto to do your sightseeing, though keep in mind that trains stop running before midnight. Here are some nearby cities where you may be able to find accommodation if Kyoto is full:

Osaka (28 minutes by JR express train, 13 minutes by *shinkansen*) Osaka is a great Plan B if Kyoto is full. Osaka is an attraction in its own right, with plenty of good hotels, restaurants, bars and shops.

Nara (44 minutes by JR express train, 35 minutes by Kintetsu express train) Nara tends to book out at the same times as Kyoto, but it's worth a try. A smaller city, it's a pleasant and relaxing place to stay.

Ōtsu (nine minutes by JR express train) Ōtsu is a small city just over the hill from Kyoto (you could even go there by taxi if you stayed out in Kyoto until after the trains stopped). There's not too much to do here, but if you're just sleeping there, it would be fine.

Nagoya (36 minutes by *shinkansen*) It's a bit of a hike from Kyoto, but if you've got a Japan Rail Pass, it would be possible to stay here while exploring Kyoto. Nagoya is a big city, so there are plenty of hotels, restaurants, bars and shops.

🛏 Kyoto Station & South Kyoto

★ LOWER EAST 9 HOSTEL   HOSTEL ¥

Map p216 (ザ ロウワー イースト ナインホステル; ☑075-644-9990; www.lowereastnine.com; 32 Minamikarasuma-chō, Higashikujō, Minami-ku; dm from ¥3800, tw ¥18,000; ⊝✳🛜; Ⓢ Karasuma line to Kujō Station) A design-savvy hostel in a quiet spot south of Kyoto Station. Dorms come with thoughtful details, while private twin rooms are a little pricey for what you get. It's kitted out with mid-century furniture and has a cool downstairs cafe-bar and communal areas. Right next to Kujō Station.

MOSAIC HOSTEL   HOSTEL ¥

Map p216 (☑075-672-0511; http://mosaichostel. jp; 4-1 Kasuga-chō, Nishikuj, Minami-ku; dm/tw/q from ¥3000/7000/16,000; ⊝✳@🛜; Ⓢ Karasuma line to Kujō Station, Ⓡ Kintetsu Kyoto line to Tōji) There's a lot to like about this new hostel close to Kyoto Station. Capsule-style dorms – a huge 30-bed, or eight-bed female only – come with details like towel hooks, charging points and a privacy curtain, and there's a mix of private rooms. Staff are friendly, the bar serves local craft beer and the rooftop terrace is perfect for a sundowner.

RYOKAN SHIMIZU   RYOKAN ¥

Map p216 (京の宿しみず; ☑075-371-5538; www. kyoto-shimizu.net; 644 Kagiya-chō, Shichijō-dōri, Wakamiya-agaru, Shimogyō-ku; r per person from ¥6000; ⊝✳@🛜; Ⓡ Kyoto Station) Just north of Kyoto Station's Karasuma central gate, this friendly ryokan has a loyal following of foreign guests; it's clean and well run. Rooms are standard ryokan style and come with TV, private bathroom and toilet. Bicycle hire is available. There is a midnight curfew.

MATSUBAYA RYOKAN   RYOKAN ¥

Map p216 (松葉家旅館; ☑075-351-3727; www. matsubayainn.com; Kamijuzūyachō-dōri, Higashinotōin nishi-iru, Shimogyō-ku; s/tw from ¥4600/8600; ✳@🛜; Ⓢ Karasuma line to Gōjō, Ⓡ Kyoto Station) A short walk from Kyoto Station, this ryokan has a range of clean, well-kept rooms and friendly staff. Some rooms look out on small gardens. Western (¥600 to ¥900) or Japanese breakfast (¥1100) is available. There are several serviced apartments in its adjoining Bamboo House section.

K'S HOUSE KYOTO   GUESTHOUSE ¥

Map p216 (ケイズハウス京都; ☑075-342-2444; www.kshouse.jp; 418 Naya-chō, Dotemachi-dōri, Shichijō-agaru, Shimogyō-ku; dm from ¥2400, s/d/tw per person from ¥3800/3250/3250; ⊝@🛜; Ⓡ Kyoto Station) A large guesthouse with private and dorm rooms, which are simple but adequate. The rooftop terrace, patio and attached bar-restaurant make this a sociable spot and a good place to meet other travellers. There's bicycle hire, internet terminals, free wi-fi and a guest-use kitchen. It's a short walk from Kyoto Station.

★ HOTEL ANTEROOM   DESIGN HOTEL ¥¥

(ホテルアンテルーム; ☑075-681-5656; https:// hotel-anteroom.com; 7 Aketa-chō, Higashi-kujō, Minami-ku; s/d from ¥5000/8000, terrace garden r from ¥12,000; ⊝✳🛜; Ⓢ Karasuma line to Kujō) If you're looking for traditional Japanese decor, Anteroom is not for you. This art-and-design hotel is contemporary from its bright lobby gallery with changing exhibitions and whitewashed warehouse building to its artist concept rooms, including a Mika Ninagawa theme room. The terrace garden rooms are the highlight with private Zen garden and a cypress wooden bathtub.

SAKURA TERRACE THE GALLERY   HOTEL ¥¥

Map p216 (☑075-672-0002; http://sakuraterrace-gallery.jp; 39 Kamitonoda-chō, Higashi-kujō, Minami-ku; d from ¥12,000; ⊝✳🛜; Ⓡ Kyoto Station) The station area might not be the most attractive side of the city but Sakura Terrace makes it feel more like you've arrived at a hip LA resort. There's an open-air lounge area with fire pit, restaurant and nightly live music to set the scene. Most of the smart modern rooms come with a balcony and there's an on-site bath.

IBIS STYLES KYOTO STATION   HOTEL ¥¥

Map p216 (イビススタイルズ 京都ステーション; ☑075-693-8444; www.ibisstyles.com; 47 Higashikujō-Kamitonoda-chō, Minami-ku; s/d from ¥7800/10,000; ⊝✳@🛜; Ⓡ Kyoto Station) While the bright, clean rooms are a tight squeeze, they're packed with features at this great business hotel just outside the south entrance to Kyoto Station. Staff and management are extremely efficient, there's free wi-fi and laundry rooms, and breakfast is included, making this fantastic for the price.

KYŌMACHIYA RYOKAN SAKURA – HONGANJI   RYOKAN ¥¥

Map p216 (京町家旅館さくら; ☑075-343-3500; www.kyoto-ryokan-sakura.com; Butsuguya-chō 228, Aburanokōji, Hanayachō-sagaru, Shimogyō-ku; tw from ¥14,000; ⊝✳🛜; Ⓡ Kyoto Station) A relatively short walk from Kyoto Station, with a mix of spotless Japanese and Western-style rooms as well as a variety of traveller-friendly extras. Staff are at home with foreign travellers and English is spoken. It's a bit over to the west side of town, but a bicycle or public transport will get you to the sightseeing spots fairly quickly.

★ **HOTEL GRANVIA KYOTO** HOTEL ¥¥¥
Map p216 (ホテルグランヴィア京都; ☎075-344-8888; www.granviakyoto.com; Karasuma-dōri, Shiokōji-sagaru, Shimogyō-ku; r from ¥28,000; ◍❋@☂❄; ℝKyoto Station) Imagine being able to step out of bed and straight into the bullet train. This is almost possible at this location directly above Kyoto Station. The rooms are clean, spacious and elegant; some get a glimpse of the *shinkansen* on the tracks while others look out directly at Kyoto Tower.

🛏 Downtown Kyoto

★ **PRIME POD** HOSTEL ¥
Map p210 (プライムポッド; ☎075-252-0341; https://theprimepod.jp; 9th fl, Felicita Sanjokiyamachi Bldg, Sanjo-dōri, Kawaramachi-dōri higashi-iru, Nagakyo-ku; small/large pods from ¥3000/4400; ◍❋☂; ⓢTōzai line to Kyoto-Shiyakusho-mae, ℝKeihan line to Sanjō) Prime Pod takes a hostel and capsule hotel and rolls them into something from a design magazine in a hard-to-beat location. Dorms come with small and large wooden 'pods', with quality mattress, laptop-sized safe, TV with headphones and light-blocking curtains. The lobby-lounge area has views, low tables and paper lanterns.

9 HOURS CAPSULE HOTEL CAPSULE HOTEL ¥
Map p210 (☎075-353-7337; https://ninehours.co.jp/en/kyoto; 588 Teianmaeno-chō, Shijō, Shimogyō-ku; capsule ¥4900; ◍☂; ℝHankyū line to Kawaramachi) If George Lucas ever designed a hotel, it might look something like this. With its sci-fi all-white design, it's easy to imagine Storm Troopers climbing into the coffin-sized capsules and waiting for the built-in ambient light system to lull them to sleep. Just pray Chewbacca's not your neighbour as you can hear a pin drop in this place.

★ **ROYAL PARK HOTEL
THE KYOTO** HOTEL ¥¥
Map p210 (ロイヤルパークホテル ザ 京都; ☎075-241-1111; www.rph-the.co.jp; Sanjō-dōri, Kawaramachi higashi-iru, Nakagyō-ku; s/d from ¥11,000/13,000; ❋@☂; ⓢTōzai line to Kyoto-Shiyakusho-mae, ℝKeihan line to Sanjō) On Sanjō-dōri, a stone's throw from the river, the Royal Park has a super-convenient location, with shops and restaurants within easy walking distance. The hotel has a boutique-business

feel, and rooms are slightly larger than most in the city. The French bakery downstairs is a perfect stop for breakfast pastries.

**LEN HOSTEL KYOTO
KAWARAMACHI** HOSTEL ¥¥
Map p210 (☎075-361-1177; https://backpackersjapan.co.jp/kyotohostel; 709-3 Uematsu-chō, Kawaramachi-dōri, Shimogyō-ku; dm/tw/d from ¥2600/6800/8800; ◍❋@☂; ℝHankyū line to Kawaramachi or Keihan line to Kiyomizu-Gojō) Another cool new hostel popping up in Kyoto, Len has minimalist yet stylish mixed dorms, as well as a female-only dorm, and private rooms with shared bathroom. Rooms are on the small side but you can hang out in the hip downstairs cafe-bar. The location is convenient for Gion and downtown.

**MITSUI GARDEN
SHINMACHI BETTEI** HOTEL ¥¥
Map p210 (三井ガーデンホテル京都新町　別邸; ☎075-257-1131; www.gardenhotels.co.jp/eng/kyoto-shinmachi; Shinmachi-dōri, Rokkaku-sagaru, Nakagyō-ku; d&tw from ¥18,000; ◍❋☂; ⓢKarasuma line to Shijō) In a quiet downtown location yet still close to the action, this chic hotel blends traditional Japanese and modern design with *shōji* (sliding rice-paper screen doors) and paper lanterns in the attractive lobby and spacious rooms. There's an on-site communal bath, a Japanese restaurant, laundry facilities and helpful staff.

UNIZO INN KAWARAMACHI SHIJO HOTEL ¥¥
Map p210 (ホテルユニゾ京都; ☎075-252-3489; www.unizo-hotel.co.jp; Kawaramachi-dōri, Sanjō-sagaru, Nakagyō-ku; s/tw from ¥9000/12,000; ◍❋@☂; ⓢTōzai line to Kyoto-Shiyakusho-mae, ℝHankyū line to Kawaramachi) They don't get more convenient than this business hotel, smack in the middle of Kyoto's nightlife, shopping and dining district. The colour scheme is a little drab, but rooms are not too poky and have everything you need. It's well run with helpful staff; there's laundry facilities and a downstairs cafe-restaurant.

KYOTO ITOYA HOTEL HOTEL ¥¥
Map p210 (京都糸屋ホテル; ☎075-365-1221; http://itoyahotel.com; 712 Yakushimae-chō, Karasuma-dōri, Shimogyō-ku; d&tw from ¥10,000; ◍❋☂; ⓢKarasuma line to Shijō) Good things come in small packages at Itoya – the rooms aren't huge but they are stylish, contemporary and excellent value. English-speaking staff go out of their way to make you feel welcome, there's an inviting lounge-cafe area with a balcony overlooking Karasuma-dōri, and bicycle rental to boot.

KAEDE GUESTHOUSE
HOSTEL ¥¥

Map p210 (☎075-344-8780; www.kaede-kyoto.jp; 465-2 Senshoji-chō, Shimogyō-ku; dm/s/d from ¥2300/7000/12,000; ☻❉☎; Ⓢ Karasuma line to Shijō) Ignore the unattractive former apartment building facade, this new hostel brightens up significantly once inside. Dorms come with everything you need, including lockers and curtains for privacy, while private rooms feature futons on raised wooden platforms, and some rooms have views of Bukkō-ji temple. The rooftop terrace is a great spot for a drink.

★TAWARAYA
RYOKAN ¥¥¥

Map p210 (俵屋; ☎075-211-5566; 278 Nakahakusan-chō, Fuyachō, Oike-sagaru, Nakagyō-ku; r per person incl 2 meals ¥49,680-86,940; ☻❉@☎; Ⓢ Tōzai line to Kyoto-Shiyakusho-mae or Karasuma-Oike) Operating for more than three centuries, this is one of the finest places to stay in Japan. From decor to service to food, everything is the best available, and this is reflected in the price. It's a very intimate, warm place that has seen many loyal guests over the years, from Marlon Brando to Steve Jobs. Rooms are kitted out in a mix of traditional Japanese-style and some mid-century decor, and the private wooden bathtubs have stunning garden views. It's centrally located within an easy walk of two subway stations and plenty of good restaurants. Book at least a few months in advance, much more if you plan to visit during peak periods.

★HIIRAGIYA RYOKAN
RYOKAN ¥¥¥

Map p210 (柊家; ☎075-221-1136; www.hiiragiya.co.jp; Nakahakusan-chō, Fuyachō, Aneyakōji-agaru, Nakagyō-ku; r per person incl 2 meals ¥34,000-90,000; ☻❉@☎; Ⓢ Tōzai line to Kyoto-Shiyakusho-mae) This elegant ryokan has long been favoured by celebrities from around the world. Facilities and services are excellent and the location hard to beat. Opt for the new wing for a polished sheen; alternatively, request an older room if you fancy some 'old Japan' *wabi-sabi* (imperfect beauty). Room 14 played host to Japanese writer Yasunari Kawabata back in the day and is around 200 years old. You'll need to reserve months in advance; reservation is preferred by email.

RITZ-CARLTON KYOTO
HOTEL ¥¥¥

Map p210 (ザ・リッツ・カールトン京都; ☎075-746-5555; www.ritzcarlton.com; 543 Hokoden-chō, Nijō-Ōhashi-hotori, Nakagyō-ku; r ¥65,000-210,000; ❉@☎☒; Ⓢ Tōzai line to Kyoto-Shiyakusho-mae, Ⓡ Keihan line to Sanjō or Jingū-Marutamachi) An oasis of luxury that commands some of the best views of any hotel in the city – it's located on the banks of the Kamo-gawa and huge windows in the east-facing rooms take in the whole expanse of the Higashiyama Mountains. The rooms are superbly designed and supremely comfortable, with plenty of Japanese touches.

YOSHIKAWA
RYOKAN ¥¥¥

Map p210 (吉川; ☎075-221-5544; www.kyoto-yoshikawa.co.jp; 135 Matsushita-chō, Tominokōji, Oike-sagaru, Nakagyō-ku; r per person incl 2 meals from ¥30,000; ❉@☎; Ⓢ Tōzai or Karasuma lines to Karasuma-Oike or Kyoto-Shiyakusho-mae) In the heart of downtown, within easy walking distance of two subway stations and the dining and nightlife district, this superb ryokan has beautiful rooms and a stunning garden. The ryokan is famous for its attached tempura restaurant (p71) and its meals are of a high standard. All rooms have private bathrooms with wooden tubs and toilets.

KYOTO HOTEL ŌKURA
HOTEL ¥¥¥

Map p210 (京都ホテルオークラ; ☎075-211-5111; http://okura.kyotohotel.co.jp; 537-4 Ichinofunairi-chō, Kawaramachi-dōri, Oike, Nakagyō-ku; s/d/ste from ¥22,000/27,000/42,000; ☻❉@☎☒; Ⓢ Tōzai line to Kyoto-Shiyakusho-mae) This towering hotel in the centre of town commands an impressive view of the Higashiyama Mountains. Rooms are clean and spacious and many have great views (7th floor and above), especially the excellent corner suites. You can access the Kyoto subway system directly from the hotel, which is convenient on rainy days or if you have luggage.

🛏 Imperial Palace & Around

BIRD HOSTEL
HOSTEL ¥

Map p220 (☎075-744-1875; www.birdhostel.com; 190 Joshinyo-chō, Marutamachi-dōri, Nagakyō-ku; dm/d/f incl breakfast from ¥2900/6800/16,000; ☻❉☎; Ⓢ Karasuma line to Marutamachi) This cool, spotless and well-run hostel is just a hop from the Imperial Palace Park and has a range of dorms, including a female-only option. Dorms are equipped with everything you need, there are a few compact double rooms and a family room with leafy views. It's rounded out with bicycle rental, a hip cafe-lounge area and laundry facilities.

NOKU KYOTO
BOUTIQUE HOTEL ¥¥

Map p220 (ノク京都, Noku Roxy ☎075-211-0222; www.nokuroxy.com; 205-1 Okura-cho, Karasuma-dōri, Maratumachi-sagaru, Nakagyō-ku; r ¥16,000-

33,000; 🌐 ✳️ 📶; §Karasuma line to Marutamachi) A stylish boutique hotel set over six floors within sight of the Imperial Palace Park and next to Marutamachi Station. The minimalist elegant rooms are all blonde wood with splashes of colour provided in the bedhead artwork. Some rooms have park views, and there is a basement bar and restaurant.

RYOKAN RAKUCHŌ
RYOKAN ¥¥

Map p220 (洛頂旅館; 📞075-721-2174; www.rakucho-ryokan.com; 67 Higashi-hangi-chō, Shimogamo, Sakyō-ku; s/tw/tr ¥5300/9240/12,600; 🌐 ✳️ @ 📶; 🚌Kyoto City bus 205 to Furitsudaigaku-mae, §Karasuma line to Kitaōji) There is a lot to appreciate about this fine eight-room ryokan in the northern part of town: there is a nice little garden; it's entirely nonsmoking; and rooms are clean and simple (no TV). Meals aren't served, but staff can provide you with a good map of local eateries. The downside is the somewhat out-of-the-way location.

PALACE SIDE HOTEL
HOTEL ¥¥

Map p220 (ザ・パレスサイドホテル; 📞075-415-8887; www.palacesidehotel.co.jp; Okakuen-chō, Karasuma-dōri, Shimotachiuri-agaru, Kamigyō-ku; s/tw/d from ¥6300/10,200/10,200; 🌐 ✳️ @ 📶; §Karasuma line to Marutamachi) Overlooking the Imperial Palace Park, this great-value hotel is looking a little dated but has friendly English-speaking staff, great service, washing machines, an on-site restaurant, well-maintained rooms and a communal guest-use kitchen. Free one-hour Japanese lessons are held in the evenings.

🛌 Gion & Southern Higashiyama

BOOK + BED HOSTEL
HOSTEL ¥

Map p218 (http://bookandbedtokyo.com/en/kyoto; 9th fl, Kamogawa Bldg, 200 Nakano-chō, Nishi-iru, Higashiyama-ku; compact/standard bed from ¥4300/4800; 🌐 ✳️ 📶; 🚆Keihan line to Gion-Shijō) With a cracking location and a 'novel' idea, this hostel is perfect budget accommodation in the heart of Gion. As expected, books dominate the decor; they hang from the ceiling and capsule-style beds nestle in among packed bookshelves. Room 19 comes with a river view, and views from the common area take in the Higashiyama mountains.

YUMIYA KOMACHI
GUESTHOUSE ¥

Map p218 (弓矢小町; 📞080-4242-9895; www.yumiyakomachi.com; 67-5 Yumiya-chō, Higashiyama-ku; r from ¥7000; 🌐 ✳️ 📶; 🚌Kyoto City bus 206 to Kiyomizu-michi, 🚆Keihan line to Kiyomizu-Gojō) Hidden a short walk from Gion, Yumiya Komachi is a delightful guesthouse run by friendly owner, Rico. The 100-year-old building is the former home of a dance teacher who taught geisha in Gion, and it offers Japanese-style rooms and one Western-style, all with shared bathroom. Curfew is 11.30pm.

JAM HOSTEL KYOTO GION
GUESTHOUSE ¥

Map p218 (JAM ジャムホステル京都祇園; 📞075-201-3374; 170 Tokiwa-chō, Higashiyama-ku; dm/d from ¥1500/4000; 🌐 ✳️ 📶; 🚆Keihan line to Gion Shijō) Has a convenient location on the edge of Gion, and a sake bar downstairs that is a convivial place for guests to mix with locals. It has simple but clean dorm rooms with lockers and power points for each bed, and a few private rooms. There is no kitchen but a fridge and kettle for guest use.

GOJŌ GUEST HOUSE
GUESTHOUSE ¥

Map p218 (五条ゲストハウス; 📞075-525-2299; www.gojo-guest-house.com; 3-396-2 Gojōbashi higashi, Higashiyama-ku; dm/tw/tr ¥2600/5500/7000; ✳️ @ 📶; 🚆Keihan line to Kiyomizu-Gojō) A fine budget guesthouse in an old wooden Japanese house, which makes the place feel more like a ryokan than your average guesthouse. There are male and female dorms, as well as private rooms. The dining area and cafe is a good place to meet other travellers. Staff speak English and can help with travel advice. They have another guesthouse nearby with private rooms and vintage furniture.

RYOKAN UEMURA
RYOKAN ¥¥

Map p218 (旅館うえむら; uemura.ryokan3hsl@gmail.com; Ishibe-kōji, Shimogawara, Higashiyama-ku; r per person incl breakfast ¥10,000; 🌐 ✳️ 📶; 🚌Kyoto City bus 206 to Higashiyama-Yasui) This beautiful little ryokan is on a quaint, quiet cobblestone alley, just down the hill from some of Kyoto's most important sights. The owner prefers bookings by fax or email. Book well in advance, as there are only four rooms. Take note: there's a 10pm curfew.

KYOTO YOSHIMIZU INN
RYOKAN ¥¥

Map p218 (京都吉水; 📞075-551-3995; www.yoshimizu.com; Maruyama-kōen, Bentendō-ue, Higashiyama-ku; r per person from ¥6900; 🌐 ✳️ @ 📶; 🚌Kyoto City bus 206 to Gion) Perched at the base of the Higashiyama mountains at the top of Maruyama-kōen, Yoshimizu is surrounded by greenery and it's like staying in the countryside (but only 15 minutes' walk to Gion). There is one room with Western-style beds instead of futons. Breakfast is included, and a few rooms look out over soothing maple leaves or bamboo groves.

★**FOUR SEASONS** HOTEL ¥¥¥
Map p218 (☎075-541-8288; www.fourseasons.com/kyoto; 445-3 Maekawa-chō, Myohoin, Higashiyama-ku; r from ¥80,000; ⊕✳🖥❄; ⓡKeihan line to Shichijō) Extravagant and contemporary yet restrained and traditional, this is an impressive new luxury hotel in the Higashiyama sightseeing district. The long bamboo-lined entrance brings you to a vast airy lobby with huge floor-to-ceiling windows looking out over the 800-year-old koi-filled pond and stunning gardens. The elegant rooms feature dark-wood floors, iPads, huge TVs, Nespresso machines and marble bathrooms.

HYATT REGENCY KYOTO HOTEL ¥¥¥
Map p218 (ハイアットリージェンシー京都; ☎075-541-1234; www.kyoto.regency.hyatt.com; 644-2 Sanjūsangendō-mawari, Higashiyama-ku; r from ¥30,000; ⊕✳@🖥; ⓡKeihan line to Shichijō) The Hyatt Regency is arguably one of Kyoto's best hotels and sits at the southern end of the Southern Higashiyama sightseeing district. Elegant and contemporary rooms feature kimono tapestry walls and traditional paper lanterns, and come packed with features including a tablet for ordering room service. The staff are extremely efficient and helpful, while the on-site restaurants and Tōzan Bar (p95) are excellent.

★**SHIRAUME RYOKAN** RYOKAN ¥¥¥
Map p218 (白梅; ☎075-561-1459; www.shiraume-kyoto.jp; Gion Shimbashi, Shirakawa hotori, Shijōnawate-agaru, higashi-iru, Higashiyama-ku; r per person incl 2 meals from ¥33,000; ✳@🖥; ⓡKeihan line to Gion-Shijō) Looking out over the Shirakawa Canal in Shimbashi, a lovely street, this ryokan offers excellent location, atmosphere and service. The decor is traditional with a small inner garden, and all five rooms have their own private bathroom with wooden bathtubs. This is a great spot to sample the Japanese ryokan experience.

★**SEIKŌRŌ** RYOKAN ¥¥¥
Map p218 (晴鴨楼; ☎075-561-1171; www.seikoro.com; 467 Nishi Tachibana-chō, 3 chō-me, Toiyamachi-dōri, Gojō-sagaru, Higashiyama-ku; r per person incl 2 meals ¥30,000-45,000; ⊕✳@🖥; ⓡKeihan line to Kiyomizu-Gojō) A classic ryokan with a grandly decorated, homey lobby. It's spacious, with excellent, comfortable rooms, attentive service and a fairly convenient midtown location. Several rooms look over gardens and all have private bathrooms featuring wooden bathtubs. Room only without meals starts from about ¥17,000.

MOTONAGO RYOKAN ¥¥¥
Map p218 (旅館元奈古; ☎075-561-2087; www.motonago.com; 511 Washio-chō, Kōdaiji-michi, Higashiyama-ku; r from ¥24,000; ⊕@🖥; ⓡKyoto City bus 206 to Gion) This ryokan may have the best location of any in the city and it hits all the right notes: classic decor, friendly English-speaking staff, nice wooden communal bathtubs and a few small Japanese gardens. There are 11 rooms; some have private bathroom, and one room has twin Western beds.

SLEEPING GION & SOUTHERN HIGASHIYAMA

STAYING IN A RYOKAN

Due to language difficulties and unfamiliarity, staying in a ryokan is not as straightforward as staying in a Western-style hotel. However, with a little education it can be a breeze, even if you don't speak a word of Japanese. Here's the basic drill.

When you arrive, leave your shoes in the *genkan* (entry area/foyer) and step up into the reception area. Here, you'll be asked to check in. You'll then be shown around the place and to your room, where you will be served a cup of tea. You'll note that there is no bedding to be seen in your room – your futons are in the closets and will be laid out later. You can leave your luggage anywhere except the *tokonoma* (sacred alcove) that will usually contain some flowers or a hanging scroll. If it's early enough, you can then go out to do some sightseeing.

When you return, you'll change into your *yukata* (light cotton kimono) and be served dinner in your room or in a dining room. After dinner, it's time for a bath. If it's a big place, you can generally bathe anytime in the evening until around 11pm. If it's a small place, you'll be given a time slot. While you're in the bath, some mysterious elves will go into your room and lay out your futon so that it will be waiting for you when you return all toasty from the bath.

In the morning, you'll be served a Japanese-style breakfast (some places these days serve a simple Western-style breakfast for those who can't stomach rice and fish in the morning). You pay at check out, which is usually around 11am.

GION HATANAKA RYOKAN ¥¥¥
Map p218 (祇園畑中; ☎075-541-5315; www.
thehatanaka.co.jp; 505 Gion-machi, Minami-gawa,
Higashiyama-ku; d from ¥31,000; ☻☎; ➡Kyoto
City bus 206 to Higashiyama-Yasui) A fine ryokan
right in the heart of the Southern Higashiyama sightseeing district (less than a minute's walk from Yasaka-jinja). Despite being
fairly large, this 21-room ryokan manages
to retain an intimate and private feeling. In
addition to bathtubs in each room, there is
a huge wooden communal bath. The rooms
are clean, well designed and relaxing.

SAKARA KYOTO INN ¥¥¥
Map p218 (桜香楽; ☎075-708-5400; www.sak
arakyoto.com; 541-2 Furukawa-chō, Higashiyama-
ku; r ¥11,000-40,200; ❋☎; ⑤Tōzai line to Higashiyama) This modern Japanese-style inn
is located in a covered pedestrian shopping
arcade just south of Sanjō-dōri, about 50m
from Higashiyama Station. It's great for couples and families; rooms are well maintained
and homey with bath/shower, kitchenette
and laundry facilities. It also has a couple of
machiya (traditional Japanese townhouse)
rental houses nearby and in Gion.

OLD KYOTO RENTAL HOUSE ¥¥¥
Map p218 (☎075-533-7775; www.oldkyoto.com;
563-12 Komatsu-chō, Higashiyama-ku; per night
from ¥31,000; ❋☎; ➡Kyoto City bus 206 to
Higashiyama-Yasui, ⑧Keihan line to Gion-Shijō)
The Old Kyoto group manages three beautiful traditional Japanese houses on the edge
of Gion that are perfect for those seeking a
more local experience. Gion House, Amber
House and Indigo House are all kitted out
stylishly in 'Japanese meets mid-century'
decor, and can accommodate up to four people. Minimum stay five nights. From each
property, a few minutes' walk will bring
you to Gion's most atmospheric lanes. The
houses come with everything you need, including a phone with a local SIM. Old Kyoto
also manages the Gion Apartments, which
are great for long-term visitors (one-month
minimum stay from ¥9800 per night).

🛏 Northern Higashiyama

GUESTHOUSE WARAKU-AN GUESTHOUSE ¥
Map p214 (ゲストハウス　和楽庵; ☎075-771-
5575; http://kyotoguesthouse.net; 19-2 Sannō-
chō, Shōgoin, Sakyō-ku; dm/d/tw from ¥2500/
6000/6500; ☻❋@☎; ➡Kyoto City bus 206 to
Kumano-jinja-mae) Convenient to Okazaki, this
traditional house has Japanese-style tatami-
mat rooms and a three-bed male and four-

bed female dorm. The deluxe double is the
pick with garden view, and the dorms come
with bamboo partitions and reading lamps.
There's a relaxing lounge area next to the
garden, no curfew and it has friendly staff.
It's close to the Kyoto Handicraft Centre.

ROKU ROKU HOSTEL ¥
Map p214 (ろくろく; www.rokuroku.kyoto.jp; 28-1
Nishiteranomae-chō, Shishigatani, Sakyō-ku; dm/
tw per person ¥2500/4300; ☻❋☎; ➡Kyoto City
bus 5 to Shinnyodo-mae or 17 to Kinrinshako-mae)
A great choice for budget digs, this modern
hostel is within walking distance of the Path
of Philosophy and many temples. Dorms
are a little cramped but have in-room bathrooms, while twin rooms have a small tatami-mat sitting area. There is a traditional
house nearby with a lounge to relax in, and it
has free laundry facilities and bicycle rental.

**KYOTO GARDEN
RYOKAN YACHIYO** RYOKAN ¥¥¥
Map p214 (旅館八千代; ☎075-771-4148; www.
ryokan-yachiyo.com; 34 Fukuchi-chō, Nanzen-ji,
Sakyō-ku; r per person ¥10,000-30,000, incl 2
meals ¥30,000-70,000; ☻❋☎; ⑤Tōzai line to
Keage) Located just down the street from
Nanzen-ji, this beautiful 20-room ryokan
has a choice of traditional or modern rooms,
all with private bathroom and TV. Some
rooms look out over private gardens and
four rooms come with an open-air wooden
bath. English-speaking staff are available.

KOTO INN RENTAL HOUSE ¥¥¥
Map p214 (古都イン; koto.inn@gmail.com; 373
Horiike-chō, Higashiyama-ku; per night for 2/3/4
people US$215/255/285; ☻❋☎; ⑤Tōzai line to
Higashiyama) Located near the Higashiyama
sightseeing district in a lovely canal setting,
this immaculate vacation rental is good for
families, couples and groups who want a bit
of privacy. It's got everything you need and
is decorated with lovely Japanese antiques.
While the building is traditionally Japanese, all the facilities are fully modernised.
There's a two-night minimum stay.

★WESTIN MIYAKO KYOTO HOTEL ¥¥¥
Map p214 (ウェスティン都ホテル京都; ☎075-
771-7111; www.miyakohotels.ne.jp/westinkyoto;
Keage, Sanjō-dōri, Higashiyama-ku; d & tw from
¥26,460, Japanese-style r from ¥24,840; ☻❋
@☎; ⑤Tōzai line to Keage, exit 2) Overlooking
the Higashiyama district (meaning it's one
of the best locations for sightseeing in Kyoto), this *grande dame* of Kyoto hotels occupies a commanding position. Rooms on the
north side have great views over the city to

the Kitayama mountains. There is a fitness centre with a swimming pool (extra charge), as well as a private garden and walking trail.

🛏 Northwest Kyoto

SHUNKŌ-IN
TEMPLE LODGE ¥

Map p222 (春光院; ☎075-462-5488; www.shun koin.com; 42 Myōshinji-chō, Hanazono, Ukyō-ku; s ¥7000, d/tr per person ¥6000/5500; ❄@🤖; 🚃JR Sagano (San-in) line to Hanazono) This is a *shukubō* (temple lodging) at a subtemple in Myōshin-ji (p115). It's very comfortable, with wi-fi and free bicycle hire, and the main priest here speaks fluent English. For an extra ¥500 you can try Zen meditation and go on a guided tour of the temple. Being in the temple at night is a very special experience.

UTANO YOUTH HOSTEL
HOSTEL ¥

Map p222 (宇多野ユースホステル; ☎075-462-2288; www.yh-kyoto.or.jp/utano; 29 Nakayama-chō, Uzumasa, Ukyō-ku; dm/tw per person ¥3390/4110; @🤖; 🚃Kyoto City bus 26 to Yūsu-Hosuteru-mae) A large, modern, well-organised and well-maintained hostel convenient for the sights of Northwest Kyoto (though it's a hike to reach other parts of town). There are a few Japanese-style tatami rooms if you prefer a more traditional feel, and friendly staff and nightly cultural events are added bonuses. There is an 11.30pm curfew.

★MOSAIC MACHIYA HOSTEL
HOSTEL ¥¥

Map p222 (☎075-466-0510; http://mosaichostel. jp/mosaic-machiya-kamishichiken; 702 Shinsei-chō, Kamigyō-ku; tw/tr from ¥8000/15,000; ❄✳🤖; 🚃Kyoto bus 50 to Kamishichiken) As the name suggests, this intimate hostel is set in a restored *machiya* on an atmospheric street in the old geisha district of Kamishichiken near Kitano Tenman-gū. It offers five simple Japanese-style rooms and there is a lovely private bath plus a courtyard garden. Mingle with the friendly staff and other travellers in the small lobby bar.

🛏 Arashiyama & Sagano

★JAPANING HOTEL LIV RANROKAKU KYOTO
HOTEL ¥¥

Map p223 (ジャパニングホテル リヴ 嵐楼閣; 54-2 Arashiyama Nakaoshita-chō, Nishikyō-ku; r ¥16,000-30,000; ❄✳🤖; 🚃Kyoto City bus 28 from Kyoto Station to Arashiyama-Tenryuji-mae, 🚃JR Sagano (San-in) line to Saga-Arashiyama or Hankyū line to Arashiyama, change at Katsura) It's not easy to find accommodation with a great location and spacious rooms for anything less than top-dollar in Arashiyama, so thankfully there is this hotel. Some rooms have separate tatami mat areas and the riverside rooms have sensational views. The on-site baths are perfect after a day on your feet.

★HOSHINOYA KYOTO
RYOKAN ¥¥¥

Map p223 (星のや京都; ☎075-871-0001; www. hoshinoyakyoto.jp; 11-2 Arashiyama Genrokuzan-chō, Nishikyō-ku; r per person incl meals from ¥81,000; ❄✳🤖; 🚃Kyoto City bus 28 from Kyoto Station to Arashiyama-Tenryuji-mae, 🚃JR Sagano (San-in) line to Saga-Arashiyama or Hankyū line to Arashiyama, change at Katsura) In a secluded area on the south bank of the Hozu-gawa in Arashiyama (upstream from the main sightseeing district), this modern take on the classic Japanese inn is becoming a favourite of well-heeled visitors in search of privacy and a unique experience. Rooms feature incredible views of the river and surrounding mountains. The best part is the approach: you'll be chauffeured by private boat from a dock near Togetsu-kyō bridge to the inn (on days following heavy rains, you'll have to go by car). This is one of the most unique places to stay in Kyoto. If you tire of relaxing with the views, it offers meditation classes as well as incense and tea ceremonies.

SUIRAN
HOTEL ¥¥¥

Map p223 (翠嵐; ☎075-872-0101; www.suiran-kyoto.com; 12 Susukinobaba-chō, Saga-Tenryū-ji, Ukyō-ku; r from ¥70,000; ❄✳🤖; 🚃Kyoto City bus 28 from Kyoto Station to Arashiyama-Tenryuji-mae, 🚃JR Sagano (San-in) line to Saga-Arashiyama or Hankyū line to Arashiyama, change at Katsura) The newest luxury hotel in Arashiyama, located in a prized riverside spot that offers complete privacy within easy walking distance to everything in town. Rooms are chic, elegant and decorated with a fusion of traditional Japanese and contemporary design. Many come with private open-air bath.

ARASHIYAMA BENKEI
RYOKAN ¥¥¥

Map p223 (嵐山辨慶旅館; ☎075-872-3355; www.benkei.biz; 34 Susukinobaba-chō, Saga Tenryu-ji, Ukyō-ku; r per person incl meals from ¥28,000; ✳🤖; 🚃Kyoto City Bus 28 from Kyoto Station to Arashiyama-Tenryuji-mae, 🚃JR Sagano (San-in) line to Saga-Arashiyama or Hankyū line to Arashiyama, change at Katsura) This elegant ryokan, with kind and friendly service, has a pleasant riverside location and serves wonderful *kaiseki* (Japanese haute cuisine). It has three riverside rooms, one comes with a private bathroom, while other rooms have calming garden views.

Understand Kyoto

Kyoto Today

Kyoto has never been more popular, which is a source of both local pride and local consternation. Like hot spots around the globe, the city has been weighing the pros and cons of its growing tourism economy and considering what steps to take towards building a sustainable future for all involved. Like the rest of Japan, Kyoto is also faced with a shrinking population and a slow-growth economy. But could a new era be on the horizon?

Best on Film

Rashomon (1950) Kurosawa Akira's classic uses the southern gate of Kyoto as the setting for a 12th-century rape and murder story told from several perspectives.
Sisters of Gion (1936) Mizoguchi Kenji's riveting B&W portrayal of two very different sisters working in the famous Kyoto geisha district.
Lost in Translation (2003) Most of this film takes place in Tokyo, but there's a lovely montage of shots of the heroine's trip to Kyoto.

Best in Print

Another Kyoto (Alex Kerr; 2016) See Kyoto through the eyes of a man who has lived and breathed the city for decades.
The Old Capital (Kawabata Yasunari; 1962) A young woman's past is disturbed by the discovery of a twin sister in another family.
Kyoto: A Cultural History (John Dougill; 2006) A sprawling study that touches on everything from courtly verse and Zen Buddhism to geisha and modern film.
The Lady and the Monk (Pico Iyer; 1991) Classic expat tale of boy comes for spiritual enlightenment and meets girl instead, against a backdrop of 1980s Kyoto.

Kyoto Welcomes the World (For the Most Part)

The number of overseas visitors to Kyoto topped three million for the first time in 2016 and hasn't backed down since. Many see the upward trend as an economic boon and welcome the interest in Japan's traditional heritage; without the global attention, they say, Kyoto might not have had the motivation and means to preserve many of its old structures and customs. Others worry that the numbers might have climbed too high: in 2017 major media outlets ran stories that gave voice to local complaints about city buses clogged with oversized suitcases and tour groups taking up sidewalks. (Here's the rub though: foreign tourists make up only a small fraction of the number of annual visitors to Kyoto.)

Much of the debate has centred around the topic of vacation rentals, called *minpaku* in Japanese. (They're legal, under certain circumstances, though most are operated without proper authorisation.) Before the advent of apartment sharing sites created a workaround, the limited number of rooms naturally kept numbers down; now, some complain, the city is flooded with visitors. Rentals are also sometimes located in communities that until now had no connection to tourism – bringing the outside world a little too close to home for some.

Towards a Sustainable City

Though Kyoto once hurried to replace its old, traditional buildings with modern concrete ones, the city now sees its restrictions on building heights and signage as a source of pride. This shift is emblematic of Kyoto's new attitude and approach to urban planning: it's a wish to see the city develop on its own terms and in its own image. The city has encouraged architects to design modern, energy-efficient homes that wouldn't look out of place next to a row of century-old wooden townhouses. It wants to reduce car traffic in favour of clean buses and expanded pedestrian walkways. And it's keen to go greener: Kyoto is a 'Model Eco-City' under the federal government's Future Cities Initiative with an ambitious plan to cut carbon emissions by 40% of 1990 levels by 2030 and 60% by 2050. If Kyoto is successful, it could be a model for other cities in Japan.

A New Era Begins

It caught everyone off guard when Emperor Akihito announced abruptly in 2016 – on TV no less – that he wished to abdicate. No emperor had abdicated since 1817, which was back in the days of the shogun. The modern constitution had no provision for what to do in this situation. For over a year, lawmakers debated whether or not Akihito, Japan's 125th emperor (according to the Imperial House Agency's record keeping), should even be allowed to abdicate. On this, the public came down decisively in favour of letting the emperor do as he pleases; he's in his mid-80s after all. Finally, a bill was passed that would allow the sitting emperor, just this once, to retire. The date is set for the end of April 2019.

What he will do afterwards remains a mystery. Some have hoped he will become a stronger voice for pacifism at a time when Japan's political leaders are becoming increasingly hawkish. The son of Japan's wartime emperor, Hirohito, Akihito has often expressed regret for Japan's actions during the war. And where will Akihito and his wife live? Kyoto has begun a campaign to bring them back to their ancestral home, the old capital. Nara, too, has expressed interest in hosting them – going so far as to promise a new palace. The Imperial Household Agency's reply so far? No comment.

When Crown Prince Naruhito ascends the chrysanthemum throne, the Heisei era will end and a new one will begin. Of course, the starts and ends of Japan's historic periods – in modern times determined by the passing of emperors – are left to nature; and yet, they really do seem to effectively bracket the culture's shifting moods. The Heisei era began in 1989, as Japan's bubble economy was collapsing. A whole generation now has come of age in a Japan where lifelong employment is no longer a guarantee and where Japan's place in the world seems increasingly uncertain. In the current, unstable global climate, everyone can't help but wonder, what changes will the new era bring?

population per sq km

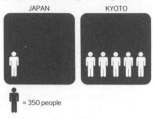

≈ 350 people

age group
(% of population)

11 — 0-14 years
62 — 15-64 years
27 — 65+ years

if Kyoto were 100 people

97 would be Japanese
2 would be Korean
1 would be Western or another nationality

History

For nearly 1000 years Kyoto was the main stage for Japan's great historical drama. It was here that emperors and shogun vied for power; the great Buddhist sects emerged; and much of what we think of today as Japanese culture developed. Though Kyoto is no longer the capital in the political sense, it remains the traditional heart of Japan. It is the city where Japanese come to learn about themselves.

Rise of the Yamato Dynasty

Japanese Historical Periods

Asuka (538–710)

Nara (710–94)

Heian (794–1185)

Kamakura (1185–1333)

Muromachi (1333–1568)

Azuchi-Momoyama (1568–1603)

Edo (1603–1868)

Meiji (1868–1912)

Taishō (1912–26)

Shōwa (1926–89)

Heisei (1989–)

The earliest traces of human life in Japan date to around 30,000 years ago, but it is possible that people were here much earlier. Until about 12,000 years ago, a number of land bridges linked Japan to the continent – Siberia to the north, Korea to the west and probably present-day Taiwan to the south. The earliest identifiable culture was that of the neolithic Jōmon who, from about 13,000 BC, inhabited settlements along coastal areas, particularly in northeastern Japan. They lived a quasi-nomadic life, gathering seaweed and wild mushrooms, hunting deer and bear, fishing and dry-farming crops like taro.

Sometime between 800 and 300 BC, settlers from China or Korea (or both; it's debated) introduced a huge game changer: wet rice farming. Not only did this labour-intensive practice demand more stable settlement, it also encouraged population growth in fertile basins, like the Kansai region (which includes Kyoto). These agriculture-based settlements led to the creation of territories and boundaries, and by 300 AD administrative and military power began to coalesce around the Yamato kingdom in Nara (also part of Kansai). By the end of the 4th century, the nascent Japanese empire, then called Wa, had established official relations with the Korean peninsula; envoys were also dispatched to the Chinese court.

Over the next 200 years, the Yamato court imported much from its neighbours, including Buddhism and written language (in the form of Chinese characters). Starting under the reign of Empress Suiko (592–628) – and her powerful regent Prince Shōtoku (573–620) – a series of administrative reforms were enacted, inspired by Tang-dynasty China, to consolidate power through taxes, land distribution and official

TIMELINE	3rd century AD	Early 7th century	710
	Queen Himiko reigns over a region called Yamatai (possibly near Nara) and is recognised by Chinese visitors as 'over-queen' of a kingdom they call 'Wa'.	The Kyoto basin is settled by the Hata clan from Korea, who established Fushimi-Inari Taisha, and the Kamo clan (of deputed origin), who established Kamo-jinja.	Japan's first permanent capital is established at Nara. By now, Japan, with its estimated five million people, has many characteristics of a nation-state.

ınks. In 710 a permanent capital was set up in Nara (Heijō-kyō), establishing Japan's first real city.

The Age of Courtiers

Kyoto is Born

The rise of the Yamato court went hand in hand with the ascendancy of Buddhism, which, by the Nara period (710–794) had become the de facto state religion. Early Buddhism in Japan was as much a vehicle of statehood as salvation. Monks were charged with praying for the health of the nation; meanwhile, Buddhist rites were incorporated into the increasingly elaborate pageantry of courtly life. Monumental works, such as Nara's Great Buddha, commissioned in the mid-8th century, gave the imperial court an essential gravitas. By the end of the 8th century, however, the clergy had become so powerful that Emperor Kammu decided to move the capital to escape it. He first settled in Nagaoka (today a suburb of Kyoto), but following several inauspicious disasters, he relocated the capital to Heian-kyō, present-day Kyoto.

The location was ideal: surrounded on three sides by gentle mountains, the site was both a natural fortress and a perfect embodiment of the principles of Chinese geomancy that were in vogue at the time. The northeast corner – where evil forces were believed to enter – was guarded by Hiei-zan (Mt Hiei). The temple Enryaku-ji, which would have a huge influence on the course of Buddhism, and politics, in Japan, was built on top of the mountain (conveniently on the edge of town) to protect the city. Two rivers, the Kamo-gawa and Katsura-gawa, provided the yin to the mountains' yang.

As with Nara, the city was laid out in accordance with a grid pattern adopted from the Tang dynasty capital, Chang'an (present-day Xi'an). Measuring 4.5km east to west and 5.3km north to south, the city was about one-third the size of its Chinese prototype. An 85m-wide, willow-lined thoroughfare, Suzaku-ōji, led from the 23m-high Rajō-mon (also known as Rashō-mon) in the south to the Imperial Palace in the north. Square plots of land (or fractions thereof) were allotted to courtiers based on rank; the most powerful among them were given land nearest the Imperial Palace.

The Rise & Fall of the Heian Court

During its foundational centuries, the Yamato dynasty drew much of its authority from institutions and ideas imported from the Asian continent. In 894, as China's Tang dynasty was on the wane and political tensions in Kyoto were at a high, the imperial court ceased its practice of sending emissaries to China. From this point forward, and for the next several centuries, Japan turned inward.

The official written language of the Heian court was Chinese characters; women, who were often shut out of formal education, employed a shorthand that would come to be known as *hiragana*, Japan's phonetic script.

794	798	805	869
The imperial capital is moved to Heian-kyō (Peaceful Capital). It is laid out in a grid according to principles of Chinese geomancy.	Kiyomizu-dera is established at the foot of the Higashiyama mountains. It is said that the location was chosen by a priest from Nara who had a vision of a holy spring at the site.	Monk Saichō, returning from Mt T'ien-t'ai in China, establishes Tendai Buddhism; the next year, monk Kūkai, returning from Chang'an (Xi'an), establishes Shingon Buddhism.	The head priest of Yasaka-jinja leads a procession through the streets of Kyoto in an effort to end a series of epidemics. This is the origin of today's Gion Matsuri.

On the one hand, from isolation was born the early inklings of Japanese culture – such as the impressions of the seasons recorded in *waka* (31-syllable poems). On the other, without an influx of new ideas, the court eventually stultified. The key check-and-balance in the Chinese system – the merit-based appointment of courtiers based on exams – was never rigorously adopted by the Japanese. As a result, increasingly powerful noble families held near-monopolies on court positions. Chief among them were the Fujiwara who, through strategic marital politics (marrying their daughters to young emperors), frequently claimed the most influence position of regent.

Meanwhile, out in the provinces dangerous military forces were developing. The court had a habit of farming out distant imperial family members – barred from succession claims – to provincial clans. These clans employed skilled warriors known as samurai (literally 'retainer'). Early on, the court called on provincial samurai to defend (and extend) Japan's borders to the northeast, fighting against peoples known as Emishi (who were most likely descended from the Jōmon). Later, they were employed to defend the capital from the belligerent bands of warrior monks who at times descended from Hiei-zan to make claims on the court.

The two main clans, the Minamoto (also known as Genji) and Taira (Heike), were enemies. In 1156 they were employed to help rival claimants to the Fujiwara family leadership, but these figures soon faded into the background when an all-out feud developed between the Minamoto and the Taira. The Taira prevailed, under their leader Kiyomori (1118–81), who based himself in the capital and, over the next 20 years, fell prey to many of the vices that lurked there. In 1180 he enthroned his two-year-old grandson, Antoku. When a rival claimant requested the help of the Minamoto family, who had regrouped, their leader, Yoritomo (1147–99), was more than ready to agree.

Both Kiyomori and the claimant died shortly afterwards, but Yoritomo and his younger half-brother Yoshitsune (1159–89) continued the campaign against the Taira, a conflict known as the Genpei War. By 1185 Kyoto had fallen and the Taira had been pursued to the western tip of Honshū. In a well-known tale, Kiyomori's widow leapt into the sea with her grandson Antoku (now aged seven), rather than have him surrender.

> People of the late Heian and early Kamakura periods were distressed by the idea of *mappō*, the 'age of the latter law', when civilisation would enter a 10,000-year period of degeneration. It was predicted to start 2000 years after the Buddha's death.

The Age of Warriors

The Kamakura Shoguns

Yoritomo did not seek to become emperor; however, he wanted the new emperor to legitimise him by conferring the title of shogun, which was granted in 1192. He left many existing offices and institutions in place in Kyoto and set up a base in his home territory of Kamakura (not far from present-day Tokyo). While in theory Yoritomo represented the

Early 1000s	1052	Mid-12th century	1168
Lady of the imperial court, Murasaki Shikibu, writes *The Tale of Genji*, considered to be the world's first novel.	The Byōdō-in Buddhist temple is established. The following year, the famous Hōō-dō (Phoenix Hall) is built. The temple is a rare remaining example of Heian-era architecture.	The name Kyoto (written with two Chinese characters that mean 'capital') starts to replace the original name of the city, Heian-kyō.	The priest Eisai travels to China and observes Ch'an Buddhism. He later introduces this as Zen Buddhism in Japan. He also brings back tea.

LIFE IN HEIAN-KYŌ

Heian-kyō was an exclusive, insular world that revolved around the court. (Interestingly, the court had no practice of executions; to be transferred to the provinces was punishment enough.) It has been estimated that the number of courtiers and courtesans hovered around 5000 to 7000; including family members, servants, merchants and artisans, it is likely that the population of the capital was at least 10 times that. Rank, largely determined by bloodlines, was everything; it determined, for example, what clothes could be worn and what kind of house could be built. High-ranking clans were granted untaxed estates (called *shōen*) from which they derived their wealth. In Heian-era Japan, women could inherit land, which gave them a degree of independence.

The women of the court wore their hair long, ideally to the ground. Both men and women dusted their faces with rice powder, for a whitening effect. Women plucked their eyebrows and painted a new set, softly shaped like clouds, higher on their foreheads; they also blackened their teeth. In the dusky luminescence of the court, lit by oil lamps and candles, the effect must have been striking. Courtiers and courtesans alike wore many layers of silken robes, their colours and patterns coordinated with the seasons.

One of the more unusual aspects of Heian-era Japan is that the nobility lived a life circumscribed by self-imposed taboos, which were initially based on Chinese systems of geomancy and astrology (but had taken on a life of their own in Japan). Prohibitions on everything from travel in certain directions to hair washing on certain days were decided by the Onmyō-ryō, the court's official Bureau of Yin and Yang, and strictly followed. Adding to this regimented life was a full calendar of annual rituals, festivals and observances at court. Though a little dated in tone, Ivan Morris' *The World of the Shining Prince* (1964) paints an evocative picture of life in the Heian court.

Of course, not everyone in Heian-kyō belonged to the court. From the diaries of courtesans we know that the city was also home to beggars and ruffians (whom the court looked upon as less than human). Meanwhile, on the outskirts, peasants worked the land at below subsistence levels on the *shōen*.

military arm of the emperor's government, in practice he was in charge of the government. The feudal age had begun.

The Kamakura shoganate, however, proved to be short-lived. The Mongols, under Kublai Khan, reached Korea in 1259 and sent envoys to Japan seeking Japanese submission. When the envoys were expelled, the Mongols sent a fleet to invade the southern island of Kyūshū in 1274. This attack, and a more determined effort in 1281, were only barely repulsed after timely storms destroyed much of the Mongol fleet.

The conflict with the Mongols produced no conquered territories or spoils with which to reward the armies for their service; the shoganate was broke, and the powerful warrior clans pulled their support. Dissatisfaction towards the Kamakura regime came to a head under the

1192	1202	Early 13th century	Mid-13th century
Minamoto Yoritomo is appointed shogun and establishes the political capital in Kamakura. While the imperial court remains in Kyoto, the real power centre of the country leaves the city.	Eisai establishes Kennin-ji, the first Zen temple in Kyoto, under sponsorship of shogun Minamoto no Yoriie.	The priest Hōnen, troubled by divisions between Japan's major Buddhist sects, establishes a new populist sect known as Jōdo (Pure Land) Buddhism. He fasts to death in 1212.	The priest Shinran preaches the radically egalitarian doctrine that becomes known as Jōdo-Shinshū (True Pure Land Buddhism).

unusually assertive emperor Go-Daigo (1288–1339). In 1333, following a failed coup that saw him exiled, Go-Daigo raised an army and toppled the government, ushering in a return of political authority to Kyoto.

The Ashikaga Shoguns

The typhoon of 1281 that expelled the Mongol invasion, believed to be sent from the gods, was called *kamikaze* (literally 'divine wind'). Later this term was used to describe Pacific War suicide pilots who, channeling divine spirit, gave their lives for the nation.

Kamakura receded but feudalism did not. Go-Daigo, and the Kyoto nobility, sought a return to the Heian-era status quo, but the warriors who fought for him – notably his general, Ashikaga Takauji – had no intention of withdrawing quietly back to the provinces. When Go-Daigo refused to name Takauchi shogun, the general revolted; Go-Daigo fled to Hiei-zan. Takauji installed a puppet emperor from a rival line, who returned the favour by declaring him shogun in 1338. He set up his base in Kyoto, at Muromachi.

The Ashikaga shoguns were great patrons of the arts, likely, in part, to shore up their authority – they were, after all, provincial warriors in aristocratic Kyoto. New cultural forms, influenced by Zen, developed during the Muromachi period (1336–1573), such as *chanoyu* (tea ceremony) and *kare-sansui* (dry landscape) gardens. Unfortunately, they were largely ineffective rulers, relying on the support of local and provincial clans to prop up their authority. Once again, a contentious succession (over the shogunate this time) turned into an all-out war between two rival clans, the Yamana and Hosokawa. Both sides amassed armies of tens of thousands and Kyoto became a battlefield. The resulting Ōnin-no-ran

MYTHIC ORIGINS

Once upon a time, the male and female deities Izanagi and Izanami came down to a watery world from Takamagahara (the Plains of High Heaven) to create land. Droplets from Izanagi's 'spear' solidified into the land now known as Japan, and Izanami and Izanagi then populated it with *kami* (gods). One of these was Japan's supreme deity, the Sun Goddess, Amaterasu (Light of Heaven) – Japan is unique in having a female solar deity. Her great-great grandson Jimmu became the first emperor of Japan, reputedly in 660 BC. This is how Japan's first historical record books, the *Kojiki* (Record of Old Things; 712) and *Nihon Shoki* (Record of Japan; 720), describe the birth of Japan. The imperial family had these works compiled in the late 7th and early 8th centuries to legitimise their power by tracing its lineage back to the divine.

Scholars are skeptical of the existence of the earliest emperors. Some believe the 10th emperor, Sujin, was the first to really exist, and was perhaps the founder of the Yamato dynasty. Different accounts place his reign in anywhere from the 1st century BC to the 4th century AD. Emperor Kinmei (509–71 AD), who reigned 539–71 AD, is the first emperor of verifiable historical record. According to the lineage of legend, he would have been the 29th emperor. Either way, the Yamoto dynasty is the longest unbroken monarchy in the world.

1333	1397	1467	1482
The Kamakura Shogunate is defeated, Emperor Go-Daigo returns from exile and the political capital is re-established in Kyoto, where it remains until 1868.	Kinkaku-ji (Golden Pavillion) is built for shogun Ashikaga Yoshimitsu to serve as a retirement villa; in accordance with his will, it is transformed into a Zen temple on his death.	The devastating Ōnin War breaks out in Kyoto, destroying the city and ushering in more than a century of near constant war.	Shogun Ashikaga Yoshimasa builds a retreat at the base of the Higashiyama mountains. After his death, the retreat is converted into Jishō-ji, a temple known today as Ginkaku-ji.

(Ōnin War; 1467–77), which produced no clear winner, all but destroyed the capital. Kyoto's population, which had hovered around an estimated 150,000 for most of its existence, had plunged to 40,000 by the year 1500.

The Ashikaga shoganate hung on for another century, but with little actual power. Throughout the period known as the Sengoku-jidai (Warring States period; 1467–1603), a protracted struggle for domination by individual *daimyō* (provincial domain lords) spread throughout Japan.

Civil War & Reunification

By the mid-16th century, Europeans had begun to arrive, bringing with them Christianity and firearms – another game changer. One of the most successful warlords to take advantage of firearms was Oda Nobunaga (1534–82). Starting from a relatively minor power base (in what is now Aichi Prefecture), he managed to outmanoeuvre rivals (including several family members), seizing Kyoto in 1568. He installed a puppet shogun from the Ashikaga clan (Yoshiaki), only to drive him out in 1573. Nobunaga was no friend of the Buddhist clergy: in 1571 he torched the temples of Hiei-zan. Although he did not take the title of shogun, Nobunaga held defacto power, ruling from his castle at Azuchi, near Biwa-ko (Lake Biwa).

Following Nobunaga's assassination (by one of his generals), another of his generals, Toyotomi Hideyoshi (1536–98), took up the torch of unification, succeeding in eight years to wrest control of Japan. The emperor crowned him regent. Hideyoshi, from surprisingly humble stock, built his showy castle – which reputedly took some 100,000 workers three years to build – in Osaka. His real interest, however, lay in ruined Kyoto. Hideyoshi took to rebuilding it, becoming the capital's second great architect, after Emperor Kammu. He altered the cityscape with new north–south roads, bridges, gates and the Odoi, an earthen rampart designed to isolate and fortify the perimeter of the city. He also rebuilt temples burned by Nobunaga, including the great Hongan-ji, and another castle for himself, Fushimi-jō, south of the city.

On his deathbed, Hideyoshi entrusted Ieyasu, who had proven to be one of his ablest generals, with safeguarding the country and the succession of his young son Hideyori (1593–1615). Ieyasu, however, had bigger ambitions and soon went to war against those loyal to Hideyori. Ieyasu's forces finally defeated Hideyori and his supporters at the legendary Battle of Sekigahara in 1600, moving him into a position of supreme power. He chose Edo (present-day Tokyo) as his base and ushered in two and a half centuries of Tokugawa rule.

Kyoto's Aoi (Hollyhock) Matsuri, held annually in May, is older than the city itself. It was first held in 544 to pray for an end to calamitous weather that had been plaguing the nascent Japanese empire.

The Tokugawa Shoguns

Having secured power for the Tokugawa, Ieyasu and his successors were determined to retain it. Their strategy was extreme micro-management.

15th–16th centuries	1568	Late 1500s	1600
Frequent peasant uprisings called *ikki* erupt, with protesters demanding tax breaks from *daimyō* (domain lords). Throughout the feudal era taxes were paid in rice.	Oda Nobunaga, son of a *daimyō* in Owari Province (now known as Aichi-ken), seizes power from the imperial court in Kyoto and begins to pacify and unify central Japan.	Sen-no-Rikyū lays down the form of the tea ceremony; the arts flourish during what is known as the Azuchi-Momoyama period, considered 'Japan's Renaissance'.	Tokugawa Ieyasu defeats Toyotomi at the Battle of Sekigahara. The Tokugawa Shogunate is established in Edo (present-day Tokyo); the capital remains in Kyoto.

They kept tight control over the provincial *daimyō*, requiring them and their retainers to spend every second year in Edo, where their families were kept permanently as hostages – an edict known as *sankin kōtai*. This policy made it hard for the *daimyō* to foment local revolt; it also ensured a steady flow of ideas and information between the capital and the provinces. Kyoto was ruled not by a *daimyō* but by a governor, appointed by the shogun, who occupied Nijō-jō, the castle that Ieyasu built in 1600.

The Tokugawa regime promoted a brand of neo-Confucianism that emphasised hierarchical order. Society was made rigidly hierarchical, comprising (in descending order of importance): *shi* (samurai), *nō* (farmers), *kō* (artisans) and *shō* (merchants). Class dress, living quarters and even manner of speech were all strictly codified, and interclass movement was prohibited. Movement in general was difficult; written authority was required for travel and wheel transport was outlawed.

Early on, the Tokugawa shogunate adopted a policy of *sakoku* (closure to the outside world). The regime was leery of Christianity's potential influence and expelled missionaries in 1614. Following the Christian-led Shimabara Rebellion, Christianity was banned and several hundred thousand Japanese Christians were forced into hiding (or worse). All Westerners except the Protestant Dutch, who were confined to a tiny trading base on the artificial island of Dejima near Nagasaki, were expelled by 1638. Trade – primarily with the Dutch, Korea, China, the Ryūkyū Kingdom (present-day Okinawa) and the Ainu (the indigenous population of present-day Hokkaidō) – was strictly controlled, with all benefit accrued to the shogunate.

For all its constraints, however, the Tokugawa period had a considerable dynamism. Japan's cities grew enormously during this period: Edo's population topped one million in the early 1700s, dwarfing much older London and Paris. Kyoto, which evolved into a production centre for luxury goods, and Osaka, a centre for trade, each hovered around 400,000 for much of the period. New art forms, such as bunraku puppet plays, kabuki theatre and wood-block prints, developed under the support of the newly prosperous merchant class.

The epic *Tale of the Heike* describes the battles of the Genpei War. It was recited by travelling monks to the accompaniment of the *biwa* (Japanese lute), spreading the Buddhist idea of impermanence (*mujō*) along with the story of the Heike's fall. It's available in translation by Royall Tyler (2014).

The Modern Era

Meiji Restoration

By the turn of the 19th century, the stagnating Tokugawa government was increasingly challenged by open criticism and peasant revolts. It is questionable how much longer the regime might have held on, but as it happened, external forces were to hasten its demise. In 1853 and again the following year, US Commodore Matthew Perry steamed into Edo-wan (now Tokyo Bay) with a show of gunships and demanded Japan open up to trade and provisioning. The shogunate, which was no

1603	1619	1620	1853
The castle known as Nijō-jō was built to serve as the official residence of the first Tokugawa Shogun, Ieyasu. The castle is a direct challenge to the emperor's power.	As part of the general purge of Christians ordered by the shogun, 52 Japanese Christians are burned alive on the banks of the Kamo-gawa in Kyoto.	Construction starts on Katsura-Rikyū Imperial Villa, considered one of the finest examples of Japanese architecture.	Succumbing to foreign pressure, after 250 years of near isolation, Japan establishes international ports at Yokohama, Hakodate, Kobe, Niigata and Nagasaki.

match for Perry's firepower, acquiesced. Soon an American consul arrived, and other Western powers followed suit. Japan was obliged to sign what came to be called the 'unequal treaties', opening ports and giving Western nations control over tariffs.

A surge of antigovernment feeling followed. The shogunate tried to backtrack, but *daimyō* in Satsuma and Chōshū, domains in western Japan, had already seized the opportunity to fan the flames of rebellion. Following a series of military clashes between the shogun's armies and the rebels – which showed the rebels to have the upper hand – the last shogun, Yoshinobu (1837–1913), agreed to retire in 1867.

In 1868 the new teenage emperor Mutsuhito (1852–1912, later known as Meiji) was named the supreme leader of the land. Feudalism was abolished and Edo was refashioned into the imperial capital and given the new name, Tokyo (Eastern Capital). In truth, the emperor still wielded little actual power; a new government was formed, primarily led by former samurai from the rebel domains. After more than a millennium as capital, the sudden changes came as a major blow to Kyoto. The city lost many great merchants and scholars, who followed the emperor to Tokyo, as well as its main employer of artists and craftsmen – the imperial court.

Buddhism, which had strong ties to the shogunate, suffered under the new government. Shintō – and particularly rituals of emperor worship – was promoted in its place following a surge of nativism. Elements of neo-Confucianism were retained for the orderliness they encouraged; new laws codified a patriarchal family system wherein women were subordinate to their husbands. The ban on Christianity was lifted (though few took advantage of it). The four-tier class system was also scrapped; after centuries of having everything prescribed for them, citizens were now free to choose their occupation and place of residence.

Westernisation

Above all, the new leaders of Japan – keen observers of what was happening throughout Asia – feared colonisation by the West. The government embarked on a grand project of industrialisation and militarisation, to prove that Japan could stand on an equal footing with the colonisers. A great exchange began between Japan and the West: Japanese scholars were dispatched to Europe to study everything from literature and engineering to nation-building and modern warfare. Western scholars were invited to teach in Japan's nascent universities. By 1889 the country had a constitution, modelled after the government frameworks of England and Prussia. Banking systems, a new legal code and political parties were established.

Read about how the landscape shaped the city and how the city shaped the landscape in *Kyoto: An Urban History of Japan's Premodern Capital* (Matthew Stavros; 2016).

HISTORY THE MODERN ERA

The waning days of the Tokugawa shogunate in the 1860s was a disorienting time. A bizarre millenarian cult spread to the cities, which saw people dancing in the streets, sometimes masked or naked, shouting *ee ja naika?* (who cares?).

1869	1895	1926	1941
The 17-year-old Emperor Meiji moves from Kyoto to Edo, renamed Tokyo the year before, where Japan's new political and economic capital is established.	Kyoto begins operation of Japan's first electric street tram service; and Heian-jingū is built re-creating Heian-era architecture.	Emperor Hirohito, the Shōwa Emperor, ascends the throne; his reign, lasting until his death in 1989, would be the longest of any Japanese emperor.	The Imperial Japanese Navy attacks the US Pacific Fleet in Pearl Harbor, Hawaii, in a strike designed to prevent American interference in Japan's territorial expansion in Asia.

Kyoto embraced modernisation. In the late 1800s it led the country in education reforms, establishing Japan's first kindergarten, primary and junior high schools, and a public library.

The Pursuit of Empire

In the 1890s Japan's growing confidence was demonstrated by the abolition of foreign treaty rights and by the ease with which it trounced China in the Sino-Japanese War (1894–95). The subsequent treaty nominally recognised Korean independence from China's sphere of influence and ceded Taiwan to Japan. Friction with Russia over control of Manchuria and Korea led to the Russo-Japanese War (1904–05), in which the Japanese navy stunned the Russians by inflicting a crushing defeat on their Baltic fleet at the Battle of Tsushima. For the first time, Japan commanded the respect of the Western powers. When Japan officially annexed Korea in 1910, there was little international protest.

In the 1920s, however, the national mood had begun to sour. A sense of unfair treatment by Western powers – and particularly by the USA, which had passed anti-Japanese immigration policies – had once again taken hold in Japan. The Washington Conference of 1921–22 set naval ratios of three capital ships for Japan to five American and five British, which upset the Japanese (despite being well ahead of France's 1.75). Around the same time, a racial-equality clause Japan proposed to the League of Nations was rejected.

By the 1930s, the military was acting on its own accord, manufacturing a conflict with China, in what came to be known as the Manchurian Incident (1931). The Japanese easily overpowered Chinese forces and within months had taken control of Manchuria and installed a puppet government. The League of Nations refused to acknowledge the new Manchurian government; in 1933 Japan left the league. By 1937, Japan had entered into full-scale hostilities against China.

Meanwhile, belief in a new world order was gaining currency in Japanese politics, one that demanded that the country look after its own

The first Europeans to arrive in Japan were the Portuguese, who landed on the island of Tanegashima, south of Kyūshū in 1543. It's believed that they introduced *peixinhos da horta* (battered and fried green beans), which evolved into tempura.

SAVING KYOTO

Kyoto's good fortune during WWII has been accredited to the efforts of American scholar Langdon Warner (1881–1955). During the latter half of the war Warner sat on a committee that endeavoured to save artistic and historical treasures in war-torn regions. He is said to have made a desperate plea to US military authorities to spare the cities of Kyoto, Nara, Kamakura and Kanazawa. A less generous theory suggests that it was a well-planned public relations stunt scripted by US intelligence officials to gain the trust of a nation that had been taught to fear and hate the American enemy.

1945	1964	1981	1994
In September, American occupation forces enter Kyoto for the first time. They maintain a headquarters in the city until January 1946.	The Tōkaidō *shinkansen* (bullet train) service opens linking Osaka and Tokyo with a station in Kyoto.	Karasuma subway starts between Kyoto and Kitaō-ji stations, allowing easy north–south travel through the city. The line later extends south to Takeda and north to Takaragaike.	Kyoto celebrates the 1200th anniversary of its founding and 17 Historic Monuments of Ancient Kyoto are registered as Unesco World Heritage sites.

interests – by securing resources not dependent on global trade – as well as those of the continent's, through a Japan-controlled Greater East Asian Co-Prosperity Sphere that would replace Western colonial interests.

WWII & Occupation

Japan signed a pact with Germany and Italy in 1940, but it was the USA, who had condemned Japan's invasion of China, that concerned Japan the most. When diplomatic attempts to gain US neutrality failed, the Japanese drew them into WWII with a surprise attack on the US Pacific Fleet in Pearl Harbor on 7 December 1941.

At first Japan scored rapid successes, pushing its battlefronts across to India, down to the fringes of Australia and into the mid-Pacific. But eventually the decisive Battle of Midway in 1942 turned the tide of the war against Japan. Exhausted by submarine blockades and aerial bombing, by 1945 Japan had been driven back on all fronts. In August the declaration of war by the Soviet Union and the atomic bombs dropped by the USA on Hiroshima and Nagasaki were the final straws: Emperor Hirohito announced Japan's unconditional surrender.

American forces, under the command of General Douglas MacArthur, occupied Japan until 1952. A new constitution was introduced that denounced war and banned a Japanese military. It also dismantled the political power of the emperor, who stunned his subjects by publicly renouncing any claim to divine origins.

Postwar Kyoto

Kyoto was spared the fate of many of Japan's cities, which had been levelled by Allied bombing. Instead, large swathes of the city were leveled by the 'economic miracle' – the trajectory of phenomenal growth that Japan experienced from the 1950s through the 1980s. Much of the city's traditional wooden buildings were scrapped in favour of contemporary concrete structures, which stood several storeys higher. It wasn't until after the economic bubble burst in 1990, and after the city celebrated the 1200th anniversary of its founding in 1994, that Kyoto began to reconsider in earnest its heritage – before it was gone for good. In September 2007 the Kyoto city government enacted new ordinances that restricted building heights and banned all rooftop and blinking advertisements. Meanwhile, down on street level, there has been a revival of interest in the city's *machiya* (traditional Japanese townhouses), and many of these fine old structures were turned into shops, restaurants and inns.

Today Kyoto is known as a centre of education (the city has 35 universities) and technology (Kyocera and Nintendo are headquartered here), in addition to its status as Japan's cultural storehouse.

HISTORY THE MODERN ERA

In the wake of the Great Kanto Earthquake of 1923, which decimated Tokyo, Japan's nascent film industry moved to Kyoto. The city's speciality was *jidaigeki* (period films), which were enormously popular at the time.

When NHK, Japan's national broadcaster, played a message prerecorded by Emperor Hirohito declaring Japan's surrender to the Allies in WWII, it was the first time the people of Japan had heard their emperor speak.

1997	1997	2011	2015
The futuristic Kyoto Station building, featuring a 60m-high atrium over the main concourse, opens in the same year as the Tōzai (east–west) line, Kyoto's second subway line.	The Kyoto Protocol, aimed at limiting greenhouse gas emissions and countering global warming, is adopted at Kyoto's Takaragaike International Conference Hall.	On 11 March the Great East Japan Earthquake strikes off the northeast coast. Kyoto suffers no damage, but sees a massive decline in tourist numbers.	On the back of a weak yen and relaxations in visa regulations for visitors from Asian countries, Kyoto sees a record number of 56.84 million tourists (including domestic visitors).

Religion

Shintō and Buddhism have historically been Japan's most important religions. Shintō ('the way of the gods') is an animist tradition indigenous to Japan. Buddhism arrived (via Korea and China) at the dawn of the Japanese empire, bringing with it a whole new worldview. Oddly enough, the two religions were not considered mutually exclusive and have long existed intertwined. Together their legacy of art, architecture and folk culture is profound.

Shintō: The Way of the Gods

Temples are great repositories of Buddhist sculpture, which enjoyed a golden age during the Nara, Heian and Kamakura eras. Unlike paintings, which are fragile, sculptures are often on public display.

Little is known of Shintō's origins; however, it likely emerged from a combination of rituals tied to the agrarian calendar and shamanistic practices. Shintō locates divinity in the natural world. Its *kami* (spirits or gods) inhabit trees, rocks, waterfalls and mountains; however, they can also be summoned through rituals of dance and music or by offerings, such as sake, into the shrines the Japanese have built for them, where they are beseeched with prayers for a good harvest, fertility and, in modern times, success in business and school entrance exams. (*Kami* can also be troublemakers and may need to be placated through rituals and offerings.)

There are innumerable deities in the Shintō pantheon, from the celebrated sun goddess Amaterasu to the humble hearth *kami*. Extraordinary people (like the warlord Toyotomi Hideyoshi, enshrined at Toyokuni-jinja) may be honoured as *kami* upon death. At shrines you may see thick ropes made of rice straw (called *shimenawa*), sometimes decorated with white paper folded in a zigzag pattern (called *shide*), which indicates a sacred space or object (such as a rock or tree).

Shintō has no doctrine and no beginning or endgame; it simply is. One important concept is *musubi,* a kind of vital energy that animates everything (*kami* and mortals alike). Impurities *(tsumi)* interfere with *musubi* so purification rituals are part of all Shintō rites and practices. For this reason, visitors to shrines first wash their hands and mouth at the *temizu* (font). Some traditional rites include fire, which is also seen as a purifying force.

Butsudō: The Way of the Buddha

Buddhism originated in northern India in the 6th century BC when a prince, Siddhartha Gautama, who had rejected his sheltered life, found enlightenment while meditating under a tree. The prince became a Buddha, an 'Awakened One'. Building on the Hindu belief of *samsara* (the cycle of death and rebirth) that is governed by karma (the law of cause and effect), he taught that we live in a temporary world of suffering, largely of our own making, and that through extinguishing our desires we can transcend this world and free ourselves from *samsara*.

Over the centuries Buddhism spread through Tibet, China and Korea and eventually reached Japan in the 6th century AD – by which time it had evolved considerably. When Buddhism entered Japan, it was part of a package that included sophisticated technologies, codes of law, competing philosophies (such as Confucianism and Taoism), superstitions and taboos from the continent. Throughout the history of the Japanese empire, the religion would be a powerful political and cultural force, not unlike the Roman church.

Japanese Buddhism

Buddhism in Japan is part of the Mahāyāna (Great Vehicle) tradition, which teaches that anyone (as opposed to just monks) can attain salvation in this lifetime. A key figure in Mahāyāna Buddhism is the *boddhisatva,* a compassionate being who, on the cusp of achieving Buddha-hood, delays transcendence in order to help others.

Two *boddhisatva* have long been revered in Japan, regardless of sect. Kannon embodies mercy and compassion and is believed to have the power to alleviate suffering in this world. Interestingly, the older, Indian version of Kannon (Sanskrit: Avalokitêśvara) is depicted as male, but in Japan Kannon appears as female, slender and with flowing robes. She takes many forms; one common one is Senjū Kannon ('thousand-armed Kannon') – the better to help all sentient beings.

Jizō is the protector of travellers and children. He is often depicted as a monk, with a staff in one hand and a jewel in the other, or roughly in stone. Parents who have lost a child or have one who is ailing may make an offering to Jizō, sometimes in the form of bib and cap (emblems of childhood).

Tendai & Shingon: Establishment Buddhism

During the Heian period, two distinctly Japanese forms of Buddhism emerged: Tendai was founded by the monk Saichō (767–822), who studied Buddhism on China's Mt T'ien-t'ai (from which Tendai gets its name). Shingon was founded by the monk Kūkai (774–835; more famously known by his posthumous name, Kōbō Daishi), who studied in Chang'an (Xi'an), the capital of Tang China. Shingon means 'true word' and is also the Japanese word for mantra, the sacred utterances of esoteric Buddhism.

Both sects, but especially Shingon, are considered esoteric, meaning they are mystical and involve teachings and practices only revealed to initiates. Shingon, which shares similarities with Tibetan Buddhism, has a sprawling cosmology represented by a *mandara* (mandala); at the centre of the *mandara* is Dainichi Nyorai, the cosmic Buddha and supreme deity in Shingon Buddhism. Dainichi's messenger is the fearsome, fire-haloed Fudō-myoō, one of the five wisdom kings – you'll recognise him when you see him. Two important Shingon temples in Kyoto are Tō-ji and Daigō-ji.

For centuries, Tendai, which is headquartered at Enryaku-ji on Hiei-zan (Mt Hiei), was the dominant sect in the capital and many members of the imperial family served in the clergy. Then, as now, Tendai monks were required to spend 12 years on Hiei-zan engaging in study, meditation and ascetic practices. In addition to Enryaku-ji, important Tendai temples in Kyoto include Shōren-in and Sanjūsangen-dō.

Pure Land & True Pure Land: Radical Buddhism

The figure of Amida (Sanskrit: Amitābha), the Buddha of Infinite Light who resides in the western paradise, the Pure Land, had been part of Japanese Buddhism from its early days. Devotees aspired to rebirth in the Pure Land, to which aim they recited the *nembutsu* mantra, *Namu Amida Butsu* ('I take refuge in Amida'). In the 12th century, Hōnen (1133–1212), a disillusioned Tendai monk, began preaching a more

During the late Heian period, it was fashionable among the aristocracy to create gardens in the image of the Pure Land; the one at Byōdō-in in Uji is a rare remaining example.

accessible form of Buddhism: that recitation of the *nembutsu* was the only thing required for liberation. This was something the common people, who didn't have the luxury of spending years in meditation, might reasonably achieve.

His disciple, Shinran (1173–1263), took this a step further, saying only faith in Amida was required. Hōnen's teachings became the basis for the Pure Land school (Jōdō-shu), while Shinran's became the foundation for the True Pure Land school (Shin Jōdō-shu). Today True Pure Land, which has no monastic orders, is the most popular sect in Japan. Chion-in is the head temple of Jōdō-shu and Nishi Hongan-ji is the head temple of Shin Jōdō-shu.

Zen & the Medieval Mind

Zen was the last major development in Japanese Buddhism. In the 12th century, after Japan resumed relations with China, Eisei (1141–1215), a Tendai priest, travelled to T'ien-t'ai to rediscover Tendai's roots only to discover that the mountain was now a centre of Ch'an (Zen) study. Ch'an or Zen comes from the Sanskrit word *dhyana* (meditation). When he returned to Japan, Eisei met only resistance among the entrenched clergy on Hiei-zan. The newly established Kamakura shogunate, however, was far more receptive; Zen, with its emphasis on discipline, proved a good match for the ascendant warrior class. Eisei's disciples had better luck in Kyoto under the Ashikaga shoguns and established the Rinzai school of Zen in the capital.

Seated meditation, called *zazen* in Japanese, is an important part of Zen practice; so is *shugyō*, self-cultivation in the practices of daily life. Both prepare the mind and the body to achieve insight into one's inner-Buddha nature. Students may also study koans (literally 'past cases' that read like riddles), which are attempts by past masters to put the inscrutable – that is, enlightenment – into words. Zen also has an irreverent streak, which some scholars have attributed to an influence of Taoism. In Zen, naturalness (rather than learnedness) is the ideal state.

Among Kyoto's many Zen temples, the most prominent are: Nanzen-ji, Tōfuku-ji, Daitoku-ji and Myōshin-ji.

Tanuki (raccoon dogs) and *kitsune* (foxes) are two popular shape-shifting (and at times devious) creatures of myth. *Kitsune* are considered messengers of Inari, the rice god. *Tanuki* love their sake and it is common to see *tanuki* statues outside restaurants.

Religion Today

Only about one-third of Japanese today identify as Buddhist, and the figure for Shintō is just 3%; however, most Japanese participate in annual rituals rooted in both, which they see as integral parts of their culture and community ties. Generally, it is said that Shintō is concerned with this life and Buddhism with the afterlife. That temple bells ring out the end of the year on 31 December (a rite called Joya-no-kane) and shrines attract visitors praying for health and happiness in the year to come on 1 January (a rite called *hatsumode*) is a perfect example of this. It is at shrines that people celebrate marriages and the milestones of childhood and where the lovelorn come to pray for a match. (And while few may truly believe in the powers of *kami* to bring people together, at the very least, many would say, it can't hurt to try.)

Temples, meanwhile, perform funeral rites and memorial services – which has given Buddhism a dour image among many younger people in Japan. The Buddhist festival of Obon, in mid-summer, is when the souls of departed ancestors are believed to pay a short visit. Families return to their hometowns to sweep gravestones, an act called *ohaka-mairi*. Even non-believers might feel a sense of foreboding at skipping such rituals. Kyoto's famous Daimon-ji Gozan Okuribi, when fires are lit in the mountains to spell out Chinese characters, is the official send-off for the spirits.

Geisha

The word geisha literally means 'arts person'; in Kyoto the term used is *geiko* – 'child of the arts'. Though dressed in the finest silks and often astonishingly beautiful, geisha are first and foremost accomplished musicians and dancers. They are also charming, skilled conversationalists. Though geisha are rarer these days, many do still work in Kyoto, in one of the historic geisha districts such as Gion and Ponto-chō. If you're lucky, you might even catch a glimpse of one.

Origins

Throughout the Edo period, courtesans called *oiran* entertained in urban pleasure districts. They were prostitutes, but the most highly sought after were also savvy entertainers and accomplished in the arts. Today, geisha – and especially *maiko* – are seen as dressing lavishly, but the *oiran* were far more ostentatious, outfitted in so many heavy robes and hair ornaments as to be rendered practically immobile. When geisha first appeared, sometime in the 18th century, in comparatively sombre dress, their faces ghostly white with just a slash of red, they were the new epitome of chic.

They were also explicitly not prostitutes; the pleasure districts had invested heavily in the *oiran* and, seeing geisha as competition, forbade them from selling sex. The geisha, who in the early days also included men, were strictly there to perform.

While geisha are the prototypical image of old, cloistered Japan, they actually hit their stride in the Meiji period. By then the *oiran* had faded and geisha districts had become the most vaunted evening destinations, drawing the leading politicians and intellectuals of the day to *ochaya* – literally 'teahouses', but in meaning more like 'salon' and rather different from the *chashitsu* of the tea ceremony (p179).

At their peak in the 1920s there were around 80,000 geisha in Japan. Today there are approximately 1000 registered geisha (including apprentices) in Japan, nearly half of whom are in Kyoto.

Life of a Geisha, Then & Now

Geisha now live a dramatically different life to their predecessors. Prior to the mid-20th century, a girl might arrive at an *okiya* (geisha living quarters) still a young child, and indeed some were sold into service by desperate families, to work as a maid. Should she show promise, the owner of the *okiya* would send her to the *kaburenjō* (school for geisha arts). She would continue maid duty, waiting on the geisha of the house, while honing her skills and eventually specialising in one of the arts, such as playing the *shamisen* (three-stringed instrument resembling a banjo) or dance. Training typically lasted about six years; those who passed exams would begin work as an apprentice under the wing of a senior geisha and eventually graduate to full-fledged geisha themselves.

Geisha were often indebted to the *okiya* who covered their board and training. Given the lack of bargaining chips that have historically been afforded women, there is no doubt that many geisha of the past, at some point in their careers, engaged in compensated relationships; this would be with a *danna* (a patron) with whom the geisha would enter a contractual relationship not unlike a marriage (and one that could be

The geisha world is known in Japanese as *karyūkai*, 'the flower and willow world'. Geisha districts are called *hanamachi* (flower towns) and the cost for an evening's entertainment is the *hanadai* (flower fee).

GEISHA MANNERS

No doubt spotting a *maiko* dressed to the hilt on the street in Kyoto is a wondrous experience, and a photo is a much-coveted souvenir of a visit to Japan. However, please keep in mind that these are young women – many of whom are minors – trying to get to work. In Kyoto the sport of geisha-spotting has gotten out of hand, with tourists sometimes blocking the women's paths in popular districts like Gion in order to get photos. Let them through; *maiko* and geisha are professionals – if you want to get close to them, support their art and go to see them perform. You can also find plenty of tourists dressed as geisha on the streets of Higashiyama during the day; many are happy to be photographed if asked.

terminated). A wealthy *danna* could help a woman pay off her debt to the *okiya* or help her start her own. Other geisha married, which required them to leave the profession; some were adopted by their *okiya* and inherited the role of house mother; still others worked until old age.

Today's geisha begin their training no earlier than in their teens – perhaps after being inspired by a school trip to Kyoto – while completing their compulsory education (in Japan, until age 15). Then they'll leave home for an *okiya* (they do still exist) and start work as an apprentice. While in the past, a *maiko* would never be seen out and about in anything but finery, today's apprentices act much like ordinary teens in their downtime. For some, the magic is in the *maiko* stage and they never proceed to become geisha; those who do are free to live where they choose, date as they like and change professions when they please.

Geisha Dress

Kimono are the visible capital in the geisha world; they are worth thousands or even hundreds of thousands of dollars and are loaned to *maiko* by their *okiya*. The colours and patterns are carefully chosen according to the season. On a rainy day, *maiko* and *geiko* are sheltered from the rain by *wagasa*, traditional Japanese umbrellas with bamboo frames and coverings of paper or silk.

Handmade boxwood combs (*kushi* in Japanese) are indispensable for creating the wonderful hairstyles of the *maiko*. One reason for using these combs, apart from their incredibly pleasing appearance, is the fact that they don't produce static electricity.

Maiko are easily distinguished by their long trailing obi and towering wooden clogs; they also wear their own hair in a dramatic fashion, accentuated with opulent (and extremely expensive) ornaments, called *kanzashi*. *Maiko* and young geisha paint their faces with thick white make-up, leaving only a suggestive forked tongue of bare flesh on the nape of the neck. Eyebrows are painted and the lower lip is coloured red.

Geisha wear more subdued robes and a simpler chignon (or a wig). As a geisha grows older her make-up becomes increasingly natural; by then their artistic accomplishments need no fine-casing.

Experiencing Geisha Culture

Historically, the geisha world was largely a closed one, requiring a personal introduction to enter. One exception has been the annual dances (known as *odori*) that geisha hold for the public – a Kyoto tradition for over a century. There are a few performances (p44) throughout the year.

As a sign of changing times, there are now a few venues, such as Maiko Theatre and Maiko Dinner Show Yasakadori Enraku, where anyone – regardless of connections – can book an evening in the presence of *maiko*. There are also regular performances of *maiko* and *geiko* at the TIC in Kyoto Tower and the Fureai-Kan Kyoto Museum of Traditional Crafts.

Arts & Crafts

Kyoto is Japan's heart and soul, a great centre for the arts for over a millennium. It was also the eastern terminus of the old Silk Road and the final repository for a continent's worth of cultural influences. Japan has at times looked outward and at times looked inwards, drawing inspiration from the world and then refining it to the nth degree. The result is a rich, sophisticated artistic tradition that transcends museum walls and seeps into daily life.

Art of the Heian Court

By all accounts, and most notably Murasaki Shikubu's 11th-century se-rialised novel, *The Tale of Genji*, life in the Heian court reached near sublime levels of aestheticism. Chief among pleasures was the compo-sition of *waka*, 31-syllable poems in Japanese (as opposed to Chinese, the language for court documents). Skill in composition, which required both a working understanding of the symbolism and themes established in classical Chinese poetry and a heightened sensitivity – ears attuned to the rustling of bamboo or the call of the cuckoo, for example – could make or break a courtier's reputation.

For the scoop on Kyoto's gallery scene, see bilingual Kansai Art Beat (www.kansaiartbeat.com).

It was also crucial in romance (a significant diversion for members of the court): lovers (and potential lovers) corresponded via handwritten poems. It was important to choose just the right colour and texture of *washi* (traditional paper usually made from mulberry). Much attention was paid to the calligraphy, as well as the seasonality and emotional sym-bolism of the sprig of leaves or blossoms that was attached to a poem. The 'morning after poem' *(kinuginu no uta),* in particular, required ex-ceptional artistic acumen.

The arts were very much a social pastime: poetry and incense-blending competitions were popular among the aristocracy; so were musical per-formances featuring instruments such as the *biwa* (lute), *shakuhachi* (bamboo flute) and *koto* (zither). Group excursions, to view the cherry blossoms in spring or the moon on an autumn evening for example, were arranged to inspire new verse. The courtesan Sei Shōnagon (966–1017) describes several such outings (and other affairs of the court) in her diary-like work, *The Pillow Book* (Makura no Shōshi). (In literature, the women of the court were at the forefront: both Murasaki and Sei were recognised in their lifetime, as was the gifted *waka* poetess Ono no Komachi.)

During the late Heian period, painting, which had until then been largely Chinese in style, became self-referential, depicting episodes of court life (like those that appear in *The Tale of Genji*). These paintings, using vivid colours and often on long scrolls that unfurled horizontal-ly, came to be called *yamato-e* ('yamato' referring to the imperial clan). Gradually a series of style conventions evolved to further distinguish *yamato-e;* one of the most striking is the use of a not quite-bird's-eye perspective peering into palace rooms without their roofs (the better to see the intrigue!).

Lacquerware techniques, *maki-e,* which involves the sprinkling of silver and gold powders onto liquid lacquer to form a picture, developed during this period to adorn boxes for scroll paintings and sutras.

The art, and indeed, the whole culture of the Heian court might have seemed frivolous were it not for Buddhism tugging on its sleeves. Buddhism taught that all things (life included) were impermanent. From this the court derived a melancholy *joie de vivre:* the present was to be cherished because it would pass all too soon. Appreciation for the cherry blossoms, which appears in poetry of the time, is in this same vein; the blossoms, though glorious, bloom only for a brief time. The inherent sorrow of nature's transient beauty is summed up in the Japanese expression *mono no aware.*

Sadly, though aptly, little remains from the Heian era, though its legacy ripples through later eras. The greatest repository of works from the period is the Kyoto National Museum; the museums at Tō-ji and Daigo-ji also have some important pieces, too.

The Medieval Arts

The rise of the warrior class heralded great changes in the arts. Japan once again turned to face the world, and new artistic styles and currents of thought – most notably Zen Buddhism – swept in from Song-dynasty China (960–1279). Gradually, the loci of culture shifted from the court to the palaces of the new rulers, the shoguns and to the monasteries. Minimalist monochrome ink wash paintings (called *sumi-e*), often painted by Zen priests, came into vogue; the decisive, intuitive brush strokes required of this style were considered a meditative exercise. Some of the best examples we have of literature of the time, such as Kamo Chōmei's *Hōjō-ki* (The Ten Foot Square Hut; 1212) and Yoshida Kenkō's *Tsurezuregusa* (Essays in Idleness; 1331), were penned by pensive monks.

The Muromachi era (1336–1573) produced two great artistic centres: Kinkaku-ji, the retirement villa of the third Ashikaga shogun, Yoshimitsu (1358–1403), and Ginkaku-ji, the retirement villa of the 8th Ashikaga shogun, Yoshimasa (1436–1490). Yoshimitsu was an early patron of *nō* theatre; Yoshimasa commissioned the first teahouse (p180).

With the development of shoin-zukuri–style architecture (p175), painting moved from scrolls to the larger canvas of *fusama* (sliding doors) and *byōbo* (folding screens). The painters of the Kano school, who would have a hand in shaping Japanese art for centuries, took the subjects and conventions of *sumi-e* and added a bolder hand – introducing colour, more pronounced outlines and eventually brilliant gold leaf. At the same time they flattened the composition for a decorative effect. (A classic example of a Kano school painting is a gnarled pine tree clearly outlined against a backdrop of solid gold.)

Following a century of intermittent war, there was a great flowering of the arts during the Azuchi-Momoyama period (1574–1600), named for the locations of two castles, at Azuchi and Momoyama, built in succession by two of Japan's great unifiers, Obu Nobunaga and Toyotomi Hideyoshi (respectively). Their hard-won (though short-lived) peace inspired a flurry of building and artistic patronage. The aesthetics of this period were broad: for public consumption Japan's new leaders commissioned ostentatious, gilded works as a display of power and for themselves, as a balm for their warrior souls, austere *sumi-e* painting. The tea ceremony (p179) also flourished during this time.

Ikebana

The Japanese art of flower arranging, ikebana (literally 'living flowers'), is thought to date back to the 6th century, when Buddhism entered the country bringing with it the tradition of leaving flowers as offerings for

Art Books

From Postwar to Postmodern, Art in Japan 1945–1989 (Dorun Chung; 2013)

Hundred Years of Japanese Film (Donald Richie; 2012)

the spirits of the dead. During the Muromachi period, flower arranging got swept up in the tea movement and developed into a fine art. One of the early innovators was Ikenobō Senno, a monk at Kyoto's Rokkaku-dō. His descendants formed the Ikenobō school (www.ikenobo.jp), which is still active today and sometimes puts on exhibitions. High-end hotels and department stores may also have ikebana displays.

The classic style of ikebana is *rikka* (standing flowers), which distills a whole world in a few blooms and sprigs placed upright in a shallow bowl. Later styles include *shōka* (living flowers), in which three elements are arranged to represent heaven, earth and mankind; and even more contemporary free-style techniques like *nageire* (throwing-in) and *moribana* (heaped flowers).

Art of the Floating World

Ukiyo was a play on words: spelt with one set of Chinese characters, it meant the 'fleeting world', our tenuous, temporary abode on earth and a pivotal concept in Japanese Buddhism for centuries; change the first character, however, and you got the homophone, the 'floating world', which was used to describe the urban pleasure quarters in Edo-era Japan. In this topsy-turvy floating world, the social hierarchies dictated by the Tokugawa shoganate were inverted: money meant more than rank, actors were the arbitrators of style and courtesans were the most accomplished of artists.

While the lords continued in their high-minded pursuits, the increasingly wealthy merchant class had become the greatest patrons of the arts. Their outré tastes (which the nobility would have considered garish, though may have secretly enjoyed) gave us two of Japan's most recognisable art forms: kabuki theatre – that of the flamboyant costumes and dramatic makeup – and *ukiyo-e*, woodblock prints. The great chronicler of the age was Ihara Saikaku (1642–93). His first novel, *Koshoku Ichidai Otoko* (The Life of an Amorous Man; 1682), reads like an updated (and funnier) *The Tale of Genji*, with the wealthy son of a 17th-century Osakan merchant as its antihero.

Ukiyo-e were literally pictures of the floating world, capturing famed beauties, pleasure boats and outings under the cherry blossoms. They were also postcards from the world beyond; at a time when rigid laws prevented much of the populace from travelling, woodblock prints presented compelling scenes from around Japan – such as The Great Wave off Kanagawa on display at the Kyoto Ukiyo-e Museum. The vivid colours, novel composition and flowing lines of *ukiyo-e* caused great excitement in the West in the late 19th century, sparking a vogue that one French art critic dubbed *japonisme*. Several shops around town, like Nishiharu, sell old prints or reproductions.

Performing Arts

Nō & Kyōgen

The oldest of Japan's performing arts that still exists today, *nō* itself began as a pastiche of earlier traditions, including Shintō rites, popular entertainments like pantomime and acrobatics, and *gagaku* (the traditional music and dance of the imperial court). It owes its form and its repertory to the artistic dynasty of Kan'ami; his son Ze'ami founded the Kanze school of *nō*, which is still active today and oversees the Kyoto Kanze Kaikan No Theatre (www.kyoto-kanze.jp).

Rather than a drama in the usual sense, *nō* seeks to express a poetic moment by symbolic and almost abstract means: glorious movements, sonorous chorus and music, and subtle expression. The stage is furnished with only a single pine tree. There are two principal characters:

Tokyo is the centre of Japan's contemporary theatre scene, but lately Kyoto is drawing focus with its edgy, new festival, Kyoto Experiment (http://kyoto-ex.jp).

Mibu kyōgen, mimed Buddhist morality plays and a kind of folk art, are performed today at Mibu-dera just as they were in Kyoto's early medieval period.

the *shite,* who is sometimes a living person but more often a ghost whose soul cannot rest or a demon; and the *waki,* who leads the main character towards the play's climactic moment.

Nō's haunting masks, carved from wood, are works of art unto themselves. Many still in use are hundreds of years old (the oil and sweat from the actors' faces keeps the wood supple). They are often designed so that tilting the masks at various angles can change the expression of the mask, an effect heightened by the lighting of the stage (which is often firelight). Masks are used to depict female or nonhuman characters; adult male characters are played without masks.

Comic vignettes known as *kyōgen* were added to programs of *nō* plays, taking the spectator from the sublime realm to the ridiculous world of the everyday. Using the colloquial language of the time and a cast of stock characters, *kyōgen* poke fun at such subjects as samurai, depraved priests and faithless women. Masks are not worn, and costumes tend to feature bold, colourful patterns.

Kabuki & Bunraku

Kabuki got its start in Kyoto when, around the year 1600, a shrine priestess named Okuni and her troupe of dancers started entertaining crowds on the banks of the Kamo-gawa with a type of dance people dubbed kabuki, a slang expression that meant 'cool' or 'in vogue'. (The performances were also a gateway to prostitution and a series of government crackdowns gave rise to one of the most fascinating elements of kabuki, the *onnagata* – adult male actors who specialise in portraying women). Kabuki later spread to Edo (Tokyo), where it would reach its golden age.

Bunraku, Japan's traditional puppet theatre developed alongside kabuki, draws upon the same body of popular themes and stories. In fact, the great playwright of the day, Chikamatsu Monzaemon, wrote first for the bunraku stage, and only later for kabuki (and many of his bunraku plays were adapted for kabuki). His specialities were tragedies of star-crossed lovers that ended with double-suicides – some based on real anecdotes. Stories of historic battles were common too, and really anything that pitted *giri* (duty) against *ninjō* (feelings) was sure to resonate with audiences.

The stories would have been well known to the audience, who took pleasure in the spectacle of it all. Kabuki is driven by its actors, who train for the profession from childhood. The highlights for many fans are the dramatic poses (called *mie*) that actors strike at pivotal moments. Every December, Tokyo's most famous kabuki actors come to Kyoto for a series of performances. While Kyoto's kabuki theatre, Minami-za, is closed for repairs, shows will be held at ROHM Theatre Kyoto.

Bunraku's puppets are sophisticated – nearly two-thirds life-sized – and manipulated by up to three black-robed puppeteers. The puppeteers do not speak; the story is provided by a narrator performing *jōruri* (narrative chanting) to the accompaniment of a *shamisen* (a three-stringed instrument resembling a lute or banjo). Bunraku was most popular in the merchant city of Osaka, where the National Bunraku Theatre keeps the torch alive.

Butō: Contemporary Japanese Dance

Butō is Japan's unique and fascinating contribution to contemporary dance. It was born out of a rejection of the excessive formalisation that characterises traditional forms of Japanese dance and of an intention to return to more ancient roots. Hijikata Tatsumi (1928–86), a dancer born in the remote northern province of Akita, founded the movement, giving his first performance in 1959.

At a time when 'Southern Barbarian' (ie European) fashion was all the rage, Okuni is reported to have sometimes danced in Portuguese dress with a crucifix around her neck. A statue of her, fan in hand and with a samurai sword slung over one shoulder, stands diagonally across from Minami-za.

During a performance, one or more dancers use their naked or semi-naked bodies to express the most elemental and intense human emotions. Nothing is forbidden in *butō* and performances often deal with taboo topics, such as sexuality and death. For this reason, critics often describe *butō* as scandalous, and *butō* dancers delight in pushing the boundaries of what can be considered beautiful in artistic performance.

Though performers have toured internationally, in Japan *butō* has remained a largely underground scene. This changed in 2016 with the opening of the Kyoto Butoh-kan (www.butohkan.jp), a dedicated performance space.

Crafts

Since its founding, Kyoto has attracted the country's most talented artisans, who came to work for the imperial court, the nobility and the Buddhist clergy (and later the warlords and wealthy merchants). Still today, the Kyoto 'brand' symbolises elegance, refinement and excellence. Items bearing the prefix *kyo,* as in *kyo-yūzen* (Kyoto dyed kimono fabric) have a natural cachet. To get a full overview of the range of Kyoto crafts, we recommend a visit to the Fureai-Kan Kyoto Museum of Traditional Crafts.

Of course, the city supports fewer artisans than it used to, as fewer people use – or can afford to use – handmade works in daily life. But

THE ART OF THE KIMONO

Kimono simply means 'thing to wear' but in the hands of Kyoto's weavers and dyers they are works of art. Heirloom pieces, and the robes worn by the city's *geiko* and *maiko* (fully fledged and apprentice geisha, respectively), are still made by hand in the city.

Nishijin is the city's historic textile district and its weaving (called Nishijin-*ori*) is internationally renowned. Originally weavers worked only with silk, but over time new methods were adopted by the Kyoto weavers and they began to experiment with materials such as gauze, brocade, damask, satin and crepe. The best known Nishijin style is the exquisite *tsuzure* – a tightly woven tapestry cloth produced with a hand loom *(tebata)* – on which detailed patterns are preset. There are demonstrations of weaving and fashion shows at the Nishijin Textile Center and examples on display at the Orinasu-kan textile museum.

Kyoto is also famous for its *kyo-yūzen* textiles. *Yūzen* is a method of silk-dyeing *(senshoku)* developed to perfection in the 17th century by fan painter Miyazaki Yūzen. *Kyō-yūzen* designs typically feature simple circular flowers *(maru-tsukushi)*, birds and landscapes, and stand out for their use of bright-coloured dyes. The technique demands great dexterity in tracing designs by hand *(tegaki)* before rice paste is applied to fabric like a stencil to prevent colours from bleeding into other areas of the fabric. By repeatedly changing the pattern of the rice paste, very complex designs can be achieved.

Traditionally, when the dyeing process was complete, the material was rinsed in the Kamo-gawa and Katsura-gawa rivers (believed to be particularly effective in fixing the colours) before being hung out to dry. Every year in mid-August this ritual is re-enacted and the fabrics flap in the wind like rows of vibrant banners.

Other techniques include stencil-dyeing *(kyō-komon)* and tie-dyeing *(kyō-kanoko shibori)*. *Kyō-komon* (komon means 'small crest') was popular in the 16th and 17th centuries with warriors, who liked to match their kimono to their armour. *Aizome* (the technique of dyeing fabrics in vats of fermented indigo plants) was traditionally used to colour the clothes of the working class. The indigo workshop Aizen Kōbō makes some beautiful indigo textiles.

If you'd like to purchase a kimono or an obi (kimono sash), you will find the best prices on used items at either the Kōbō-san or the Tenjin-san markets. If you're after a new kimono, try Erizen or Takashimaya.

there are always those willing to try, and Kyoto has a vibrant scene of contemporary artisans building on tradition and working towards something new. See some of their creations at Kyoto Design House.

Pottery & Ceramics

At the height of productivity, in the mid-1600s, there were more than 10 different kilns active in and around the city. Of these, however, only Kiyomizu-yaki remains today. This kiln first gained prominence through the workmanship of potter Nonomura Ninsei (1596–1660), who developed an innovative method of applying enamel overglaze to porcelain. This technique was further embellished by adding decorative features such as transparent glaze *(sometsuke)*, as well as incorporating designs in red paint *(aka-e)* and celadon *(seiji)*.

Many shops on the streets below Kiyomizu-dera, like Asahi-dō, sell Kiyomizu-yaki and other types of Japanese pottery. Tōki Matsuri is Kyoto's annual ceramics fair.

The *mingei* (folk crafts) movement in the early 20th century promoted the works of artisans over cheaper, mass-produced goods. Central to the *mingei* philosophy is *yono bi* (beauty through use). Potter Kawai Kanjirō was one of the movement's founders; his studio is now the Kawai Kanjirō Memorial Hall.

Lacquerware

Known in Japan as *shikki* or *nurimono*, lacquerware is made using the sap from the lacquer tree *(urushi)*, a close relative of poison oak. Raw lacquer is actually toxic and causes severe skin irritation in those who have not developed immunity. It's an ancient technique, to protect and enhance the beauty of wood, that's been refined over the centuries. Lacquer is naturally clear; pigments such as iron oxide (which produces vermillion) are added for colour. Multiple layers are painstakingly applied and left to dry, and finally polished to a luxurious shine; once hardened, lacquerware is extraordinarily durable. Zōhiko has a beautiful selection.

Fans

Originally made from the leaves of the cypress tree, *kyō-sensu* (Kyoto fans) are now primarily made with paper fixed onto a skeleton of delicate bamboo ribs. The paper can feature decorations from simple geometric designs to courtly scenes from the Heian period and are often sprinkled with gold or silver leaf powder. Some fans are designed to be practical; others are for use in ceremonies and the arts (such as *nō* drama or the traditional dances performed by geisha). Kyōsen-dō is a fan speciality shop.

Washi

The art of making paper by hand was introduced to Japan from China in the 5th century. *Washi* (traditional Japanese paper) is normally produced using mulberry, but it can also be made from mountain shrubs and other plants. One distinctive type of *washi* found in Kyoto is *kyō-chiyogami,* which has traditionally been used by Japanese to wrap special gifts.There are several fine *washi* shops in Kyoto, including Wagami no Mise and Kamiji Kakimoto. *Washi* is also used to make traditional lights like those sold at Miura Shōmei.

Architecture & Gardens

Japan's traditional design aesthetic of clean lines, natural materials, heightened spatial awareness and subtle enhancement has inspired artists and designers around the world. Kyoto has many outstanding examples in its centuries-old shrines, temples and teahouses, but also in modern works that riff on the old while striving for the new. Since ancient times in Japan, landscape design has been inseparable from architecture, and Kyoto has the greatest collection of gardens in the country.

Traditional Japanese Architecture

Early Japanese architecture was greatly indebted to Chinese building technology, design motifs and geomancy. From the introduction of Buddhism in the 6th century through the medieval period, temples *(tera* or *ji)* were Japan's most important works of architecture and exerted a strong stylistic influence on all other types of structures; it was often through Buddhism that new styles and techniques entered Japan from the continent.

The construction of Shintō shrines (called *jinja, jingū, gū* or *taisha)* predates the arrival of Buddhism; however, there is little evidence of what shrines looked like before they were influenced by Buddhist architecture. One hint is the forked finials (called *chigi)* that appear on the roofs of some of the oldest shrines, such as Nara's Kasuga Taisha. (In truth most temple buildings aren't that old either, having been rebuilt many times over the years, sometimes in the existing style and sometimes in a new style.)

In the late Heian era, a style of architecture called *shinden-zukuri* emerged, with structures consisting of a series of halls connected by covered corridors. While rooted in the old continental framework, this style introduced a lightness and flexibility – by way of sliding doors and screens – that the monumental structures in the Chinese style lacked. There are no *shinden-zukuri* structures that remain standing in Kyoto, although Heian-jingū is designed to replicate a Heian-era palace.

Shion-zukuri & Sukiya-zukuri

Much of what we think of today as traditional Japanese architecture came into being in the Muromachi period. A new style, called *shoin-zukuri,* developed under the influence of Zen Buddhism. What distinguished it from *shinden-zukuri* was a preference for naturalness, asymmetry and restraint, achieved by extracting, in equal parts, beauty and function from locally abundant natural materials. A key feature of *shoin-zukuri* (and later *sukiya-zukuri)* is the *tokonoma,* an alcove for displaying a scroll painting or ikebana arrangement, and accentuated with a *tokobashira,* a decorative wooden column.

The principles and features of *shoin-zukuri* were refined in *sukiya-zukuri,* a style that developed in tandem with the tea ceremony during the Azuchi-Momoyama and Edo periods. *Sukiya* means 'abode of refinement', though spelled with a different character it can also mean 'abode of emptiness' – which has a nice Buddhist ring to it. *Sukiya-zukuri* was well suited to intimate spaces, as it favoured details over grand statements. It doubled

Books

Japanese Architecture (Mira Locher; 2010)

What is Japanese Architecture? (Nishi Kazuo and Hozumi Kazuo; 1996)

Japan-ness in Architecture (Arata Isozaki; 2006)

down on the beauty inherent in natural materials: the result could be exceedingly elegant, as in a ceiling of woven wooden slats, or totally rustic, as in a *tokobashira* with the bark left intact. To show a little eccentricity – as befitting a cultured Kyotoite – was encouraged; it worked, because by then, Japan's master carpenters had worked out the ideal proportions for all the structural components.

Sukiya-zukuri was the last major development in Japanese architecture before Western ideas entered Japan. Many older inns in Kyoto are in this style. Sumiya Pleasure House, an Edo-era salon in Shimabara where geisha and courtesans entertained, is an example of the elegant *sukiya*-style architecture twinned with the decadent tastes of the night world.

Katsura Rikyū, which has structures in both *shoin-zukuri* and *sukiya-zukuri* styles, is often considered the finest existing example of traditional Japanese architecture.

Natural Materials

Japan's abundant forests were an easy source of wood, which has historically been the building material of choice. *Hinoki* (cypress) and more recently *sugi* (cryptomeria) are often used structurally; more valuable woods, like red pine and cherry, might be used for the floors, or ornamentally. Stone (usually granite) appears in foundations, bridges or castle ramparts; however, the frequency of earthquakes in Japan made it an unsuitable material for walls. Instead, timber frames were filled in with mud plaster, which might be covered with a final coat of lime (for a uniform, white finish) or mixed with pigment, sand or straw (for colour and texture). Today's buildings often use textured wallpaper to mimic this effect. Bamboo has traditionally been used for rafters, gutters and fencing; dried reeds were woven into floor mats (tatami) and window shades.

Gates & Roofs

A prominent feature of any monumental structure is its *mon* (gate), which may be even more impressive than the structures behind it. With the exception of shrines, which have a unique style of gate called *torii* (that looks like the symbol for 'pi' with an extra lintel), *mon* are constructed of several pillars or casements joined at the top by a roof. Gates in Japan are rich in symbolism: their size and design elements correspond to strict regulations on rank and importance; in the case of temples or shrines, they represent the boundary between the sacred and

---

MACHIYA: KYOTO'S TRADITIONAL TOWNHOUSES

Machiya are wooden row houses that functioned as both homes and workplaces for Japan's bourgeousie, a class that grew in prominence during the Edo period. The shop area was located in the front of the house, while the rooms lined up behind it formed the family's private living quarters. This elongated shape, which came about because homes were once taxed according to the size of their street frontage, earned *machiya* the nickname '*unagi no nedoko*' (eel bedrooms). The affluent among Kyoto's merchants adopted design elements from *sukiya-zukuri*, such as delicate latticework. Even with space at a minimum, many *machiya* have small courtyard gardens, called *tsubo-niwa* – one *tsubo* being the standard size of two tatami mats.

Although well suited to Kyoto's humid, mildew-prone summers, a wooden *machiya* has a limited lifespan of about 50 years. In the decades after WWII, many families chose not to rebuild them and instead put up multistorey concrete buildings. In many ways this made sense: modern buildings were simpler to maintain and could easily be fitted out with the latest mod-cons, like air-conditioning; they were cheaper to build, as the cost of traditional materials and workmanship was rising; and the hardship of Japan's steep inheritance tax could be offset by income generated by rental units. The pendulum swung back around in the 1990s, when it became clear that the city was losing something dear. Since then there have been numerous efforts to restore old *machiya;* many of them now house restaurants, cafes and boutiques. Judith Clancy's *Kyoto Machiya Restaurant Guide* (2012) has over one hundred suggestions.

PAGODAS

••

A pagoda *(to)* is a tower with stacked eaves, each one smaller than the one below. It is a style of Buddhist architecture that evolved in China from the Indian stupa, which originally functioned as a reliquary. Wooden pagodas may be anywhere from one to seven storeys tall. On top is a spire that usually has nine tiers, representing the nine spheres of heaven. They are constructed around a central pillar (called a *shimbashira*) that acts as a counterweight when the structure sways – making them very earthquake resistant. (Tokyo's Skytree, the world's tallest freestanding tower, built in 2012, uses this same technology.)

Early on in Japanese Buddhism, the pagoda was a temple's most important structure; older Tendai and Shingon temples may have one, but Zen temples usually don't. The oldest building in Kyoto is the five-storey pagoda at Daigo-ji. Constructed in 951, it is one of only a few buildings to survive the Onin War. The 57m-tall pagoda at Tō-ji is the tallest in Japan.

the mundane. It is not uncommon for a structure to have more than one gate; perhaps unintuitively, the gates are usually freestanding, unconnected to border walls.

Temple complexes are typically designed on a north–south axis (though there are plenty of exceptions); for this reason, the *nandai-mon* (southern gate) is usually the main gate. Most temples have a *niō-mon* (guardian gate), which houses the frightful-looking statues of gods, such as Raijin (the god of thunder) and Fū-jin (the god of wind), between the main gate and the *hondō* (main hall; also sometimes called *honden*). Temples built in the Zen style will have a grand *san-mon* (short for *sangedatsumon;* 'gate of the three emancipations'), which may be two storeys tall. A *kara-mon* ('Chinese' gate) is an elaborately decorated gate with a curving bargeboard; only the most important structures – say, a palace – will have a *kara-mon*.

Another hallmark of traditional architecture is a strong roof, which may be straight, curved or cusped and covered in clay tiles, cedar shingles or, in the case of farmhouses or teahouses, rice straw thatch. Long overhanging eaves shelter the verandahs from the elements. All told, a structure might appear to be half roof. Temples usually have hipped roofs while shrines usually have gabled roofs (or hip-and-gable roofs). Shrines in the *nagare-zukuri* style (the most common style) have gabled roofs that extend, on one side only, over the verandah where worshippers approach.

Design Elements

Traditional Japanese constructions use a post and lintel system, which, when combined with the gridlike composition of latticed screens and tatami-mat floors, give buildings an overwhelmingly rectilinear appearance. Outer walls may be fitted with *shoji,* sliding wooden screens covered with translucent *washi* (Japanese handmade paper), which allows a soft light to filter in. They can also be opened (or even removed), eliminating the barrier between inside and outside. Inside, heavy-duty sliding screens covered with opaque *washi,* called *fusama,* are used to partition rooms; like *shoji,* these can be removed. Another defining feature of traditional buildings is that they are designed for a life largely lived on the floor. Tatami mats cushion the floor where people sit on *zabuton* (floor pillows) around low tables and sleep on futon (floor mattresses).

Gardens

Flowering plants are only one component of the Japanese garden, which may be composed of any combination of vegetation (including trees, shrubs and moss), stones of varying sizes, and water. Some gardens are not limited to that which falls within their walls, but take into account the scenery beyond (a technique called *shakkei* or 'borrowed scenery'). Often they are meant to evoke a landscape in miniature, with rocks standing in

Garden Books

••••••••••••••••••••••

Zen Gardens & Temples of Kyoto (John Dougill; 2017)

••••••••••••••••••••••

The Art of the Japanese Garden (David and Michiko Young; 2005)

••••••••••••••••••••••

Japanese Stone Gardens (Stephen Mansfield; 2009)

TEMPLE OR SHRINE?

Buddhist temples and Shintō shrines were historically intertwined, until they were separated by government decree in 1868. But centuries of coexistence means the two resemble each other architecturally. The easiest way to tell them apart is to check the gate. The main entrance of a shrine is a *torii* (gate) – usually two upright pillars joined at the top by two horizontal crossbars. *Torii* are often painted bright vermilion. In contrast, the *mon* (main entrance gate) of a temple is constructed of several pillars or casements, joined at the top by a multitiered roof. *Mon* often contain guardian figures, usually Niō (deva kings).

Neighbourhood Shrines

Shrines aren't always grand structures; all over the city you can spot small wooden ones, sometimes no bigger than a doll's house. They're maintained by members of the local community, who take up collections for their upkeep and leave fresh offerings, such as fruit, flowers or sake. The shrines are located at auspicious points, based on ancient geomancy, and for that reason aren't moved – even if it means constructions have to go up around them.

The garden on the north side of the Hōjō at Tōfuku-ji, created by landscape artist Shigemori Mirei in 1939, is an example of modern Japanese garden design.

for famous mountains of myth or literature; raked gravel may represent flowing water. Garden elements are arranged asymmetrically and shapes, such as the outline of a pond, are often irregular. The idea is that the garden should appear natural, or more like nature in its ideal state; in reality most gardens are meticulously maintained – and entirely by hand. Gardens may be designed as spaces of beauty, for leisure and entertainment purposes, or they might be a designation of sacred space (most fall somewhere in between). The white gravel that appears in some temple gardens is rooted in Shintō tradition: there are gravel courtyards at Ise-jingū, which dates to the 3rd century and is considered Japan's most sacred spot.

Kare-sansui: 'Dry' Landscape Gardens

Equally iconic and enigmatic, *kare-sansui* are gardens composed of rocks and raked gravel. They may also have moss or shrubbery, but there is no water element and none of the lushness that you might associate with gardens. They are designed to be viewed from a single vantage point – usually that of an adjacent hall; this style is known as *kanshō* (contemplation garden). *Kare-sansui* gardens are rooted in the culture of the Zen monastery. Monks would meditate on them and in them – as tending to the garden was also considered a form of meditation. Some bear a resemblance to nature scenes depicted in monochrome ink wash paintings; the garden of 15 stones at Ryōan-ji is famously abstract (and, like Zen, resists interpretation). Daitoku-ji has several *kare-sansui* gardens spread among its many subtemples.

Strolling Gardens

The gardens of Muromachi-era Kyoto were largely built by a class of Kyotoites called *kawara-mono* (river people) who lived in settlements on the banks of the Kamo-gawa and were considered outcasts.

Strolling gardens *(shūyū)* are meant to be entered and viewed from multiple vantage points along a meandering path. This style falls towards the leisure side of the spectrum and can often be found on imperial or feudal estates. In the Edo period, *kaiyū* ('many-pleasure') gardens came into fashion; these were like several gardens in one, set around a central pond. Such gardens have a number of interesting architectural elements, such as bridges, which may be a graceful sloping arch or a simple slab of stone, and pavilions, which were created as places for rest or for moon-viewing. Some may employ a technique called *shin-gyō-sō* (formal-semiformal-informal; the *sō* is the same as in *sōan*, the 'grass cottage' of the teahouse), meaning the garden takes on a more and more intimate feeling as the visitor heads deeper. The ideal garden is designed to be attractive in all seasons, though most are associated with a particular time of year (be it the blooming of the azaleas in April or the turning of the maples in November).

The Tea Ceremony

Chanoyu (literally 'water for tea') is usually translated as 'tea ceremony', but it's more like performance art, with each element – from the gestures of the host to the feel of the tea bowl in your hand – carefully designed to articulate an aesthetic experience. It's had a profound and lasting influence on the arts in Japan; whether you take part in a ceremony or simply pause to admire a teahouse, *sadō* (the way of tea) will colour your Kyoto experience.

The Story of Tea

By at least the 9th century tea had arrived in Japan from Tang-dynasty China, though it wasn't until the 12th century that it really took off. This was when Buddhist monks returned from what had since become Song-dynasty China with two important new developments: Zen Buddhism and a loose, powdered tea that came to be known in Japan as *matcha*. Unlike the typical infusions of today (and a vast improvement over the earlier boiled tea), *matcha* is whisked into an emulsion and drunk unstrained.

Monks used it for its medicinal properties, and also to help them power through long meditation sessions. Like everything else in monastic life – the sweeping of the temple grounds and the tending of the garden, for example – the preparation of tea was approached as a kind of working meditation.

In the Muromachi period, when there was a great flow of ideas between the monasteries and the feudal elite, *sadō* became part of the larger culture. To be sure, tea wasn't an entirely high-minded pursuit: it was also an excuse for a social gathering and an opportunity to demonstrate one's taste (and affluence) – in the selection of utensils prepared, the artwork displayed, even the teahouse itself. Eventually various styles of *sadō* emerged, which were codified into schools; many are still active today, including Urasenke, which runs the Urasenke Chadō Research Center.

> Most often *matcha* (powdered green tea) is served as *usucha* ('thin' tea), which is already much thicker than an infusion. At formal tea ceremonies (and at some tea shops) it is also served as *koicha* ('thick' tea), which is as thick as cream.

Wabi-sabi & the Art of Tea

Wabi-sabi is an aesthetic that embraces the notion of ephemerality and imperfection and is Japan's most profound – though hardest to pin down – contribution to the arts. *Wabi* roughly means 'rustic' and connotes the loneliness of the wilderness, while *sabi* can be interpreted as 'weathered', 'waning' or 'altered with age'. Together the two words signify an object's natural imperfections, arising in its inception, and the acquired beauty that comes with the patina of time. What makes *wabi-sabi* so important, in addition to its novelty, is that it percolated through all the divergent arts wrapped up in the tea ceremony: architecture, landscape design, ikebana (flower arranging), ceramics and calligraphy.

Sen no Rikkyū (1522–1591), personal tea master to both Oda Nobunaga and Toyotomi Hideyoshi, is credited with laying down the foundations of *wabi-sabi* – and with raising tea to the level of art form. Like all of the prominent tea masters of the era, he was a student of Zen (at Daitoku-ji) and its influence shows in his preference for naturalness and unaffected vitality.

Teahouse Architecture

The classic *chashitsu* (teahouse), as established by the old medieval masters, had an area of 4½ tatami mats, or nearly 7½ sq metres (though they could be even smaller). Made of earth and wood, with a thatched roof, teahouses often look more like hastily thrown-together shelters than intentional works of art – which was exactly the point. The most rustic extreme (and the truest embodiment of *wabi-sabi*) are called *sōan*, literally 'grass cottages'. More than just a place to drink tea, a Japanese teahouse is a distillation of an artistic vision; even today, no architect would turn down a commission to work on one.

Visitors to a teahouse approach via the *roji* ('dewy' path), formed by irregular stepping stones. The path represents a space of transition – a place to clear one's mind and calm one's spirit before entering the teahouse. The doorway is purposely low, causing those who enter to stoop, and thus humble themselves. All are considered equal inside the teahouse (swords were to remain outside). Inside, the sole decoration is a spray of seasonal flowers or leaves and a hanging scroll in the *to-kanoma* (alcove).

Tea grown in Uji, south of Kyoto, is said to be the best in Japan; according to lore, the first tea bushes planted there were from seeds brought back from China by the monk Eisei (who also introduced Zen).

Chadōgu: Tools of the Tea Ceremony

Every devotee of the way of tea is a curator of tea utensils, which include *chawan* (tea bowls), *chigusa* (jars for storing tea), *chashaku* (bamboo scoops for measuring tea) and *chasen* (bamboo whisks for mixing the *matcha*). In the spirit of *wabi-sabi,* ceramics for the tea ceremony are often dented, misshapen or rough in texture, with drips of glaze running down the edges.

Raku-yaki, a style of hand-formed earthenware first commissioned by Sen no Rikkyu, is particularly prized. It's rapidly cooled – creating an opportunity for spontaneous (and prized) imperfections to arise – and is often glazed black or red. *Raku-yaki* is still made in Kyoto today by 15th-generation artisan, Raku Kichizaemon; the Raku Museum displays works by successive generations. The Kyoto National Museum also has an excellent collection of tea utensils.

With its long history of *chanoyu,* Kyoto is the best place in Japan to shop for tea utensils. Recommended shops include Asahi-dō and Kaikadō.

Experiencing a Tea Ceremony

All of this – the careful design of space and selection of utensils, good company and, of course, good tea – comes together in the tea ceremony. A formal tea ceremony might last hours and include several courses of food and drink, like a dinner party. The actual preparation and drinking of the tea follows a highly ritualised sequence: the utensils are carefully washed and presented; the tea bowl is held just so. It's an insistence on correctness that infuses much of the arts in Japan.

For a small taste of the experience, several establishments offer short versions geared towards travellers. Try En, Club Ōkitsu Kyoto or Camellia Tea Experience.

Survival Guide

Transport

ARRIVING IN KYOTO

Most foreign visitors arrive in Kyoto via Kansai International Airport (KIX; Kyoto's main international entry point). Kyoto is also within reach of two other airports and it's sometimes cheaper to fly into Tokyo than into KIX.

Kansai International Airport

Built on an artificial island in Osaka Bay, Kansai International Airport (KIX) is about 75 minutes away from Kyoto by direct express trains.

At KIX, there is a tourist information counter operated by the Osaka prefectural government. It's located roughly in the centre of the international arrivals hall, and can supply maps and answer questions.

If you'd prefer not to lug your bags into Kyoto, there are several luggage delivery services in the arrivals hall.

When it comes time to depart, those travelling on Japanese airlines (JAL and ANA) can make use of an advance check-in counter inside the JR ticket office in Kyoto Station. This service allows you to check in with your luggage at the station, which is a real bonus for those with heavy bags.

Train

The fastest and most convenient way to move between KIX and Kyoto is the special JR Haruka airport express (reserved/unreserved ¥3370/2850, 1¼ hours). It's actually cheaper to buy a JR West Kansai Area Pass as this is valid for unreserved seats on the JR Haruka express to KIX and costs ¥2300. Buy tickets at the JR ticket office inside the north entrance of Kyoto Station, to the left of the platform ticket gates (you'll need to show your passport).

First and last departures on the JR Haruka express from KIX to Kyoto are at 6.30am and 10.16pm Monday to Friday (6.40am on weekends); first and last departures from Kyoto to KIX are at 5.45am and 8.30pm.

If you have time to spare, you can save money by taking the *kankū kaisoku* (Kansai airport express) between the airport and Osaka Station, and then taking a regular *shinkaisoku* (special rapid train) to Kyoto. The total journey by this route takes about 95 minutes with good connections and costs around ¥1750.

Bus

Kansai International Airport Limousine Bus (☑075-682-4400; www.kate.co.jp/en; one way adult/child ¥2550/1280) runs frequent buses between Kyoto and KIX (about 1½ hours). Buses from Kyoto Station to the airport depart from the **Hachijo-guchi exit** (Map p216) in front of the

---

CLIMATE CHANGE & TRAVEL

Every form of transport that relies on carbon-based fuel generates CO_2, the main cause of human-induced climate change. Modern travel is dependent on aeroplanes, which might use less fuel per kilometre per person than most cars but travel much greater distances. The altitude at which aircraft emit gases (including CO_2) and particles also contributes to their climate change impact. Many websites offer 'carbon calculators' that allow people to estimate the carbon emissions generated by their journey and, for those who wish to do so, to offset the impact of the greenhouse gases emitted with contributions to portfolios of climate-friendly initiatives throughout the world. Lonely Planet offsets the carbon footprint of all staff and author travel.

Avanti department store and Keihan Hotel every 20 to 40 minutes. There are also pick-up points at Shijō Karasuma and Sanjō Keihan departing roughly every 60 minutes. Purchase tickets from the ticket window near the boarding point.

Taxi

Perhaps the most convenient option is the **MK Taxi Sky Gate Shuttle limousine van service** (☑075-778-5489; www.mktaxi-japan.com; one way to Kansai airport ¥4200, to Itami airport ¥2900), a door-to-door service that will drop you off at most places in Kyoto – simply go to the staff counter at the south end of the KIX arrivals hall and they will do the rest. From Kyoto to the airport it is necessary to make reservations two days in advance to arrange pickup from your hotel in Kyoto.

A similar service is offered by **Yasaka Taxi** (☑075-803-4800; www.yasaka.jp; adult/child one way to/from Kansai airport to Kyoto ¥4200/2100). Keep in mind that these are shared taxis (actually vans), so you may be delayed by the driver picking up or dropping off other passengers.

Kyoto Station

Kyoto Station is linked to nearby cities by several excellent train lines, including Japan Railways (JR). JR also has links to cities further afield, many of which are served by super-fast *shinkansen* (bullet trains). If you plan to do a lot of train travel around the rest of Japan, consider buying a Japan Rail Pass.

Private lines connect Kyoto Station with Nagoya, Nara, Osaka and Kōbe. Where they exist, private lines are always cheaper than JR. In particular, if you're travelling between Kyoto Station and Nara, you'll probably find a *tokkyū* (limited express) on the Kintetsu line to be faster and more comfortable than JR.

Osaka International Airport

Osaka International Airport, commonly known as Itami (ITM), is closer to Kyoto than KIX, but it handles only domestic traffic. Still, you might find that your international carrier will tack on a domestic leg from Tokyo to Itami.

There's an info counter with English-speaking staff in the main arrivals hall. There are several luggage delivery services in the arrivals hall if you don't want to carry your bags to Kyoto.

Bus
Osaka Airport Transport (☑06-6844-1124; www.okkbus.co.jp; one way Itami to Kyoto ¥1310) runs frequent airport limousine buses between Itami and Kyoto Station (55 minutes). There are less-frequent pickups and drop offs at some of Kyoto's main hotels. The Itami stop is outside the arrivals hall – buy your ticket from the machine near the bus stop and ask one of the attendants which stand is for Kyoto. The Kyoto Station stop is in front of Avanti department store, which is opposite the Hachi-jo-guchi exit of the station.

Taxi
MK Taxi Sky Gate Shuttle limousine van service (☑075-778-5489; www.mktaxi-japan.com; one-way to Kansai airport ¥4200, to Itami airport ¥2900) travels to/from the airport. Call at least two days in advance to reserve.

Central Japan International Airport

Nagoya's Central Japan International Airport (NGO; www.centrair.jp), commonly known as Chubu Centrair, may seem a long way from Kyoto, but if you're travelling with a Japan Rail Pass, you'll find that it can be a good option, especially if you get a good deal on your flight.

Train
The Meitetsu Tokoname Railroad line connects Centrair with Nagoya Station (¥870, 30 minutes), which connects to the Tōkaidō *shinkansen* (bullet train) line. It is therefore possible to use Centrair as your gateway to Kyoto.

The *shinkansen* (¥5590, 35 minutes) goes to/from Nagoya Station to Kyoto Station. You can save around half the cost by taking regular express trains, but you will need to change trains at least once and can expect the trip to take about three hours.

Narita & Haneda International Airports

It's perfectly possible to fly to/from Tokyo via either Narita International Airport (NRT) or Haneda International Airport (HND) when visiting Kyoto. You can catch domestic flights from either airport on to Kansai International Airport (KIX) or Osaka International Airport (ITM).

Train

You can go by train from Narita or Haneda to Kyoto. From Narita, take the Narita Airport Express (N'Ex) to Tokyo Station then switch to a *shinkansen* to Kyoto. The total journey will take about four hours and cost ¥16,000. From Haneda, take airport transport (there are several options) between the airport and either Tokyo Station or Shinagawa Station and switch to a *shinkansen*. The total journey will take about three hours and cost ¥14,000.

GETTING AROUND

Bus

Kyoto has an intricate network of bus routes providing an efficient way of getting around at moderate cost. Most routes used by visitors have announcements and bus stop information displays in English. Most buses run be-tween 7am and 10pm, though a few run earlier or later.

Bus Terminals

Kyoto's main bus terminals are also train stations: Kyoto Station, Sanjō Station, Karasuma-Shijō Station and Kitaōji Station. The bus terminal at Kyoto Station is on the north side and has three main departure bays (departure points are indicated by the letter of the bay and number of the stop within that bay).

Bus stops usually have a map of destinations from that stop and a timetable for the buses serving that stop.

Bus Fares

Bus entry is usually through the back door and exit is via the front door. Inner-city buses charge a flat fare (¥230 for adults, ¥120 for children ages six to 12, free for those younger), which you drop into the clear plastic receptacle on top of the machine next to the driver on your way out. A separate machine gives change for ¥100 and ¥500 coins or ¥1000 notes. On buses serving the outer areas, take a *seiri-ken* (numbered ticket) on boarding. When alighting, an electronic board above the driver displays the fare corresponding to your ticket number (drop the *seiri-ken* into the ticket box with your fare).

Maps & Information

The main **bus information centre** (京都バス案内所; Map p216; ⏰city bus office 7.30am-7.30pm, JR office 9am-6pm; 🚉Kyoto Station) is in front of Kyoto Station. You can pick up bus maps, purchase bus tickets and passes (on all lines, including highway buses), and get additional information. The Kyoto Tourist Information Center (p192) stocks the *Bus Navi: Kyoto City Bus Sightseeing Map*, which shows the city's main bus lines.

City Loop Bus

In addition to the regular city buses, Kyoto has an

JAPAN RAIL PASS

The Japan Rail Pass is a must if you're planning extensive train travel within Japan. It will save you both money and the need to carry change each time you board a train. The pass covers all *shinkansen* (bullet train) travel, except for the super-express *nozomi shinkansen* service. There are two types of passes available, ordinary and green. A 'green' pass covers rides in 1st-class 'green' train cars.

In the past, JRPasses could only be purchased outside of Japan but they are now also available to buy within Japan. The price is slightly higher if bought in Japan – a seven-day ordinary pass costs ¥29,110 if purchased outside of the country and ¥33,000 if purchased in Japan. Passes can be bought at the ticket office in Kansai international airport, as well as at Narita and Haneda international airports in Tokyo. They can also be bought at Tokyo, Shinjuku and Osaka stations but are not yet available to buy at Kyoto Station.

As a one-way reserved-seat Kyoto–Tokyo *shinkansen* ticket costs ¥13,910, travelling from Kyoto to Tokyo return will make a seven-day pass come close to paying off. Note that the pass is valid only on Japan Railways services (ie you still have to pay for private train services).

If buying outside of Japan, in order to get a pass you must first purchase an 'exchange order' at JAL and ANA offices or major travel agencies. Once you arrive in Japan, you have to bring this order to a JR Travel Service Centre (found in most major JR stations and at Narita and Kansai international airports). You'll need to show your passport when you validate your pass. Choose the date on which your pass becomes valid carefully: if you plan to spend several days in Tokyo or Kyoto before setting off to explore Japan, set your pass to become active on the morning you leave those cities.

For more information on the pass and overseas purchase locations, visit the Japan Rail Pass website (www.japanrailpass.net). The prices listed right are for passes bought outside Japan.

unlimited hop-on, hop-off sightseeing bus that operates on Saturday, Sunday and holidays (adult/child one-day pass ¥2000/500, two-day pass ¥3000/500). **K'Loop** (http://kloop.jp/en) travels around the city's World Heritage Sites, starting from the Hachijo-guchi exist of Kyoto Station. Audio guides are ¥500.

Subway

Kyoto has two efficient subway lines, operating from 5.30am to 11.30pm. Minimum adult fare is ¥210 (children ¥110).

The quickest way to travel between the north and south of the city is the Karasuma subway line. It has 15 stops and runs from Takeda in the far south, via Kyoto Station, to the Kyoto International Conference Hall (Kokusai-kaikan Station) in the north. The east–west Tōzai subway line traverses Kyoto from Uzumasa-Tenjingawa Station in the west, meeting the Karasuma subway line at Karasuma-Oike Station, and continuing east to Sanjō-Keihan, Yamashina and Rokujizō in the east and southeast.

The Kyoto City Subway Pass (adult/child ¥600/300) allows unlimited travel on the city's subway for one day, plus discounts on some sights. You can buy it from the Kyoto Tourist Information Center or any subway ticket office.

Bicycle

Kyoto is a great city to explore on a bicycle. With the exception of the outlying areas, it is mostly flat and there is a useful bike path running the length of the Kamo-gawa.

Many guesthouses hire or lend bicycles to their guests and there are also hire shops around Kyoto Station, in Arashiyama and in Downtown Kyoto. With a decent bicycle and a good map, you can easily make your way all around the city. Dedicated bicycle tours are also available.

Bicycle helmets are only required to be worn by law by those 12 years and under.

Cycling on the following streets is prohibited:

➡ Kawaramachi-dōri, between Oike-dōri and Bukkoji-dōri

➡ Shijo-dōri, between Higashioji-dōri and Karasuma-dōri

➡ Sanjo-dōri, between Kiyamachi-dōri and Kawaramachi-dōri

For more information, visit Cycle Kyoto (www.cyclekyoto.com).

Bicycle Rental

A great place to hire a bicycle is the **Kyoto Cycling Tour Project** (京都サイクリングツアープロジェクト, KCTP; Map p216; ☎075-354-3636; www.kctp.net; 552-13 Higashi-Aburanokoji-chō, Aburanokōji-dōri, Shiokōji-sagaru, Shimogyō-ku; ⊗9am-7pm; ⓇKyoto Station). These folk hire bikes (¥1000 per day) that are perfect for getting around the city. KCTP also conducts a variety of bicycle city tours with English-speaking guides, which are an excellent way to see Kyoto (check the website for details).

For exploring the Northern Higashiyama area, check out **Rent a cycle EMUSICA** (Map p214; ☎075-200-8219; www.emusica-dmcy.com/en; 24 Tanaka Kamiyanagi-chō, Sakyō-ku; per day from ¥700; ⊗9am-11.30pm Mon-Fri, 9am-10.30pm Sat & Sun; ⓇKeihan line to Demachinayagi), which is conveniently located right outside the Keihan Demachinayagi Station and with access to the river and sightseeing areas.

Most rental outfits require you to leave a deposit and ID, such as a passport.

Parking

Kyoto's bike parking facilities are pretty average. Many bikes end up stolen or impounded in regular sweeps of the city (particularly near

JAPAN RAIL PASS PRICES

DURATION (DAYS)	REGULAR ADULT (¥)	REGULAR CHILD (¥)	GREEN ADULT (¥)	GREEN CHILD (¥)
7	29,100	14,550	38,880	19,440
14	46,390	23,190	62,950	31,470
21	59,350	29,670	81,870	40,930

KANSAI THRU PASS

The Kansai Thru Pass is a real bonus to travellers who plan to do a fair bit of exploration in the Kansai area. It enables you to ride on city subways, private railways and city buses in Kyoto, Nara, Osaka, Kōbe, Kōya-san, Shiga and Wakayama. It also entitles you to discounts at many attractions in the Kansai area. A two-day pass costs ¥4000 and a three-day pass costs ¥5200. It is available at the Kansai International Airport tourist information counter on the 1st floor of the arrivals hall and at the main bus information centre in front of Kyoto Station, among other places. For more, visit www.surutto.com.

entrances to train/subway stations). If your bike does disappear, check for a poster (in both Japanese and English) in the vicinity indicating the time of seizure and the inconvenient place you'll have to go to pay the ¥2300 fine and retrieve your bike. If you're just riding around to temples, you shouldn't have a problem as there are generally parking areas at the entrance to most temples.

If you don't want to worry about your bike being stolen or impounded, we recommend using one of the city-operated bicycle parking lots. There is one downtown (Map p210) on Takakura-dōri north of Shijō-dōri, another near Kyoto Station (Map p216), and another in the north of town (Map p214) near the Eizan Densha Station at Demachiyanagi. These charge ¥150 per day (buy a ticket from the machine on your way in or out). Also look for Eco Stations around town where you can usually park free for two to three hours and then be charged an hourly rate thereafter.

Train

The main train station in Kyoto is Kyoto Station, which is in the south of the city, just below Shichijō-dōri and is actually two stations under one roof: JR Kyoto Station and Kintetsu Kyoto Station.

In addition to the private Kintetsu line that operates from Kyoto Station, there are two other private train lines in Kyoto: the Hankyū line running from Downtown Kyoto along Shijō-dōri and the Keihan line that operates from stops along the Kamo-gawa.

Buying a Ticket

All stations have with automatic ticket machines, which are simple to operate. Destinations and fares are posted above the machines in Japanese and English – once you've figured out the fare to your destination, insert your money and press the yen amount. Most machines accept paper currency in addition to coins (usually just ¥1000 notes). If you've made a mistake, press the red tori-keshi (cancel) button. There's a help button to summon assistance.

If you happen to purchase the wrong ticket or change your mind about which station to get off at mid-journey (or miss the stop, get on an express train by accident etc), don't stress as most stations have a fare adjustment machine when exiting. Simply pop your ticket into the machine and it will calculate how much extra you need to pay. Pay the amount and your new ticket will be issued to then put through the exit barriers.

Taxi

Taxis are a convenient, but expensive, way of getting from place to place about town. A taxi can usually be flagged down in most parts of the city at any time. There are also a large number of takushī noriba (taxi stands) in town, outside most train/subway stations, department

TRAINS: USEFUL WORDS & PHRASES

Train Types

shinkansen	新幹線	bullet train
tokkyū	特急	limited express
shinkaisoku	新快速	JR special rapid train
kyūkō	急行	express
kaisoku	快速	JR rapid or express
futsū	普通	local
kaku-eki-teisha	各駅停車	local

Other Useful Words

jiyū-seki	自由席	unreserved seat
shitei-seki	指定席	reserved seat
green-sha	グリーン車	1st-class car
ōfuku	往復	round trip
katamichi	片道	one-way
kin'en-sha	禁煙車	nonsmoking car
kitsuen-sha	喫煙車	smoking car

KYOTO TRANSPORT PASSES

There's a one-day card valid for unlimited travel on Kyoto City buses and some of the Kyoto buses (these are different companies) that costs ¥600 and a one-day subway pass that also costs ¥600. The **Kyoto Sightseeing Pass** allows unlimited use of the Kyoto City buses, subway and some of the Kyoto bus routes for one day ¥900 or two days ¥1700. One-day bus and Kyoto Sightseeing passes can be purchased at major bus terminals, at the Kyoto bus information centre (p184) at Kyoto Station or at the Kyoto Tourist Information Center (p192). The one-day subway pass can be bought at subway ticket windows and the Kyoto Tourist Information Center.

The prepaid rechargeable **ICOCA card** has a magnetic chip, which you wave over the reader at the ticket gates, and it is valid on most trains, subways and buses in the Kansai region (Osaka, Kyoto, Nara etc). It can be bought from ticket machines and at the Kansai International Airport and costs ¥2000, including ¥500 refundable deposit. The **ICOCA & Haruka** (¥3600) is a set including the ICOCA card preloaded with ¥1500 (including ¥500 refundable deposit) plus a discounted ticket for the JR Haruka Express train from Kansai International Airport to Kyoto Station.

Kansai One Pass (https://kansaionepass.com/en), an ICOCA card (¥2000, including ¥500 refundable deposit) with an image of Astro Boy on it specifically for foreigners, offers discounts at selected tourist attractions and some temples.

stores etc. There is no need to touch the back doors of the cars at all – the opening/ closing mechanism is controlled by the driver.

Foreigner-Friendly Taxis

In March 2016, Kyoto introduced a foreigner-friendly taxi service. The service aims to make the taxi system more accessible to tourists, with drivers who can speak other languages, such as English and Chinese, and accepting payment by credit card. The taxis are clearly marked as 'foreigner friendly' and there are separate taxi stands in front of the JR Kyoto Station north (Map p216) and south (Map p216) exits.

Car & Motorcycle

Kyoto's heavy traffic and narrow roads make driving in the city difficult and stressful. You will almost always do better riding a bicycle or catching public transport. Unless you have specific needs, do not even entertain the idea of renting a car to tour the city – it's far more cost and headache than any traveller needs (plus parking fines start at ¥15,000).

However, it makes sense to rent a car if you plan to explore certain rural areas that aren't serviced by train lines (such as Miyama-chō). Driving is on the left-hand side in Japan.

Driving Licence & Permits

Travellers from most nations are able to drive in Japan with an International Driving Permit (IDP) backed up by their own regular driving licence.

Travellers from Switzerland, France and Germany (and others whose countries are not signatories to the Geneva Convention of 1949 concerning international driving licences) are not allowed to drive in Japan on a regular international licence. Rather, travellers from these countries must have their own licence backed by an authorised translation of the same licence. These translations can be made by their country's embassy or consulate in Japan, or by the **Japan Automobile Federation** (JAF; ☑03-6833-9100, emergency roadside help 0570-00-8139; www.jaf. or.jp; 2-2-17 Shiba, Minato-ku; ☺9am-5.30pm Mon-Fri; ⑤Mita line to Shiba-kōen, exit A1).

Hire

There are several car-hire agencies in Kyoto. **Nissan Rent-a-car** (Map p216; ☑075-661-4123; https:// nissan-rentacar.com/english; 41-4 Nishikujō Kitanouchi-chō, Minami-ku; 12/24hr from ¥5076/6156; ☺8am-10pm Mon-Fri, 9am-6pm Sat & Sun) and **Toyota Rentacar Kyoto Eki Shinkansen-guchi Branch** (Map p216; ☑075-365-0100, toll free within Japan 0800-7000-815; https://rent.toyota.co.jp/en; Kamitonoda-chō 31-1, Higashi-Kujō, Minami-ku; 12/24hr from ¥5400/7020; ☺8am-9pm) are both a short walk from the south (Hachijō) exit of Kyoto Station. The **Toyota Rentacar Hyakumamben Branch** (Map p214; ☑075-702-8100, toll free within Japan 0800-7000-815; https:// rent.toyota.co.jp; 103-31 Tanakamonzen-chō, Sakyō-ku; 12/24hr from ¥5400/7020; ☺8am-8pm; ⑤Kyoto City bus 206 to Hyakumamben) at the Hyakumamben intersection in Northern Higashiyama is good for those heading north into the Kitayama area.

Some car-hire agencies, including Toyota, have *some* cars with English GPS systems (called 'car navi' in Japanese). Be sure to ask when making reservations.

Directory A-Z

Customs Regulations

Alcohol	up to three 760cc bottles
Gifts/ souvenirs	up to ¥200,000 in total value
Perfume	2oz
Tobacco products	100 cigars/400 cigarettes/500g loose

Electricity

100V/50Hz/60Hz

The Japanese electric current is 100V AC. Kyoto and Osaka are on 60Hz.

Most electrical items from elsewhere in the world will function on Japanese current.

Both transformers and plug adaptors are readily available at Bic Camera and Yodobashi Camera near Kyoto Station, and there's a small range at Tokyu Hands downtown.

Emergency

Ambulance & Fire	☑119
Police	☑110

Health

Japan has high standards of hygiene, few endemic diseases and medical care is reasonably priced. The quality of care in Kyoto is generally very good at the main hospitals.

It's a good idea to bring any medications you might need as pharmacies in Japan don't stock foreign medications.

Tap water is safe to drink.

Internet Access

It's getting much easier for travellers to get online in Kyoto, with almost all hotels and hostels offering free wi-fi for their guests. If you want constant access to wi-fi when you're out and about, your best bet is either renting a portable device or buying a data-only SIM for an unlocked smartphone.

Wi-fi

Almost all Starbucks in Japan offer free wi-fi for their customers, as do most modern cafes and some restaurants.

Wi-fi Hotspots Kyoto City Free Wi-fi Service has hot spots across the city, mainly at bus and train stations. Unfortunately, this is not at all as convenient as it sounds. First, you have to email to get the access code, so you need to be somewhere with internet access. Go to http://kanko. city.kyoto.lg.jp/wifi/en/to find a map of hotspots and sign up. Note that access is limited to 30 minutes, so once 30 minutes is up, you'll need to email again for another access code. Freespot Map (www.freespot. com/users/map_e.html) has a list of internet hot spots, too. It's not exhaustive.

Pocket Wi-fi You can rent portable pocket wi-fi devices from various phone-rental companies in Japan, including Sakura Mobile (www.sakuramobile.jp), Puuru (www.pupuru. com/en) and Rentaphone (www.rentafonejapan.com). They start at around ¥5000 for one week and most companies can arrange for airport pick-up or delivery to your hotel.

Data SIM cards If you're travelling with an unlocked smartphone, you can buy data-only SIM cards from major electronics shops, including Yodobashi Camera and Bic Camera near Kyoto Station, or order online for delivery to your hotel. Bic Camera has a bigger range. Options include the B-Mobile Visitor SIM (www.bmobile.ne.jp/english), Freetel (www.freetel.jp/prepaid) and Iijmio Japan Travel SIM (https://t.iijmio.jp/en/index.html). Freetel is generally the easiest to set up. Cards start at around ¥2280 for 1GB for seven days.

Internet Cafes

Tops Café (トップスカフェ; Map p216; ☑075-681-9270; www.topsnet.co.jp/5/; 2F Daiichi Doboku Bldg, 53-1 Higashikujo-Kamitonoda-chō, Minami-ku; per 15min ¥140, plus ¥216 registration fee; ⊗24hr; 圓Kyoto Station) An all-night manga/internet cafe where you can actually spend the night in the booths if you want. It's just outside the south (Hachijō) exit of Kyoto Station.

Kinko's (キンコーズ; Map p210; ☑075-213-6802; 651-1 Tearaimizu-chō, Karasuma-dōri, Takoyakushi-sagaru, Nakagyō-ku; 1st 20min ¥250, every subsequent 10min ¥200; ⊗24hr; ⑤Karasuma line to Shijō or Karasuma-Oike) Copy shop with several terminals where you can log on to the internet. It's expensive but conveniently located and open 24 hours.

LGBT Travellers

With the possible exception of Thailand, Japan is Asia's most enlightened nation with regard to the sexual preferences of foreigners. Some

travellers have reported problems when checking into love hotels with a partner of the same sex, and it does pay to be discreet in rural areas. Apart from this, same-sex couples are unlikely to encounter too many problems.

While there is a sizeable gay community in Kyoto, the gay and lesbian scene is very low-key. There is a monthly 'Diamonds are Forever' drag queen event at Metro, but there is a more active scene in Osaka and many of Kyoto's gay residents make the trip there. Lesbians are poorly served in Kyoto and Osaka and it's difficult to find specifically lesbian-friendly venues.

Utopia (www.utopia-asia.com) is the site most commonly frequented by English-speaking gay and lesbian people.

Maps

Available free at the Kyoto Tourist Information Center (p192), the *Kyoto City Map* is a decent map of the city with several detailed insets of the major sightseeing districts. Also available is the *Bus Navi: Kyoto City Bus Sightseeing Map*, which has detailed information on bus routes in the city and some of the major stops written in both English and Japanese.

Medical Services

Kyoto University Hospital (京都大学医学部附属病院; Map p214; ☑075-751-3111; www.kuhp.kyoto-u.ac.jp; 54 Shōgoinkawahara-chō, Sakyō-ku; ⊗walk-in appointments 8.15am-11am Mon-Fri; 圓Keihan line to Jingū-Marutamachi) is the best hospital in Kyoto. There is an information counter near the entrance on the ground floor that can point you in the right direction.

Kyoto Prefectural University Hospital (Map p220; ☑075-251-5111; www.h.kpu-m.ac.jp/en; Kawaramachi-Hirokoji, Kamigyō-ku; ⊗walk-in appointments 8.45am-11am Mon-Fri; 圓Keihan line to Demachiyanagi) can try to provide English-speaking staff to assist you and has English-speaking doctors.

Money

The currency in Japan is the yen (¥). The Japanese pronounce yen as 'en', with no 'y' sound. The kanji for yen is: 円.

Yen coins come in the following denominations:
➡ ¥1 lightweight, silver colour
➡ ¥5 bronze colour, hole in the middle, value in Chinese character
➡ ¥10 copper colour
➡ ¥50 silver colour, hole in the middle
➡ ¥100 silver colour
➡ ¥500 large, gold colour

Yen banknotes come in the following denominations:
➡ ¥1000
➡ ¥2000 (rare)
➡ ¥5000
➡ ¥10,000

ATMs

ATMs are almost as common as vending machines in Japan. Unfortunately, many do not accept foreign-issued cards. Even if they display Visa and MasterCard logos, most accept only Japan-issued versions of these cards.

Fortunately, 7-Eleven stores and Japan Post Bank ATMs accept cards that belong to the following international networks: Visa, Plus, MasterCard, Maestro, Cirrus, American Express, JCB, Union Pay, Discover and Diners Club.

7-Eleven stores The most convenient option; these are found everywhere in Kyoto and the

ATMs are open 24 hours and have English instructions.

Japan Post Bank ATMs You'll find postal ATMs in almost all post offices. These ATMs have instructions in English. Most open 9am to 5pm on weekdays, 9am to noon on Saturday, and are closed on Sunday and holidays. Some postal ATMs in very large central post offices are open longer hours. If you need cash outside these hours, try the Kyoto central post office, next to Kyoto Station.

SMBC (シティバンク; Map p210;☑075-212-5387; Shijo Bldg, 88 Kankoboko-chō, Shijō-dōri, Muromachi higashi-iru, Shimogyō-ku; ⓢKarasuma line to Shijō) Has a 24-hour ATM in its lobby that accepts most foreign-issued cards.

Changing Money

You can change cash or travellers cheques at most banks, major post offices, some large hotels and most big department stores. World Currency Shop, operated by Tokyo-Mitsubishi UFJ (MUFG) bank, is located on the 8th floor of the Kyoto Station building and usually has a broader range of currencies. It's only open on weekdays.

Most major banks are located near the Shijō-Karasuma intersection, two

stops north of Kyoto Station on the Karasuma subway line. Of these, **Bank of Tokyo-Mitsubishi UFJ** (三菱東京ＵＦＪ銀行; Map p210; ☑075-211-4583; ⓢKarasuma line to Shijō) is the most convenient for changing money and buying travellers cheques.

Exchange rates for the US dollar and the euro are reasonable in Japan. All other currencies, including the Australian dollar and the currencies of countries near to Japan, fetch very poor exchange rates. If you want to bring cash to Japan, we suggest US dollars or euros.

Credit Cards

Credit cards are not as widely accepted in Japan as they are in other places but more businesses are accepting them these days. It's always a good idea to ask in advance, though. Visa is the most widely accepted, followed by MasterCard, American Express and Diners Club.

Opening Hours

Following are typical business hours in Kyoto. Restaurants and shops sometimes close irregularly. Note that many temples have shorter opening hours during winter, typically closing 30 minutes to one hour earlier.

Banks 9am–3pm Monday to Friday

Bars 6pm–late

Department stores 10am–8pm or 9pm

Post offices local 9am–5pm Monday to Friday; central post offices 9am–7pm Monday to Friday and 9am–3pm Saturday

Restaurants 11.30am–2pm and 6pm–10pm. Last orders are usually taken 30 minutes to one hour before closing.

Shops 9am–5pm

Post

Japan's postal service is reliable efficient. The symbol for post offices is a red T with a bar across the top on a white background (〒). Mail can be sent to, from or within Japan when addressed in English (Roman script). One peculiarity of the Japanese postal system is that you will be charged extra if your writing runs over onto the address side (the right side) of a postcard.

The **Kyoto central post office** (京都中央郵便局; Map p216; ☑075-365-2471; 843-12 Higashishiokōji-chō, Shimogyō-ku; ⓧ9am-9pm Mon-Fri, to 7pm Sat & Sun, ATMs 12.05am-11.55pm Mon-Sat, to 9pm Sun & holidays; ℝKyoto Station) is on the north side of Kyoto Station. There's a service counter on the south side of the building open after hours for airmail, small packages and special express mail services.

Nakagyō post office (Map p210;☑075-255-1112; cnr Sanjō-dōri & Higashinotoin; ⓧ8am-9pm Mon-Fri, to 3pm Sat, closed Sun; ⓢKarasuma line to Karasuma-Oike), at the Nishinotōin-Sanjō crossing in Downtown Kyoto, has a 24-hour service window on the west side of the building.

Public Holidays

When a public holiday falls on a Sunday, the following Monday is taken as a holiday. If that Monday is already a holiday, the following day becomes a holiday as well. If a public holiday falls on a Monday, most museums and restaurants that normally close on Mondays will remain open and close the next day instead.

Ganjitsu (New Year's Day) 1 January

Seijin-no-hi (Coming-of-Age Day) Second Monday in January

Kenkoku Kinem-bi (National Foundation Day) 11 February

Shumbun-no-hi (Spring Equinox) 20 or 21 March

Shōwa-no-hi (Shōwa Emperor's Day) 29 April

Kempō Kinem-bi (Constitution Day) 3 May

Midori-no-hi (Green Day) 4 May

Kodomo-no-hi (Children's Day) 5 May

Umi-no-hi (Marine Day) Third Monday in July

Yama-no-hi (Mountain Day) 11 August

Keirō-no-hi (Respect for the Aged Day) Third Monday in September

Shūbun-no-hi (Autumn Equinox) 22 or 23 September

Taiiku-no-hi (Health-Sports Day) Second Monday in October

Bunka-no-hi (Culture Day) 3 November

Kinrō Kansha-no-hi (Labour Thanksgiving Day) 23 November

Tennō Tanjōbi (Emperor's Birthday) 23 December

Taxes & Refunds

There is an 8% consumption tax on retail purchases in Japan (scheduled to increase to 10% in October 2019). Many shops in Kyoto offer tax-free shopping for purchases over ¥5000 (look for a sticker in the window). You must show your passport to prove that you have a short-stay visa.

There is no need to collect a refund when leaving the country; however, you should hand in a form affixed to your passport to customs officials when you depart. For details see http://enjoy.taxfree.jp

Telephone

The country code for Japan is 81 and the area code for greater Kyoto is 075. Japanese telephone codes consist of an area code plus a local code and number. You do not dial the area code when making a call in that area. When dialling Japan from abroad, the country code is 81, followed by the area code (drop the 0) and the number.

Mobile Phones

Japan's mobile-phone networks use 3G technology. Prepaid SIM cards that allow you to make voice calls are not available in Japan, though Iijmio Japan Travel SIM (https://t.iijmio.jp/en) cards offer a dedicated app that allows calls to be made and received through your own 050 telephone number. They partner with telecommunications company Brastel and the Travel SIM card comes with a Brastel card you can top up.

For most people who want to use a mobile phone for voice calls while in Japan, the only other solution is to rent one. Several telecommunications companies in Japan specialise in short-term mobile-phone rentals. Rentafone Japan (www.rentafonejapan.com) rents mobile phones for ¥3900 per week and offers free delivery of the phone to your accommodation. Domestic rates are from ¥35 per minute and overseas calls are ¥45 per minute.

Otherwise, you can buy a prepaid data-only SIM card from electronics stores, such as Bic Camera and Yodobashi Camera, and use communication apps, such as Skype and What's App. Some companies offer SIM cards where these apps don't count against your data. Note the Line app is the most commonly used messaging app in Japan.

Directory Assistance

Local directory assistance
☑104 (¥60 to ¥150 per call)

Local directory assistance in English ☑0120-36-4463 (9am to 5pm Monday to Friday)

International directory assistance in English ☑0057

Useful International Numbers

Direct-dial international numbers include the following. There's very little difference in their rates. Dial one of the numbers, then the international country code, the local code and the number.

➡ ☑001-010 (KDDI)
➡ ☑0033-010 (NTT)
➡ ☑0041-010 (SoftBank Telecom)

For international operator-assisted calls dial 0051 (KDDI; operators speak English).

Prepaid International Phone Cards

Public phones do still exist and they work almost 100% of the time; look for them around train stations. Ordinary public phones are green; those that allow you to call abroad are grey and are usually marked 'International & Domestic Card/Coin Phone'. Because of the lack of pay phones from which you can make international phone calls in Japan, the easiest way to make an international call is to buy a prepaid international phonecard. Most convenience stores carry a couple of different types of phonecards. These cards can be used with any regular pay phone in Japan.

Local Calls

Local calls from pay phones cost ¥10 per minute; unused ¥10 coins are returned after the call is completed but no change is given on ¥100 coins.

In general it's much easier to buy a telephone card (terehon kādo) when you arrive rather than worry about always having coins on hand. Phonecards are sold in ¥500 and ¥1000 denominations (the latter earns you an extra ¥50 in calls) and can be used in most green or grey pay phones.

Time

Kyoto local time is nine hours ahead of GMT/UTC. There is no daylight saving time.

Toilets

➜ You'll come across a range of toilets when visiting Kyoto, from futuristic gadget-laden loos to old-school squat style. When using squat toilets, the correct position is facing the hood, away from the door.

➜ Public toilets are free and generally clean and well maintained. Most convenience stores have them, along with train stations and department stores. They will usually be stocked with toilet paper but it doesn't hurt to carry small tissue packets on you just in case.

➜ The most common words for toilet in Japanese are トイレ (pronounced 'toire') and お手洗い ('o-te-arai'); 女 (female) and 男 (male) will also come in handy.

➜ Toilet slippers are provided in many bathrooms. They are only to be used in the toilet so don't forget to take them off before you leave.

Tourist Information

Kyoto Tourist Information Center (京都総合観光案内所, TIC; Map p216; ☑075-343-0548; 2F Kyoto Station Bldg, Shimogyō-ku; ◷8.30am-7pm;

🚇Kyoto Station) Stocks bus and city maps, has plenty of transport info and English speakers are available to answer your questions.

JTB Kansai Tourist Information Office (Map p216; ☑075-341-0280; www.tourist-information-center.jp/kansai/en/kyoto; 3rd fl, Karasuma-dōri, Shichijō-sagaru, Shimogyō-ku; ◷10am-6pm; 🚇Kyoto Station) On the 3rd floor of the Kyoto Tower building, this tourist office can help with booking day trips and tours, as well as general information on Kyoto and the Kansai region.

Kansai International Airport Tourist Information Counter (関西国際空港関西観光情報センター; ☑072-456-6160; Central 1F, Terminal 1 Bldg, 1 Senshu-kuko-naka, Tajiri-chō, Sennan-gu; ◷7am-10pm) On the 1st floor of the international arrivals hall. Staff can provide information on Kyoto, Kansai and Japan.

Kyoto International Community House (京都市国際交流会館, KICH; Map p214; ☑075-752-3010; 2-1 Torii-chō, Awataguchi, Sakyō-ku; ◷9am-9pm Tue-Sun; ⑤Tōzai line to Keage, exit 2) An essential stop for those planning a long-term stay in Kyoto, KICH can also be quite useful for short-term visitors. It has a library with maps, books, newspapers and magazines from around the world, and a board displaying messages regarding work, accommodation, rummage sales etc. You can use the wi-fi and also pick up a copy of its excellent Guide to Kyoto map and its Easy Living in Kyoto book (note that both of these are intended for residents). You can also chill out in the lobby and watch CNN news.

You'll find other small tourist offices dotted around the downtown area along

Kawaramachi-dōri, such as the following office:

Kawaramachi Sanjo Tourist Information Center (Map p210; ☑075-213-1717; 1st fl, Kyoto Asahi Kaikan Bldg, 427 Ebisu-cho, Kawaramachi-dōri, Sanjō-agaru; ◷10am-6pm; ⑤Tōzai line to Kyoto-Shiyakusho-mae) Convenient tourist information with plenty of brochures and maps, and helpful staff.

Travellers with Disabilities

Although Kyoto has made some attempts at making public facilities more accessible, its narrow streets and the terrain of sights, such as temples and shrines, make it a challenging city for people with disabilities, especially for those in wheelchairs. Let staff at temples and shrines know someone in your party is travelling in a wheelchair as some may have a separate accessible route.

If you are going to travel by train and need assistance, ask one of the station workers as you enter the station. There are carriages on most lines that have areas set aside for those in wheelchairs. Those with other physical disabilities can use one of the seats set aside near the train exits; these are called yūsen-zaseki and are usually a different colour from the other seats in the carriage, making them easy to spot. Major train stations have elevators to the platform but many stations don't.

MK Taxi (☑075-778-4145; www.mktaxi-japan.com) can accommodate wheelchairs in many of its cars.

Facilities for the visually impaired include musical pedestrian lights at many city intersections and raised bumps on railway platforms for guidance.

AD-Brain (the same outfit that publishes the monthly

Kyoto Visitor's Guide) has produced a basic city map for people with disabilities and senior citizens. It shows wheelchair-access points in town and gives information on public transport access etc. The map is available at the Kyoto Tourist Information Center.

Another useful resource is the Japan Accessible Tourism Center (www.japan-accessible.com/city/kyoto.htm), with a rundown of accessible sights and hotels in Kyoto.

Download Lonely Planet's free Accessible Travel guides from http://lptravel.to/AccessibleTravel.

Visas

Generally, visitors who are not planning to engage in income-producing activities while in Japan are exempt from obtaining visas and will be issued a *tanki-taizai* (temporary visitor) visa on arrival. Nationals of Australia, Canada, France, Ireland, Italy, the Netherlands, New Zealand, Spain, the UK and the USA are eligible for this visa.

Stays of up to six months are permitted for citizens of Austria, Germany, Ireland, Liechtenstein, Mexico, Switzerland and the UK. Citizens of these countries will almost always be given a 90-day temporary visitor visa upon arrival, which can usually be extended for another 90 days at an immigration bureau inside Japan.

Japanese law requires that visitors to the country entering on a temporary visitor visa possess an ongoing air or sea ticket or evidence thereof. In practice, few travellers are asked to produce such documents, but to avoid surprises it pays to be on the safe side.

Note that upon entering Japan, all short-term foreign visitors are required to be photographed and fingerprinted. This happens when you show your passport on arrival.

Women Travellers

Kyoto is generally a very safe city for women travellers, though it's best not to be lulled into a false sense of security by Japan's image as one of the world's safest countries. Women travellers are occasionally subjected to some form of verbal harassment or prying questions in Japan, so take the normal precautions you would in your home country.

The Hankyū and Keihan line commuter trains in Kyoto have women-only cars to protect female passengers from *chikan* (men who grope women and girls on packed trains). These cars are usually available during rush-hour periods on weekdays on busy urban lines. There are signs (usually pink in colour) on the platform indicating where to board, and the cars themselves are usually labelled in pink in both Japanese and English.

Language

Japanese is spoken by more than 125 million people. While it bears some resemblance to Altaic languages such as Mongolian and Turkish and has grammatical similarities to Korean, its origins are unclear. Chinese is responsible for the existence of many Sino-Japanese words in Japanese, and for the originally Chinese kanji characters which the Japanese use in combination with the homegrown hiragana and katakana scripts.

Japanese pronunciation is easy to master for English speakers, as most of its sounds are also found in English. If you read our coloured pronunciation guides as if they were English, you'll be understood. In Japanese, it's important to make the distinction between short and long vowels, as vowel length can change the meaning of a word. The long vowels, shown in our pronunciation guides with a horizontal line on top of them (ā, ē, ī, ō, ū), should be held twice as long as the short ones. It's also important to make the distinction between single and double consonants, as this can produce a difference in meaning. Pronounce the double consonants with a slight pause between them, eg sak·ka (writer).

Note also that the vowel sound ai is pronounced as in 'aisle', air as in 'pair' and ow as in 'how'. As for the consonants, ts is pronounced as in 'hats', f sounds almost like 'fw' (with rounded lips), and r is halfway between 'r' and 'l'. All syllables in a word are pronounced fairly evenly in Japanese.

WANT MORE?

For in-depth language information and handy phrases, check out Lonely Planet's *Japanese phrasebook*. You'll find it at **shop. lonelyplanet.com**, or you can buy Lonely Planet's iPhone phrasebooks at the Apple App Store.

BASICS

Japanese uses an array of registers of speech to reflect social and contextual hierarchy, but these can be simplified to the form most appropriate for the situation, which is what we've done in this language guide too.

Hello.	こんにちは。	kon·ni·chi·wa
Goodbye.	さようなら。	sa·yō·na·ra
Yes.	はい。	hai
No.	いいえ。	ī·e
Please. (when asking)	ください。	ku·da·sai
Please. (when offering)	どうぞ。	dō·zo
Thank you.	ありがとう。	a·ri·ga·tō
Excuse me. (to get attention)	すみません。	su·mi·ma·sen
Sorry.	ごめんなさい。	go·men·na·sai

You're welcome.
どういたしまして。 dō i·ta·shi·mash·te

How are you?
お元気ですか? o·gen·ki des ka

Fine. And you?
はい、元気です。 hai, gen·ki des
あなたは? a·na·ta wa

What's your name?
お名前は何ですか? o·na·ma·e wa nan des ka

My name is ...
私の名前は wa·ta·shi no na·ma·e wa
…です。 ... des

Do you speak English?
英語が話せますか? ē·go ga ha·na·se·mas ka

I don't understand.
わかりません。 wa·ka·ri·ma·sen

Does anyone speak English?
どなたか英語を do·na·ta ka ē·go o
話せますか? ha·na·se·mas ka

ACCOMMODATION

Where's a ...?	…が ありますか?	... ga a·ri·mas ka
campsite	キャンプ場	kyam·pu·jō
guesthouse	民宿	min·shu·ku
hotel	ホテル	ho·te·ru
inn	旅館	ryo·kan
youth hostel	ユース ホステル	yū·su· ho·su·te·ru

Do you have a ... room?	…ルームは ありますか?	...·rū·mu wa a·ri·mas ka
single	シングル	shin·gu·ru
double	ダブル	da·bu·ru

How much is it per ...?	…いくら ですか?	... i·ku·ra des ka
night	1泊	ip·pa·ku
person	1人	hi·to·ri

air-con	エアコン	air·kon
bathroom	風呂場	fu·ro·ba
window	窓	ma·do

DIRECTIONS

Where's the ...?
…はどこですか?　　　　　... wa do·ko des ka

Can you show me (on the map)?
(地図で)教えて　　　(chi·zu de) o·shi·e·te
くれませんか?　　　　ku·re·ma·sen ka

What's the address?
住所は何ですか?　　　jū·sho wa nan des ka

Could you please write it down?
書いてくれませんか?　　kai·te ku·re·ma·sen ka

behind ...	…の後ろ	... no u·shi·ro
in front of ...	…の前	... no ma·e
near ...	…の近く	... no chi·ka·ku
next to ...	…のとなり	... no to·na·ri
opposite ...	…の 向かい側	... no mu·kai·ga·wa
straight ahead	この先	ko·no sa·ki

Turn ...	…まがって ください。	... ma·gat·te ku·da·sai
at the corner	その角を	so·no ka·do o
at the traffic lights	その信号を	so·no shin·gō o
left	左へ	hi·da·ri e
right	右へ	mi·gi e

KEY PATTERNS

To get by in Japanese, mix and match these simple patterns with words of your choice:

When's (the next bus)?
(次のバスは)　　　(tsu·gi no bas wa)
何時ですか?　　　nan·ji des ka

Where's (the station)?
(駅は)どこですか?　(e·ki wa) do·ko des ka

Do you have (a map)?
(地図)　　　　　　(chi·zu)
がありますか?　　　ga a·ri·mas ka

Is there (a toilet)?
(トイレ)　　　　　(toy·re)
がありますか?　　　ga a·ri·mas ka

I'd like (the menu).
(メニュー)　　　　(me·nyū)
をお願いします。　　o o·ne·gai shi·mas

Can I (sit here)?
(ここに座って)　　(ko·ko ni su·wat·te)
もいいですか?　　　mo ī des ka

I need (a can opener).
(缶切り)　　　　　(kan·ki·ri)
が必要です。　　　　ga hi·tsu·yō des

Do I need (a visa)?
(ビザ)　　　　　　(bi·za)
が必要ですか?　　　ga hi·tsu·yō des ka

I have (a reservation).
(予約)があります。　(yo·ya·ku) ga a·ri·mas

I'm (a teacher).
私は(教師)　　　　wa·ta·shi wa (kyō·shi)
です。　　　　　　des

EATING & DRINKING

I'd like to reserve a table for (two people).
(2人)の予約を　　(fu·ta·ri) no yo·ya·ku o
お願いします。　　　o·ne·gai shi·mas

What would you recommend?
なにが　　　　　　na·ni ga
おすすめですか?　　o·su·su·me des ka

What's in that dish?
あの料理に何　　　a·no ryō·ri ni na·ni
が入っていますか?　ga hait·te i·mas ka

Do you have any vegetarian dishes?
ベジタリアン料理　be·ji·ta·ri·an ryō·ri
がありますか?　　　ga a·ri·mas ka

I'm a vegetarian.
私は　　　　　　　wa·ta·shi wa
ベジタリアンです。　be·ji·ta·ri·an des

I'm a vegan.
私は厳格な　　　　wa·ta·shi wa gen·ka·ku na
菜食主義者　　　　sai·sho·ku·shu·gi·sha
です。　　　　　　des

Signs

入口	Entrance
出口	Exit
営業中/開館	Open
閉店/閉館	Closed
インフォメーション	Information
危険	Danger
トイレ	Toilets
男	Men
女	Women

I don't eat ...	…は 食べません。	... wa ta·be·ma·sen
dairy products	乳製品	nyū·sē·hin
(red) meat	(赤身の) 肉	(a·ka·mi no) ni·ku
meat or dairy products	肉や 乳製品は	ni·ku ya nyū·sē·hin
pork	豚肉	bu·ta·ni·ku
seafood	シーフード 海産物	shī·fū·do/ kai·sam·bu·tsu

Is it cooked with pork lard or chicken stock?
これはラードか鶏の
だしを使って
いますか？
ko·re wa rā·do ka to·ri no
da·shi o tsu·kat·te
i·mas ka

I'm allergic to (peanuts).
私は
（ピーナッツ）に
アレルギーが
あります。
wa·ta·shi wa
(pī·nat·tsu) ni
a·re·ru·gī ga
a·ri·mas

That was delicious!
おいしかった！
oy·shi·kat·ta

Cheers!
乾杯！
kam·pai

Please bring the bill.
お勘定をください。 o·kan·jō o ku·da·sai

Key Words

appetisers	前菜	zen·sai
bottle	ビン	bin
bowl	ボール	bō·ru
breakfast	朝食	chō·sho·ku
cold	冷たい	tsu·me·ta·i
dinner	夕食	yū·sho·ku
fork	フォーク	fō·ku
glass	グラス	gu·ra·su
grocery	食料品	sho·ku·ryō·hin
hot (warm)	熱い	a·tsu·i
knife	ナイフ	nai·fu
lunch	昼食	chū·sho·ku
market	市場	i·chi·ba
menu	メニュー	me·nyū
plate	皿	sa·ra
spicy	スパイシー	spai·shī
spoon	スプーン	spūn
vegetarian	ベジタリアン	be·ji·ta·ri·an
with	いっしょに	is·sho ni
without	なしで	na·shi de

Meat & Fish

beef	牛肉	gyū·ni·ku
chicken	鶏肉	to·ri·ni·ku
duck	アヒル	a·hi·ru
eel	うなぎ	u·na·gi
fish	魚	sa·ka·na
lamb	子羊	ko·hi·tsu·ji
lobster	ロブスター	ro·bus·tā
meat	肉	ni·ku
pork	豚肉	bu·ta·ni·ku
prawn	エビ	e·bi
salmon	サケ	sa·ke
seafood	シーフード 海産物	shī·fū·do/ kai·sam·bu·tsu
shrimp	小エビ	ko·e·bi
tuna	マグロ	ma·gu·ro
turkey	七面鳥	shi·chi·men·chō
veal	子牛	ko·u·shi

Fruit & Vegetables

apple	りんご	rin·go
banana	バナナ	ba·na·na
beans	豆	ma·me
capsicum	ピーマン	pī·man
carrot	ニンジン	nin·jin
cherry	さくらんぼ	sa·ku·ram·bo
cucumber	キュウリ	kyū·ri
fruit	果物	ku·da·mo·no
grapes	ブドウ	bu·dō
lettuce	レタス	re·tas
nut	ナッツ	nat·tsu
orange	オレンジ	o·ren·ji
peach	桃	mo·mo

peas	豆	ma·me
pineapple	パイナップル	pai·nap·pu·ru
potato	ジャガイモ	ja·ga·i·mo
pumpkin	カボチャ	ka·bo·cha
spinach	ホウレンソウ	hō·ren·sō
strawberry	イチゴ	i·chi·go
tomato	トマト	to·ma·to
vegetables	野菜	ya·sai
watermelon	スイカ	su·i·ka

Other

bread	パン	pan
butter	バター	ba·tā
cheese	チーズ	chī·zu
chilli	唐辛子	tō·ga·ra·shi
egg	卵	ta·ma·go
honey	蜂蜜	ha·chi·mi·tsu
horseradish	わさび	wa·sa·bi
jam	ジャム	ja·mu
noodles	麺	men
pepper	コショウ	koshō
rice (cooked)	ごはん	go·han
salt	塩	shi·o
seaweed	のり	no·ri
soy sauce	しょう油	shō·yu
sugar	砂糖	sa·tō

Drinks

beer	ビール	bī·ru
coffee	コーヒー	kō·hī
(orange) juice	（オレンジ）ジュース	(o·ren·ji·)jū·su
lemonade	レモネード	re·mo·nē·do
milk	ミルク	mi·ru·ku
mineral water	ミネラルウォーター	mi·ne·ra·ru·wō·tā

Question Words
How?	どのように?	do·no yō ni
What?	なに?	na·ni
When?	いつ?	i·tsu
Where?	どこ?	do·ko
Which?	どちら?	do·chi·ra
Who?	だれ?	da·re
Why?	なぜ?	na·ze

red wine	赤ワイン	a·ka wain
sake	酒	sa·ke
tea	紅茶	kō·cha
water	水	mi·zu
white wine	白ワイン	shi·ro wain
yogurt	ヨーグルト	yō·gu·ru·to

EMERGENCIES

Help!
たすけて! — tas·ke·te

Go away!
離れろ! — ha·na·re·ro

I'm lost.
迷いました。 — ma·yoy·mash·ta

Call the police.
警察を呼んで。 — kē·sa·tsu o yon·de

Call a doctor.
医者を呼んで。 — i·sha o yon·de

Where are the toilets?
トイレはどこですか? — toy·re wa do·ko des ka

I'm ill.
私は病気です。 — wa·ta·shi wa byō·ki des

It hurts here.
ここが痛いです。 — ko·ko ga i·tai des

I'm allergic to ...
私は…アレルギーです。 — wa·ta·shi wa ... a·re·ru·gī des

SHOPPING & SERVICES

I'd like to buy ...
…をください。 — ... o ku·da·sai

I'm just looking.
見ているだけです。 — mi·te i·ru da·ke des

Can I look at it?
それを見てもいいですか? — so·re o mi·te mo ī des ka

How much is it?
いくらですか? — i·ku·ra des ka

That's too expensive.
高すぎます。 — ta·ka·su·gi·mas

Can you give me a discount?
ディスカウントできますか? — dis·kown·to de·ki·mas ka

There's a mistake in the bill.
請求書に間違いがあります。 — sē·kyū·sho ni ma·chi·gai ga a·ri·mas

ATM	ATM	ē·tī·e·mu
credit card	クレジットカード	ku·re·jit·to·kā·do
post office	郵便局	yū·bin·kyo·ku
public phone	公衆電話	kō·shū·den·wa
tourist office	観光案内所	kan·kō·an·nai·jo

Numbers

1	一	i·chi
2	二	ni
3	三	san
4	四	shi/yon
5	五	go
6	六	ro·ku
7	七	shi·chi/na·na
8	八	ha·chi
9	九	ku/kyū
10	十	jū
20	二十	ni·jū
30	三十	san·jū
40	四十	yon·jū
50	五十	go·jū
60	六十	ro·ku·jū
70	七十	na·na·jū
80	八十	ha·chi·jū
90	九十	kyū·jū
100	百	hya·ku
1000	千	sen

TIME & DATES

What time is it?
何時ですか？ — nan·ji des ka

It's (10) o'clock.
(10)時です。 — (jū)·ji des

Half past (10).
(10)時半です。 — (jū)·ji han des

am	午前	go·zen
pm	午後	go·go

Monday	月曜日	ge·tsu·yō·bi
Tuesday	火曜日	ka·yō·bi
Wednesday	水曜日	su·i·yō·bi
Thursday	木曜日	mo·ku·yō·bi
Friday	金曜日	kin·yō·bi
Saturday	土曜日	do·yō·bi
Sunday	日曜日	ni·chi·yō·bi

January	1月	i·chi·ga·tsu
February	2月	ni·ga·tsu
March	3月	san·ga·tsu
April	4月	shi·ga·tsu
May	5月	go·ga·tsu
June	6月	ro·ku·ga·tsu
July	7月	shi·chi·ga·tsu

August	8月	ha·chi·ga·tsu
September	9月	ku·ga·tsu
October	10月	jū·ga·tsu
November	11月	jū·i·chi·ga·tsu
December	12月	jū·ni·ga·tsu

TRANSPORT

boat	船	fu·ne
bus	バス	bas
metro	地下鉄	chi·ka·te·tsu
plane	飛行機	hi·kō·ki
train	電車	den·sha
tram	市電	shi·den

What time does it leave?
これは何時に — ko·re wa nan·ji ni
出ますか？ — de·mas ka

Does it stop at (...)?
(…)に — (...) ni
停まりますか？ — to·ma·ri·mas ka

Please tell me when we get to (...).
(…)に着いたら — (...) ni tsu·i·ta·ra
教えてください。 — o·shi·e·te ku·da·sai

A one-way/return ticket (to Tokyo).
(東京行きの) — (tō·kyō·yu·ki no)
片道/往復 — ka·ta·mi·chi/ō·fu·ku
切符。 — kip·pu

first	始発の	shi·ha·tsu no
last	最終の	sai·shū no
next	次の	tsu·gi no

aisle	通路側	tsū·ro·ga·wa
bus stop	バス停	bas·tē
cancelled	キャンセル	kyan·se·ru
delayed	遅れ	o·ku·re
ticket window	窓口	ma·do·gu·chi
timetable	時刻表	ji·ko·ku·hyō
train station	駅	e·ki
window	窓側	ma·do·ga·wa

I'd like to hire a ...	…を借りたい のですが。	... o ka·ri·tai no des ga
bicycle	自転車	ji·ten·sha
car	自動車	ji·dō·sha
motorbike	オートバイ	ō·to·bai

For additional Transport words and phrases, see p186.

GLOSSARY

agaru – north of

ageya – traditional banquet hall used for entertainment

bashi – bridge (also *hashi*)

bentō – boxed lunch or dinner, usually containing rice, vegetables and fish or meat

bosatsu – a Bodhisattva, or Buddha attendant, who helps others to attain enlightenment

bugaku – dance pieces played by court orchestras in ancient Japan

bunraku – classical puppet theatre that uses life-size puppets to enact dramas similar to those of *kabuki*

chadō – tea ceremony, or 'The Way of Tea'

chanoyu – tea ceremony; see also *chadō*

chō – city area sized between a *ku* and a *chōme*

chōme – city area of a few blocks

dai – great; large

daimyō – domain lords under the *shōgun*

dera – temple (also *ji* or *tera*)

dōri – street

futon – cushion-like mattress that is rolled up and stored away during the day

gagaku – music of the imperial court

gaijin – foreigner; the contracted form of *gaikokujin*

gawa – river (also *kawa*)

geiko – Kyoto dialect for *geisha*

geisha – a woman versed in the arts and other cultivated pursuits who entertains guests

gū – shrine

haiden – hall of worship in a shrine

haiku – 17-syllable poem

hanami – cherry-blossom viewing

hashi – bridge (also *bashi*); chopsticks

higashi – east

hiragana – phonetic syllabary used to write Japanese words

honden – main building of a shrine

hondō – main building of a temple (also *kondō*)

ikebana – art of flower arrangement

izakaya – Japanese pub/eatery

ji – temple (also *tera* or *dera*)

jingū – shrine (also *jinja* or *gū*)

Jizō – Bodhisattva who watches over children

jō – castle (also *shiro*)

JR – Japan Railways

kabuki – form of Japanese theatre that draws on popular tales and is characterised by elaborate costumes, stylised acting and an all-male cast

kaiseki – Buddhist-inspired, Japanese haute cuisine; called *cha-kaiseki* when served as part of a tea ceremony

kaisoku – rapid train

kaiten-zushi – automatic, conveyor-belt sushi

kampai – cheers, as in a drinking toast

kanji – literally, 'Chinese writing'; Chinese ideographic script used for writing Japanese

Kannon – Buddhist goddess of mercy

karesansui – dry-landscaped rock garden

kawa – river (also *gawa*)

kayabuki-yane – traditional Japanese thatched-roof farmhouse

ken – prefecture, eg Shiga-ken

kimono – traditional outer garment similar to a robe

kita – north

KIX – Kansai International Airport

Kiyomizu-yaki – a distinctive type of local pottery

ko – lake

kōen – park

koma-inu – dog-like guardian stone statues found in pairs at the entrance to *Shintō* shrines

kondō – main building of a temple (also hondō)

ku – ward

kudaru – south of (also *sagaru*)

kyōgen – drama performed as comic relief between *nō* plays, or as separate events

kyō-machiya – see *machiya*

kyō-ningyō – Kyoto dolls

kyō-ryōri – Kyoto cuisine

Kyoto-ben – distinctive Japanese dialect spoken in Kyoto

live house – a small concert hall where music is performed

machi – city area (for large cities) sized between a *ku* and a *chōme*

machiya – traditional wooden townhouse, called *kyō-machiya* in Kyoto

maiko – apprentice *geisha*

maki-e – decorative lacquer technique using silver and gold powders

mama-san – older women who run drinking, dining and entertainment venues

matcha – powdered green tea served in tea ceremonies

matsuri – festival

mikoshi – portable shrine carried during festivals

minami – south

minshuku – Japanese equivalent of a B&B

mizu shōbai – the world of bars, entertainment and prostitution

mon – temple gate

mura – village

ningyō – doll (see also *kyō-ningyō*)

niō – temple guardians

nishi – west

nō – classical Japanese mask drama

noren – door curtain for restaurants, usually labelled with the name of the establishment

obanzai – Japanese home-style cooking (the Kyoto variant of this is sometimes called *kyō-obanzai*)

obi – sash or belt worn with *kimono*

Obon – mid-August festivals and ceremonies for deceased ancestors

okiya – old-style *geisha* living quarters

okonomiyaki – Japanese cabbage and batter dish cooked on an iron griddle with a variety of fillings

onsen – mineral hot spring with bathing areas and accommodation

pachinko – vertical pinball game that is a Japanese craze

ryokan – traditional inn

ryōri – cooking; cuisine (see also *kyō-ryōri*)

ryōtei – traditional-style, high-class restaurant; *kaiseki* is typical fare

sabi – a poetic ideal of

finding beauty and pleasure in imperfection; often used in conjunction with *wabi*

sagaru – south of (also *kudaru*)

sakura – cherry trees

sama – a suffix even more respectful than *san*

samurai – Japan's traditional warrior class

san – a respectful suffix applied to personal names, similar to Mr, Mrs or Ms

sen – line, usually railway line

sensu – folding paper fan

sentō – public bath

setto – set meal; see also *teishoku*

shakkei – borrowed scenery; technique where features outside a garden are incorporated into its design

shamisen – three-stringed, banjo-like instrument

shi – city (to distinguish cities with prefectures of the same name)

shidare-zakura – weeping cherry tree

shinkaisoku – special rapid train

shinkansen – bullet train

Shintō – indigenous Japanese religion

shōgun – military ruler of pre-Meiji Japan

shōjin-ryōri – Buddhist vegetarian cuisine

shokudō – Japanese-style cafeteria/cheap restaurant

soba – thin brown buckwheat noodles

tatami – tightly woven floor matting on which shoes should not be worn

teishoku – set meal in a restaurant

tera – temple (also *dera* or *ji*)

tokkyū – limited express train

torii – entrance gate to a *Shintō* shrine

tsukemono – Japanese pickles

udon – thick, white wheat noodles

wabi – a Zen-inspired aesthetic of rustic simplicity

wagashi – traditional Japanese sweets served with tea

wasabi – spicy Japanese horseradish

washi – Japanese paper

yudōfu – bean curd cooked in an iron pot; common temple fare

Zen – a form of Buddhism

MENU DECODER

Rice Dishes

katsu-don (かつ丼) – rice topped with a fried pork cutlet

niku-don (牛丼) – rice topped with thin slices of cooked beef

oyako-don (親子丼) – rice topped with egg and chicken

ten-don (天丼) – rice topped with tempura shrimp and vegetables

Izakaya Fare

agedashi-dōfu (揚げだし豆腐) – deep-fried tofu in a dashi broth

chiizu-age (チーズ揚げ) – deep-fried cheese

hiya-yakko (冷奴) – a cold block of tofu with soy sauce and spring onions

jaga-batā (ジャガバター) – baked potatoes with butter

niku-jaga (肉ジャガ) – beef and potato stew

poteto furai (ポテトフライ) – French fries

shio-yaki-zakana (塩焼魚) – a whole fish grilled with salt

tsuna sarada (ツナサラダ) – tuna salad over cabbage

Sushi & Sashimi

ama-ebi (甘海老) – shrimp

awabi (あわび) – abalone

hamachi (はまち) – yellowtail

ika (いか) – squid

ikura (イクラ) – salmon roe

kai-bashira (貝柱) – scallop

kani (かに) – crab

katsuo (かつお) – bonito

sashimi mori-awase (刺身盛り合わせ) – a selection of sliced sashimi

tai (鯛) – sea bream

toro (とろ) – the choicest cut of fatty tuna belly

uni (うに) – sea urchin roe

Yakitori

gyū-niku (牛肉) – pieces of beef

hasami/negima (はさみ/ねぎま) – pieces of white meat alternating with leek

kawa (皮) – chicken skin

piiman (ピーマン) – small green peppers

sasami (ささみ) – skinless chicken-breast pieces

shiitake (しいたけ) – Japanese mushrooms

tama-negi (玉ねぎ) – round white onions

tebasaki (手羽先) – chicken wings

tsukune (つくね) – chicken meat balls

yaki-onigiri (焼きおにぎり) – a triangle of rice grilled with *yakitori* sauce

yakitori (焼き鳥) – plain, grilled white meat

Tempura

kaki age (かき揚げ) – tempura with shredded vegetables or fish

shōjin age (精進揚げ) – vegetarian tempura

tempura moriawase (天ぷら盛り合わせ) – a selection of tempura

Rāmen

chānpon-men (ちゃんぽん麺) – Nagasaki-style *rāmen*

chāshū-men (チャーシュー麺) – *rāmen* topped with slices of roasted pork

miso-rāmen (みそラーメン) – *rāmen* with miso-flavoured broth

rāmen (ラーメン) – soup and noodles with a sprinkling of meat and vegetables

wantan-men (ワンタン麺) – *rāmen* with meat dumplings

Soba & Udon

kake soba/udon (かけそば/うどん) – *soba/udon* noodles in broth

kata yaki-soba (かた焼きそば) – crispy noodles with meat and vegetables

kitsune soba/udon (きつねそば/うどん) – *soba/udon* noodles with fried tofu

soba (そば) – thin brown buckwheat noodles

tempura soba/udon (天ぷらそば/うどん) – *soba/udon* noodles with tempura shrimp

tsukimi soba/udon (月見そば/うどん) – *soba/udon* noodles with raw egg on top

udon (うどん) – thick white wheat noodles

yaki-soba (焼きそば) – fried noodles with meat and vegetables

zaru soba (ざるそば) – cold noodles with seaweed strips served on a bamboo tray

Unagi

kabayaki (蒲焼き) – skewers of grilled eel without rice

una-don (うな丼) – grilled eel over a bowl of rice

unagi teishoku (うなぎ定食) – full-set *unagi* meal with rice, grilled eel, eel-liver soup and pickles

unajū (うな重) – grilled eel over a flat tray of rice

Kushiage & Kushikatsu

ginnan (銀杏) – ginkgo nuts

gyū-niku (牛肉) – beef pieces

ika (いか) – squid

imo (いも) – potato

renkon (れんこん) – lotus root

shiitake (しいたけ) – Japanese mushrooms

tama-negi (玉ねぎ) – white onion

Okonomiyaki

gyū okonomiyaki (牛お好み焼き) – beef *okonomiyaki*

ika okonomiyaki (いかお好み焼き) – squid *okonomiyaki*

mikkusu (ミックスお好み焼き) – mixed fillings of seafood, meat and vegetables

modan-yaki (モダン焼き) – *okonomiyaki* with *yaki-soba* and a fried egg

negi okonomiyaki (ネギお好み焼き) – thin *okonomiyaki* with spring onions

Kaiseki

bentō (弁当) – boxed lunch

take (竹) – special course

matsu (松) – extra-special course

ume (梅) – regular course

Alcoholic Drinks

chūhai (チューハイ) – *shōchū* with soda and lemon

mizu-wari (水割り) – whisky, ice and water

nama biiru (生ビール) – draught beer

oyu-wari (お湯割り) – *shōchū* with hot water

shōchū (焼酎) – distilled grain liquor

whisky (ウィスキー) – whisky

Coffee & Tea

american kōhii (アメリカンコーヒー) – weak coffee

burendo kōhii (ブレンドコーヒー) – blended coffee, fairly strong

kafe ōre (カフェオレ) – *café au lait*, hot or cold

kōcha (紅茶) – black, British-style tea

kōhii (コーヒー) – regular coffee

Japanese Tea

bancha (番茶) – ordinary-grade green tea, brownish in colour

matcha (抹茶) – powdered green tea used in the tea ceremony

mugicha (麦茶) – roasted barley tea

o-cha (お茶) – green tea

sencha (煎茶) – medium-grade green tea

Behind the Scenes

SEND US YOUR FEEDBACK

We love to hear from travellers – your comments keep us on our toes and help make our books better. Our well-travelled team reads every word on what you loved or loathed about this book. Although we cannot reply individually to your submissions, we always guarantee that your feedback goes straight to the appropriate authors, in time for the next edition. Each person who sends us information is thanked in the next edition – the most useful submissions are rewarded with a selection of digital PDF chapters.

Visit **lonelyplanet.com/contact** to submit your updates and suggestions or to ask for help. Our award-winning website also features inspirational travel stories, news and discussions.

Note: We may edit, reproduce and incorporate your comments in Lonely Planet products such as guidebooks, websites and digital products, so let us know if you don't want your comments reproduced or your name acknowledged. For a copy of our privacy policy visit lonelyplanet.com/privacy.

WRITER THANKS

Kate Morgan

Thank you to my family and my partner, Trent, for all the support. Big thank you to destination editor, Laura, for sending me off again to one of my favourite cities in the world. Thank you to Kengo Nakao from the Kyoto Tourist Information Center and Michelle Montpetit from the Kansai Tourist Office for all of your assistance. Also thank you to Yoshiko and David, Yoshiko Sato and Rico for your help, and to my friend Yuki Okabe for boozy nights out in Osaka.

Rebecca Milner

Thank you to LC for giving me the excuse to spend a leisurely summer reading books on classical Japanese literature and the arts, and to my husband for ceding the living room to my piles of books. To KM for giving me the scoop on her fantastic new finds. And to Maya and Will, my sources for all things Kansai. I am indebted to the many great scholars of Japan, whose works sustain my interest in the country, even after all these years.

ACKNOWLEDGMENTS

Cover photograph: Geisha, Kyoto, Japanese Temples/Alamy ©

THIS BOOK

This 7th edition of Lonely Planet's *Kyoto* guidebook was researched and written by Kate Morgan and Rebecca Milner. The previous two editions were written by Chris Rowthorn. This guidebook was produced by the following:

Destination Editor Laura Crawford
Product Editors Kate James, Tracy Whitmey
Senior Cartographer Diana Von Holdt
Assisting Cartographer Anita Banh
Book Designer Katherine Marsh

Assisting Editors Andrea Dobbin, Kristin Odijk
Cover Researcher Naomi Parker
Thanks to Ronan Abayawickrema, Naoko Akamatsu, Shona Gray, Fran Miller, Catherine Naghten, Claire Naylor, Karyn Noble

Index

See also separate subindexes for:

🍴 **EATING P205**

🍷 **DRINKING & NIGHTLIFE P206**

☆ **ENTERTAINMENT P206**

🔒 **SHOPPING P206**

🛏 **SLEEPING P206**

🏃 **ACTIVITIES P207**

Kyoto Maps

Sights

- Beach
- Bird Sanctuary
- Buddhist
- Castle/Palace
- Christian
- Confucian
- Hindu
- Islamic
- Jain
- Jewish
- Monument
- Museum/Gallery/Historic Building
- Ruin
- Shinto
- Sikh
- Taoist
- Winery/Vineyard
- Zoo/Wildlife Sanctuary
- Other Sight

Activities, Courses & Tours

- Bodysurfing
- Diving
- Canoeing/Kayaking
- Course/Tour
- Sento Hot Baths/Onsen
- Skiing
- Snorkelling
- Surfing
- Swimming/Pool
- Walking
- Windsurfing
- Other Activity

Sleeping

- Sleeping
- Camping
- Hut/Shelter

Eating

- Eating

Drinking & Nightlife

- Drinking & Nightlife
- Cafe

Entertainment

- Entertainment

Shopping

- Shopping

Information

- Bank
- Embassy/Consulate
- Hospital/Medical
- Internet
- Police
- Post Office
- Telephone
- Toilet
- Tourist Information
- Other Information

Geographic

- Beach
- Gate
- Hut/Shelter
- Lighthouse
- Lookout
- Mountain/Volcano
- Oasis
- Park
- Pass
- Picnic Area
- Waterfall

Population

- Capital (National)
- Capital (State/Province)
- City/Large Town
- Town/Village

Transport

- Airport
- Border crossing
- Bus
- Cable car/Funicular
- Cycling
- Ferry
- Metro/MTR/MRT station
- Monorail
- Parking
- Petrol station
- Skytrain/Subway station
- Taxi
- Train station/Railway
- Tram
- Underground station
- Other Transport

Routes

- Tollway
- Freeway
- Primary
- Secondary
- Tertiary
- Lane
- Unsealed road
- Road under construction
- Plaza/Mall
- Steps
- Tunnel
- Pedestrian overpass
- Walking Tour
- Walking Tour detour
- Path/Walking Trail

Boundaries

- International
- State/Province
- Disputed
- Regional/Suburb
- Marine Park
- Cliff
- Wall

Hydrography

- River, Creek
- Intermittent River
- Canal
- Water
- Dry/Salt/Intermittent Lake
- Reef

Areas

- Airport/Runway
- Beach/Desert
- Cemetery (Christian)
- Cemetery (Other)
- Glacier
- Mudflat
- Park/Forest
- Sight (Building)
- Sportsground
- Swamp/Mangrove

Note: Not all symbols displayed above appear on the maps in this book

MAP INDEX

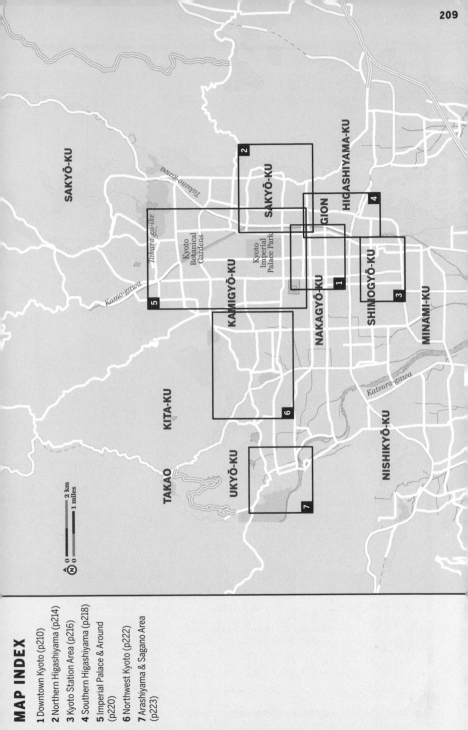

DOWNTOWN KYOTO *Map on p210*

NORTHERN HIGASHIYAMA *Map on p214*

DOWNTOWN KYOTO

Key on p213

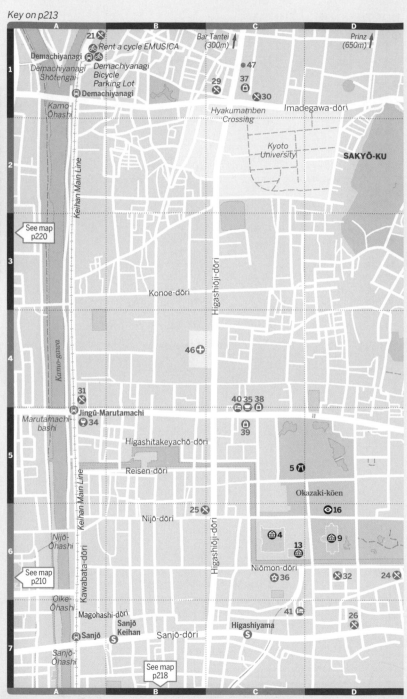

NORTHERN HIGASHIYAMA

0   500 m
0   0.25 miles

Shisen-dō (2km);
Enkō-ji (2.1km);
Shūgaku-in Rikyū
Imperial Villa (4km)

Shira-kawa

Ginkaku-ji-Michi

Kagura-oka-dōri

22

28

17

1 Ginkaku-ji

6

Daimonji-yama
(1.5km)

19

43

18

8

Shirakawa-dōri

Shira-kawa

Tetsugaku-no-Michi
(Path of Philosophy)

15

Marutamachi-dōri

23

Shira-kawa

3

Nijō-dōri

14

27

Biwa-ko Sosui Canal

2 Nanzen-ji

10

45

42

20

7

11

12

Shirakawa-dōri

Sanjō-dōri

44

Keage

33

HIGASHIYAMA-KU

KYOTO STATION AREA

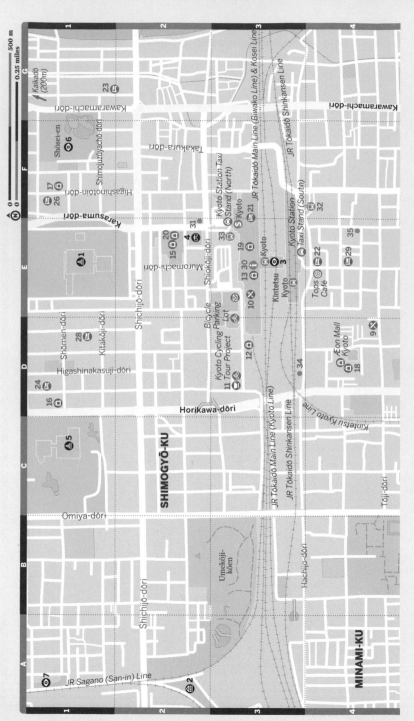

⊙ Sights p57
1 Higashi Hongan-ji............................E1
2 Kyoto Railway Museum.....................A2
3 Kyoto Station..................................E3
4 Kyoto Tower Observation Deck.........E2
5 Nishi Hongan-ji...............................C1
6 Shōsei-en......................................F1
7 Sumiya Pleasure House....................A1
8 Tō-ji...B5

🍴 Eating p59
9 Arata..D4
10 Cube..E3
Eat Paradise..............................(see 10)
Kyoto Ramen Kōji.......................(see 10)
Kyoto Tower Sando.......................(see 4)

🍷 Drinking & Nightlife p60
11 Kurasu..D3
Roots of all Evil..........................(see 4)

🛍 Shopping p61
12 Bic Camera....................................D3
13 JR Isetan Department Store............E3
14 Kōbō-san Market...........................B5
15 Kōjitsu Sansō................................E2
16 Kungyoku-dō.................................D1
17 Kyōsen-dō....................................F1
18 Popondetta Æon Mall Kyoto Shop....D4
19 Porta Shopping Mall.......................E3
20 Yodobashi Camera.........................E2

😴 Sleeping p144
21 Hotel Granvia Kyoto.......................F3
22 Ibis Styles Kyoto Station.................E4
23 K's House Kyoto.............................G1
24 Kyomachiya Ryokan Sakura – Honganji....D1
25 Lower East 9 Hostel........................F5
26 Matsubaya Ryokan.........................F1
27 Mosaic Hostel................................D5
28 Ryokan Shimizu..............................D1

29 Sakura Terrace the Gallery.............E4

ℹ️ Information p192
JTB Kansai Tourist Information Office.......(see 4)
30 Kyoto Tourist Information Center......E3
31 Tōkai Discount Ticket Shop.............E2

ℹ️ Transport p182
32 Airport Limousine Bus Stop.............F4
33 Kyoto Bus Information Centre...........E3
34 Nissan Rent-a-Car..........................D3
35 Toyota Rentacar Kyoto Eki Shinkansen-guchi
Branch.......................................E4

Kyoto Brewing Company (550m)

Tofuku-ji (1.2km);
Vermillion Bar Espresso (1.8km);
Fushimi Inari-Taisha (2km)

Hotel Anteroom (450m)

Tōji

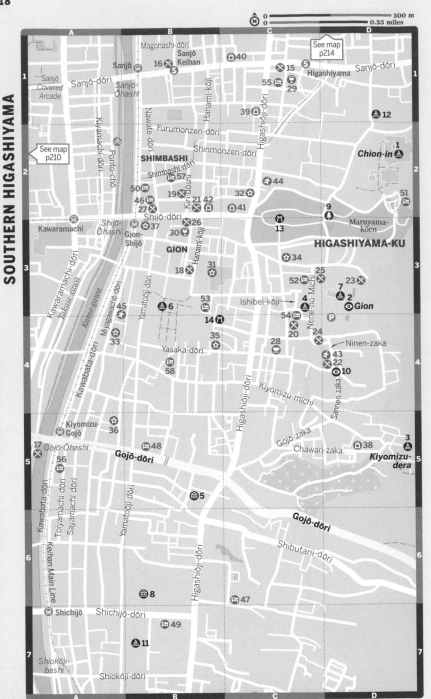

SOUTHERN HIGASHIYAMA

0   500 m
0   0.25 miles

See map
p214

Sanjō Covered Arcade

Magohashi-dōri

Sanjō
Keihan

Sanjō

16

40

15

Higashiyama

Sanjō-dōri

Sanjō-dōri

Sanjō-Ōhashi

55

29

Furumonzen-dōri

39

12

See map
p210

Shinmonzen-dōri

SHIMBASHI

Shimbashi-dōri

57

50

19

21 42

32

44

Chion-in

51

46

27

41

13

9

Maruyama-kōen

Kawaramachi

Shijō-Ōhashi

Gion-Shijō

37

30

26

GION

HIGASHIYAMA-KU

18

31

34

25

52

23

7

45

6

53

Ishibei-kōji

4

2

Gion

33

14

54

20

24

Nene-no-Michi

35

Yasaka-dōri

28

43

22

10

Ninen-zaka

58

Kiyomizu-michi

Kiyomizu-Gojō

36

Gojō-zaka

3

17

Gojō-Ōhashi

48

38

Kiyomizu-dera

56

Gojō-dōri

Chawan-zaka

5

Gojō-dōri

Shibutani-dōri

8

Higashiōji-dōri

47

Shichijō

Shichijō-dōri

49

11

Shiokōji-bashi

Shiokōji-dōri

SOUTHERN HIGASHIYAMA

SOUTHERN HIGASHIYAMA

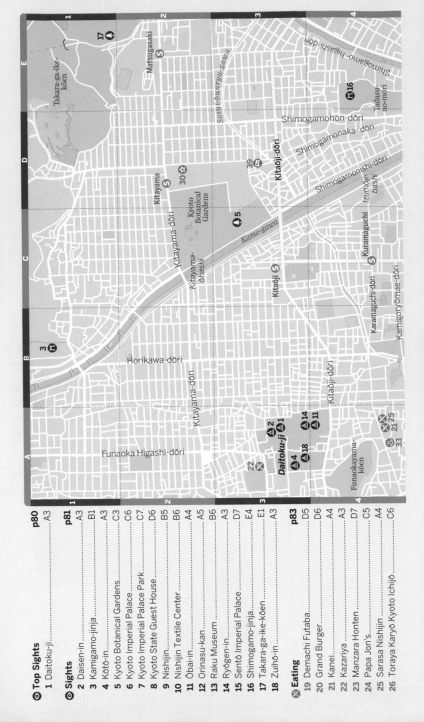

IMPERIAL PALACE & AROUND

KAMIGYŌ-KU

NISHIJIN

Map labels: Eizan Railway Line, Izumo-ga-ku (Izakaya Line), Aoi-bashi, Kamo-kaidō, 34, Demachiyanagi, 19, 20, Kamo-Ōhashi, Kyoto Prefectural University Hospital, Kawaramachi-dōri, Keihan Main Line, Jingu-Marutamachi, Marutamachi-bashi, Reisen-dōri, See map p214, 27, Kojinguchi-dōri, Shimogamohon-dōri, 23, Teramachi-dōri, Imadegawa-dōri, 24, Karasuma-dōri, Doshisha University, Imperial Household Agency, Kyoto Imperial Palace Park, 8, 6, 15, Kyoto-Shiyakusho-mae (Kyoto City Hall), Kyoto-Oike, Imadegawa, 26, 28, 32, 7, Marutamachi-dōri, Marutamachi, 38, 36, 37, Karasuma-dōri, Kamitachiuri-dōri, Nakachōjamachi-dōri, Shinmachi-dōri, Takeyamachi-dōri, Horikawa-dōri, 35, 31, 10, 13, Nakatachiuri-dōri, Horikawa-dōri, Inokuma-dōri, 29, Nijō-jō, Nijō-jō-mae, Omiya-dōri, Chiokoin-dōri, Demizu-dōri, Shimotachiuri-dōri, Sawaragichō-dōri, Sasayachō-dōri, Ichijo-dōri, Jofukuji-dōri, 9, 12, Teranouchi-dōri, Senbon-dōri, Nijō, Nijō Train Station, See map p210

Drinking & Nightlife p84
27 Kamogawa Cafe.................... D7

Entertainment p85
28 ALTI C6
29 Jittoku............................... B7
30 Kyoto Concert Hall D2

Shopping p85
31 Aizen Kōbō......................... B6
Nishijin Textile Center........ (see 10)

Sports & Activities p85
32 Club Ōkitsu Kyoto................ C6
33 Funaoka Onsen................... A4
34 Haru Cooking Class............. D5
35 Urasenke Chadō Research Center..... B5

Sleeping p146
36 Bird Hostel.......................... C7
37 Noku Kyoto C7
38 Palace Side Hotel................ C7
39 Ryokan Rakuchō................... D3

NORTHWEST KYOTO

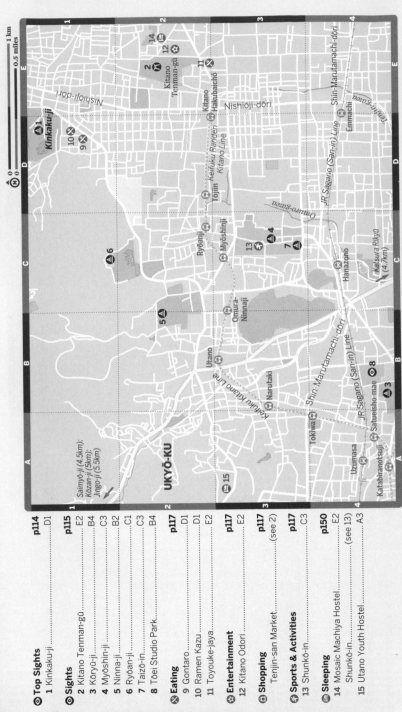

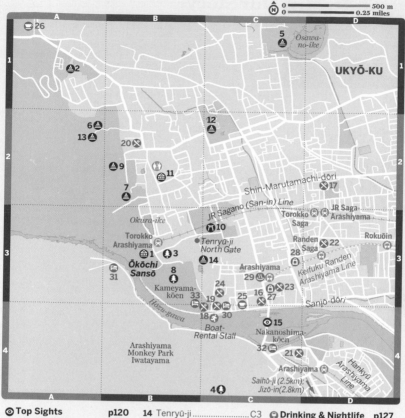

Our Story

A beat-up old car, a few dollars in the pocket and a sense of adventure. In 1972 that's all Tony and Maureen Wheeler needed for the trip of a lifetime – across Europe and Asia overland to Australia. It took several months, and at the end – broke but inspired – they sat at their kitchen table writing and stapling together their first travel guide, *Across Asia on the Cheap.* Within a week they'd sold 1500 copies. Lonely Planet was born.

Today, Lonely Planet has offices in Franklin, London, Melbourne, Oakland, Dublin, Beijing and Delhi, with more than 600 staff and writers. We share Tony's belief that 'a great guidebook should do three things: inform, educate and amuse'.

Our Writers

Kate Morgan

Having worked for Lonely Planet for over a decade, Kate has covered plenty of ground working as a travel writer on destinations such as Shanghai, Japan, India, Russia, Zimbabwe, the Philippines and Phuket. She has done stints living in London, Paris and Osaka but these days is based in one of her favourite regions in the world – Victoria, Australia. In between travelling the world and writing about it, Kate enjoys spending time at home working as a freelance editor.

Rebecca Milner

California born, longtime Tokyo resident (15 years and counting!), Rebecca has co-authored Lonely Planet guides to Tokyo, Japan, Korea and China. A freelance writer covering travel, food and culture, she has been published in the *Guardian,* the *Independent,* the *Sunday Times Travel Magazine,* the *Japan Times* and more. After spending the better part of her twenties working to travel – doing odd jobs in Tokyo to make money so she could spend months at a time backpacking around Asia – she turned the tables in 2010, joining Lonely Planet's team of authors.

Published by Lonely Planet Global Limited
CRN 554153
7th edition – Aug 2018
ISBN 978 1 78657 063 5
© Lonely Planet 2018   Photographs © as indicated 2018
10 9 8 7 6 5 4 3 2 1
Printed in China

Although the authors and Lonely Planet have taken all reasonable care in preparing this book, we make no warranty about the accuracy or completeness of its content and, to the maximum extent permitted, disclaim all liability arising from its use.